Kevin Hatch

PostNuke
Content
Management

SAMS

800 East 96th Street, Indianapolis, Indiana 46240

PostNuke Content Mangement

Copyright © 2005 by Sams Publishing

International Standard Book Number: 0-672-32686-8

Library of Congress Catalog Card Number: 2004091351

Printed in the United States of America

First Printing: December 2004

07   06   05   04   4   3   2   1

Trademarks

Warning and Disclaimer

Bulk Sales

Sams Publishing offers excellent discounts on this book when ordered in quantity for bulk purchases or special sales. For more information, please contact

U.S. Corporate and Government Sales
1-800-382-3419
corpsales@pearsontechgroup.com

For sales outside of the U.S., please contact

International Sales
international@pearsoned.com

Acquisitions Editor
Shelley Johnston

Development Editor
Mark Cierzniak

Managing Editor
Charlotte Clapp

Project Editor
Andy Beaster

Copy Editor
Karen Annett

Indexer
Larry Sweazy

Proofreader
Tricia Liebig

Technical Editor
Steve Heckler

Publishing Coordinator
Vanessa Evans

Book Designer
Gary Adair

Page Layout
Kelly Maish
Julie Parks

Contents at a Glance

Table of Contents

About the Author

Kevin Hatch is a professional web developer specializing in user interface design. With more than a decade of experience on the Internet, he has worked with the Web since its beginning and served in a variety of roles, ranging from graphic designer and interface systems analyst to webmaster and network architect. Originally a graduate with a combined Computer Science and English degree, Kevin has also been a technical writer and editor, and aspires to publish his fiction. He currently lives in eastern Iowa with his wife and their nine pets. He can be reached via email at kevin@kevinhatch.com.

Dedication

To my patient wife, Alissa.

Acknowledgments

I'd like to express my thanks to the core PostNuke Team who is ultimately responsible for the PostNuke CMS. Without their ongoing efforts, PostNuke would not be what is it today. Special recognition is also due for the tireless work of Mark West and Andreas Krapohl (also known as larsneo), the two Lead Developers. In addition, I'd like to acknowledge the outstanding PostNuke community of developers and users who regularly contribute to PostNuke through third-party modules, blocks, and themes and with their active participation in the PostNuke forums where the user-to-user support is simply amazing.

We Want to Hear from You!

As the reader of this book, *you* are our most important critic and commentator. We value your opinion and want to know what we're doing right, what we could do better, what areas you'd like to see us publish in, and any other words of wisdom you're willing to pass our way.

You can email or write me directly to let me know what you did or didn't like about this book—as well as what we can do to make our books stronger.

Please note that I cannot help you with technical problems related to the topic of this book, and that due to the high volume of mail I receive, I might not be able to reply to every message.

When you write, please be sure to include this book's title and author as well as your name and phone or email address. I will carefully review your comments and share them with the author and editors who worked on the book.

Email: webdev@samspublishing.com

Mail: Mark Taber
         Associate Publisher
         Sams Publishing
         800 East 96th Street
         Indianapolis, IN 46240 USA

Reader Services

For more information about this book or another Sams title, visit our website at www.samspublishing.com. Type the ISBN (excluding hyphens) or the title of a book in the Search field to find the page you're looking for.

Introduction

Welcome to *PostNuke Content Management*. The information contained within this book is designed to be a resource and reference, a guide to one of the most popular and powerful open source Content Management Systems (CMSs) available.

In this introduction, you learn

- Why you should read this book

- What you can achieve using this book

- About PostNuke and Content Management Systems

- How this book is organized

Let's begin.

Why You Should Read This Book

This book covers all aspects of PostNuke website development from initial hardware preparation to advanced customization and hacks. It shows you how to use PostNuke as a tool to develop and manage a professional website.

This book is structured primarily for technical readers who are comfortable with programming and site management. It's not necessary for you to have specific experience with Extensible Hypertext Markup Language (XHTML), the PHP scripting language, or database development, only that you are prepared to pick up any missing knowledge along the way. The basics of everything you need are covered swiftly. Beginning developers are pointed in the right direction to learn more if needed, and experienced developers can proceed to advanced topics more quickly.

The biggest complaint developers have had with PostNuke is the lack of current and comprehensive documentation. I have personally experienced similar frustrations with the CMS, and I hope this text solves this key problem so that many more developers can see what a great product PostNuke is.

What You Can Achieve Using This Book

Reading this book empowers you with everything you need to know to install, customize, and manage a PostNuke website. Your site can include easy, form-based content management, a built-in user login system, news and article submission, instant community features, ad support, and much more. You learn how to apply themes and additional third-party modules to modify PostNuke for any site application.

PostNuke is an open source program. Features and capabilities not currently available in the default install of PostNuke can be added using code edits or "hacks." This book explains many of the most popular hacks and teaches you what you need to know to edit any file in the PostNuke package.

PostNuke enables you to develop a complex, dynamic website very quickly, but the limitless flexibility can itself be overwhelming with all of the available choices. This book covers PostNuke customization in real-world site examples using Case Studies at the end of each major section. This shows you how to make the right choices for your website.

PostNuke and Content Management Systems

PostNuke is a Content Management System (CMS). A *CMS* is essentially software that allows you to add and edit content existing on a website. Most CMS systems provide tools to manage content without knowledge of Hypertext Markup Language (HTML) or programming.

PostNuke has also been described as a "Community, Content, and Collaborative Management System," or C3MS. The additional Cs refer to the specific additional community-building tools PostNuke includes and the large community and user base PostNuke enjoys.

Why PostNuke Is the Right Choice

PostNuke is an open source CMS. The obvious benefit of open source is cost; although some open source products do have useful support licensing, open source implementations are usually only a fraction of the cost of their fully commercial counterparts.

Some might point out that the real cost of open source is in the support, or lack thereof, for a given product. That is an especially positive feature of PostNuke, which has a huge online community with hundreds of thousands of site developers. The PostNuke website, which hosts the primary support forums, receives well over a million visitors each month.

Open source solutions are also often criticized as untested in the corporate commercial environment, but that is a myth. A growing trend among large businesses and organizations is to switch from proprietary applications to General Public License (GPL) and open source.

Worldwide, governments are regularly announcing that they are evaluating open source solutions and in many cases performing a complete switch to open source products.

But even if you are sold on open source, why PostNuke specifically? First, PostNuke is well established with over three years of development history, longer than nearly every other active open source CMS.

Of all the open source Content Management Systems, PostNuke and PHP-Nuke are by far the most popular and established with the most sites, modules, and community support. PHP-Nuke is also released under the GPL but charges to download the latest version. PostNuke proponents generally agree that PostNuke aims for a higher level of code quality than PHP-Nuke, resulting in a more stable, secure, and modular program.

PostNuke's large centralized community ensures continual growth and support. Hundreds of third-party module developers exist, and this veritable army provides a development power large enough to challenge any commercial competitor. Perhaps due to the large community involvement, PostNuke has uniquely been focused on user needs and support among similar CMS projects.

The bottom line is that when you need a feature for your PostNuke site, odds are you will have a choice of multiple modules that already perform the task. And for entirely new features, explaining the benefit of your need in the support forums is likely to generate interest leading to new module development.

History and Development Forks

PostNuke was born as a development fork from PHP-Nuke (www.phpnuke.org) early in the summer of 2001. Developers had become increasingly frustrated with code inconsistencies and security issues plaguing PHP-Nuke at the time, but the often closed team structure of PHP-Nuke made it impossible to remedy the known problems. As a result, many of the active PHP-Nuke developers left that project to form PostNuke.

This forking of development groups is far from uncommon in the open source world. PHP-Nuke itself was a fork of Thatware (www.thatware.org), and subsequent forks of PostNuke, notably Envolution (www.envolution.com), Xaraya (www.xaraya.com), and MD-Pro (www.maxdev.com).

In September of 2004, PostNuke 0.75 was released as a major step toward version 1.0. It provides support for legacy modules written before 0.75, but also contains the new pnRender and Xanthia modules that enable developers of third-party modules and themes to convert their code over to the new cleaner and more modular PostNuke system before 0.8 is released. Version 0.75 is a turning point in PostNuke's development, designed to ensure smooth transition to this and all future versions.

How This Book Is Organized

This book is divided into four main sections. The first part is basically an introduction to PostNuke with general installation and setup information. The other three sections offer progressively more advanced discussion of additional features and options.

- Part I, "Exploring PostNuke," takes you from server setup to the full install. There is a general overview of PostNuke terminology and all of the core modules and blocks.

- Part II, "Basic PostNuke," covers commonly used core and third-party modules and how to set up basic permissions and application of a site theme. This section's Case Study documents an Online Club, a very popular application of the PostNuke program.

- Part III, "Custom PostNuke," expands the module selection to include other useful components, such as commercial tools. Advanced theme design is covered and the sometimes complex permission system is explained. An Information Resource Site is the topic of this section's Case Study.

- Part IV, "Advanced PostNuke," provides general instructions for fitting PostNuke into any site model. Selective application of PostNuke components is discussed, and walk-throughs of a variety of changes and hacks of the code are covered. A customized Business Intranet is the subject of this section's Case Study.

You'll also find extensive reference information in the concluding appendixes. Appendix A, "Speed Up PostNuke," covers methods and tools you can use to optimize your site's performance. Appendix B, "PostNuke Modules List," provides an extensive list of PostNuke modules arranged both alphabetically and in functional category groups. The glossary and links in Appendixes C and D, "Glossary of Terms" and "Web Resources," respectively, can help you get up to speed with any technologies with which you're not familiar. And Appendix E lists the functions of the PostNuke Application Programming Interface (API) for those wanting to dig deeper into the PostNuke system. A collection of downloads for this book is available online at www.samspublishing.com/title/0672326868. There, you'll find source code, image samples, and downloads of the various modules discussed in this book.

PART I

Exploring
PostNuke

Preinstallation Requirements

This chapter covers the required hardware and software you need to install PostNuke. It's important to know what PostNuke requires to operate to prevent any slowdowns or setbacks. In this chapter, you learn about the following major topics:

- Hardware requirements

- Software requirements

- Helpful optional software

> **Tip**
>
> You can simplify your setup efforts by going with a professional host, such as HostNuke (www.hostnuke.com) or Simply Hosting (www.simplyhosting.ws).

Hardware Requirements

Every PostNuke site is different. The choice of installed modules and components, operating system (OS), database, and other services can greatly alter the needs of a given PostNuke site. Popular websites with a great deal of traffic need a more robust server than a small club site with few hits. As a result, you must take into account how you want to apply PostNuke to your needs and adjust your server's hardware accordingly.

> **Note**
>
> Experienced server administrators should be able to skip down to the "Software Requirements" section, if desired. PostNuke's hardware requirements are no greater than the average server's needs.

Those of you already familiar with the computer hardware and the components usually required to run a server will be pleasantly surprised that configuring a PostNuke server does not require any special considerations. The hardware required to run the other applications, such as the web server and database, is, in most cases, more than sufficient for PostNuke's needs. The majority of professional hosting services have the required systems.

If you have never run a server before, or if you are simply experimenting with PostNuke on your home PC, expect that most modern personal computers can run the software you need. If your system is a few years old, you might need to upgrade. Unless you see any concerns with the requirements mentioned in the following sections, I suggest you try to get things running with what you have, even if you find yourself on the borderline of the recommendations.

CPU and Memory

Your server's CPU and memory are very important to having quality site performance. PostNuke is known to be a bit of a CPU hog at times. If you know your site will be under a great deal of regular load, you might want to consider having a dual-processor server; however, most PostNuke servers run with a single processor, and unless you are certain you have a need for the extra power, just stick with one processor.

You should plan to run at least a 1GHz processor. A Linux install on 1GHz runs very well; Windows XP usually has a little more overhead and might need a respective boost in the processor. 1GHz processors are inexpensive and even if you are upgrading an older system for PostNuke, it should be fairly easy to get a good CPU for an older mainboard.

Note

PostNuke scales quite well with higher-end hardware. One popular PostNuke site, www.flashflashrevolution.com, has more than 375,000 members and more than 13 million page views each month. The site runs on a Dual Xeon 2.0GHz Linux server, which also simultaneously hosts more than 200 smaller sites.

PostNuke can also eat up a server's memory; if you have to choose between upgrading your CPU or RAM, go for the memory. PostNuke can be served on only 256MB, but more is always better. If you are running Windows, consider that Windows XP needs 128MB minimum just to run the main OS with all its features. After you move up to server status, 256MB should be your baseline for Linux, and XP users should consider 384MB. A popular PostNuke site benefits from 512MB, and a heavy server, especially one running multiple sites, is recommended to have at least 1GB.

Tip

1GB of memory might seem like overkill. If you are running a clean install of all your server applications, and nothing else, it might indeed be more than you need. To reduce system requirements, don't bog your server down with unnecessary files, media, applications, shells, and so on.

Memory can be a costly component to upgrade, but the good news is PostNuke running with only 1GB of RAM has been proven to handle impressive traffic numbers. The PostNuke site www.patriotsforpeace.org was mentioned during *The Oprah Winfrey Show* when the organization's leader appeared as a guest. The website received 21,000 PostNuke page views over a two and a half hour period. The server had been prepared for the traffic with static Hypertext Markup Language (HTML) versions of major pages, including the home page, all of which were not counted by PostNuke. The server load statistics showed neither the static pages nor the separate database server it employed were needed at the time.

It's clear that most single-site PostNuke servers do fine with 512MB, especially if they are running Linux. If you are in doubt, try running with less first to confirm load issues before upgrading. Even if your server is showing some wear, try the options discussed in Appendix A, "Speed Up PostNuke," to get the most out of your existing hardware.

Drive Space

The base PostNuke install itself only requires 20MB of hard drive space. You need extra space for any additional modules you want to install. If you plan to run multiple PostNuke sites, be aware that each site is a separate install and requires an additional 20MB, and most modules also require duplication as each site is customized. A good rule of thumb is to set aside 30MB for any given PostNuke install.

Windows XP and Linux servers both require a couple GB of space for their major OS components. Unless your site is very large, the database is unlikely to consume more than 50MB. A server with a 20GB hard drive is fine for most applications.

Network Connections

Because PostNuke is served up through the type of web server you are running, PostNuke itself does not have any special network requirements. A PostNuke site with modest traffic can be hosted easily on a business-class Digital Subscriber Line (DSL) connection, just like any other website. As a site's traffic grows, it needs a faster, T1 or better, connection. Intranet sites especially should see no traffic issues.

The Choice of OS

Many operating system options are available for PostNuke. You can host a PostNuke site using Unix, Linux, FreeBSD, Mac OS X (which is based on Berkeley Software Distribution [BSD]), Solaris, Advanced Interactive eXecutive (AIX), Windows 98, Windows Me, Windows NT, Windows 2000, Windows XP, or Windows Server 2003. The vast majority of PostNuke servers are running Windows and Linux, the two systems on which this book focuses.

PostNuke is stable on the supported operating systems and runs for as long as your database and web servers keep going. Linux has the reputation for being a very robust OS, but Windows is no slouch either.

The best choice is probably to start with whatever OS you are most familiar. That way, should you have any trouble, you can quickly resolve any problems. If you don't have a preference and/or much experience, consider that Linux can be downloaded for free, but Windows is easier to learn. The OS that suits your needs will also work fine for PostNuke.

Crash Course in Linux

If you choose to work with Linux and are new to the operating system, you need to know a few things. First, many different kinds of Linux are available. The most popular distributions are Red Hat (www.redhat.com), Debian (www.debian.org), and Mandrake (www.mandrakesoft.com). It's a good idea to start with one of these three if you are new to Linux; many books and online resources are available for these distributions.

All distributions have generally the same capabilities, just with differing interfaces and tools. Linspire (www.linspire.com), Lycoris (www.lycoris.com), and Xandros (www.xandros.com) are distributions designed to be very user-friendly, especially for Windows users, but they are not free, and, for example, both Linspire and Xandros are based on Debian. Also, it's important to note that the well-known Linux company Red Hat has changed the way they handle their distribution. Their commercial Linux is still branded Red Hat, but to get their free download-able Linux, you must go to The Fedora Project (fedora.redhat.com), which is the Red Hat-sponsored open source version.

Note

Choosing a custom install for your Linux distribution provides you with many more options. Many useful tools might not be installed by default. Even if you don't make any changes to the choices, reading through your options during a custom install can help ensure you're not missing anything later.

All major Linux distributions come with an X Windowing system and either or both of the main desktops—GNU Network Object Model Environment (GNOME; www.gnome.org) and K Desktop Environment (KDE; www.kde.org). Your distribution should install a graphical interface by default, and you have access to various system utilities you can use to manage your web and database servers on Linux. Although very handy, you should keep in mind that the easy graphical tools do not effectively replace standard command-line Linux management from a terminal. Many configuration options are simply not available in the graphical tools. They can get you started, but keep a terminal window handy for when you need it.

Tip

Even if you never do any application development yourself, it is a good idea to install the base set of development tools with any Linux distribution. It enables you to compile any additional programs you might need without the hassle of having to add the tools later when you need them.

The following list contains some of the basic terminal commands you might need. To get more information about these or any other commands, simply type man [command name] at the command prompt.

- `cat`—Concatenates and displays a file
- `cd`—Changes the working directory
- `chmod`—Changes the permissions mode of a file

- **chown**—Changes the owner and/or group of a file

- **cp**—Copies a file

- **diff**—Displays differences between pairs of text files

- **exit**—Terminates a process

- **find**—Finds a file by name or by other characteristics

- **grep**—Searches a file for a specific text string

- **gzip**—Compresses and uncompresses files in the gzip format

- **ifconfig**—Displays current network settings

- **ls**—Lists the contents of a directory

- **man**—Displays a reference manual page

- **mkdir**—Makes a directory

- **more**—Displays a text file

- **mv**—Moves or renames a file

- **passwd**—Creates or changes a password

- **pwd**—Displays the current directory pathname

- **rm**—Removes a file

- **rmdir**—Removes a directory

- **tar**—Compresses and uncompresses files in the Tape ARchive format

- **vi**—Starts a simple ASCII text editor

Crash Course in Windows XP

Using Windows XP can be the easiest and fastest way to get PostNuke up and running. It installs generally without a hitch, and is easy to work with. You have the choice between the Windows XP Home (http://www.microsoft.com/windowsxp/home/), Windows XP Professional (http://www.microsoft.com/windowsxp/pro/), and Windows Server 2003 (http://www.microsoft.com/windowsserver2003/) editions. They are all essentially the same operating system, but Windows XP Professional and Windows Server 2003 both include a number of additional features you might find useful, such as remote desktop management, increased security and networking options, backup and recovery software, and Internet Information Services (IIS). If you plan to run a public website with regular traffic, you should go with Windows XP Professional or Windows Server 2003. Windows XP Professional IIS server does have a session limit, but you can use Apache for your production site. If you just want to try PostNuke or do some at-home development, Windows XP Home Edition should work fine.

Tip

After installing Windows XP, be certain to do the major updates. You can click on Windows Update on the Start menu, or simply browse with Internet Explorer to windowsupdate.microsoft.com. Some updates can only be installed individually, so you might have to run Windows Update multiple times to get what you need.

As a web server on Windows Server 2003, IIS is actually a really good choice. Windows XP Professional also comes with Personal Web Server (PWS), but there is really no reason to use PWS when IIS is an option. Of course, the Apache Web Server (httpd.apache.org) can also be installed on both Windows XP editions and is the logical choice for Windows XP Home and Windows XP Pro users.

Note

IIS in Windows XP Professional is limited to running one server at a time with 10 concurrent connections, just like Windows 2000 Professional. If you want to run multiple servers with IIS, you must use Windows Server 2003. Apache serves multiple virtual servers on any version of Windows.

It's a good idea when installing Windows XP that you go through the custom options. Windows XP has less optional components than Linux does, but you can add in extras such as IIS, which is not installed by default.

Tip

To install IIS on a Windows XP machine that's already running, from the Start menu, click Control Panel, and then click Add or Remove Programs (choose Settings first if you are using the Classic Start menu interface). Click the Add/Remove Windows Components option and check the Internet Information Services (IIS) check box. Then click Next to complete the changes.

The following list contains some useful commands you can use from the Windows XP command prompt. You can type /? after a command to see more options.

- **bootcfg**—Views and sets up boot options
- **cd**—Changes the working directory
- **copy**—Copies a file
- **del**—Deletes a file
- **dir**—Lists the contents of a directory
- **gpresult**—Views user and group policy settings
- **ipconfig**—Displays current network settings
- **md**—Makes a directory
- **mmc**—Starts the Microsoft Management Console (MMC)
- **move**—Moves or renames a file
- **msconfig**—Manages the services and utilities that start with Windows
- **netsh**—Configures network interfaces, protocols, folders, and routes
- **pathping**—Combines the traceroute and ping utilities
- **quit**—Ends current process
- **rd**—Removes a directory
- **regedit**—Starts the Windows Registry Editor
- **sfc**—Scans system files and can replace those with errors
- **systeminfo**—Displays general configuration information, such as processor and memory
- **type**—Displays a text file

Software Requirements

PostNuke is a great Content Management System (CMS), but it's only one piece in the server puzzle. It requires a database to store content and a web server to serve pages to the world. You should have all of the associated software installed and configured before placing PostNuke on your server. Failure to properly set up a required component can prevent the success of your PostNuke install, and you might have to completely reinstall PostNuke again, after fixing the other software.

Databases

PostNuke currently only runs with the MySQL database engine (www.mysql.com). You need to have MySQL version 3.23 or higher to interface properly with PostNuke. When the system was originally designed, specific Structured Query Language (SQL) code was used that limited PostNuke to MySQL. The PostNuke SQL is now being generalized to enable a wider range of databases. The next database that will be supported is PostgreSQL (www.postgresql.org), another open source engine.

There are plans to have eventual support for mainstream commercial database engines, such as Microsoft SQL Server and Oracle. Being noncommercial themselves, the PostNuke developer community has not had easy access to those environments.

PHP

PostNuke is written entirely in the PHP scripting language (www.php.net). Your server needs PHP version 4.0.1pl2 or higher installed to render PostNuke pages. PHP 4 has built-in MySQL support and uses the Zend Engine 2 (www.zend.com), which are both important to PostNuke.

When you install PHP, you have the option of letting PHP make web server setting changes for you. To take advantage of this convenience, you need to install your web server software first.

Tip

You might need to stop your web server before installing PHP. The install might not be completed properly with the service still running. IIS and PWS specifically do not have this issue and can remain running.

Web Servers

PostNuke runs on any web server that has PHP support. The vast majority of web servers in the world use the Apache Web Server (httpd.apache.org), and you certainly can't go wrong with that choice. If you are using Windows XP, you might want to use IIS instead, which is included with the OS.

Tip

Need a little more security? Try the Apache-SSL Server (www.apache-ssl.org). It is based on Apache and OpenSSL and includes 128-bit encryption.

Combined Server Packages

You might find it more convenient to install one of the combined server packages. Most packages at least include the Apache HTTP Server, PHP, and MySQL. Some have added additional features and tools, such as the Zend Optimizer (see Appendix A) in FoxServ and phpMyAdmin (see the "Administration Tools" section later in this chapter) with PHP Triad.

- ApacheToolbox (www.apachetoolbox.com)

- AppServ (www.appservnetwork.com)

- EasyPHP (www.easyphp.org)

- FoxServ (www.foxserv.net)

- NuSphere TechPlatform (www.nusphere.com)

- PHP Triad (sourceforge.net/projects/phptriad/)

Tip

Mitel Networks' SME Server (www.e-smith.org) can get you up and running in a flash. The package includes a modified Red Hat Linux installation with web, File Transfer Protocol (FTP), and mail servers, Samba file sharing, and a firewall all installed and configured for you. And it's all in one easy ISO.

Helpful Optional Software

Many other applications and utilities can make management of PostNuke much easier. Besides having the everyday compression and FTP tools needed to install and maintain PostNuke, some really great applications and scripts are available that you can use to easily resolve any problems that might come up.

FTP Applications

PostNuke content is updated mainly through the built-in online web forms, but even after the install, you still need to transfer files directly to the server. If your server is local on your local area network (LAN), you can do this using a drive share or mount, but in most cases, your server will be hosted remotely and you need to use FTP.

A variety of clients are available for both Linux and Windows XP. Windows users should start with one of these popular FTP utilities:

- CoffeeCup FTP (www.coffeecup.com)

- CuteFTP (www.globalscape.com)

- FTP Voyager (www.ftpvoyager.com)

- SmartFTP (www.smartftp.com)

- WS_FTP Pro (www.ipswitch.com)

Tip

Many Unix servers run Secure SHell (SSH) and require you to connect with SSH File Transfer Protocol (SFTP) or Secure Copy Protocol (SCP). If you need an SFTP-capable client, try WinSCP (winscp.sourceforge.net).

For Linux users, if you are not running X Windows, you are probably already familiar with the FTP that comes standard. Whether you prefer X or not, you might still want a more full-featured FTP client, such as one of the following:

- AxY FTP (www.wxftp.seul.org)

- gFTP (gftp.seul.org)

- GNU wget (wget.sunsite.dk)

- ProFTPD (www.proftpd.org)

- Pure-FTPd (pureftpd.sourceforge.net)

Editors

PostNuke is incredibly powerful right out of the proverbial box, but if you expect to make a site yours both in form and function, you must do some web development. And that means you need an HTML/PHP editor. Developers with web experience undoubtedly already have their personal set of tools installed and ready, but if you're new to the Web, you certainly have plenty of options.

Note

PostNuke is a tool for rapid website development, but like any tool, you must put it to work to see a real benefit. That means customizing. The more effort you put into the postinstall development, the better your website becomes.

Some of the applications in the following list are full-featured Integrated Development Environments (IDEs), and some are simple text editors. Selection of an editor that's right for you is very much a personal choice. Try many editors before you settle; the differences are often subtle but very important.

Those developing on a Windows XP platform can start with one of these handy applications:

- AceHTML (freeware.acehtml.com)
- Arachnophilia (www.arachnoid.com)
- CoffeeCup HTML Editor (www.coffeecup.com)
- HomeSite (www.macromedia.com)
- PHPEdit (www.phpedit.com)
- UltraEdit-32 (www.ultraedit.com)
- Zend Studio (www.zend.com)

HomeSite, PHPEdit, and Zend all have support for PHP, whereas the others are more strictly HTML focused. Simple Windows Notepad is fine for edits if you have to use it, but it's generally easier and faster to have an application that includes at least some syntax highlighting.

> **Note**
>
> Other larger-scale development suites, such as Dreamweaver and FrontPage were purposely left out of the list of recommended tools. Although WYSIWYG (What You See Is What You Get) code-generating applications can be easy to use, they can also be "too smart," adding or changing code for you. Unless you are very comfortable and familiar with the application and how it performs, unexpected changes such as these might end up hindering your development with PostNuke.

The vi editor will always be popular with diehard Unix and Linux users, but if you prefer a Linux editor with an X Windows graphical user interface (GUI), try one of these:

- Bluefish (bluefish.openoffice.nl)
- CoffeeCup HTML Editor (www.coffeecup.com)
- Kate (kate.kde.org)
- PhpED (www.nusphere.com)
- Quanta Plus (quanta.sourceforge.net)
- Vim (www.vim.org)
- Zend Studio (www.zend.com)

Compression Tools

You need a compression tool to extract PostNuke and additional separate modules for install. Windows XP and Linux both provide this standard utility, but many users have found other third-party applications to be more full-featured or user-friendly. Good options for Windows XP include the following:

- 7-Zip (www.7-zip.org)

- WinRAR (www.rarlabs.com)

- WinZip (www.winzip.com)

Linux users might want to try out one of the following:

- gnochive (gnochive.sourceforge.net)

- GnoZip (www.geocities.com/SiliconValley/9757/gnozip.html)

- RAR (www.rarlabs.com)

Mail Servers

It's a good idea to have a working mail system installed or at least available to your PostNuke server. Integrated components of PostNuke, such as the account registration module, use mail, and you might find it easier to have a server running on the same host.

Both Linux and Windows XP provide mail servers you can use. Alternate standalone mail servers for Windows XP include the following:

- 602LAN SUITE (www.software602.com)

- DeskNow Mail (www.desknow.com)

- Kerio MailServer (www.kerio.com)

- WorkgroupMail (www.workgroupmail.com)

Any of these Linux alternatives are equally effective:

- acmemail (www.astray.com/acmemail/)

- eXtremail (www.extremail.com)

- Kerio MailServer (www.kerio.com)

- qmail (www.qmail.org)

PostNuke uses PHP to send mail. You need to edit your php.ini file to make changes to how PostNuke sends out email, including the setup of a separate mail server. A full mail module with more configuration options is planned for the next release of PostNuke, 0.8. The default mail server setting in PHP is localhost, so having a local mail server might be easier for you.

Administration Tools

You need a tool to easily manage your PostNuke MySQL database. One commercial option is cPanel (www.cpanel.net) and if you are using an external hosting service, you might find that cPanel support is part of your package.

phpMyAdmin (www.phpmyadmin.net) is another very popular management option and is distributed under the General Public License (GPL). It provides a web-based client for administration from any location.

The MySQL Control Center (MySQLCC; www.mysql.com) is a client application, also available under the GNU GPL, which provides even more features in a platform-independent GUI.

Other MySQL management options include

- MySQL Manager (ems-hitech.com)
- Navicat (www.navicat.com)

Troubleshooting

This chapter contains a large amount of setup, but as this book is about PostNuke and not operating systems or servers, it is important to jump through the material fairly quickly. The following sections discuss some common issues you might come across.

Common Linux Issues

If you are installing MySQL and Apache on an existing Linux workstation and are having problems, you should first remove any existing MySQL or Apache packages on the system. Many Linux installations include both servers in their distribution and perform updates with the Red Hat Package Manager (now simply RPM and used with many distributions). You can get a list of existing installations using these commands:

```
# rpm -qa grep ¦ mysql
# rpm -qa grep ¦ apache
```

This command searches for "mysql" or "apache" in existing package names. For relevant software found, use the following example command to remove it:

```
# rpm -e mysql-3.23.58-4
```

This helps clean up your system prior to installation. You might also receive warnings about dependent packages. If this is the case, you should remove those packages first.

For best results, the servers should be installed in the following order: MySQL, Apache, PHP. Wait until after installing all servers before customizing any settings.

Common Windows XP Issues

You might find that Apache 2 and PHP 4 do not work automatically after installation on Windows XP. The PHP 4 install does not make all changes to Apache's httpd.conf file, and you have to manually complete the install setup. Open the httpd.conf file and make the following additions in their respective sections:

```
ScriptAlias /php/ "c:/php/"
AddType application/x-httpd-php .php
Action application/x-httpd-php "/php/php.exe"
```

This enables PHP through Apache 2 as a Common Gateway Interface (CGI). You can also use a more complicated set of steps to set up PHP as an Apache Module. If you have any problems getting them to work together or want to see the alternatives, go to www.php.net for current documentation.

Those familiar with Windows 2000 Server web services might find it easy to use IIS, but Windows XP Professional has the same single-server limitation found in Windows 2000 Professional. You can use a workaround that allows you to run multiple servers on IIS in Windows XP Professional, but only one server can be running at a given time. From a command prompt, type the following lines:

```
cd \Inetpub\AdminScripts
adsutil.vbs create_vserv W3SVC/2
adsutil.vbs copy W3SVC/1 W3SVC/2
```

This creates a new virtual server and seeds it with the information from the default server. Now reopen your IIS Manager console and you see two "Default Web Site" servers. You can rename the second server and change other settings, such as port, as needed. To start the additional server, simply first stop the one currently running.

Other General Troubleshooting

Remember that PostNuke is written with PHP, and all default directory files are called index.php. Be certain your web server is configured to use index.php as a valid default file when a directory is browsed, and index.php should be listed before other index files. You might also find index.html missing from the list (if you are using IIS, for example).

If you've installed a given server but can't seem to get it to work at all, check to see if it's running. A common mistake is assuming that an installed server is set up to run automatically when the OS starts up. You can check the settings by looking at the Services utility for current status and startup type.

Next

In the next chapter, you look at the install of PostNuke itself, including differences in the choice of OS and ensuring your MySQL database is properly configured.

Install PostNuke

2

In this chapter, you walk through the steps to a successful install of PostNuke. Both new installs and upgrades for existing PostNuke systems are covered with the following topics:

- Database preparation

- PostNuke distribution

- Language packs

- Backing up PostNuke

It's a good idea to have any of the extra applications described in Chapter 1, "Preinstallation Requirements," ready before beginning the install. If you will be using an external host for your PostNuke server, you definitely need to have a File Transfer Protocol (FTP) or Secure SHell (SSH) client available as part of the install process. An externally hosted database also requires an administration tool, such as phpMyAdmin mentioned in Chapter 1, unless you have direct access to the machine through a terminal or virtual connection.

> **Tip**
>
> PostNuke requires site names to be fully qualified, as in http://www.myname.com/, unless you are running in Intranet Mode (not recommended for public sites). That means using http://localhost/ or http://myname.com/ does not work. If you are installing locally but do not have your own Domain Name System (DNS) server setup, you can edit your local hosts file to simulate the domain name. In Linux, the file is at /etc/hosts, and in Windows XP the file is at \windows\system32\drivers\etc\hosts. Use any ASCII text editor to edit the file.

New Installation

PostNuke is written in PHP and interpreted live when browsed, so in a sense, the program itself is not actually installed. The files are simply copied to the web server directory. However, PostNuke is a database-driven application, and that is the key to getting it to work.

Two main actions must happen to complete your PostNuke install: The PostNuke database must be created with a user given administrative rights, and the database must be populated with PostNuke tables seeded with default data. The former is usually accomplished manually; you set up the tables and data using the automated installer.

Database Preparation

The PostNuke install includes scripts to automatically create the database and all the tables the program needs to operate. That said, what you need to do to prepare MySQL for use by PostNuke varies a great deal depending on how your server is set up.

If you are running on an external host and do not have direct access to the server, you need to request the creation of the database. A user account also needs to be set up to access the new database. You might be allowed to choose the names of the database and user and select the password. After this is done, you need to keep this information available during the install process. If your database and users have already been created, you can skip the following, more detailed steps.

Your host might provide a remote database administration tool, such as phpMyAdmin or cPanel, set up with your database. In this case, some things might already be done for you, such as the creation of the main database, but you have access to other features, such as table and user management.

If your server is locally installed or if you have direct access to the server and want to create the database yourself, you can still use a locally installed tool, such as phpMyAdmin, or you can create the database and users using the MySQL command-line interface.

Before going through the steps, it's important to know that the absolute minimum database preparation PostNuke needs is a user account on the MySQL server with privileges to create and manage a database. For example, a default root user is created during the MySQL install; you could use the root account for the install and let PostNuke create all the rest, but that is not very secure. It's strongly recommended that you at least create a new user specifically set up for PostNuke. This account will be used continually by PostNuke after the install to interact with the database.

Database Creation

The most popular graphical user interface (GUI) for database administration with PostNuke is phpMyAdmin, and so it is specifically covered here. If your host uses a different tool, they should provide you with any directions you might need.

phpMyAdmin is installed by default with the root account settings of MySQL. If you have changed the root account password, you also need to edit the config.inc.php settings file for phpMyAdmin to enable access. The application files should simply be placed in a browsable location on your web server, preferably a virtual host location. At this point, you should be able to bring up the main phpMyAdmin page in your browser, as shown in Figure 2.1.

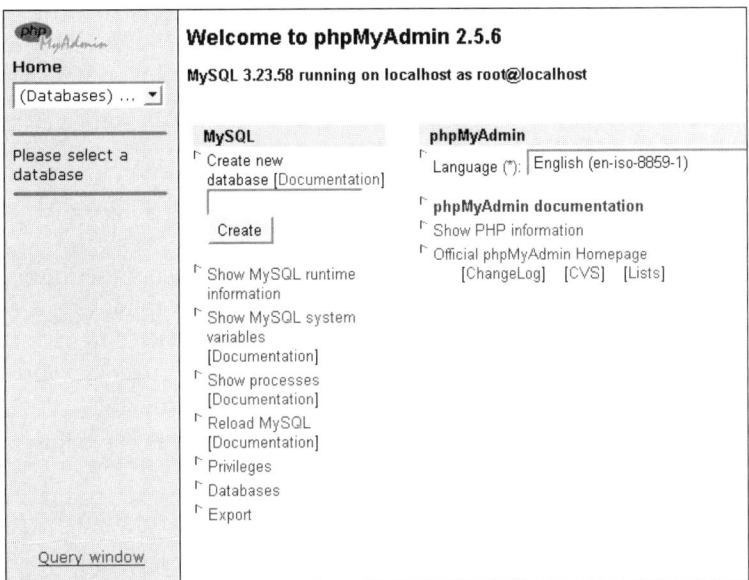

Figure 2.1   phpMyAdmin starting page.

The first item under the MySQL column is conveniently Create New Database. Type in the name you want for the PostNuke database and click the Create button. The screen then updates to the administration subpage specific to your database, which initially gives you the option to create a new table. Do not create any tables at this time.

> **Note**
>
> You can navigate around phpMyAdmin databases using the left frame in the interface. A drop-down list box contains the names of every database. The number in parentheses by each name signifies the number of tables within a given database. If you select the first item in the list: (Databases) ..., you are taken back to the main starting page for phpMyAdmin.

To create a database manually using console commands, you first need to enter the MySQL Monitor shell. From a Linux terminal prompt, type the following:

```
# mysql -u root -p
```

It should be in your path and prompts you for the root password. Windows XP users most likely need to change to the `c:\mysql\bin\` directory from the command prompt before running the `mysql` command.

Now that you are at the shell prompt, type the following:

```
mysql> create database [your database name];
```

You should see the message `Query OK, 1 row affected` to confirm its creation.

Database User Creation

When a user is created in MySQL, you can grant the account specific rights. For security purposes, when you have an account that is created only for PostNuke to use, it is a good idea to give the account access to only the PostNuke database. If you choose to only set up a user account prior to your PostNuke install, you must grant the user the ability to make a database. But, if you make the PostNuke database yourself, the user can be restricted to only the tables within the one database. That is why the database creation steps are covered before user creation in this text, and it's recommended you create both database and the user account before installing PostNuke.

> **Tip**
>
> If PostNuke creates your database for you using an account with open database creation privileges, it's a good idea after the install to restrict the user's abilities. It is more secure to grant the PostNuke user access to only the one database containing the PostNuke tables.

Open phpMyAdmin to the main administration page, as shown in Figure 2.1. Click the Privileges link (third from the bottom in the MySQL column) to get to the user administration page. Your screen should now look similar to Figure 2.2.

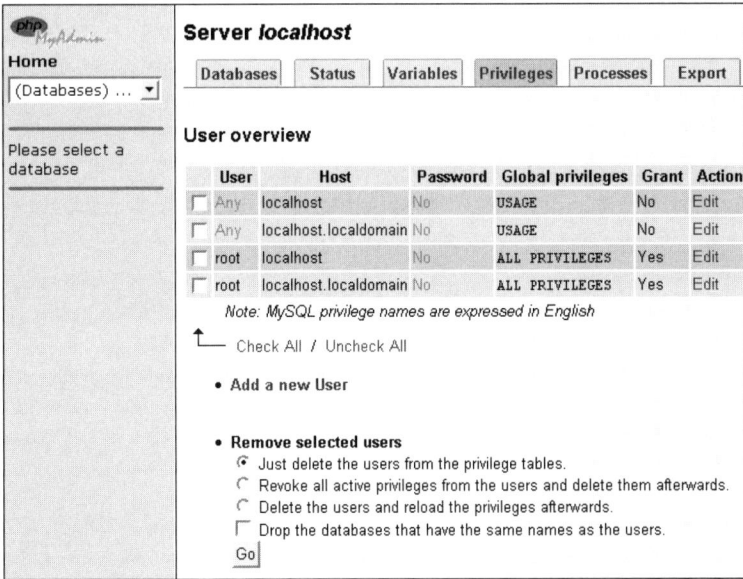

Figure 2.2 phpMyAdmin privileges administration screen.

Click the Add a New User link. Two tables are available: Login Information and Global Privileges. Complete the text fields for the Login Information. You can use localhost for the Host field. If you have created a database already, you should leave the Global Privileges table blank for security. Click the Go button to create the user.

The resulting screen is the administration page for the new user. Besides the same Global Privileges table from the creation screen, this page allows you to grant database-specific access (see Figure 2.3). In the Database-Specific Privileges section, choose the existing PostNuke database from the drop-down list box, and click the Go button.

On the next screen, you see a series of check boxes you can enable to grant specific rights to the database. At minimum, you must check the boxes by SELECT, INSERT, UPDATE, DELETE, CREATE, ALTER, and DROP. If your user will be restricted to just the PostNuke database, you can select all 10 of the privilege options for the database to keep it simple. Now submit the form. Your user now has all the access it needs for the PostNuke install.

To create a user manually using console commands, reenter the MySQL Monitor shell, as described in the previous "Database Creation" section, and use the Grant command to create a new user as follows:

```
mysql> GRANT SELECT,INSERT,UPDATE,DELETE,CREATE,ALTER,DROP ON [database name].* TO
[username]@localhost IDENTIFIED BY '[password]';
```

Figure 2.3 phpMyAdmin user management screen.

The command for creating a user with complete access to a database is as follows:

```
mysql> GRANT ALL PRIVILEGES ON [database name].* TO [username]@localhost IDENTIFIED BY
'[password]' WITH GRANT OPTION;
```

Most MySQL command statements are documented with keywords in uppercase, but it is not required to type them that way. Replace the noted variables with the names and password you have chosen, and don't forget the single quotation marks around the password. This creates a user with complete access to the one database.

You might also need to change a user's password. This can also be accomplished using Structured Query Language (SQL) at the command prompt with the following command:

```
mysql> SET PASSWORD FOR [username]@localhost = PASSWORD('[password]');
```

> **Note**
>
> It is possible to install PostNuke into an existing database containing data for another application, such as a forum. PostNuke installs with a prefix before each table name to prevent any confusion with other tables that might exist in the database. It's strongly recommended you back up your data before the install.

The PostNuke Distribution

The most recent (stable) release of PostNuke is version 0.726-1 Phoenix. It can be found on the PostNuke site at download.postnuke.com under PostNuke, Main Releases, or alternatively there is always a direct link from the PostNuke home page on the right. Archived older versions are available, but there is no benefit to running an older version.

Decompress the file to a directory on your server. The distribution package files are contained in two main subdirectories. The `html` directory has all of the files that you must place in your server's web path. The `phoenix-sql` directory contains the MySQL dump of the default install structure. If you are using the automated install of PostNuke, which is recommended, you can ignore and/or delete the `phoenix-sql` data.

PostNuke File Placement

It's important to know how a web server works to place the PostNuke files in the right place. This is often one of the more tricky parts for new users. When you make a request for a web page from a site, a server pulls the file from a specific location on its hard drive. A server might be filled with other directories and applications and files, including its main operating system files, but the web server program knows to look in a specific spot for web pages. If you are running multiple virtual servers, each one is defined with a different specific directory for its files. You need to place the PostNuke application files in the web server directory you want to use for PostNuke.

Apache installs by default to `/usr/local/Apache2/` on Linux. Web files are served from the `/user/local/Apache2/htdocs/` directory. If you are using the default Apache `httpd` included with your Linux distribution, the path might be integrated more into the operating system, such as having server and configuration files in `/etc/httpd/` and having web files served from `/var/www/html/`. You might also find that the web root is called `public_html`.

Apache on Windows XP installs to `c:\program files\apache group\apache2\` and web files are placed by default in `c:\Program Files\Apache Group\Apache2\htdocs\`. Microsoft IIS is integrated with Windows XP and creates a directory off the root for web files. The full path for IIS is `c:\Inetpub\wwwroot\`.

The configuration files for any web server can be modified to move the default web file location to any location you desire. You can even run multiple, different server services that point to a custom web file directory tree.

If you browse a file with the uniform resource locator (URL) of http://www.mywebsite.com/mypage.html, the file `mywebpage.html` must be in the root of the web server. So, for example, if your server path was `/var/www/html/`, the file would be at `/var/www/html/mypage.html`. The path is equal to the server name, no matter how deep the path might be on the hard drive partition.

The PostNuke files are contained in the html directory, but if you copy the html directory itself into the web root, you have a path like this: /var/www/html/html/nukefile.php, and your browser URL looks like this: http://www.mynukesite.com/html/nukefile.php. The point is that the html directory itself does not need to be copied; only the directory's contents should be copied. You can install PostNuke into a subdirectory, and in more advanced website configurations, this might be advisable. However, if you want to use PostNuke as your site, where PostNuke appears as your home page, you only want to move the files inside the html directory.

If you are using an external host, your provider tells you where those web files need to be placed. It might be the directory to which you FTP, or it might be a subdirectory off your user account.

You should move the files to the appropriate web server directory now. The SQL folder is only included for those users who want to install PostNuke manually. If you plan to use the automated install, you can ignore this directory; it does not need to be moved to the web server.

You can now test the files and your web server setup. Open a browser and go to your server's URL. You should see the PostNuke "problem" page, as shown in Figure 2.4.

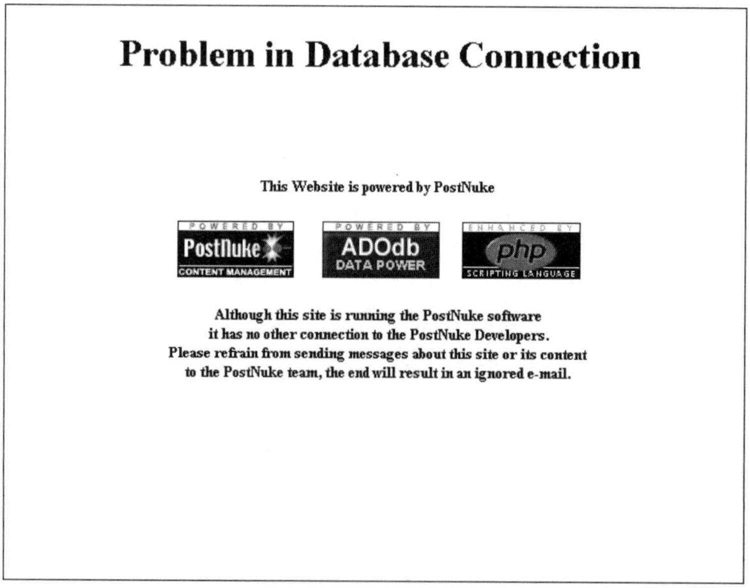

Figure 2.4   PostNuke home page before install.

Even though PostNuke has not been installed, the PostNuke program only needs a web server with PHP to run its code. The actual install process now creates the database and completes the PostNuke setup.

PostNuke Config Permissions

The final change you need to make to files before running the setup is to confirm access permissions to your PostNuke configuration files. These are called `config.php` and `config-old.php` and are also located in the PostNuke root. If your server is a Windows XP system, you should have full access to the files automatically. Linux users, however, need to use `chmod` to open the permissions.

Change to the root directory of your PostNuke files, which at this time is your web server's root, if you expect to run PostNuke as your home page. If you have terminal access to your server, type the following from a Linux command prompt:

```
# chmod 666 config.php config-old.php
```

If you are using an FTP or SSH client to remotely access your server, it should have the ability to set permissions for Unix files. You might have to select a file and click a permissions button or right-click to bring up options. The 666 permissions setting grants both Read and Write access to everyone. Select the options available to give Owners, Group Members, and Other users both Read and Write access.

The access markers, if you have the ability to see them, for those two files now look something like this:

```
-rw-rw-rw-
```

Note

You can also grant access up to 777, additionally giving Execute permission for the two files, but the install process itself does not require it. Full access is marked like this: `-rwxrwxrwx`.

Automated PostNuke Install

In your browser, go to the `index.php` file in the root of your PostNuke install. If you moved the files into your web's root, the address is something like http://www.yourwebsite.com/install.php. If you have moved the files to a subdirectory off your web root, it is http://www.yourwebsite.com/directoryname/install.php. You now see the page in Figure 2.5.

Select your language for the install. Additional languages are available for PostNuke and can be installed later. Click the Set Language button to continue.

The next screen presents you with the GNU General Public License (GPL), which you must accept to complete the install. If you are not familiar with the GPL, you should read through the document to be certain the licensing fits your needs. Click Next to continue.

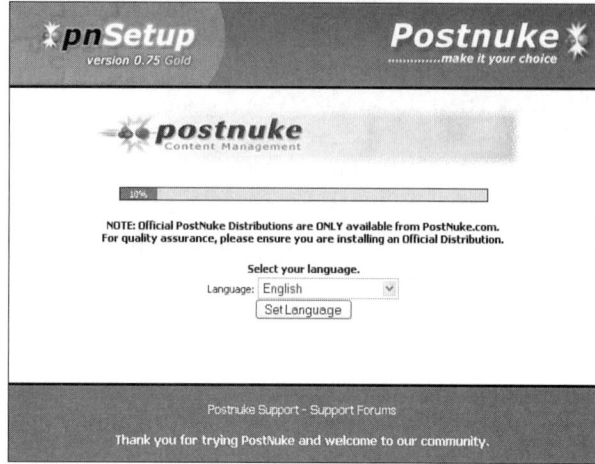

Figure 2.5   Selecting your language to begin.

PostNuke now performs a CHMOD Check on the two configuration files you fixed earlier. The permissions levels are displayed with check marks by each item, as shown in Figure 2.6.

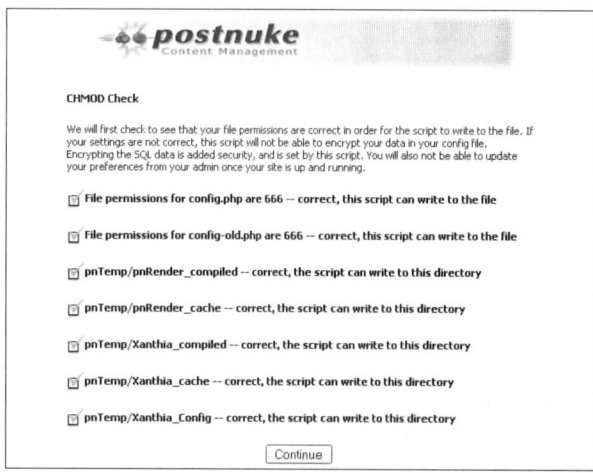

Figure 2.6   Configuration file permissions are correct.

You are now 40% through the PostNuke install process, and it's time to enter all the database information you have collected. Here, you need to enter the Database Username, Database Password, and Database Name information into their respective fields. If you do not specifically know what other fields need to be altered, leave them at their defaults.

Some remote hosts might require that you enter a specific server name in the Database Host field. Some are configured to use localhost or 127.0.0.1. You need to check with your host if you are uncertain. If you are installing PostNuke locally, you should leave the field set to localhost.

The Table Prefix field contains the word inserted at the start of every table name. This is to prevent any confusion between tables in a shared database. For example, you can install multiple copies of PostNuke into the same database using different table prefixes (nuke2, nuke3, and so on).

After you have completed your changes to the Database Information form, click Submit to continue with the install. You have the opportunity on the next screen to confirm the information you have entered. At this point, you determine whether the process should be completed as a New Install or Upgrade. Click New Install.

At the 60% point in the process, you are presented with the option of creating the database. If you have already made a database for PostNuke using the steps described previously, do not check this box. Most external hosts have created a database for you and provided the name, and, in that case, also do not check the box. If you have server access but have left it up to PostNuke to create the database for you, check the box. The install still creates all the tables to populate the database without the box being checked. If you do check the box but have given the install the name of a database that already exists, the install fails.

The next screen has a long list of table creation messages such as the following:

- nuke_autolinks made.

- nuke_autonews made.

- nuke_banner made.

- nuke_bannerclient made.

- and so on

Depending on whether you have made the database prior to installation, you might see the phrase No database made. at the top of the line. It is not an error message unless you were trying to create the database at this time.

The PostNuke administrative account is set up at 80% (see Figure 2.7). Change the two Admin Password fields to something difficult (preferably impossible) to guess but that you can remember. The default Admin password for the automated install is "Password" (and is case sensitive). You must change the password before making your site public or you risk losing control of the site.

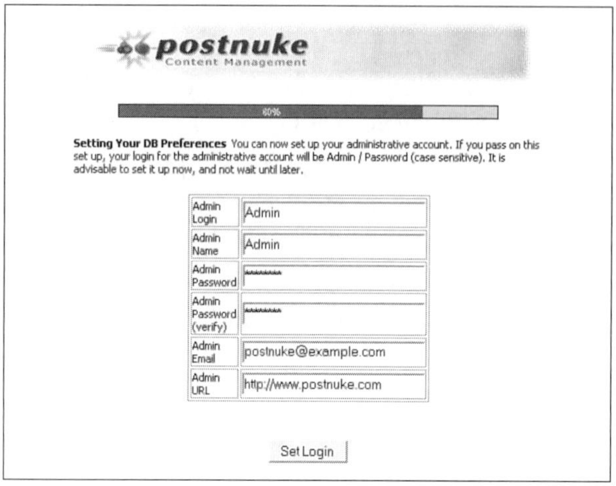

Figure 2.7   Setting the Admin account password.

The Admin URL field is used to identify your PostNuke website in automated correspondence generated by the PostNuke administrative system. It does not need to be the exact address of your PostNuke site, but you should enter the main URL to your overall site so the address can be used to focus your site's visitors to the right location.

The next screen confirms that the administration account is created with another list of database change messages:

- nuke_blocks updated.
- nuke_counter updated.
- nuke_headlines updated.
- nuke_message updated.
- and so on

You can click the Finish button, and at the bottom of the PostNuke credits page is a link to your new PostNuke site's home page. The page looks similar to Figure 2.8.

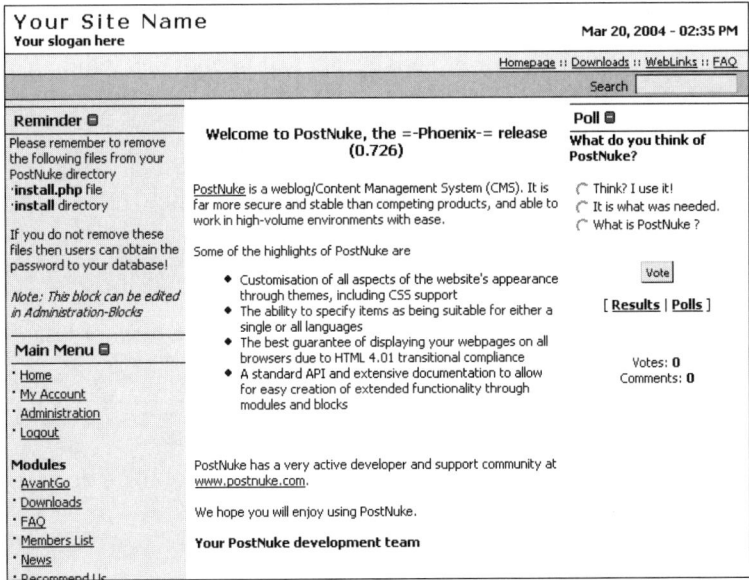

Figure 2.8 Your PostNuke home page.

Manual PostNuke Install

If you prefer to do the manual PostNuke installation, you need to use the SQL file included in the zip under the phoenix-sql directory. You also need direct access to the server to issue the required shell commands.

First, manually edit the config file before install. Open config.php in an ASCII editor and under Database & System Config, look for the following section of code:

```
$pnconfig['dbtype'] = 'mysql';
$pnconfig['dbtabletype'] = 'MyISAM';
$pnconfig['dbhost'] = 'localhost';
$pnconfig['dbuname'] = '';
$pnconfig['dbpass'] = '';
$pnconfig['dbname'] = 'Phoenix';
$pnconfig['system'] = '0';
$pnconfig['prefix'] = 'nuke';
$pnconfig['encoded'] = '1';
```

You can enter your username and database name into the dbuname and dbname lines, respectively. The single quotation marks around your names are required, and, of course, delete "Phoenix" from the dbname when you are entering yours.

File permissions must be set to 666 for both of the config files as outlined previously.

Change to the directory containing the SQL file, or be certain that is it in your path, and type the following command:

```
# mysql [database name]<Phoenix-0.7.2.6.sql
```

This populates the PostNuke database using the configuration files and defaults.

Note

The default administration account in the SQL dump is still called "Admin," but the password is instead set to "God." Both are case sensitive.

Be certain to change your Admin password using the PostNuke interface after you are up and running. "God" is also a common password that is easily guessed.

Language Packs

PostNuke is a global application used on thousands of websites all over the world. Fifteen language options are available from the main install of PostNuke, but you can find more language packs at the PostNuke Language Project (http://sourceforge.net/projects/ pnlanguages/).

As of this writing, 32 language packs are available. You can also download an additional translation tool pack called Nukelang for the development of other language versions.

You will learn more about site setting changes and the install of additional packages in upcoming chapters.

Upgrade Installation

Upgrading PostNuke to the most current version is recommended to ensure you have all the latest security fixes installed. You also have access to the continual code improvements, and new features are added with each release.

PostNuke supports upgrading from all earlier official versions of PostNuke. You can also upgrade from many versions of PHP-Nuke and MyPHPNuke.

Back Up Everything

The first step in an upgrade process should always be to back up of all your current data. You never know what might go wrong, and without a backup, you might have to rebuild everything on your site from scratch.

If you have problems and your upgrade fails, you can use your backup to restore your old site to the point at which you made the backup. In addition, if you find the problem was something wrong with PostNuke itself, you can offer to provide your backup to the development team so they can reproduce the problem themselves, track down what's causing it, and fix it so it never happens again.

Tip

It's also recommended that you back up if you are installing into an existing database that contains previous data. Safety first!

You might find your host does regular backups of all files and database data for you. If this is the case, you are probably covered. If you need to perform the backup manually, you can simply copy the website files to another location for safekeeping. The database content can be backed up using your database administration tool, such as on the Export tab in phpMyAdmin. You can save the database to a file and copy it elsewhere too.

Second, you should specifically copy your `config.php` file. This file is used with the new install. You can use the `config.php` pulled from your backup location if you have it handy.

Third, delete all of the PostNuke files from your web server's directory. The new version's files replace them all. You can also rename the main directory, for example from `html` to `html2`, if you want to keep the files around a little while longer, or to serve as your file backup. Uncompress the new PostNuke archive and place all the files in the main directory.

The fourth and last step before running the upgrade install is to copy the old `config.php` file back into the main directory and overwrite the existing default `config.php` that came with your new PostNuke version.

Note

The permissions for the config files must be set to at least 666 or `rw-rw-rw-` just like a new install. The install process needs to update the files, and you can restrict access for them after the upgrade is complete.

PostNuke Distribution Update

Complete the install process outlined previously until you reach the 50% point, when you can select the Upgrade option. You see the screen in Figure 2.9.

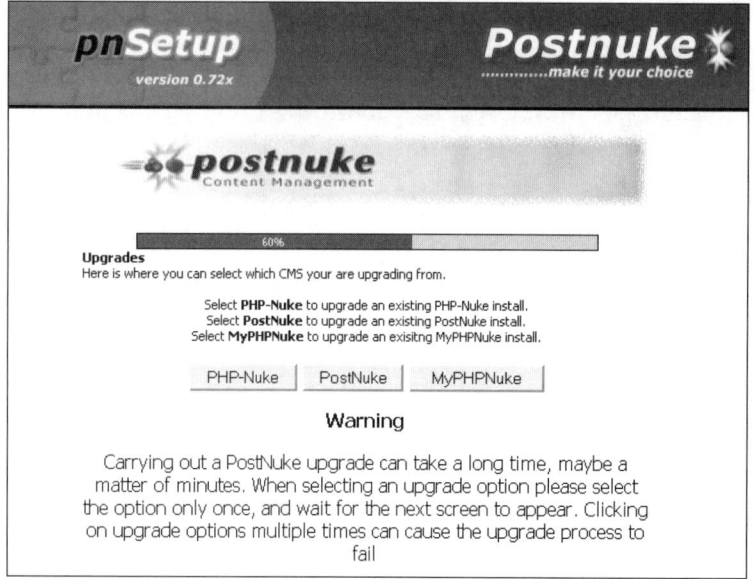

Figure 2.9   Updating your previous website.

Select the Content Management System (CMS) from which you are upgrading, and then select the version of your old site from the list provided. The rest of the install is completely automatic.

Any custom modules you added to your old install need to be added again now. If you are upgrading from a variant of PostNuke, you might find that some noncore modules do not have versions that work with PostNuke. In addition, any custom code changes or hacks must be made once again.

Troubleshooting

The PostNuke install process can be tricky, especially for new developers with little or no previous website experience. The following sections provide examples and answers to some of the more common problems, and places where you can get additional help, if needed.

The Directory Name Is Invalid

For some users of Windows XP Professional and IIS 5.1, running PHP scripts produces only the error "The Directory Name is invalid." This problem is fixed through a setting in IIS. Bring up the properties of the virtual directory where the problem occurs. Select the Virtual Directory tab and click the Configuration button in the dialog box.

You now see a list of Application Mappings. Find the entry for .php, select the row, and then click the Edit button. On the bottom left, check the Check That File Exists check box to turn that option on. Then exit the dialog boxes saving the change.

All I See Is PHP Code

If you find that when you try to preview your PostNuke site's root after moving the files into the web directory, all you see is raw PHP script, the problem is most likely that PHP is not properly installed on your web server. The server needs the PHP service installed and running to understand PHP when you browse a page. This problem also causes code to display for the install.php and every other PHP file. You need to go back over your PHP server settings and confirm that you have it running properly.

I Installed PostNuke to the Wrong Place

If you find you've placed your PostNuke files in the wrong directory, your browser URL might be different than you planned. For example, instead of having http://www.yournukesite.com/, you might have to use http://www.yournukesite.com/html/. This is not as bad a problem as it might seem. PostNuke is not dependent on the directory location, and references have been programmed to be relative, so you can just move all those files up one directory (or to wherever you want them), and PostNuke works.

The Install Says My Config Files Are Not World-Writable

If your permissions settings are not correct, the install process cannot make the changes necessary to complete the install. Read/Write access should be enough for most systems. On Linux, this is accomplished with the chmod 666 command. If you find that you have set your config file permissions but still see this error, increase the access to include Execute permissions—chmod 777 on Linux.

The Install Has Problems Creating/Populating the Database

Most likely, this problem is caused by a problem with your user's MySQL privileges. If your user was set up by your external host, you might need them to increase your user's access. If you have direct shell access to your server, you can also try to log in and create table data.

I Know I've Created My User Perfectly, But the Account Does Not Work

If you know you have created the database user correctly, but the user does not seem to be accessible, stop and restart your MySQL server. Though this happens rarely, some systems seem to need a server restart for MySQL to properly initialize changes that have been made.

My Install Worked But Now I Can't Log In

First, did you change the Admin password? If not, your password is "Password" if you used the automated install or "God" if you did the manual install from the SQL file.

Your problem might be that you are not using a fully qualified domain name (FQDN) consisting of a hostname, domain, and top-level domain. These site names are good:

- www.mynukesite.com
- www.clubfun.org
- nuke.mydomain.com

These examples are not fully qualified:

- mynukesite.com
- localhost

Documentation for setting up your server's hostname can be found at the pnDocs site (docs.postnuke.com).

If you need to run PostNuke without an FQDN, you need to use the Intranet option during your install. After the install, you can use the PostNuke Swiss Army Knife tool (http://download.postnuke.com/pafiledb.php?action=category&id=47) to change to Intranet Mode and regain access to your site. Place the psak.php file in your site's root directory and browse to it. The PostNuke Swiss Army Knife is covered in greater detail later in this book.

Getting More Help

The absolute first place you should go to get more help with PostNuke is the online forum community (forums.postnuke.com). Thousands of forum members are out there, and anything and everything related to PostNuke is discussed.

The forums are also searchable, and it's a good idea to look for your question in previous posts before creating a new one. Odds are your questions have already been asked and answered, dozens of times. Please be courteous when asking questions.

You can also find information in the official PostNuke documentation area (docs.postnuke.com). The site contains a large and growing repository of information on both current and future releases of PostNuke. The pnDocs site is also where you can find the main PostNuke frequently asked questions (FAQs; http://docs.postnuke.com/modules.php?op=modload&name=FAQ&file=index).

Live help can be obtained on Internet Relay Chat (IRC). The PostNuke IRC server is irc.postnuke.com, and you might want to try one of the following channels:

- #postnuke-support

- #postnuke-chat

- #postnuke

Next

Congratulations, you have installed PostNuke! In the next chapter, you discover steps you can take to confirm your site is set up properly and securely.

PostNuke Essentials

3

It's time to start making the PostNuke site truly yours by customizing the global website settings. PostNuke includes a central administrative area where you can configure nearly everything about your site, from its name displayed in the browser's title bar to the footer code displayed on every page. But first, you need to understand the naming conventions and terms used throughout PostNuke. Generally, language should not be a barrier to using PostNuke, but you do need to know about a few terminology quirks. In this chapter's upcoming sections, you learn about

- PostNuke terminology

- Working with the administration system

- Site settings

PostNuke Terminology

A number of terms and conventions used with PostNuke can be confusing to a new user of the application. To minimize any problems you might encounter with some of the words, this section covers the most common issues.

Modules and Blocks

You will see the terms *modules* and *blocks* universally throughout PostNuke. PostNuke is essentially developed in a modular way and each component of PostNuke is called a module. Many modules do their job unseen, working seamlessly as part of the overall PostNuke system. Some modules interact with users and administrators, and some have what are called blocks. Blocks are smaller components of modules that display module content for your site.

Core modules specifically refer to those components included with the PostNuke package itself. *Third-party modules* are written by other developers outside of the main PostNuke team and are released separately from PostNuke. Many third-party modules are exceptionally helpful and widely used, and some of them have been incorporated into PostNuke itself, becoming core modules.

International Spellings

It's very important to note that in addition to PostNuke's worldwide usage, the application is also developed internationally. Other language options allow you to change from the English default, but there are currently no dialect choices for English in the default install. English words are just as likely to appear with British spellings as they are with American.

> **Note**
>
> PostNuke 0.8, predicted to be available sometime in the later half of 2005, will include a completely reworked pnLanguages module that will centralize the settings for a site and make it much easier to create support for additional languages and dialects.

Themes

PostNuke separates its content from presentation using *themes*. Many applications now allow this kind of visual customization, and you might also be familiar with the term *skin*, where "skinning an application" is equivalent to applying a theme to change its appearance. Though some Content Management Systems (CMS) use skin to describe their presentation layer, in PostNuke the standard is theme. PostNuke's themes are made using one or more web files containing Hypertext Markup Language (HTML), PHP code, or both. The creation of PostNuke themes is covered in Chapter 10, "Themes," and Chapter 15, "Customized Themes."

Stories, Articles, and News

Some PostNuke terms are also used interchangeably in what can be an inconsistent or unclear manner. This is likely due to the large number of different developers who have worked on the PostNuke application over the years. The most commonly confused example is the use of *stories*, *articles*, and *news*. All three words refer to items posted and managed through the same tools. For example, when you post information through a form, you have the choice of displaying it on the home page or simply adding it to the site. If you show the item on the home page, it's considered "news." Old news is cycled off the home page over time. Regardless of whether an item is displayed on the home page, it is still part of the collection of permanent "articles."

The term "story" is used in PostNuke to identify the administrative management of news and articles. In PostNuke usage, a site administrator adds or approves a story for the home page news, whereas a general site visitor submits news for the site. In both cases, a given story can also be sidelined as simply an article and never appear on the home page at all. So, a given posting that appears on the home page can, at any point, be referred to as a story, article, or news item. Even old articles are called past news or news stories. There's very little clear distinction. Many have commented upon this issue, and there will hopefully be a more clear usage of those terms in a future release.

Topics, Categories, and Sections

Another sometimes-confusing usage in PostNuke is found with the terms *topics*, *categories*, and *sections*. Topics are a way of grouping news articles. When an article appears, it is usually accompanied by a graphic; the graphic is defined by the topic with which the article is associated. Every article must have a topic. Categories also group articles, but a category is only displayed as text, usually before an article's title. A default category called "Articles," which when chosen essentially means an article is not in any category, is in the general "Articles" pool. Topics and categories have similar names and duties, but topics are what add the icon to an article.

Sections might seem to be related to topics and categories, but they are actually completely separate and should not be a problem after you understand their function. A section is a kind of alternative article, but its format is more for long, multipage documents. These long documents are grouped by section name. General site users cannot submit a section document for inclusion on a site. Section documents are also named articles, but section articles are not connected in any way to news/story articles.

Hacks

And, finally, you will be reading a great deal about PostNuke *hacks*. A hack in PostNuke is a manual change or rewriting of the PHP code that alters the function of the application. These changes do not carry the negative connotation often associated with hacking. PostNuke is open source, which means its code is legally open to any changes you want to make. PostNuke hacks are often publicized and recommended by other developers and users as a means to extend PostNuke's default capabilities. Popular hacks can be chosen to be included with future releases of PostNuke just like popular third-party modules. Throughout this book, you will discover the custom changes that you too can make to PostNuke's source code to maximize its use.

Working with the Administration System

The Administration system provides access to all of the configurable modules and settings of PostNuke. Access to the system is achieved through the Administration link found in the Main Menu on the left in Figure 3.1. You can move or add additional links to access the Administration area, including incorporating them into your theme, which is covered in Chapter 15.

If you install additional modules, they automatically appear on the same Administration Menu page with all of the core modules. In the current version of PostNuke, modules are arranged in alphabetical order by module name (see Figure 3.1), but to make them easier to understand, you can group the modules into three main categories: System, Utility, and Content.

> **Note**
>
> PostNuke version 0.8 will include the ability to create physical categories to group the modules for easier management.

Figure 3.1   Main PostNuke Administration Menu.

System Modules

System modules are the sole domain of the site administrator and are used to directly change how PostNuke works and who can use it. The system modules from version 0.750 include

- Admin Messages
- Blocks
- Groups
- Languages
- Modules
- Permissions
- Settings
- User Administration

Utility Modules

The following utility modules are grouped with the criteria that they enhance given content but do not themselves create content, or they are tools that are not related to the direct management of the site but are still useful to site managers. The utility modules are

- Autolinks
- Censor
- Mail Users
- Ratings
- HTTP Referer
- Topics
- Top List

Content Modules

Content modules allow the direct creation of additional content for a given site. Some of these modules require an administrator's approval for their content to go live, and others interact with site visitors immediately. PostNuke content modules include

- Add Story
- Banners

- Comments

- Downloads

- Ephemerids

- FAQ

- Polls

- Quotes

- Reviews

- Sections

- Submit News

- Web Links

All of these modules are explained in detail in the forthcoming chapters, and where applicable, various third-party modules you might find useful are also discussed. Main site configuration is done through the Settings module, discussed later in this chapter.

Displayed on the Administration Menu page beneath the list of modules are three sections. The Programmed Articles section lists any articles scheduled for future release on the site. The Last 20 Articles section shows the most recent postings and provides an easy edit form. The name of the Current Online Poll can be found in the last section at the bottom of the page.

Role of the Site Administrator

The primary job of a PostNuke site administrator is really little different from any website manager. Websites contain content, and users of the Internet access content. A site manager controls the connection between the users and the content leading them to visit the site.

But the relationship between sites and users is more complex than that. Users expect content to be current and relevant, but they also expect it to be of good quality and easy to find. If you are new to website management, consider these concepts carefully, and take them to heart. Understanding and accounting for the needs of your users is necessary to have a successful PostNuke site.

PostNuke provides tools to create content, but it also is a system that allows you as an administrator to customize the interface to the site information. You can perform simple editing functions, such as profanity reduction and keyword linkage. You can create custom content hierarchies for grouping articles and links. You can even design a unique theme with user-friendly navigation for immediate access to site content.

Users can be grouped using the permission system to allow access to specialized areas of the site. Some sections can be made dynamically visible only to a select group. A special group of users could be given partial administrative privileges to distribute the management of the site.

It's important to keep in mind what you are building with PostNuke. Remember your target visitors and what their needs are expected to be. A good PostNuke site administrator takes the system as only a beginning, a foundation on which to build a new, larger website.

Site Settings

The *Settings module* allows you to administer all general website configuration options in PostNuke. In the way that a given module might allow you to configure a particular site feature included with the module, the Settings module configures global variables for PostNuke itself. There are currently six main parts to the one long form:

- General Site Info
- Footer Messages
- Backend Configuration
- Security Options
- Run on Intranet
- HTML Options

When you submit your changes, anything altered in any of the six parts is submitted together.

General Site Info

The *Site Name* field allows you to place the name of your site into the PostNuke database, as shown in Figure 3.2. This is a very important field. Many themes, including the default ones included with PostNuke, use the Site Name field as a variable to dynamically display the name of your site in the page header. Your site's name also displays in the browser's title bar, and it is used to name the bookmarks visitors make to your site. Even if you decide later to use a graphic for your title, you should always have this field populated.

The *Site Logo* field names a file that should be a small version of your logo (no larger than 300px wide and 80px tall). The graphic must be placed in the main PostNuke images directory. You can find the default logo.gif file there as an example. The format of this graphic should be GIF, JPG, or PNG, just like any web image.

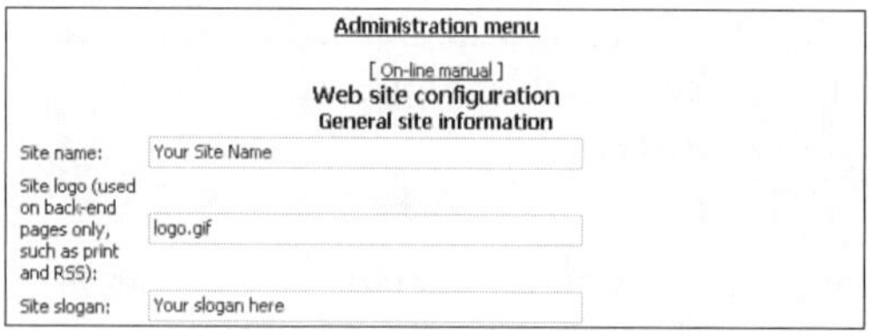

	Administration menu
	[On-line manual]
	Web site configuration
	General site information
Site name:	Your Site Name
Site logo (used on back-end pages only, such as print and RSS):	logo.gif
Site slogan:	Your slogan here

Figure 3.2   Describing your site.

This logo filename can also be referenced in a theme, just as the site name mentioned previously, and some of the default themes previously used the file in the site header. In the current PostNuke release, the Site Logo field has two functions. When a user views content in the Printer Friendly Page format, all normal images and theme structure are removed from the page. The resulting content only includes the Site Logo file above the text. Second, when a website gets a Really Simple Syndication (RSS) news feed from a PostNuke site, the Site Logo image can optionally display with the news to identify where it comes from. It's recommended that you keep this image as small as possible to make a minimal impact on printing and news feed usage. For additional information on the later feature, see the "Backend Configuration" section later in this chapter.

The *Site Slogan* field is used to describe your site further. It appears in all the default themes, usually after or under the site name. You can code this variable out of your theme, but it's a good idea to leave it in the browser's title bar. PostNuke 0.750 does not provide a field for creating and editing your site's meta description tag. You can hack PostNuke to include additional meta tags (see Chapter 21, "General PostNuke Hacks"), but if you leave the page header information as the default, your site's title becomes very important for search engine indexing.

The *Meta Keywords* field, shown in Figure 3.3, allows you to populate the standard keyword tag used to describe your site to a search engine. The words and phrases should be separated by commas. Search engines usually give priority to the earlier words over the latter, so place your main words first. In addition, it is best to avoid word repetition, as many engines penalize you with a reduced ranking if they believe you are trying to abuse the keyword system.

You also have the option to turn on PostNuke's *Dynamic Meta Keywords*. With this feature enabled, the Meta Keywords for a given page are determined by the content displayed on the page. For example, if you are viewing a news article, the article's content is parsed by PostNuke, and the most commonly used words are applied to the page's keywords.

Metakeywords: nuke, postnuke, postnuke, free, community, php, portal, opensource, open source, gpl, mysql, sql, database, web site, website, weblog, content management, contentmanagement, web content management, webcontentmanagement

Figure 3.3   Managing Meta Keywords.

Tip

The use of the Dynamic Meta Keywords feature can result in reduced performance for your site. If you are using this setting and find your site is running slow, try turning it off and test for speed improvement. See Appendix A, "Speed Up PostNuke," for more performance tips.

PostNuke's *Site Start Date* field describes the date your PostNuke site itself goes live. Even if your website existed before you installed and began using PostNuke, this date should reflect when PostNuke itself became active. It is displayed on the built-in statistics module, and that information only relates to PostNuke itself no matter how long your site existed previously. The date is actually a regular text field, so you can write the date in whichever manner you prefer, such as any of the following examples:

- July 15, 2010
- July 2010
- 2010-07-15
- 15/07/2010
- 07.2010
- Thursday, July 15th 2010, 10:30am

The *Administrator Email* field is used with any correspondence you initiate using the PostNuke mailing features. The contents of this field appear as the "From" address in the sent email. You might want to set up a special email address for administrative PostNuke messages to help protect your personal address from unwanted posts, such as spam solicitations or virus mailers.

> **Note**
>
> PostNuke cannot send email if you have not configured one of the transport options in the Mailer module. Simple Mail Transfer Protocol (SMTP) services defined in your php.ini file are used by default. If you do not plan to have a mail server set up for your PostNuke site, you can leave the Administrator Email field blank.

Your site's global theme is chosen using the Default Theme For Your Site drop-down list box. The theme you choose here is the first thing all users see when they visit your website. PostNuke includes one basic theme, ExtraLite, enabled by default, and six different Xanthia themes. You can test each of the themes by simply selecting them and saving your changes in this form.

> **Tip**
>
> Click the Inactive Xanthia Themes Are Not Included in This List link by the Default Theme list box to jump to the Xanthia module administration page where you can easily add the other default themes.

The default themes are all similar, and you should have no trouble getting back to the settings form after testing. The theme shown in this book's figures is called simply "PostNuke" (see Figure 3.4).

Site users can be allowed to customize their own site interface by selecting a different theme in their personal account preferences. If you prefer to restrict the site to only your main theme, you can select "No" for the Allow Users to Override Theme option. The theme list is dynamically generated using the theme directories found in the /themes/ directory in your PostNuke site; if you remove a theme from that directory, it is also removed from the list box for both users and your website settings form. Users without an account or those who are not currently logged on will always see the default theme.

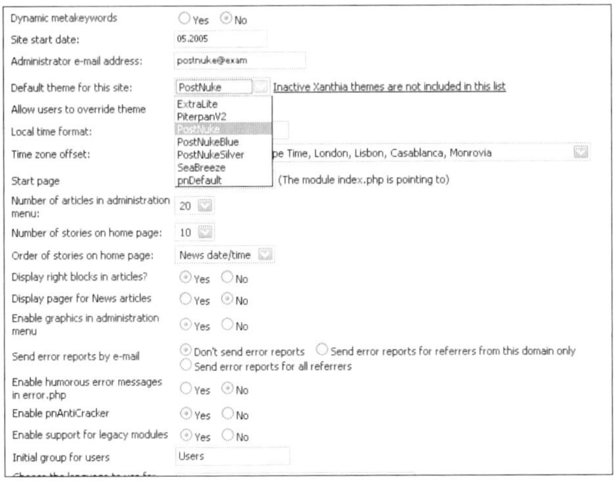

Figure 3.4 Choosing your site's theme using the drop-down list box.

Note

If you initially allow users to select personal themes, but later turn off this option, all users automatically see the site's default theme. If you rename or remove a theme previously chosen by a user, the user also automatically sees the default site theme until their chosen theme is replaced or renamed.

The *Local Time Format* field determines how date and time references are displayed throughout your site. It is mainly tied to the language setting. It's recommended that you leave this setting at your installed default, such as en_US. To alter the way dates appear on pages, go to your language directory and edit the configuration files manually. For example, with a site using English, edit /language/eng/global.php. The code you need to look for is as follows:

```
define('_DATEBRIEF','%b %d, %Y');
define('_DATELONG','%A, %B %d, %Y');
define('_DATESTRING','%A, %B %d @ %H:%M:%S');
define('_DATETIMEBRIEF','%b %d, %Y - %I:%M %p');
define('_DATETIMELONG','%A, %B %d, %Y - %I:%M %p');
```

The dates are defined using standard PHP time/date character variables. A complete listing of what characters are possible, what each means, and how to use them is available online in the official PHP documentation at http://www.php.net/manual/en/function.date.php.

The *Time Zone Offset* field should be set to the server's local time zone. The positive/negative hour offset is based on Greenwich mean time (GMT), which is the default setting. Every time PostNuke displays date or time information, it is in reference to this setting. Individual users with accounts can select their respective local time zone in their personal preferences. A user's local time is then computed using the server's Time Zone Offset and hardware time setting as a basis.

Your site's *Start Page* is determined by the next selection box. By default, all PostNuke sites use the News module as a home page. The drop-down list box provides a list of other modules you can use instead. News is still available to site visitors through the news link, just as other sections are always available from the Main Menu.

As mentioned previously, when you browse to the main site Administration Menu page, additional information areas are below the icons. One of those sections lists recent articles posted to your site. By default, only 20 articles are shown, but you can change that amount from 10 to 50 using the Number of Articles in Administration Menu field.

Similar to the Number of Articles in Administration Menu option, you can also set the number of posts visible on the main news page using the Number of Stories on Homepage list box. The default is 10 news articles, but you can increase it up to 30 by using this form.

Tip

A large number of news articles displayed at once can result in slower page display. If you are using News as your site's home page, it's better to keep the article number low so your site's most-visited page remains fast for your visitors.

The *Order of Stories on Homepage* option selects the criteria PostNuke uses to determine the age and importance of articles for display. By default, this field is set to News Date/Time. Each article has a time of creation associated with it, and normally the default setting is what you want to use. Alternatively, you can select the News ID to determine display order. Most PostNuke content is given a unique ID number as the content is created. The numbers are incremental and respective to the section where the content belongs. If you feel you cannot trust the time stamps placed on your articles, for example if your server's time setting has changed, using the ID number displays the articles in their creation order.

The *Display Right Blocks in Articles* option relates only to how a story article is displayed when read fully. For example, if you click on the name of a news posting, you are sent to a page containing just the one article. PostNuke articles have extra "right blocks" that can be displayed for extra information, such as to show other articles related to the one being viewed. If you turn this setting off, articles are automatically displayed in the full width available.

Note

Do not confuse the Right Blocks in Articles option with the overall positioning of blocks in a theme. PostNuke themes have content locations with names such as "left," "right," and "center," and those positions are used to describe module blocks. But the name similarity with right-side article blocks is not meant to relate them.

You can make lengthy News articles easier to read using the Display Pager in News Articles option. Toggling the radio buttons to "Yes" breaks up lengthy articles into multiple pages with a dynamic numbered navigation bar.

PostNuke also allows you to turn off all those icons on the main Administration Menu page. Select "No" for the Graphics in Administration Menu option, and you receive a text-only page, as shown in Figure 3.5. The display is dynamic, and the icons return just as easily. This feature is only visible to those with access to the Administration Menu.

Tip

You can also change the administration icons to use other graphics. The icon for a given module is kept in the `images` directory of the module and is always called `admin.gif`.

The *Send Error Reports by Email* feature relates to users' attempted browsing to pages that do not exist. When a site visitor browses to an invalid uniform resource locator (URL), an email can be generated and mailed to the site administration address. Three different configurations for this feature are as follows:

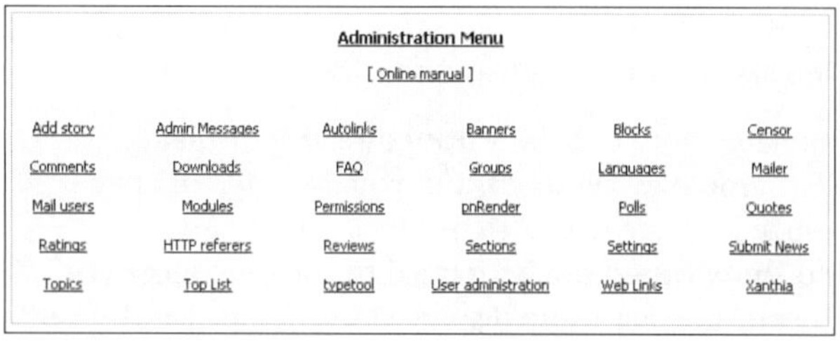

Administration Menu

[Online manual]

Add story	Admin Messages	Autolinks	Banners	Blocks	Censor
Comments	Downloads	FAQ	Groups	Languages	Mailer
Mail users	Modules	Permissions	pnRender	Polls	Quotes
Ratings	HTTP referers	Reviews	Sections	Settings	Submit News
Topics	Top List	typetool	User administration	Web Links	Xanthia

Figure 3.5   The Administration Menu without graphics.

- **Don't Send Error Reports**—Selecting this option disables error reporting for your site.

- **For Referrers from This Domain Only**—This option generates an email when a visitor clicks an invalid link within your site. The broken links reside on your site itself, and this report shows you what needs to be fixed.

- **For All Referrers**—All referrers report all failed page-viewing attempts from any source. This option is useful if other sites often link deeply into your site; their links might become invalid as you make changes. The report shows what old moved or deleted pages you might need to replace with a redirect.

All web servers allow you to create customized error pages for your site. The PostNuke developers have created a humorous variation of the standard 404 Page Not Found message, and you can turn on this feature using the Enable Funny Error Message in error.php option. This feature is more humorous than useful and consists of a series of JavaScript-generated messages meant to be from the server that explains how sad and depressed the server is that it has failed to find your requested page. If your PostNuke site is of a commercial or professional focus, you should leave this feature turned off. An example of the message can be seen at http://www.postnuke.com/error.php?error=404.

Your website will be more secure if you leave the Enable pnAntiCracker feature on as the default. This PostNuke security module runs invisibly as part of the site subsystem and constantly watches for potential break-in or hack attempts on your PostNuke website via the use of GET, POST, and Cookie (GPC) variables. If an attack on your site triggers pnAntiCracker, the site administrator's email you configured previously is sent a message containing the ENV variables, such as IP address, browser, operating system, and so on, of the suspected assailant. The message also includes the module and script information relating to the attack. PostNuke 0.8 will include additional custom configuration options for pnAntiCraker.

Enable Support for Legacy Modules is a very important setting for your site. When set to "yes," it allows modules that are not fully pnAPI compliant to function with PostNuke. As PostNuke .750 is a release designed to transition users to version 0.8, many current modules for PostNuke are not yet compliant, including some core modules. Unless you are certain all of the modules are pnAPI compliant, keep this option set to "yes."

The *Initial Group for Users* field allows you to change the group setting for newly created accounts. When a new user account is created, whatever you have typed into that field is the group name given to the new account. Site permissions and user management are covered in Chapter 9, "Users and Permissions," but it's important to note that you must be careful when setting this field. It is a test field and does not provide a drop-down list of group names. If you mistype a group name, so that new users are assigned to a group that does not exist, those new users are locked out of your site. All modules and blocks outside of the most basic HTML in your theme are not displayed, and a locked-out user might not even be able to log back out of your site.

The *Choose the Language to use for Your Website* field determines the default language setting for all pages. Users with PostNuke accounts can select their personal language preference. This setting does not mean your pages are automatically translated into a newly chosen language. Each piece of content you create is associated with a given language (or with all languages), and the setting determines which content is displayed based upon the contents' association. You need to install additional language packs to have translations of PostNuke itself. Language options are covered in Chapter 4, "Modules and Blocks."

If you *Activate Compression* for your PostNuke website, you enable the GZIP compression option of PHP. Basically, a given page is compressed at the server before it is sent to a visitor's browser. The change offers a relatively small speed improvement for pages with many images, but it is noticeable on text-laden sites. This feature also only works with browsers that support GZIP-compressed pages; older browsers that cannot handle the compression receive pages normally.

Footer Messages

This section of the Site Settings has only one large text area field titled Footer Line. Here, you should enter any information you want to appear on the bottom of all pages on your site. Suggestions include copyright and legal notices, disclaimer information, contact links, and perhaps a miniature navigation bar for access to major areas of your site. You can include HTML in this footer field; the default footer is formatted with HTML and provides copyright and licensing information, as well as links to technologies used to create PostNuke (see Figure 3.6).

Figure 3.6   Default PostNuke footer.

Backend Configuration

PostNuke includes support for RSS news feeds. RSS is a universal and popular Extensible Markup Language (XML) format used to share news headlines and similar timely content between websites. You can include other sites' content on your website, and other sites can list "what's new" from your PostNuke site. The Backend options here allow you to define the content you send.

The *Backend Title* field should be populated with a short description of your site or the type of news you provide. Your site name is automatically sent with a feed, and this is the title of the news being sent.

The *Backend Language* field identifies your content using the RSS listing. The language most commonly used in your news should be set here.

Tip

Your site provides RSS feeds automatically by default. If you want to turn off this feature, you need to rename or delete the `backend.php` file found in your PostNuke directory root. You can also edit this file manually for more advanced configuration options.

You can add news from another site by installing an RSS block. More information on RSS can be found at the following links:

- http://blogs.law.harvard.edu/tech/rss
- http://www.webreference.com/authoring/languages/xml/rss/intro/
- http://www.xml.com/pub/a/2002/12/18/dive-into-xml.html
- http://bdn.borland.com/article/0,1410,31981,00.html

Security Options

This section determines how user accounts interact with PostNuke. When a user logs in to his account, he has the option to be "remembered." Checking that box in the form places a cookie on the user's machine to authenticate him automatically when he returns to the website. This can be a security risk in shared computer environments in which a different user visiting the same PostNuke site might have access to areas where they would normally not be allowed.

Three basic Security Level options are available to you:

- **High**—Users must log in each time they return to the site.

- **Medium**—Users stay logged in for a set number of days.

- **Low**—Users stay logged in forever.

Medium security is selected by default, and you can set the specific number of days before a user is required to log in again using the text field beneath the list box.

Users are also tracked by session, so that as users travel throughout your site, they are known by the site and automatically have access to available areas. If a user goes idle too long, the user's session can be ended, and this way PostNuke auto-logs out a given account. This setting is dependent on the security level, in that a low Security Level might still allow access through a new login.

The *Check Referer on Printer Friendly Page* option logs the source of traffic going to your site's print-ready pages. This setting is off by default, and unless you have security worries, it is best left that way. Under normal circumstances, all traffic to a printer page comes from links on your site.

Run on Intranet

This single radio button selection determines whether PostNuke is running in Intranet Mode. When turned on, the Intranet option reduces the amount of security PostNuke uses by default.

This option usually comes up in reference to the use of fully qualified domain names (FQDNs) with sites. For example, your full domain might be http://www.mypostnukesite.com/, but if you use http://mypostnukesite.com/, the URL is not fully qualified. The complete name helps ensure a site is identified correctly. Users on an intranet might simply use http://intranet/ to get to the site. Internally, behind a secure firewall, having an unqualified domain is fine. If your site is available to the general public, it is strongly recommended you leave this setting turned off.

HTML Options

PostNuke is a form-driven application, but when a user submits content that contains HTML, a bad choice of tags, by accident or intent, can break the overall site shell when the content is later rendered. Because of this common problem, PostNuke has implemented a detailed set of HTML tag controls you can customize through the Site Settings page (see Figure 3.7).

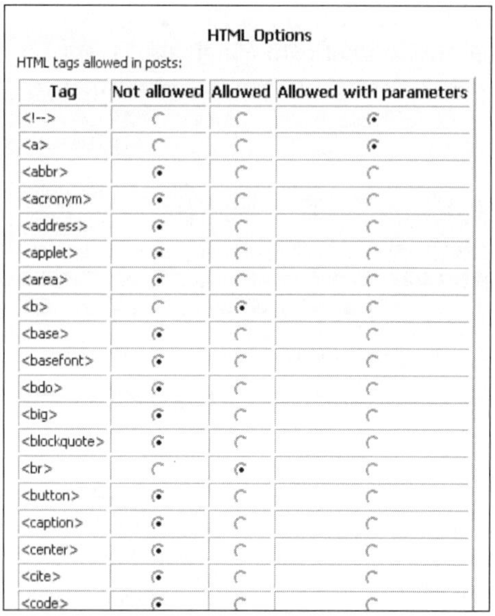

	HTML Options		

HTML tags allowed in posts:

Tag	Not allowed	Allowed	Allowed with parameters
<!-->	○	○	●
<a>	○	○	●
<abbr>	●	○	○
<acronym>	●	○	○
<address>	●	○	○
<applet>	●	○	○
<area>	●	○	○
<b>	○	●	○
<base>	●	○	○
<basefont>	●	○	○
<bdo>	●	○	○
<big>	●	○	○
<blockquote>	●	○	○
 	○	●	○
<button>	●	○	○
<caption>	●	○	○
<center>	●	○	○
<cite>	●	○	○
<code>	●	○	○

Figure 3.7 Global HTML tag settings.

For a given tag, you have three options:

- Not Allowed
- Allowed
- Allowed with Parameters

Not Allowed means the tag typed into a form with regular content is visible when the content is read. *Allowed* tags are rendered, but only the tag itself is parsed. *Allowed with Parameters* enables tags to be used normally and completely with all attributes.

You can see in Figure 3.8 that the article has two tags in it, a comment and a hyperlink. The comment is restricted by default, so it and the text inside it both appear. The hyperlink anchor, on the other hand, is allowed with full parameters, so the tag can be typed and the HREF attribute in the anchor is rendered making the link active.

Note

Tag settings are globally applied to the site and are in effect for all user accounts regardless of group or permission settings. Even the Admin account must follow these HTML rules.

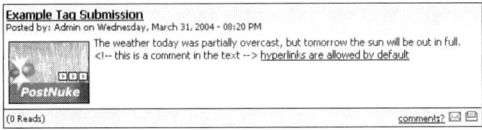

Figure 3.8   Tag settings article example.

If you trust your site users to not damage the operation of PostNuke with bad tag usage, you can relax the HTML restrictions. Many of the tags can add a lot of functionality to a PostNuke site. It mainly depends on what abilities you grant your users. If, for example, you restrict posting to only a special power users group, this smaller approved group might be fine with all HTML open to use. An intranet environment is also a good example of an environment with a known user group.

Also as stated in the warning on the page, the <img>, <span>, <marquee>, <script>, <embed>, <object>, and <iframe> tags all pose a potential security hazard. Those tags can be used in inappropriate ways to gain access to user information or outright break your site. Do not allow potentially dangerous tags unless your site is otherwise secure through other settings or a known user base.

The final option, *Translate Embedded HTML Entities into Real Characters*, converts and displays standard foreign language characters from the &#xxx; entities to real characters. This option is only important if your site uses a foreign language and you're having problems getting the special characters of the language to display on your PostNuke site.

When you have completed your changes to the Website Configuration screen, simply click the Save Changes button at the bottom of the page to apply the settings.

Troubleshooting

If you've never worked with a CMS or portal site system before, you might find some of the features and settings a bit complicated. But keep in mind, after you have done the initial setup, the majority of those options will not change often during the life of your site, if they change at all. Try out different settings to see what works best for your site.

For most of the site settings, making changes will not outright break your site. But there are some circumstances where you might have problems making changes, or even accidentally lock yourself out of your own site. Three common concerns with initial setups are discussed in the following sections.

No Authorization as Administrator

A very common problem when navigating through the PostNuke administration system is the appearance of the error message "No Authorization to Carry Out Operation" after submitting a form. Secure operations are accomplished using authids created for you when you log in using an administrative account. The message occurs when you use browser navigation buttons instead of in-page navigation links. PostNuke is designed to work this way as an additional security feature to prevent URL data submissions.

For example, suppose you filled out a form, clicked the Submit button, and then clicked the Back button to make a change and submit again. The second submit is not valid because you did not go to the form page in a legal way. To prevent this from happening, you must use the navigation links built in to PostNuke whenever possible.

Locked Out Without Intranet Mode

If your PostNuke site is running on an intranet and you accidentally turn the Intranet Mode setting off, you might find yourself locked out of your site if your only browsing option is to use an unqualified domain. A quick fix for this problem is to set an FQDN for your server's IP in your local machine's host file. Then, you can use a complete name from your local machine, and the server will respond to you, allowing you to turn Intranet Mode back on. Your Windows XP hosts file is found at c:\windows\system32\drivers\etc\hosts, and in Linux, the file is usually at /etc/hosts. You can edit the file with any text editor. The hosts entry would look something like this:

```
192.168.0.20    www.myserver.com
```

Bad Default User Account Group

You can easily fix a user account locked out due to a group name error by going to Administration Menu, and click on the Groups link. Select the *Group Name* to which you want to add the lost account, and choose the user account from the list provided. After being added to a valid group, the user account can log in normally.

Next

The next chapter finally dives into the real heart of PostNuke: modules and blocks. You learn how they work and what modules come standard with PostNuke.

Modules and Blocks

4

Modules and blocks are the core components that make PostNuke work, and this chapter explains what each of the two elements means to PostNuke and how you can manage them as effective parts of your PostNuke site. This chapter covers only three main sections, but each contains a fair amount of depth. Though generally an overview of information, this is perhaps the most important chapter for new PostNuke administrators to read. This chapter discusses the following topics:

- How modules work
- Core modules overview
- How blocks work

How Modules Work

It could be said that PostNuke is simply a collection of modules, and, for the most part, that is true. If you look through the PostNuke install directory, you see there are more files and content in the one modules folder than all the others combined. Each module performs one or more tasks for the system, and it's PostNuke's component structure that allows you to customize your site to such a high degree. If you don't need a specific module, remove it. If you need additional functionality, add a new module. Modules are what give PostNuke its functionality.

Module files are all found in the /modules/ directory off your site root. You can install a new module by simply copying its files into the module directory. Modules are removed in the same way by deleting them from the folder. But in either case, you must let PostNuke know about your module changes through the main Module Administration screen, detailed later in this chapter.

Configuring Modules

You can configure PostNuke modules in many different ways. When you were making changes to the Website Configuration page in Chapter 3, "PostNuke Essentials," you were updating information in the Settings module. In fact, all of the icons found on the Administration Menu are links to configure their respective modules. There is even a module that controls all PostNuke modules' install and activation levels; it is appropriately called Modules and is also found on the Administration Menu.

Click into the Modules page, and you see a relatively blank page containing just two links: *List* and *Regenerate*. Either link choice generates a listing of modules you can manage from this page. List shows all of the modules currently installed and running on your PostNuke site, sorted alphabetically by name. It queries the database only for this information.

Regenerate looks first to the PostNuke file folders and tallies all of the modules it can find that have been loaded onto the server. It then compares that listing with the database entries and produces an updated list of all existing and new modules. If you have not installed any new or removed existing modules since you last generated a list, there will be no difference in the resulting list shown by either link. Using the Regenerate link every time to create a current listing does not harm your site.

> **Note**
>
> When you regenerate the listing, new modules added to your PostNuke `/modules/` folder are shown with an *Initialize* option. You must initialize new modules before they can be activated.

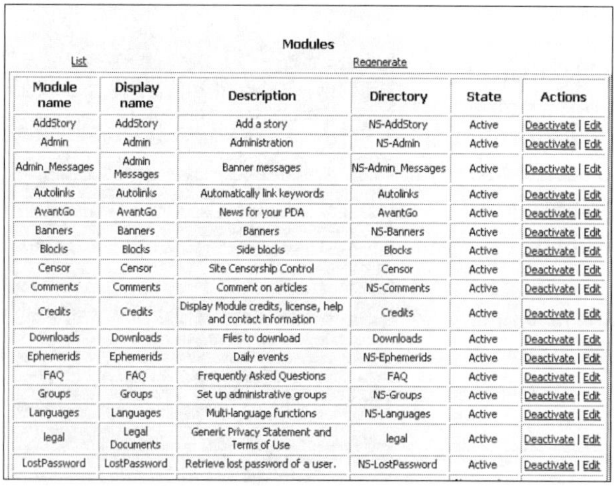

Modules

List Regenerate

Module name	Display name	Description	Directory	State	Actions
AddStory	AddStory	Add a story	NS-AddStory	Active	Deactivate | Edit
Admin	Admin	Administration	NS-Admin	Active	Deactivate | Edit
Admin_Messages	Admin Messages	Banner messages	NS-Admin_Messages	Active	Deactivate | Edit
Autolinks	Autolinks	Automatically link keywords	Autolinks	Active	Deactivate | Edit
AvantGo	AvantGo	News for your PDA	AvantGo	Active	Deactivate | Edit
Banners	Banners	Banners	NS-Banners	Active	Deactivate | Edit
Blocks	Blocks	Side blocks	Blocks	Active	Deactivate | Edit
Censor	Censor	Site Censorship Control	Censor	Active	Deactivate | Edit
Comments	Comments	Comment on articles	NS-Comments	Active	Deactivate | Edit
Credits	Credits	Display Module credits, license, help and contact information	Credits	Active	Deactivate | Edit
Downloads	Downloads	Files to download	Downloads	Active	Deactivate | Edit
Ephemerids	Ephemerids	Daily events	NS-Ephemerids	Active	Deactivate | Edit
FAQ	FAQ	Frequently Asked Questions	FAQ	Active	Deactivate | Edit
Groups	Groups	Set up administrative groups	NS-Groups	Active	Deactivate | Edit
Languages	Languages	Multi-language functions	NS-Languages	Active	Deactivate | Edit
legal	Legal Documents	Generic Privacy Statement and Terms of Use	legal	Active	Deactivate | Edit
LostPassword	LostPassword	Retrieve lost password of a user.	NS-LostPassword	Active	Deactivate | Edit

Figure 4.1 Managing your installed modules.

As you can see in Figure 4.1, the modules table has six columns. The meanings and functions of each column are as follows:

- **Module Name**—This is the real name of the module as it's referenced in the code. There are no spaces in the name, so words can be run together or joined with an underscore. When you need to reference a module name in a site setting, this is the name you need to use.

- **Display Name**—This is the user-friendly name of a module. In some listings, such as the Main Settings page, the Display Name is used to identify its respective module.

- **Description**—This column lists a short description for each module to clarify its function.

- **Directory**—This column allows you to identify different modules when you are doing file management. Modules' physical folder locations on your server are defined here.

- **State**—This is the current status for a given module. Possible states include Active, Inactive, New Version Installed, and Uninitialized.

- **Actions**—The links in this column allow you to edit the operation of their respective modules. The first option is coordinated with the *state* of a module; for example, an active module has the Deactivate link in the Actions column. The last link allows you to edit the modules operation. Modules with an inactive or uninitialized state also have a Remove option. Removed modules are dropped from the PostNuke system at the database level. The source files remain, and the modules can be immediately reinitialized, but all previous data is gone. Selecting Edit allows you to configure how the module interacts with PostNuke. From the Edit page, you can usually rename the module, change its description, and toggle the activation of additional hook features, such as Autolinks, Ratings, or Wiki support.

To see the options in action, deactivate the Polls module and return to your site's Administration Menu. Notice the Polls icon and link are missing. Activate the module again and you see Polls reappear on the Administration Menu. Other modules you install also appear as they are added.

Note

Deactivating the wrong module here can completely take down your site, requiring a reinstall if you are unable to manually make database changes to recover. The Admin, Groups, Permissions, Settings, and User modules are specifically ones you should never disable without accounting for the missing functionality beforehand with replacement modules or hacks.

You might also have noticed that even though the Polls module is deactivated, the poll on the home page remains. That is because the home page poll is an instance of a *block*, and not the module itself. Some blocks have functionality that can exist even if their module is removed. You learn more about blocks after covering the PostNuke core modules in the following section.

Core Modules Overview

All of the modules that come installed and configured as part of the PostNuke system are considered *core modules*. They are fully integrated and tested with each other to ensure the proper operation of your site. In addition, many custom modules, written by other PostNuke site developers, are available for download that can extend the functionality of your default install. These components are considered *third-party modules*, but be aware they are not guaranteed to work perfectly with your site.

Tip

Development announcements and links to many third-party modules can be found on the PostNuke website at http://mods.postnuke.com/.

Very popular third-party add-ons are often promoted by the PostNuke team, and many have been integrated into the PostNuke core system for distribution with upcoming version releases. The following sections provide short overviews of each of the core modules included with PostNuke.

Add Story

This module adds articles to PostNuke. They can optionally appear on the News page, and articles submitted through this module do not require approval to go live. In addition, a link inside Add Story allows you to review articles currently waiting on approval that were submitted using the Submit News module. See Chapter 5, "Article Modules," for more information on Add Story.

Admin

Admin is a module that creates and controls the Administration Menu.

Admin Messages

Admin Messages are static posts that appear above the changing articles on the News page. The News page is usually the default home page for a PostNuke site, and the Admin Messages are intended to display announcements or other important information to users.

The messages appear on the News page through a block. It is, of course, possible to create other blocks or customize a theme's display to allow Admin Messages to appear anywhere and in any form on the site. See Chapter 5 for more information on Admin Messages.

Autolinks

You can set up special links for keywords you feel are important for your site's users. When a keyword appears on a news article or section page, for example, it is automatically changed to be a hyperlink to the site address you configured in the Autolinks module settings.

Autolinks must be activated for specific individual modules. By clicking Edit under the Actions column on the Modules Management page, you see an Activate Autolinks for This Module check box. Enabling this option and submitting the form associates the linking system to the module.

Although it is a handy feature, the Autolinks module is a known cause of speed reduction for PostNuke sites. If your visitors don't really need the links, it's recommended you disable this module.

AvantGo

AvantGo is a free service that allows a user to have access to a website's news articles and other content through a Personal Digital Assistant (PDA) or smartphone. The AvantGo module in PostNuke allows your site's information to be served to users using the AvantGo software.

If your visitors do not use PDAs or smartphones to access your site information, this module is best removed. For more information on AvantGo, visit the official site at www.avantgo.com.

Banners

The Banners module is a well-featured advertising system that controls and monitors ads for your site. You can set up client accounts and then define each banner with a run schedule for a given client. Statistics are logged for each banner, including impressions and click-throughs. In addition, your clients can visit your site to see their ads' performance. See Chapter 13, "Money-Making Modules," for more information on banners.

Blocks

The Blocks module controls the existence and appearance of blocks on your site. More in-depth information on blocks can be found at the end of this chapter.

Censor

Objectionable content submitted to your site can be managed using the Censor module. Words added to the censor table are dynamically replaced when they appear on a page. The word shown in place of the questionable words can be changed; by default, five asterisks appear. In addition, you can turn the Censor Mode on or off at any time.

Tip

Keep in mind that anything can be censored, but you have to be specific. Use varied and creative spellings of words with which you are concerned. In addition, you can enter a site name or uniform resource locator (URL) if your site allows open posting and someone keeps spamming his site to your users.

Comments

The Comments module allows visitors to add their own opinions or clarifications to articles. Comments appear below the full article view and can be moderated by users or administrators. The Reviews module also allows comments, but review comments are part of the Reviews module. The Comments module only manages article comments. See Chapter 6, "User Interaction Modules," for more information on Comments.

Credits

Credits is a simple module tool that lists all of the modules currently installed on your site with the version, description, author, documentation, and licensing information provided by the modules' developers. You can link to the module from any menu with {Credits} or by simply using the URL /index.php?module=Credits.

Downloads

Files can be distributed from your site using the Downloads module. You can reference files stored locally on your server or remotely on a different server. Each download can also be rated with user votes. The Downloads module also has support for multiple category levels to group files. The upcoming PostNuke 0.8 will also include a sitewide category system, which will be available for the Downloads module and the very similar Web Links module. See Chapter 6 for more information on Downloads.

Ephemerids

An Ephemerid is something that is short-lived, often used to describe insects. Ephemerids in PostNuke act as a "this day in history" feature, in that you can create entries that appear just for the day in question.

FAQ

FAQ is an acronym that stands for frequently asked questions. Websites often have FAQ pages with helpful content in a question-and-answer format. Users can submit questions to the FAQ module; the questions wait for an administrator to answer them and submit them to the site. The PostNuke FAQ system also allows you to create categories to organize the questions. See Chapter 14, "Support and Statistics Modules," for more information on FAQ.

Groups

Groups are used to define site permissions for user accounts. Their function is similar to every other user groups system; specific users are grouped for easy reference by group name, and resources are restricted or permitted by groups.

By default, PostNuke only comes with the groups Admins and Users, but you can add as many more custom groups as you want. It's also possible to assign permissions to individuals, but, in general, the group system is always preferable. See Chapter 9, "Users and Permissions," for more information on Groups.

Languages

The Languages module allows you to define the primary language for your site. PostNuke can also run in a multilingual mode if you want to have multiple language packs installed simultaneously. Flag images are also included to make language selection easier.

Legal

The Legal module is an integrated part of the core PostNuke system that manages the display of legal information for the site, such as the privacy policy, user registration, access requirements, and terms of use statement. The text for your site can be changed by editing the file `/modules/legal/lang/eng/global.php`.

Lost Password

This module works with the User module to allow your site's users to retrieve their password if they have forgotten it. PostNuke initiates an email to the user with a confirmation code. The user can then enter the code on your site, and a new password is generated for her account and mailed again to the user's address. The user can log back in with the random password, just as a new user does.

Mailer

The PostNuke Mailer manages the way your site sends email. You can select SendMail, Qmail, SMTP, or the default PHP Mail() for your site's mail transport, and the module allows you to enter in an SMTP username and password to authenticate with a secure mail server.

Mail Users

Administrators can communicate with registered users using the Mail Users module. You have the option to select a specific user to contact or email all registered users with a single check box. Users must have a current valid email address in their account to receive a message, and you must have email capability configured with PHP for your PostNuke site.

Members List

Members List is a simple module that provides directory access to all registered user accounts. Users are listed with their account name, real name, an avatar if one has been selected, and a status marker to show whether they are currently online. If the user entered a personal website URL, a link is available to it. In addition, PostNuke has a built-in message system in which you can enter a message to a user through this module, which is available to him the next time he logs in.

This module also provides search capability. Users can search by nickname, real name, or website URL. Alternatively, all users are browsable through the alphabetical navigation links.

Messages

The Messages module allows personal messages to be sent from one user to another. This is the same message system mentioned in the preceding Members List section.

Modules

The Modules module manages the existence and configuration of all modules in your PostNuke site. To add, remove, update, or edit a module, use this module.

Multisites

Multisites is a complex module that allows you to create multiple PostNuke websites, each with a separate domain and look, but which share some database tables. It allows you to share content between sites on the same server that are otherwise independent. See Chapter 25, "Multisites," for more information.

News

The News module contains the backend functionality to site articles. News items are mainly configured through related modules, such as Add Story and Submit News. See Chapter 5 for more information on News.

New User

The New User module handles the account sign-up and creation for new users to your site. When users register with PostNuke, they must enter basic account information and are emailed their introductory random password to confirm their address. All new user functionality is handled through the New User module. See Chapter 9 for more information on New User.

Past Nuke

This module was written to include administrative compatibility for older PostNuke modules that are no longer available with the current release. This module is disabled by default, and is only important if you need the backward compatibility.

Permissions

Access to all PostNuke content happens through the Permissions module. Groups or individual users can be given authorization for site resources. Each permission setting is ordered with precedence to higher entries. Care must be taken when making changes to this module. See Chapter 9 for more information on Permissions.

pnRender

The pnRender module is a component of the Xanthia Templating Environment (XTE). It's a subclass of the Smarty Templating Engine for PHP (smarty.php.net) and provides a framework for automating and modularizing the presentation of PostNuke modules. All new PostNuke modules should be developed using pnRender, but not all current modules employ pnRender. pnRender itself is used by other modules that depend on pnRender's tools to function. See Chapter 10, "Themes," for more information on pnRender.

Polls

The Polls module adds simple radio button surveys to PostNuke. Although not entirely scientific, the polls might provide some insight into your users and often can be a form of entertaining content. See Chapter 6 for more information on Polls.

Quotes

Quotes blocks added to your site display a random quote and its author from those you have added to the database. The selection is only random; to create an assigned daily quote, try the Ephemerids module.

Ratings

Ratings are available for modules throughout your PostNuke installation. You must enter the configuration screens under the Modules Management page to enable the Activate Ratings for This Module check box.

Ratings can be recorded with a variety of different styles, such as percentage, number out of ten, number out of five, stars out of ten, or the default stars out of five. You can also set security levels ranging from multiple votes allowed from a user to only one vote ever.

Recommend Us

The Recommend Us module allows users to email someone they know about your PostNuke site. This feature is common on many websites and is often called "Send to a Friend." The resulting email simply directs its recipient to visit the source site. See Chapter 13 for more information on Recommend Us.

Referers

A page's "referer" is the link on whichever other page a user followed to get to your site. The misspelling of the term is intentional and part of the Hypertext Transfer Protocol (HTTP) standard. PostNuke counts all HTTP referers, the URL or bookmark where the link originated, and shows the percentage of hits from a given referer.

Reviews

The Review module allows users to submit their opinions about products or places to your site. Ratings, a related web link, and an image can also be included with the review. User-submitted reviews sit in a queue until they are approved for the site. See Chapter 6 for more information on Reviews.

Search

The Search module enables a comprehensive keyword search of all content in your site's database. Returns are grouped by respective content area, such as articles together and reviews together.

Sections

Sections are designed to handle lengthy articles set up by the site administrator. They are intended to be more permanent fixtures to your site, unlike news articles that "get old." You can create multiple sections that act like categories to group your articles. Each section has its own header with an image. See Chapter 5 for more information on Sections.

Settings

The Settings module manages the global PostNuke site settings as described in Chapter 3.

Stats

The PostNuke Stats module provides visitor traffic information similar to most website log systems. The following categories are tracked:

- Browsers
- Operating Systems
- Visitors by Hour
- Visitors by Day of the Week
- Visitors by Month
- Miscellaneous Stats

The final category includes general totaled information, such as total members, stories published, topics, and comments. See Chapter 14 for more information on Stats.

Submit News

Submit News allows administrators to post articles without passing them to the approval queue first, and articles awaiting approval can be reviewed from the Submit News module as well. See Chapter 5 for more information on Submit News.

Template

The Template module is not a real module and only exists as a guide for other developers who want to build their own module. It's not used by PostNuke in an active way. This directory can and should be removed from your live PostNuke site as part of postinstall cleanup.

Top Lists

Similar to the Stats module, Top Lists displays the most popular items for a given set of categories. The default categories listed are as follows:

- Most Read Stories
- Most Commented Stories
- Most Voted On Polls
- Most Active Authors
- Most Read Reviews

The Top Lists module is initially set to show the top ten items for each category, but this number is variable and can be set to anything.

Topics

Topics are categories used to group articles. Each topic is identified by an icon graphic that is displayed with its article. You can create as many different topics for articles as you want. See Chapter 5 for more information on Topics.

TypeTool

TypeTool is a universal WYSIWYG Hypertext Markup Language (HTML) editor for PostNuke. WYSIWYG is an acronym for What You See Is What You Get, and when you enable the TypeTool module in PostNuke, every time you click on a text area form box in the pages of other modules, you have the option to enter a Visual Mode. Choosing "No" keeps the field as standard HTML. Selecting "Yes" converts the text area into a simple WYSIWYG editor where you can click buttons for HTML instead of typing the tags manually.

The editor is handy in environments in which users who don't know HTML are expected to add site content with HTML formatting. It is also compatible with current browsers, including Mozilla Firefox and Microsoft Internet Explorer.

Users

The Users module allows you to add new users and edit existing accounts. Through this module, you can also change the way accounts work, such as altering the requirements for registration and adding additional fields to capture more user information. See Chapter 9 for more information on Users.

Web Links

The Web Links module is very similar to the Downloads module. You can enter links to other sites with a title and description for each entry. The Configuration page provides a large variety of other options, such as how many links to display per page, voting and Top Links setup, and whether links can be posted anonymously. The Web Links module also has support for multiple category levels to group links. The upcoming PostNuke 0.8 will also include a sitewide category system that will be available for the Web Links module as well as its cousin, the Downloads module. See Chapter 6 for more information on Web Links.

Wiki

WikiWiki is Hawaiian for "quick." The original WikiWikiWeb system was an online database in which any visitor could make and edit web page content using only a browser. Now shortened to just Wiki, the open website concept is now very widespread.

The open and editable page feature is already built in to PostNuke (by relaxing user permissions), so PostNuke supports Wiki by allowing Wiki formatting characters in content submission forms using a hook that can be enabled for the individual modules that support it. Wiki code can then be used as an alternative to HTML, and for those already familiar with Wiki, it can be much easier to enter content. Wiki formatting is translated and stored as regular HTML.

More information on Wiki and how to use it can be found on the original WikiWiki website at http://c2.com/cgi/wiki/. The PhpWiki formatting rules are hosted on the SourceForge website at http://phpwiki.sourceforge.net/phpwiki/TextFormattingRules.

Xanthia

Xanthia is the core theme module for PostNuke and part of the XTE package. It uses the pnRender module to create a system for managing the appearance of your PostNuke website. Themes created to work with the Xanthia module are specifically labeled Xanthia Themes. PostNuke provides one static theme and six Xanthia themes by default. See Chapter 10 for more information on Xanthia.

XML-RPC

This is the XML-RPC specification for PostNuke. It facilitates the creation of XML-encoded Remote Procedure Calls between PostNuke and other external web services, such as w.Blogger. At this time, the XML-RPC module only works with PostNuke news articles.

Your Account

The Your Account module is another backend system integrated with the user modules. The My Account link on the Main Menu accesses the features of the Your Account module and allows users to change their personal information, including password and email, set their home page, manage comments, or simply log out.

How Blocks Work

Modules perform the content management, but blocks visually display modules' content and allow a site user to interact with the modules underneath the blocks. The name "block" is used to label both the positioning of content, for example "left block" or "center block." It's used to describe the separate functions you can display to interact with site users, for example the Polls module allows you to create polls for your site, but a Poll block displays a specific poll for voting.

Look at your site's home page; the menus, poll, messages, and login form are all content blocks. The blocks can be placed anywhere on your site, and you can create multiple instances of blocks tied to the same module with different display settings. Not all modules require blocks to function and display content, but nearly all blocks are tied to their parent modules for at least their creation.

Managing Blocks

Click on the Blocks module link in the Administration Menu. You see a table layout like the one in Figure 4.2. It's very similar to the Modules configuration page, but blocks are actually a bit more complicated.

Order	Position	Title	Module	Name	Language	State	Options
	Centre	Administration Messages	Admin_Messages	messages	All	Active	Deactivate | Edit | Delete
⇩	Left	Reminder	Core	html	All	Active	Deactivate | Edit | Delete
⇧⇩	Left	Main Menu	Core	menu	All	Active	Deactivate | Edit | Delete
⇧⇩	Left	Incoming	Core	menu	All	Active	Deactivate | Edit | Delete
⇧⇩	Left	Online	Core	online	All	Active	Deactivate | Edit | Delete
⇧⇩	Left	Users Block	Core	user	All	Active	Deactivate | Edit | Delete
⇧	Left	Languages	Core	thelang	All	Active	Deactivate | Edit | Delete
⇩	Right	Other Stories	Core	stories	All	Active	Deactivate | Edit | Delete
⇧⇩	Right	Categories Menu	Core	category	All	Active	Deactivate | Edit | Delete
⇧⇩	Right	Poll	Core	poll	All	Active	Deactivate | Edit | Delete
⇧⇩	Right	Todays Big Story	Core	big	All	Active	Deactivate | Edit | Delete
⇧⇩	Right	Login	Core	login	All	Active	Deactivate | Edit | Delete
⇧	Right	Past Articles	Core	past	All	Active	Deactivate | Edit | Delete

Figure 4.2   Building your site with blocks.

The title navigation bar contains four links: New Block, View Blocks, Show All Blocks, and Configure. *New Block* takes you to an input form where you can generate a new block. *View Blocks* takes you back to the table listing that you see when you first enter the blocks administration area.

Show All Blocks produces the complete list of blocks. The default listing is simplified to only active blocks. When viewing the complete list, the Show All Blocks link changes to Show Active Blocks.

Configure lets you change global block settings. The only global option in the current release is to enable/disable the collapsible menu icons. These are the little squares by each block title with a plus or minus in them that allow you to shrink a block up to only its title bar.

There are eight columns containing information about the configured blocks. The basic meaning of each column is as follows:

- **Order**—This column allows you to change the positioning of your site's blocks.
- **Position**—This column names the location where your block appears.

- **Title**—A block's title appears with its content on your site. This is the plain text users see.

- **Module**—Every block is part of a module. This column names which module the block is part of, but note the name might be cropped for space.

- **Name**—A block's name is determined by the parent module itself, and whatever name has been set appears here. This is mostly for reference should the Module column not provide clear enough information about what the block does.

- **Languages**—This marks which languages have been chosen for this block. It does not mean the block is written in that language, only with which languages the block appears.

- **State**—This column displays the current activity level for a given block. Blocks are listed as either active or inactive.

- **Options**—The block options allow you to change the state of a given block.

Blocks are always grouped by position, and they appear on your pages in the order defined here. For example, in Figure 4.2 you see the Left positioned blocks begin with Reminder, Main Menu, and Incoming. This means in the left column, the first block to appear is the Reminder; the Main Menu is below it on the page, and so on. If you click on the up arrow by Incoming, it moves up in position and appears above the Main Menu. Both Incoming and Main Menu are still below Reminder. If you click Incoming's up arrow again, it exchanges places with Reminder. You can sort all the blocks this way, but you cannot sort between positions.

> **Note**
>
> PostNuke provides only the Left, Center, and Right position options by default. The names are actually arbitrary. You can develop custom themes that place both left and center blocks on the left side of your pages. Third-party modules are also available that have positions simply numbered, so you can place the numbered areas in your theme wherever you like.

Click *Deactivate* for a block and it goes offline. Subsequent visitors automatically do not see an inactive block. The block is not deleted; you need only activate it for it to appear once more.

The *Edit* link lets you change a block's current settings. You can change a block's position here. In addition, an option in the Edit screen allows you to set the refresh time for a block. This feature is relevant only for blocks that pull their content from outside sources, such as Really Simple Syndication (RSS) news feeds. The default setting is once every 30 minutes. For some blocks, the Edit screen contains additional options specific to its module function.

Creating New Blocks

The *New Block* link takes you to the Add Block page. This form only has four fields, as shown in Figure 4.3. *Title* should be populated with the plain English title you want to appear with your live block. The drop-down list box contains all of the currently installed and available block types for every module. They are shown here with Module/Name designation. The *Position* selection provides current grouping options, by default the three mentioned earlier. *Language* determines when a block should appear. "All" is the recommended choice unless you are building language-specific versions of your site.

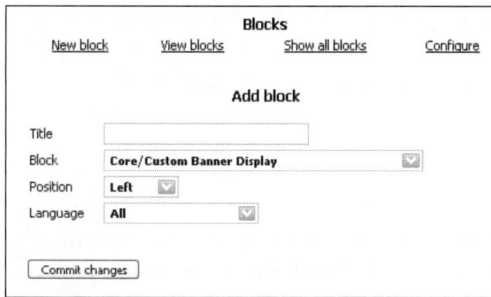

Figure 4.3 Adding a new PostNuke block.

After creating a new block, you automatically see the Modify Block screen for your new block. This allows you to configure the additional options many blocks possess, and many blocks do not function properly without the additional settings.

Troubleshooting

Some modules might give you trouble when you are adding or removing them. It's possible that a module-gone-bad can confuse PostNuke and blank out the Modules Administration page completely, preventing you from disabling the bad module. If this occurs, just rename the suspect module's directory. This breaks PostNuke's connection to the module. Then, when you go back to the Modules Administration page, PostNuke is unable to see the confusing module code, and you can remove the now-defunct entry.

You can also install multiple modules with otherwise similar names, functions, and directories by using different main folder names. pnAPI-compliant modules are added and referenced by their folder name. For example, if you are trying out a number of different weather modules, but each, by default, wants to use "weather" for its main directory, just call the second install "weather2," and so on. After you have finished your testing, it's easy to remove a module, rename everything back the way you want it, and then re-add the module for permanent use.

Next

In the next chapter, you dive into Part II, "Basic PostNuke." Now that you have a general idea how PostNuke functions, you can put it to work as a real site. The next chapter looks at some of the most popular core modules: News, Polls, Downloads, and Comments.

PART II

Basic PostNuke

Article Modules

5

The complex articles system built in to PostNuke is often the hub around which all other site features seem to revolve. It is the module set to home page by default, and nearly every PostNuke site uses it that way. It's very natural that content-centered information portal websites would want a news system up front, and most likely you will want to use articles in your site as well.

You should be aware that many third-party alternatives to core modules are available, some of which are discussed in later chapters. But it is easiest to first use the standard modules before branching out. Though some outside modules have many more options and features over core systems, they can also be more complex and require greater time overhead to maintain. See if these primary PostNuke modules meet your needs before extending your system.

In this chapter, you look over the main types of article modules included with the core PostNuke system. These modules are designed to communicate directly with site users and nearly every PostNuke website utilizes them. In this chapter, you learn about

- Topics
- News articles
- Sections
- Admin messages

Topics

Before adding news articles, you need to configure your topics. Article topics visually define your posts through the use of icons displayed with the text. Go to the Administration Menu and click the Topics link. You can see the two default topics, Linux and PostNuke, in Figure 5.1.

Figure 5.1   The Topics Manager.

You can replace those icons with topics of your own. Topics can relate to any subject, the content, or groups of articles, but it's best to make your topics similar to one another. Too many topics can make it hard for your visitors to use, so try to balance your content to group ratio carefully. Topic images can also be any file size or dimension, but smaller images load faster and take up less page space.

If your site is about general computer hardware, for example, you probably want a topic for each of the different types of cards and drives. You probably do not want or need a topic for every specific brand and model of video card—just a "video cards" topic that covers them all.

First, remove the two demonstration topics. Click on one of the topics under the Current Active Topics header. You see a screen similar to Figure 5.2.

Figure 5.2 Editing an existing topic.

You can see each topic has a number of information fields associated with it. The first three fields describe the topic by *Topic Name*, *Topic Text*, and *Topic Image*. The fourth area titled *Add Related Links* lets you define additional offsite uniform resource locators (URLs) that relate to the topic's content. The Related Links appear in the right-side article blocks mentioned in Chapter 3, "PostNuke Essentials."

Click the Delete link at the bottom of the form. You have the opportunity to confirm the removal, and note the warning that is displayed:

```
Are you sure you want to delete topic Linux?
This will delete ALL its stories and comments!
```

This illustrates how tied articles and topics are. Removing a topic also deletes all articles attached to it. That is why it's very important to set up your topics before you add articles. You can add more topics, reassign article/topic connections, and rename topics in an existing PostNuke site, but it's much easier to do a little planning beforehand and get them set up right before your site goes live.

Click Yes to remove the topic. Then select the other topic and remove it as well. For this example, three images of major pieces of computer hardware are included with the book materials. You can download these sample images from this book's online materials, or simply create your own images to try out. The images provided are 100 pixels by 90 pixels GIFs named

- `icon-harddrive.gif`
- `icon-mainboard.gif`
- `icon-videocard.gif`

Though not required, it's a good rule of thumb to use a consistent naming convention with your image files. That way, references to your files are consistent, and it is easy to identify images at a later time.

PostNuke topics are stored in the `/images/topics/` folder off your web root. Copy the new topic images to that directory on your server. You might notice that four other files are already present. The `linux.gif` and `PostNuke.gif` files were the ones previously used by topics, and there is an additional `AllTopics.gif` sample icon. If you have no plans to use those in the future, they can be deleted now. Leaving them is also harmless; they only take up minimal server space. The `index.html` file is blank and meant to deter directory browsing. It should be left intact.

Return to the Topics Manager page shown in Figure 5.1 and fill out the *Add a New Topic* section. For the hard drive topic, enter "harddrives" in the Topic Name text box. This name cannot contain spaces and is the name used in PostNuke's code. The Topic Text field contains the plain-English description of the topic that will appear with the icon; enter "Hard Drives." Finally, type the topic's icon filename, `icon-harddrive.gif`, in the Topic Image text box. When done, click the Add Topic button.

You now see your new topic displayed under the Current Active Topics header. It should look similar to Figure 5.3.

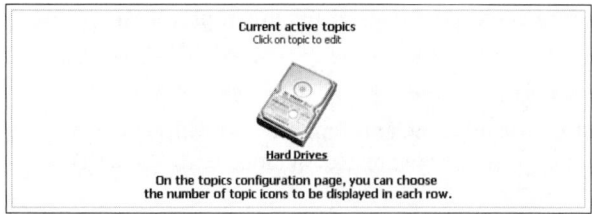

Figure 5.3   Your first topic.

Use the Add a New Topic form to to add at least two more topics using the other computer hardware images or your own to complete the initial topic setup. When you have completed them, your Topics Manager page should look similar to Figure 5.4.

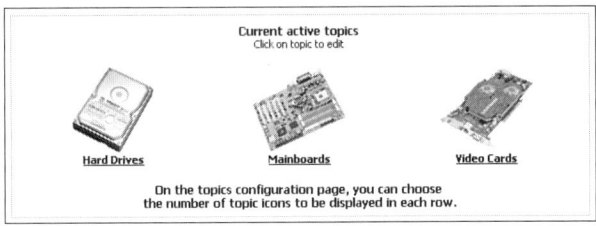

Figure 5.4   Custom article topics ready for use.

News Articles

Now, you can add some articles using these new topics. Two main module forms are used to manage submitted news articles: *Add Story* and *Submit News*. (In the example, you use the latter form first because it's simpler and what most site users will be seeing.) First click the Submit News link in the Administration Menu (see Figure 5.5). You are taken to the Submit News Configuration page that allows you to receive an email notification every time someone submits a news article. You can configure who gets the email and what the message says. This tool is disabled by default, but if you do not plan to check for new submissions regularly, this can be a handy reminder.

Next click the Submit News link in the Main Menu. You see the standard Submit News form (displayed in Figure 5.6) with only five fields to complete. The Title text box should contain a short, clear description of your content. For a sample submission, enter "Bigabyte Announces New Mainboard." Look at the Topic drop-down list box options. Notice the topics you created earlier automatically appear in this listing. Select a topic.

The Language drop-down list box defaults to the site's Language setting. For most sites, ignoring this option is fine. If you plan to use multiple languages, however, you need to select the language preference with which this article should be shown. In this way, you can enter multiple versions of a given article, each in a different language.

ADD STORY
Add story
ADMIN ANC
Admin Messages
AUTO-LINKS
Autolinks
BANNERS
Banners
BLOCKS
Blocks
CENSOR
Censor
COMMENTS
Comments
DOWNLOADS
Downloads
FAQ
FAQ
GROUPS
Groups
LANGUAGES
Languages
MAILER
Mailer
MAIL USERS
Mail users
MODULES
Modules
PERMISSION
Permissions
pnRender
pnRender
POLLS
Polls
QUOTES
Quotes
RATINGS
Ratings
REFERRALS
HTTP referers
REVIEWS
Reviews
SECTIONS
Sections
SETTINGS
Settings
SUBMITNEWS
Submit News

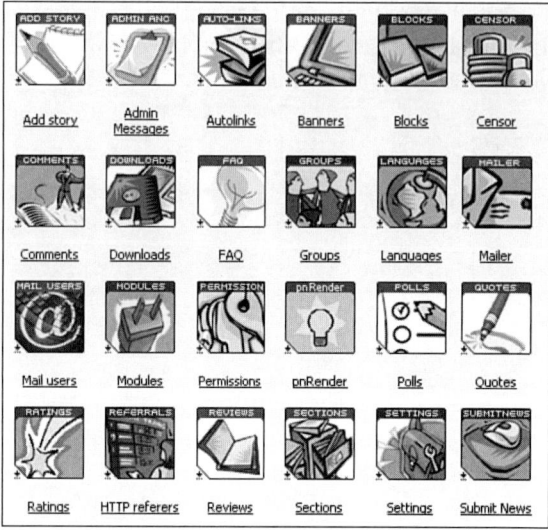

Figure 5.5 Adding news articles to PostNuke.

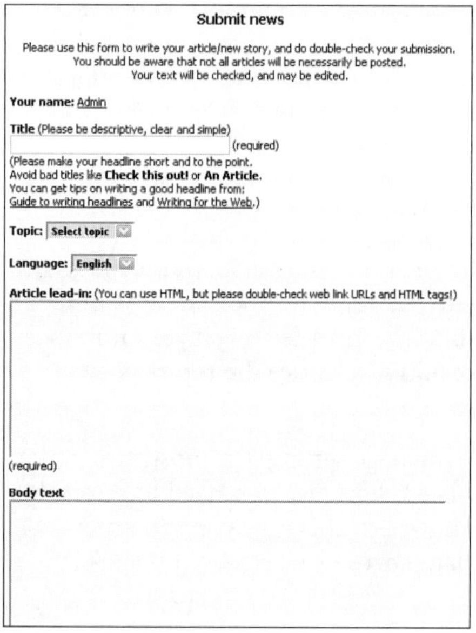
Submit news
Please use this form to write your article/new story, and do double-check your submission.
You should be aware that not all articles will be necessarily be posted.
Your text will be checked, and may be edited.
Your name: Admin
Title (Please be descriptive, clear and simple)
(required)
(Please make your headline short and to the point.
Avoid bad titles like Check this out! or An Article.
You can get tips on writing a good headline from:
Guide to writing headlines and Writing for the Web.)
Topic: Select topic
Language: English
Article lead-in: (You can use HTML, but please double-check web link URLs and HTML tags!)
(required)
Body text

Figure 5.6 Submitting a news article.

Lastly, two main text areas are provided for the article body. The first field, the *Article Lead-In* field, is required and displays whenever multiple articles are being viewed. For example, on a site's home page, different news postings are listed together. The information should be short and to the point so as not to bog down article browsing.

The second field, the *Body Text* field, is not required and is meant to contain the rest of the story, if the short first field is not completed. When an article is selected by a user, it is opened into its own page and the entire contents of the article are available for reading.

The two boxes are *not* different versions of the same information. The first field is the intro- duction, and it is displayed above the extended text when the complete article is being read. If the article information can be contained completely in the main article text field, the extended text is not required. The short introduction field is always displayed.

Now enter some text into both fields and submit the form. The only option at this point is to preview the submission before it's posted; click the Preview button. You should now see a page that includes your populated form and has a short sample preview of your posting at its top (see Figure 5.7). At the bottom of the form, the Submit button is now available; click the button to add your article to PostNuke.

Figure 5.7   A short article preview.

Tip

You can change the messages displayed with the Submit News module by editing the module's language file. The standard path to this file is /modules/Submit_News/lang/eng/global.php. Change the wording in the single quotation marks under each `define` line to alter text displayed by the module.

Browse your site's News page and you see the article is not yet visible. Notice a new block automatically appears under the Main Menu called *Incoming*. This block now displays the text:

```
Waiting Content
* Submissions: 1
```

The article you submitted is now in a queue waiting for approval by a site administrator. You could click that link to approve the article, but first return to the Administration Menu page; this time, click the Add Story link. The Add New Article form is basically a copy of the Submit News form with an additional five options. You can see this form in its entirety in Figure 5.8.

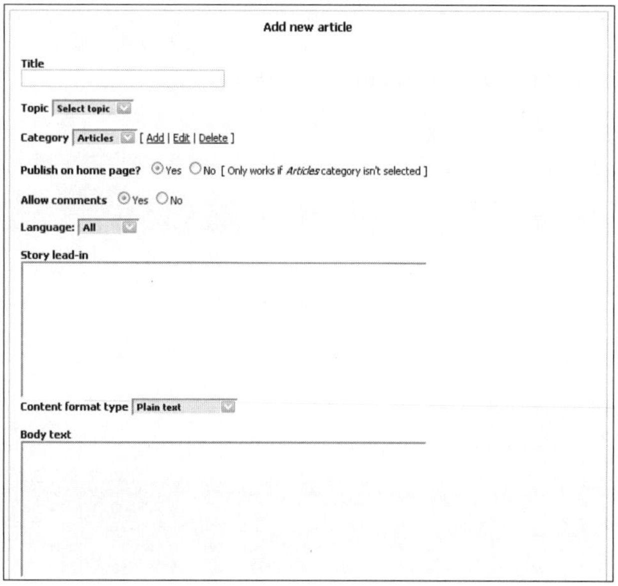

Figure 5.8   Administrator's Article/Stories submission form.

At the top of the page is an unassuming link under Articles/Stories Administration called *New Story Submissions*. Select this link to review articles waiting in the submission queue. You must preview an article before posting it, so choose Preview in the left drop-down menu and click the Go button.

Now, the same Add Story long form appears, but it is populated with the contents of the article submitted earlier. Any content or choices made during the story submission can be changed now during the review process. If a user submitted a story under the wrong topic, just change it before approving the post. The additional fields function as described in the following sections.

Category

An article category is very similar to a topic. Both divide articles into different groups. Topics display the icons, but categories are listed with an article's title. Categories provide another overlapping level of grouping.

Take our computer hardware example. If each topic is concerned with physical components, the categories could be Announcements, Product Previews, Reviews, Benchmarks, and so on. The sample posting has a Mainboard topic and is in the Announcements category. In this way, you can create a more versatile interface to your site's content for your users.

The category *Articles* is a default entry that basically means "no category." Selecting this option publishes an article without any connection to category listings.

Publish on Homepage

This option lets you file a posting into the live site, but not display it on the home page. This is great for adding information that is important but no longer timely. It's expected that users will find older articles by the category headings. For this reason, the Publish on Homepage switch only works if you have also selected a category other than the Articles default.

Allow Comments

Comments are a standard feature of most Content Management Systems (CMSs) that allow readers of an article to comment on its contents. The feature is turned on by default, and submitted comments appear beneath an article when read in its full-page format.

Content Format Type

Administrators have the ability to choose how an article is parsed by the PostNuke engine. In this way, you can take a submitted article and clean up any formatting issues that might be unprofessional or simply inconsistent with your site's styling.

Select Plain Text and lines are broken at each return. Any Hypertext Markup Language (HTML) in a submission is displayed and not rendered. Select HTML-Formatted and only legal HTML tags are used to format the content. A document might have clear returns to break up paragraphs, but without the tags to support them, all the text runs together.

> **Note**
>
> When HTML-Formatted is selected, only tags approved in the HTML Options section of the Website Settings page are rendered. Restricted tags are ignored.

The option you choose is dependent on your own styling for your site, and you can select either format for every article. The setting choice is remembered in the PostNuke database and remains with the content.

Notes

Notes are meant to be treated like an editor's comments or clarifications. They appear in italicized text below the article in both the short and full-page versions. Notes should be kept short, such as a single paragraph in plain text.

Program This Story

PostNuke allows you to program a story to appear at a scheduled time. By setting this field to Yes, the following Hour, Day, Month, and Year fields are checked to confirm when the article should be displayed. An article can currently only be scheduled to appear, not expire, so all live articles are designed to be permanent on your site unless manually removed.

When you have completed your review of the article, change the final drop-down list box to Post Story and click the Submit button. Your article now appears on the News home page formatted similarly to Figure 5.9.

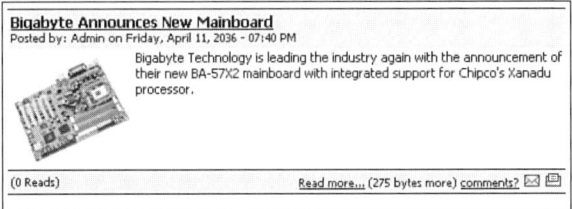

Figure 5.9   News added to the home page.

Sections

Longer articles that don't have a timely nature, such as guides, opinions, or other relatively static content, can be placed in the Sections module. Sections can each have a graphical header image displayed over article selections, and multiple pages are supported for section articles using a page break tag.

Section articles are completely unconnected to the news story modules. They can be searched together using the global site search, but the news topics and categories do not apply to section articles.

When you first enter the Sections Administration area, you only see a simple form prompting you to create a section. You must have at least one section created before you can add articles to the module. Create a new example section called "Section 1." You can rename an existing section later. Look at the complete Sections Administration page shown in Figure 5.10. The page has four main areas. The first and last, Active Sections and Add a New Section, allow you to edit the sections themselves, whereas the second and third, Add a New Article Under a Section and Last 20 Articles, relate to the articles present within sections.

The areas of the page are arranged by live site usage, with more commonly needed areas on top. But to set up your sections, you need to scroll to the bottom of the page to Add a New Section.

Look in your site's /images/sections/ directory. Three files are included there as part of the PostNuke package. The transparent.gif image is a spacing shim used by the Sections module; do not remove it from this folder. index.html is provided as a security measure against directory browsing, and it should also remain.

The template.gif image is a simple empty frame drawn in the blocky image style used with other built-in PostNuke images. You can use it to make section header images that match the rest of PostNuke. If you are customizing your site fully, you do not need this template file. A sample header image using the template file is available in the book's downloads. It is called guides-mainboards.gif and can be downloaded with this chapter's online materials.

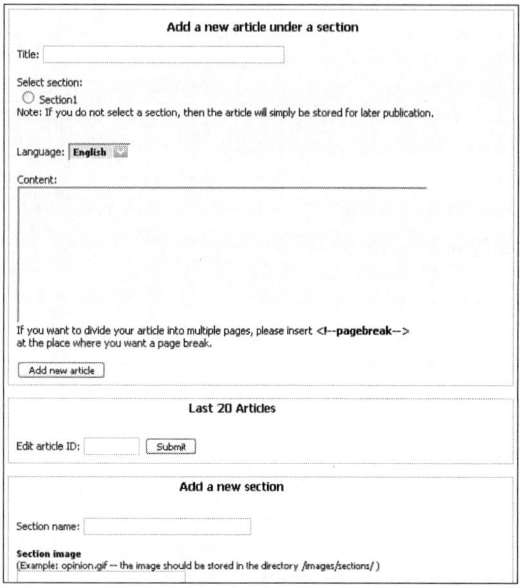

Figure 5.10   Sections Administration page.

Type a section name, such as "Mainboard Guides," in the Section Name text box, and enter in the name of a section image in the Section Image text box. Click the Add Section button to complete the form. The page refreshes and you see your new section listed under Active Sections at the top.

Now add a new section article. The Add a New Article Under a Section form is very simple; you need to enter a title for the article in the Title text box, and pick your section name from the list provided. Language is the same here as it was with the News Articles module; choose the language that best describes the content. Enter your complete article text in the Content field. Pages are divided using the <!--pagebreak--> tag comment described on the page.

Following a click on the Add New Article button, the page refreshes again, and you see your article listed in the Last 20 Articles area. The Last 20 Articles area also has a useful form for editing past articles by their ID. The ID number for any PostNuke content can be easily determined by the item's URL. For sections, look for &artid= in the URL address. The number after that is the ID of the section article you are viewing.

> **Tip**
>
> You can quickly check the ID of an article without reading it by mousing over a link to the article and looking at your browser's status bar, which displays the link in full.

If you need to edit an article, but don't have a link handy, you can also click the article's section link under Active Sections. The Edit Section page allows you to edit a section's name and image, or you can edit any article contained within the section using the article title drop-down list box (see Figure 5.11).

Figure 5.11 Edit Section and its articles.

It is also possible to extend the functionality of the Sections module using hacks and third-party add-ons. You can hack sections to include categories similar to the News Article module. In addition, static web pages can be pulled into the PostNuke shell using a wrapper, such as Nuke Wrapper or Post Wrap. These techniques and third-party modules are discussed in Chapter 18, "Static XHTML and PostNuke."

Admin Messages

It is often necessary to post an important message to site users that must remain above normal dynamic content. The Admin Messages module provides that functionality to

PostNuke. A perfect example of an admin message is the Welcome to PostNuke posting on your site's home page (see Figure 5.12).

Welcome to PostNuke, the =-Phoenix-= release (0.750)

PostNuke is a weblog/Content Management System (CMS). It is far more secure and stable than competing products, and able to work in high-volume environments with ease.

Some of the highlights of PostNuke are

- Customisation of all aspects of the website's appearance through themes, including CSS support
- The ability to specify items as being suitable for either a single or all languages
- The best guarantee of displaying your webpages on all browsers due to HTML 4.01 transitional compliance
- A standard API and extensive documentation to allow for easy creation of extended functionality through modules and blocks

PostNuke has a very active developer and support community at www.postnuke.com.

We hope you will enjoy using PostNuke.

Your PostNuke development team

Figure 5.12   Welcome to PostNuke.

Click on Admin Messages in the Administration Menu to get to the Messages Administration page. A table containing all admin messages is in the top area, and below that is a simple form where you can add new messages (see Figure 5.13).

Different from other main content forms, this module contains an active/inactive switch for its content. Admin messages can be written and stored for use whenever you need them. Click the Edit link in the table for the Welcome to PostNuke message. Change the Active setting to No and click the Save Changes button. Now when you look at your home page, you see the Welcome message is gone, and your test news posts are at the top.

The Message module also has the ability to set an audience for each message. The Who Can View This drop-down list box has the following options:

- **All Visitors**—Messages with this setting are seen by every user browsing the site, no matter their registration or login status.

- **Registered Users Only**—Only users who are currently registered and logged in to your site see these messages.

- **Anonymous Users Only**—This audience setting is great for promoting site registration. You can mention the great content and features only available to logged-in users.

- **Administrators Only**—PostNuke sites with multiple administrators need this audience setting to easily communicate important announcements or tasks to the administration team.

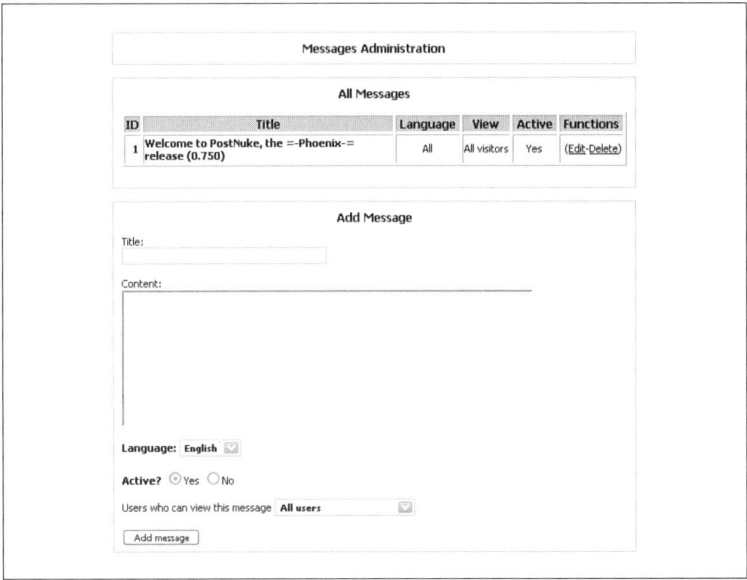

Figure 5.13   Managing admin messages.

Troubleshooting

The PostNuke article modules are the most popular and most commonly used modules on websites, and as a result they also tend to produce the most problems and support requests. The following sections discuss a few of the more common problems you might encounter with articles.

Missing Topic Icons

Adding new topic icons is often one of the first trouble spots because it is usually also the first time a new user works with both web forms and files together. The system also simply has users type in the filename—expecting the file to be there—with no browsing operation to allow definite selection of the image.

If you find your icons are simply not appearing, first check your directory location. Placing your images in the root /images/ folder is not enough; they must be in /images/topics/. Then, after the images are confirmed in the right folder, verify that you referenced them in the topic creation form correctly. Look again at Figure 5.2. Your filename must be written fully, including the extension, which is hidden on some machines.

Linux servers are case sensitive, so the name you type into the topic form must match the physical filename if your PostNuke is running on Linux. Even if it is not running on Linux, you should always maintain case consistency. PostNuke is portable; you can export your database and literally just copy the files to a new server and go. However, if you previously used inconsistent casing on a Windows server, you will have many updates to do before it will work on a new Linux machine.

If your files are named well and in the correct location, but you still can't get them to show, check your Topics Configuration settings at the bottom of the Topics Manager page. The directory path to your topics images can be set there. If you inadvertently changed it, none of your images show.

Missing Article Image

You can add images to your articles so they appear like any standard news article, with captioned photos or supporting diagrams on the side. But, often when new PostNuke administrators test this capability, they find their images do not show up with their article text. The word content appears fine, but not the side photo.

This problem is usually caused by restricted HTML options. By default, PostNuke prevents certain tags from being rendered for security reasons. The <img> tag is one of those tags. If you are the only poster, or you know you can trust your posters to not harm your site, relaxing the HTML restrictions should be fine. Go to the long HTML Options table under your global Site Settings page. You need to allow the <img> tag with parameters so the image source can be defined.

Missing New Submission Email

You might have turned on the Notify of New Submissions by Email option in your Submit News Configuration page, but you still don't receive any email. First return to the configuration page and check the email you entered into the form. A mistype in the address field could be the problem. If this is not the case, you probably have not configured the PostNuke Mailer properly. PostNuke uses the basic Simple Mail Transfer Protocol (SMTP) PHP mail() function by default to generate messages.

If you are using an external host, you might not have access to the server's PHP configuration file. If this is the case, contact your host and ask about the email setting on the server. If you have access, open your php.ini file and look for this section of the code:

```
[mail function]
; For Win32 only.
;SMTP = localhost ; for Win32 only
;sendmail_from= me@localhost.com ; for Win32 only

; For Win32 only.
;sendmail_from = me@example.com

; For Unix only. You may supply arguments as well (default: "sendmail -t -i").
;sendmail_path =
```

The semicolons are comment markers. You need to remove the semicolons by the lines relevant for your server type, and enter in the appropriate sendmail information for your mail server.

PostNuke alternately allows you to use a standalone SendMail, Qmail, or SMTP server, which can on a separate physical machine. If you have selected one of those options in your PostNuke Mailer Configuration, you need to verify that the separate mail server is running and configured properly.

Next

In the next chapter, you learn about User Interaction modules. You discover additional common core PostNuke modules, such as Polls and Downloads, which are designed to work directly with site users. In addition, you learn how to enable the Comments features for different modules to allow your users to enhance content throughout your website.

User Interaction Modules

This chapter looks at both core and third-party modules that get your site users involved. The majority of high-traffic websites are fully interactive with regular visitors generating most site content. Users adding content to a site have a vested interest in seeing it succeed and return to the site to add more content. In this chapter, you look at the following main user interaction components:

- Polls
- Downloads
- Web Links
- Reviews
- Comments

Polls

PostNuke's built-in polling module provides a very quick and easy way to get feedback from your site users. It doesn't provide many options or features, but the simplicity is also an aid to lowering the maintenance needs of the module. You can see an immediate example of the Polls module by looking at your site's home page. In the right column, a default poll is created as part of your installation, titled "What do you think of PostNuke?"

Now, you can replace that demo poll with one of your own. Click the Polls link in the Administration Menu. The Polls Administration page appears, as shown in Figure 6.1.

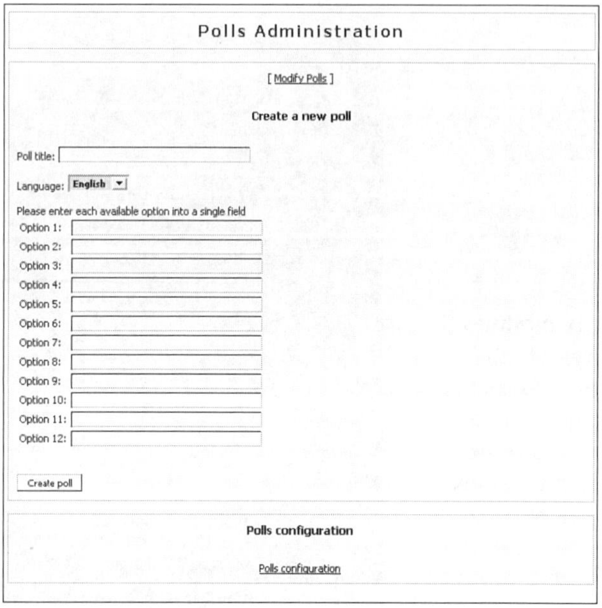

Figure 6.1   Creating polls for your site.

This example assumes you are making a site about books. The poll will ask users what fiction genre they like the most. In the Poll Title text box, enter "What's your favorite fiction genre?" Set the Language to All so the poll will always appear. For each of the Option # text boxes, use the following entries:

- Mystery
- Science Fiction
- Fantasy
- Romance
- Western
- Historical
- Other Fiction

Options 8–12 are still blank. You don't need to use all of the choice fields. Any extras left blank are automatically deleted. Now click the Create Poll button. The page refreshes and clears, and it might appear nothing has happened, but your poll has now been added to the system and made live automatically. Go back to your site's home page to see your new poll on the right. It should look similar to Figure 6.2.

Figure 6.2
Learning about
your users.

You cannot schedule the poll; after it's submitted, it is live to the public and replaces whatever poll was previously live. The most recent poll is always displayed.

From the poll interface, users can also click Results or Polls. The Results link allows users to see the current poll numbers without first casting a vote. The Polls link returns a list of the older polls that users can view. They can see the results of those polls and even cast their own votes.

> **Tip**
>
> Like the article modules covered in Chapter 5, "Article Modules," you can also enable comments for the polls that allow users to talk about their choices in a thread beneath the results.

Advanced Polls

Advanced Polls is a third-party module developed by Mark West of the PostNuke development team. Version 1.1 is available with the online book materials, or you can check for a more current version of the module at Mark West's website (markwest.me.uk).

By decompressing the archive files, you see the module's files are already arranged in the folders modules/advanced_polls/. Copy the entire advanced polls directory to your server under your PostNuke modules directory.

When you regenerate your modules list, you see the Advanced Polls module near the top of the table. Select *Initialize* under the module actions to create the new database tables. Next click to *Activate* the module to make it available for use. The state should now read Active.

Back on the main Administration page, a new link and icon appear called Advanced Polls. Enter the Modules Management area and select the New Poll link. Though their basic functions are very similar, the Advanced Polls module clearly has a great deal more options (see Figure 6.3).

The Date and Time fields allow you to schedule a poll's appearance. Through the *Poll Authorization Method*, you can manage or prevent duplicate votes by User ID, IP, or Cookie. Polls can be scheduled to recur automatically after expiration so your site can monitor the changing opinions of your visitors. In addition, you can configure exactly how a tie is handled in the results.

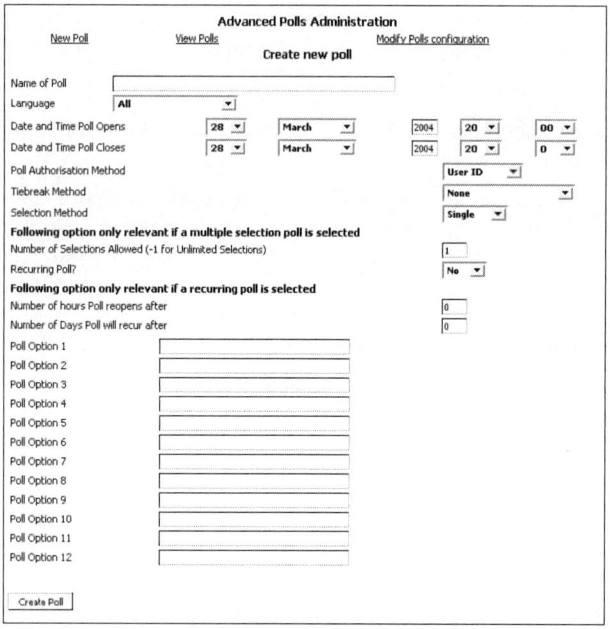

Figure 6.3   Adding an advanced poll.

Create an advanced poll for comparison using the same data we applied earlier to the stock PostNuke Poll module: "What's your favorite fiction genre?" with the options:

- Mystery
- Science Fiction
- Fantasy
- Romance
- Western
- Historical
- Other Fiction

Choose the other options as you see fit. They are fairly straightforward, and if you regularly use polls on your site, you should have no problems applying them all to other examples.

Your poll won't display without a block for an interface. So go to the Blocks Administration page and click the New Block link. Fill in the title for your poll and choose a position of Right for your block. The Advanced Polls module is chosen using the Block drop-down menu. Scroll to the bottom of the list and you see the following options:

- **advanced_polls/Show a Poll**—Displays your poll for voting; is identical to the core Poll block.

- **advanced_polls/Display List of Open Polls**—Allows users to have easy access to multiple active polls simultaneously.

- **advanced_polls/Show Results of the Most Recently Closed Poll**—Is great for sites that don't run an active poll regularly or for keeping important results posted.

- **advanced_polls/Warns if Poll Is Unanswered**—Prompts users to answer important polls.

For the standard poll, you use the first option. After the block is created, it has additional configuration options for you to manage. You can display a specific poll only, the latest poll, or a random poll from those you've created. From this screen, you can choose to display the poll based on its programmed dates, or you can override the dates and permanently display the block. Choose the set of options you want to test first, and commit the changes. You have now created a Poll block, such as the one in Figure 6.4.

Blocks

New block	View blocks	Show all blocks	Configure

View blocks

Order	Position	Title	Module	Name	Language	State	Options
	Centre	Administration Messages	Admin_Messages	messages	All	Active	Deactivate | Edit | Delete
⇩	Left	menu3	Core	menu	eng	Active	Deactivate | Edit | Delete
⇧⇩	Left	Reminder	Core	html	All	Active	Deactivate | Edit | Delete
⇧⇩	Left	Main Menu	Core	menu	All	Active	Deactivate | Edit | Delete
⇧⇩	Left	Incoming	Core	menu	All	Active	Deactivate | Edit | Delete
⇧⇩	Left	Online	Core	online	All	Active	Deactivate | Edit | Delete
⇧⇩	Left	Users Block	Core	user	All	Active	Deactivate | Edit | Delete
⇧	Left	Languages	Core	thelang	All	Active	Deactivate | Edit | Delete
⇩	Right	Advanced Poll	advanced_polls	poll	eng	Active	Deactivate | Edit | Delete
⇧⇩	Right	Yahoo Technology	Core	rss	eng	Active	Deactivate | Edit | Delete
⇧⇩	Right	Other Stories	Core	stories	All	Active	Deactivate | Edit | Delete
⇧⇩	Right	Categories Menu	Core	category	All	Active	Deactivate | Edit | Delete
⇧⇩	Right	Poll	Core	poll	All	Active	Deactivate | Edit | Delete
⇧⇩	Right	Todays Big Story	Core	big	All	Active	Deactivate | Edit | Delete
⇧⇩	Right	Login	Core	login	All	Active	Deactivate | Edit | Delete
⇧	Right	Past Articles	Core	past	All	Active	Deactivate | Edit | Delete

Figure 6.4 Blocks let users access your poll.

Your block is added to the table and grouped with the other Right Position blocks. Notice the poll appears on the top of the listing (see Figure 6.4). All new blocks appear at the top of their position's list and must be moved to their permanent location.

Tip

If you are moving blocks around, or just setting up a new block you've just added, disable the block to take it offline. Then, site users cannot see the blocks moving around, and you can reactivate the block(s) after everything is in the correct place.

Now return to the home page and try out your new poll. It essentially acts much like the core Poll module, but the advanced system provides much greater control over how the poll functions.

pnESP

This third-party module gives you the ability to create a complete survey for site visitors, with multiple database-driven questions, custom permissions, and results analysis. pnESP's full name is the Easy Survey Package for PostNuke.

It is more advanced than the Advanced Polls module, but to be fair in the comparison, the difference in the modules is more that pnESP allows you to survey your users with *depth*. The two modules are applicable to different types of polling that for the most part do not overlap. Both can be installed and used at the same time to poll for different types of information.

pnESP 1.0 is provided with this text's materials, or you might want to check the module's website (pnesp.sourceforge.net) for the latest version. Decompress pnESP's files and copy them to your server's modules directory. After you regenerate your module list, you see the regular Initialize option for the new module. You do not have to activate pnESP after initialization; it does that part for you automatically.

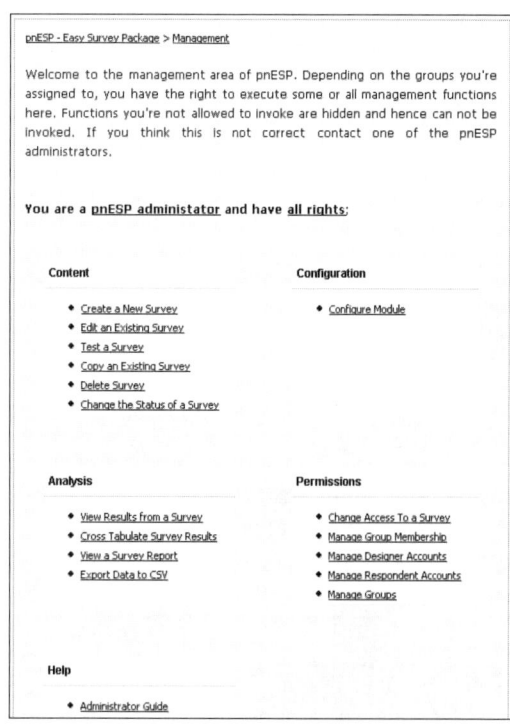

Click the new pnESP Administration icon, and you see the full configuration for the module (see Figure 6.5). Options are divided into five sections:

- **Content**—Creates and manages user surveys

- **Configuration**—Configures pnESP module settings

- **Analysis**—Reviews and exports survey results

- **Permissions**—Changes survey access rights

- **Help**—Learns about module features and terms

pnESP does have a lengthy setup time to prepare a survey, and it is strongly recommended that you plan out all questions and answers, including question types and layout styles, before you even begin with pnESP. It will save you a lot of time.

Figure 6.5 Detailed surveys made easy.

Figure 6.6 A survey with three sample questions.

pnESP surveys do not generally appear in side blocks; users reach the survey pages through links in blocks. By default, questions appear in one long page, as shown in Figure 6.6, but you can also add breaks to give each question its own view.

When you create a new survey, it must be activated to become available for public display. After being activated, it cannot be edited. In this way, pnESP's mode system allows you to maintain professional surveys with clean results.

For the sake of space, this chapter does not cover this entire module's setup. The majority of questions you might have about the product are likely answered in its included documentation. Just walk through the creation of a new survey and you will quickly see how it can work for you. Extensive information is also included in the module's documentation files (`/modules/pnESP/pndocs/`).

Downloads

You can add files to your site and make them available to your users through the Downloads module. You can allow any file type, and the module supports the creation of categories and subcategories to organize your files. Each file object includes a number of informative fields, such as Description and Filesize.

Continuing with your book site example, create a Downloads section that allows site visitors to browse and select different texts. Edit the Downloads module settings through the Administration page. Your initial screen looks similar to Figure 6.7. All uploaded files must be grouped by categories, so you must first create a main category before any files can be added for download.

For this example, use selected classic works no longer in copyright, which are in this text's additional materials, and they can be found at their original source in the Project Gutenberg site (www.gutenberg.net).

Create a main category called Shakespeare with the description "Selected works from the 16th century playwright." Upon submission, the page expands to include three new forms: Add Subcategory, Add a New Download, and Modify a Category. To see how the structure works, add two more main categories using the top form called "Lewis Carroll" and "Sir Arthur Conan Doyle" using the respective descriptions "Classics from the writer of *Alice's Adventures in Wonderland*" and "Stories including the famous Sherlock Holmes."

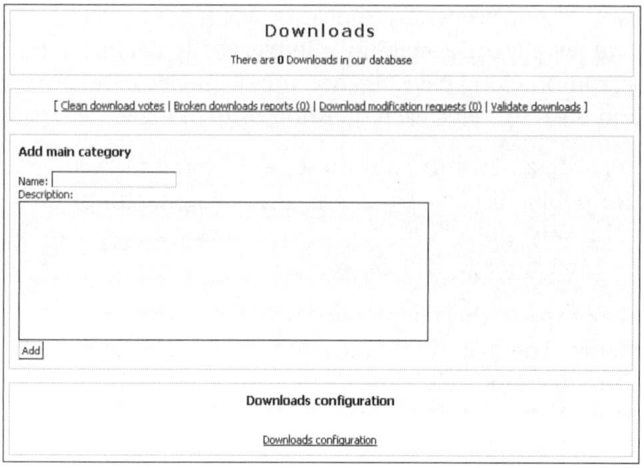

Figure 6.7   Grouping your downloads by category.

Next create three subcategories under Shakespeare named Comedies, Histories, and Tragedies. You need to use the second form for this operation, and with subcategories, descriptions are not required. Downloads categories are always displayed alphabetically, so you don't need to be concerned with the order in which you add them to PostNuke.

Note

When you delete a download link, the file is not deleted. If it resides on your server, you must delete it separately.

The stock Downloads module references files as though they are web-accessible. This means your files need to be uploaded to your server to complete the module form and add the file to your site. Connect to your server using File Transfer Protocol (FTP) or your local share, and create a directory called downloads at your root web folder. Place the files you will be linking to in that folder.

Now use the third form to add a new download to your site. This module was originally designed to link to application downloads; the Program Name text box is a legacy of the older design. In the Program Name text box, type "The Tragedy of Hamlet."

The next text box, File Link, defines the file location. Clear the default http:// and enter the web path to your file. For this example, the path is /downloads/Shakespeare-Hamlet.txt. The http:// is also a clue for you that you can also link to external files. Many PostNuke sites use their Downloads module to provide handy links to files on other websites.

Tip

You could also use your server's fully qualified domain name (FQDN) in the link, such as http://www.yourserver.com/downloads/Shakespeare-Hamlet.txt, but the full domain is not necessary with local references, and it hard-codes that domain into your links permanently. If, at a later time, you want to change your domain or share your links between multiple domains using the Multisites module, you must update every link to get them to work. Using the simplified, shorter link is easier in the long run.

Place the file link into a category using the drop-down menu. Using the examples outlined previously, you should now see six choices in the drop-down menu (see Figure 6.8). Subcategories are listed under their parent group alphabetically. Choose Shakespeare/Tragedies from the list.

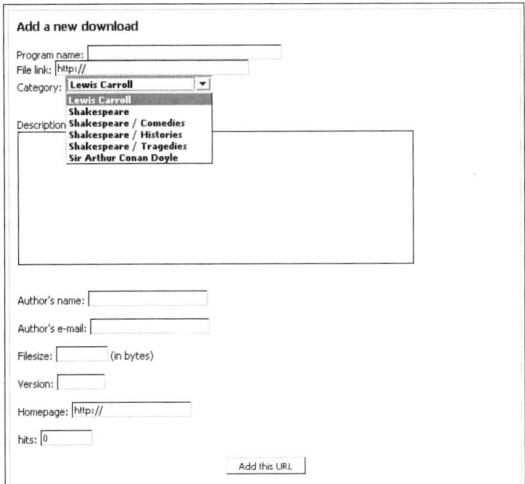

Figure 6.8 Picking a category for your link.

The Description field is also required, so type in a short comment about the file. The remaining six fields are not required to complete the link, but they do add additional description for your file. The Filesize and Version text boxes appear with the link and are blank if no information is entered. To keep your site looking polished, you should, at a minimum, complete these two additional fields.

Add additional links to the module structure using the files provided or by adding more files of your own. After you are done, click the Downloads link in your site's Main Menu to go to the module's user interface. The page should look similar to Figure 6.9.

Tip

The Hits text box is automatically incremented as your files are browsed, but if you have to move links or rebuild your site, the count might be lost. You can manually populate a link's hits using this form. Enter in your link's old hit total to create continuity between site changes.

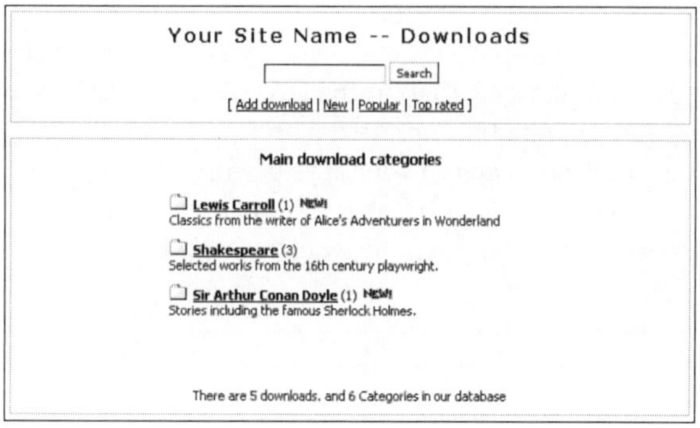

Figure 6.9   User's view of your downloads.

The New! image is automatically placed by sections with recently added links. The number in the parentheses is the current total count of links within the category. Subcategories are not visible until a user clicks into one of the main sections. Within a main category, links are listed with their short information and any subcategories are available at the top of the page.

For the sake of example, the Hamlet document was added twice, once under the Tragedies subcategory and once under the main Shakespeare category (see Figure 6.10). This illustrates how files are displayed using this system.

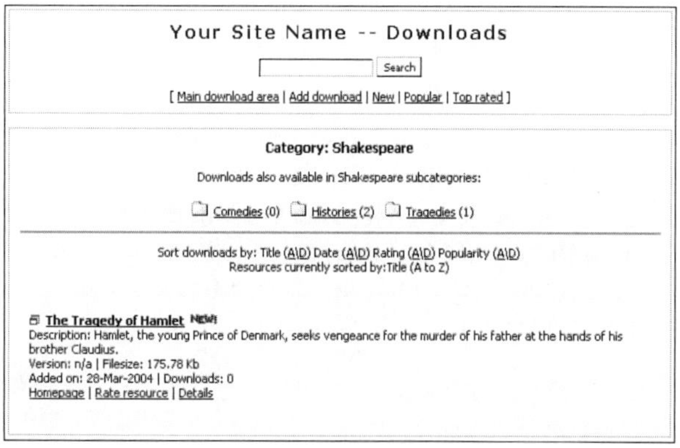

Figure 6.10   Files and subcategories in Downloads.

Users can submit links to your site using the Add Download link beneath the top search form. Their suggestions are queued just like news article submissions, and you can approve them individually through the Administration page. The only limitation to this system is that files cannot be physically uploaded to your server using the module, so users must suggest links to files hosted remotely on other web servers.

UpDownload

UpDownload is designed to solve the file upload problem with the Downloads module. It provides users with the ability to transfer a file to your server using a web form. Version 1.82 is included with this book's materials, and the module's current home is found at http://www-users.rwth-aachen.de/jens.goebbert/, where a new version might be available.

Copy the module files into your PostNuke's `modules` directory. This module needs to be activated after initialization to make it available for use. Next go into the Administration page for the UpDownload notice; it appears identical to the regular Downloads, even having the title of "Downloads" on the page.

Tip

Look at the UpDownload module files in the folder path `UpDownload/docs/extra_features/`. You can unlock additional features using those files; you can add UpDownload files to the site search and add blocks that show recently added or popular files.

The UpDownload module is not an add-on to Downloads; it's an alternative module that can completely replace the core Downloads. To see exactly how UpDownload is different, duplicate your category structure used with the Downloads module.

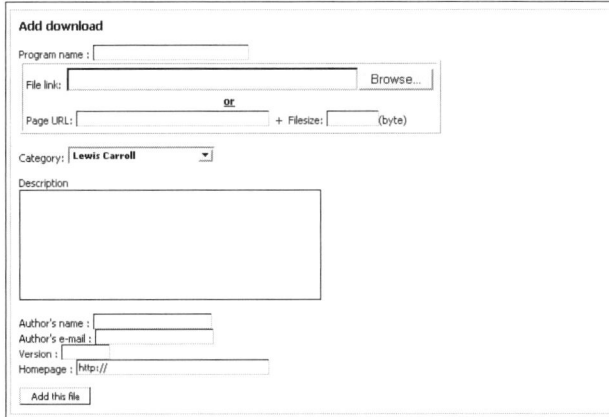

Figure 6.11   Adding an UpDownload.

Compare Figures 6.11 and 6.8. The UpDownload form in Figure 6.11 has boxed out its key difference. Files can be linked using the same system possible with Downloads, or the new Browse feature allows files to be uploaded directly to the server.

UpDownload files are kept in the `store_folder` in the module's directory. Browsing the folder also shows how files are placed in a directory tree mirroring your category structure. When users submit new downloads, they queue up just like the link versions. When you have approved them, they finally go live and are visible to everyone.

For security reasons, a few file types are restricted from being sent to your server using the UpDownload module. Those types are

- Macromedia Flash files (`.swf`)
- JavaServer Pages (`.jsp`)
- PHP pages (`.php`, `.php3`, `.php4`, `.phtml`)
- Perl files (`.pl`)
- Compiled executable files (`.com`, `.exe`)
- Batch files (`.bat`)

These formats are also listed for users in the user upload screen (see Figure 6.12), and an automatic limit for uploads is set at 2MB.

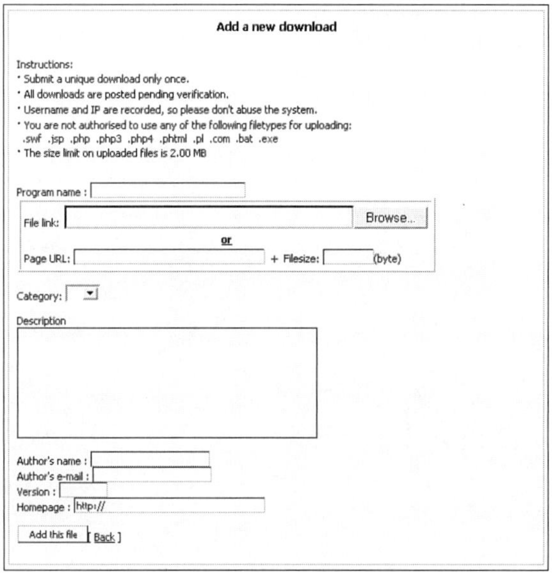

Figure 6.12 Now, users can upload files directly.

Web Links

The Web Links module is essentially a copy of the Downloads module. It has the same main categories and subcategories, and links to web pages can just as easily link to files.

However, the cousin modules have numerous differences. The Filesize, Version, Homepage, and Hits fields found in the Downloads module are not present for Web Links. The Description field for Main Categories is not required for Web Links, although the specific links themselves do require it.

Unlike Downloads, Web Links listings are not maintained in alphabetical order. This is true throughout the module for both categories and links. Web Links are displayed by ID in the order items are added. It can be a bit of a flaw, hindering this module's usability, but if you plan out your Web Link categories well and in advance of creating the structure, you will not need to make changes later affecting the order. It's also a known issue that will likely be fixed in future releases.

> **Note**
>
> Deleting subcategories also permanently removes all links contained within them. Deleting main categories removes all links, subcategories, and the subcategories' links. Be careful when removing categories.

Compare Figure 6.13 with Figures 6.9 and 6.10. Web Links subcategories are displayed on the main page beneath their parent categories. It has the benefit of giving users immediate access to deeper content, but many PostNuke site managers have felt the page becomes visually unbalanced very quickly the more subcategories you add.

Figure 6.13   Categories displayed in Web Links.

The Web Links module might have a few issues, but it is a clean, stable module that can also be used as a built-in spare Downloads module. PostNuke's easy-to-edit source also ensures you can make whatever changes you need to customize and polish its display.

Reviews

Another original core component of PostNuke is the Reviews module. It allows users to submit their opinions and rating of any item or topic. User-submitted reviews are placed in a queue and wait for an administrator's approval before being displayed publicly.

To see how the review process works, first go to the Administration Menu page and click Reviews. The Reviews Administration page has two main sections. The first lets you retitle the Reviews page and provide a description of the reviews you publish on your site. The second area lists all the reviews currently awaiting approval and has a link where you can add a new review. Click the Write a Review link to go to the Review Submission page (as shown in Figure 6.14).

Write a review for Your Site Name

Please enter all information in accordance with the stated requirements

Review title:

Name of the reviewed item.

Language: All

Review:

This is the review you submitted. Please use proper grammar, and please write at least 100 words. You can also include HTML tags.

Permitted HTML tags:
<!--> <a> <b>
 <em> <hr> <i> <li> <ol> <p> <pre> <strong> <table> <td> <th> <tr> <tt> <ul>
If you want to divide your article into multiple pages, please insert <!--pagebreak-->
at the place where you want a page break.

Your name:
Admin
Your full name (required)

Your e-mail address:

Your e-mail address is required.

Score:
(10) 5 Stars   *This item's score*

Figure 6.14   Adding a review to your site.

To edit or delete an existing review, you need to browse the Reviews Section as any user. Administrative accounts are automatically detected and provide additional links to manage review content.

Many PostNuke sites focus on technical content, and on those sites, reviews usually relate to software or hardware products. But the Reviews module can apply to any topic, and continuing with the book example in this chapter, enter a review of Isaac Asimov's book *The Robots of Dawn.*

In the Product Title text box, enter *"The Robots of Dawn* by Isaac Asimov." Enter your own text for the Review field, or you can use this text from the publisher, Spectra Books: "A puzzling case of roboticide sends New York Detective Elijah Baley on an intense search for a murderer. Armed with his own instincts, his quirky logic, and the immutable Three Laws of Robotics, Baley is determined to solve the case. But can anything prepare a simple Earthman for the psychological complexities of a world where a beautiful woman can easily have fallen in love with an all-too-human robot...?"

As you can see in Figure 6.14, a limited selection of Hypertext Markup Language (HTML) tags are allowed to format reviews, and multiple pages are supported using a special page break comment.

Enter your name, email, and the star rating you want to use. The Related Link text box allows reviewers to link to outside sources for more information, such as a manufacturer, a movie's official website, or in your book example's case, an author's or publisher's website. Enter Asimov's official site: http://www.asimovonline.com/.

After populating the Related Link text box, the URL needs a title. Enter "Isaac Asimov's Home Page" into the Link Title text box.

Though not required, users also have the ability to display an image with their review. The image must be located on your server in the `/modules/Reviews/images/` folder. You cannot upload the image into that directory, so users need to provide images to the site administrator separately, or when an item is approved, the administrator can find an appropriate image and add it to the review.

The image `Asimov-Cover.gif` is in the book materials and you can copy it to your server to see how the image addition works. Be certain to pay attention to the filename case when referencing files on Linux servers.

Submit the form and click the Reviews link in the Main Menu to see how reviews are listed. Click your review to see how it looks. If you used the sample content given previously, it should look similar to Figure 6.15.

Note

Reviews can be removed by clicking Delete on a review's page, while logged in with administrative access. There is no confirmation check, so be certain you want to remove the item before clicking the Delete link.

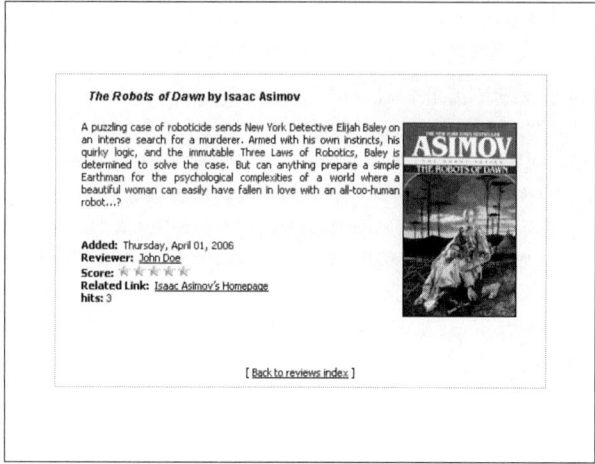

Figure 6.15 A simple book review.

No categories are built in to the Reviews modules to group the different entries. They are simply listed by the title letter. It is, however, possible to sort a given list of reviews in ascending or descending order by title, reviewer's name, rated score, or hits using the arrows in the title row.

Comments

The Comments module is not so much a single component of PostNuke as it is an add-on to modules throughout the application. The module allows users to add their own statements on whatever post they are reading. New comments appear beneath the source document in a treaded format.

Figure 6.16 A sample reader comment.

You can see in Figure 6.16 a simple sample posting using the news posting from Chapter 5.

Comments can be deleted individually to allow you to moderate postings. They can be disabled altogether through the respective Administrative settings of those modules that use the Comments module.

Troubleshooting

Integrating third-party modules can often be very complicated. Development cycles differ between product releases, and sometimes, you have to consider compatibility issues with an install. Be certain to carefully read the installation instructions that accompany each module to ensure you have completed all the preparation steps before initializing a new module.

If you find you missed something, don't panic. PostNuke is very forgiving. You can remove the module, delete and replace the files if necessary, and reinitialize the module a second time. It's also possible to go into your PostNuke database using an admin tool such as phpMyAdmin and remove any tables belonging to a damaged module. But be careful because deleting the wrong table might result in a need to reinstall PostNuke completely.

> **Tip**
>
> To be certain your site is protected, back up your database tables before making direct changes.

As with all active third-party modules, you can consult the developer of the application for support. Many module developers are active in the PostNuke forums (forums.postnuke.com), and the forums are the main place to get support for discontinued modules.

Advanced Poll Does Not Allow Votes

One common bit of confusion with advanced polls happens when you make a new poll using the Advanced Polls module. You might select it for appearance in a block for your site, and the poll displays in the block perfectly, but the options are missing the radio buttons or check boxes required to place votes.

This is most likely happening because the poll is expired. New polls' date fields are automatically populated with the current date and time. If you do not change the expiration date to a later time, it very quickly expires and no one can vote.

Surveys Disappearing in pnESP

pnESP is sometimes too smart for its own good. At times, surveys seem to disappear from the Content listings. The key to keeping track of your pnESP content is the Survey Status page. The other listings only show those surveys that are relevant to its subject. You can't edit a survey that's active, and you can't test a survey that's still in editing. Just check your status list to see what stage your surveys are in, and you'll never lose track of them again.

Fatal Error with UpDownload

UpDownload uses the store_folder directory to house files uploaded to the module. For the upload process to work, it's required that your web server can write to that directory. With write access, you will likely be seeing the Fatal Error: Call to a Member Function message.

Install packages compressed using .zip generally lose any permission settings when used on a Linux server. It's not required that you pick up the .tar.gz version of the module, but you do need to fix the directory permissions.

If you are using a special user account for access to the folder, be certain that account has read, write, and access permissions. If giving the single account permissions does not work, you can also try opening the access up in general, for example with chmod 777 on Linux, which gives complete access. It's not a good idea to leave directories fully open, but it can help you test the access and verify that the module is otherwise working before you go back to fixing the web server account.

Next

The next chapter looks at more third-party modules that can greatly enhance your site through community building. Five of the most popular calendar, forum, and newsletter modules are reviewed.

Community Building Modules

7

Three of the most important community building tools for any website are calendars, forums, and newsletters. With any of the applications, you can create a system in which users regularly return for new dynamic content, and these tools can become self-perpetuating when users themselves help to generate more new content.

PostNuke does not currently include a calendar, forum, or newsletter module with its core package, but a number of third-party modules are available for PostNuke that work quite well.

This chapter examines the following five third-party community modules you can use with your PostNuke website:

- PostCalendar
- pnConcert/pnEvent
- PNphpBB2
- XForum
- pnTresMailer

Calendars

Calendars can be a very important tool for generating traffic and building an online community. Users who are granted access to post events to a calendar can set dates and create events so others in the community can come together and interact. Visitors are encouraged to return to see the updated future events, and new entries ensure your site remains current.

PostCalendar

PostCalendar is a very popular third-party module for many PostNuke sites. It has been released by its original developer and adopted by some of the core PostNuke developers. PostCalendar itself is not yet a core module, but it's likely that the module will eventually be part of the PostNuke package.

Version 4.0.1 is included with this book's additional materials. Current versions of PostCalendar are available on the PostNuke Network Operations Center (NOC) project site at http://noc.postnuke.com/projects/postcalendar/. Uncompress the archive and move the resulting PostCalendar directory tree over to your server's /modules/ folder.

> **Note**
>
> PostCalendar must have write access to these directories:
>
> /modules/PostCalendar/pntemplates/compiled
> /modules/PostCalendar/pntemplates/cache
>
> If you are using a specific server account for Web access, the account must be given permissions to write to both folders. On a Windows server, the web server process must have access.

Regenerate the module table and *Initialize* PostCalendar. You also need to click the Activate link to complete the install. The PostCalendar main administration screen has eight sections:

- **Settings**—Shows the default Global Settings page
- **Add**—Adds new events to the calendar
- **Clear Smarty Cache**—Forces a recompile of event information
- **Test System**—Lists system details and checks for permissions
- **Categories**—Defines color-coded groups for events
- **Queued**—Shows events waiting for approval
- **Approved**—Lists only the events currently approved
- **Hidden**—Displays all the currently nonvisible events

Click Test System first to be certain all your permissions are working. You need to fix any issues found in the test before testing out the calendar's options.

PostCalendar has an extensive manual available at http://www.postcalendar.tv/wiki/. Most of the module's features are intuitive and require no explanation, but if you don't understand how something works, try the information found in the manual first because it's very complete.

Now, you can add some events to PostCalendar. For this chapter, the examples center on live music performances. Table 7.1 displays two data examples used throughout the chapter. Click the Add link and enter both of these events into PostCalendar. Change the Month and Year fields to match the current date, and be certain to set the Sharing field to either "Public," for registered users, or "Global," for all users.

TABLE 7.1
Data Examples

Performer/Band:	Billy Plays Sax	Jenna Marx
Date:	February 10, 2006	February 11, 2006
Time:	8:00pm	7:00pm
Venue:	Blue 44	Boulevard Café
Address:	500 44th Street	938 E. Lincoln Blvd.
City/State:	Metropolis, ZA 12345	Metropolis, ZA 12345
Phone:	(123) 555-1234	(123) 555-5678
Contact:	John Smith	Jenna Marx
Email:	jsmith@billy-plays-sax.com	jenna@jennamarx.com

Users cannot see the events without making a PostCalendar block. Make a new block called Event Calendar and add it to your site with a Right position and the block name PostCalendar/Calendar Block.

You are presented with an additional screen of options; for this example, you need to check the Display the Calendar? and Display Upcoming Events in Block? check boxes. Set the Display How Many Events? field to 5 and the How Many Months Ahead to Query for Upcoming Events? field to 1. When you are done, it should look like Figure 7.1.

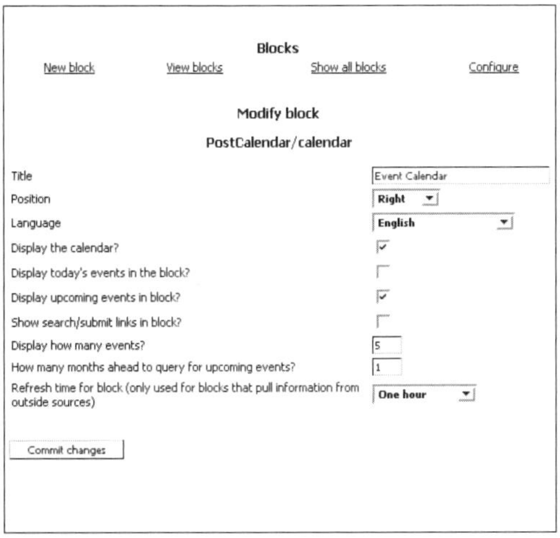

Click the Commit Changes button, and return to your site's home page. Your calendar should appear with your other right blocks and have the information shown in Figure 7.2.

Click on the calendar month, and you are presented with the full-page version. Events are boxed in a color matching their category. The default category is red. You can see from this view that the default heading does not look attractive over events, so you should develop your own custom categories for your calendar to keep your site polished.

Figure 7.1 PostCalendar block settings.

> **Note**
>
> The calendar display works off of the server's system date settings. If your server date and/or time is not correct, PostCalendar does not display the current date.

Figure 7.2
Calendar with upcoming events.

By default, the calendar uses variables defined in the site's theme for its only colors and interface. PostCalendar is fully configurable and you can develop a theme just for PostCalendar that is not connected with your site's theme.

pnConcert/pnEvent

pnConcert is a simplified event module designed to provide concert information in a calendar format. It is a much simpler module than PostCalendar, and if you find you don't need all the features of the larger module, pnConcert might work better for you. pnEvent is a hacked version of pnConcert that has all references to "concert" replaced with "event" to make it more general. Both modules install the same and have all the same interface screens.

pnConcert 0.4 is the version included with this text's online materials. At the time of this writing, the module is still very young with many as yet unimplemented features. The module developer has plans to port pnConcert to the upcoming PostNuke 0.8 where the module's development will be continued from there. You can check for a more recent version at http://sourceforge.net/projects/pnconcert/.

If your events are not related to music, you should try the pnEvent 0.4 that has also been made available with this book's materials.

Uncompress the pnConcert archive to a temporary folder location. The resulting pnConcert folder has two paths:

```
pnconcert/html/includes/search/
pnconcert/html/modules/event/
```

The entire directory tree is not needed on your server; it was included in the archive as a guide to show you where to place the module files. The actual pnConcert module is contained in the concert directory. Copy the concert directory over to your site's modules folder.

Your PostNuke install already has a directory path of /includes/search/ off its root. The concert.php file must be copied to your server and into the matching location from the archive (/includes/search/concert.php). This file allows pnConcert content to be included in general PostNuke site searches.

Now, you can Initialize the module on the Modules Administration page. After regeneration of the list, pnConcert appears simply as *concert*, whereas pnEvent displays as *event*. The new module needs to be activated after installation.

Go to your main Administration page, and you see a new icon and link. pnConcert and pnEvent both use the same guitar icon. Inside the pnConcert administration, you have the following five options:

- Add Concert
- Approve Concerts
- Show Only Next Concerts
- Show All Concerts
- Edit Module Configuration

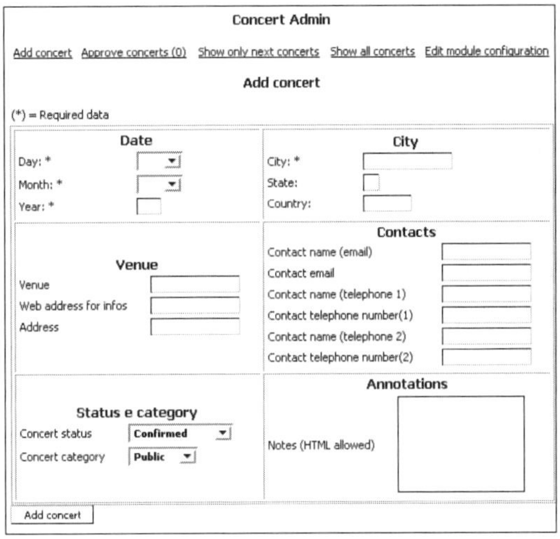

Figure 7.3 Adding a simple concert event.

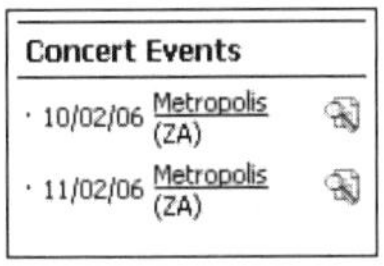

Figure 7.4
A pnConcert events block.

To see how pnConcert works, add in the two sample events you used earlier (see Figure 7.3).

Edited events are placed back into the approval queue—even if you are an administrator—when making changes. It might seem like your event disappears from the listing after an edit, but the listing views only display approved events. Click the Approve Concerts link to preview and approve an event.

The Module Configuration page lets you adjust how many concerts you want to display per page and has a check box for enabling user submission of events. The current release of pnConcert doesn't have settings for separated permissions between users and site administrators. If you allow users to submit their own events, they can also edit or delete existing events.

Make a new block called Concert Events with the block selection of Concert/Show Next X Concerts Scheduled. Commit your changes and view the new block from the home page. You can see from Figure 7.4 that the events listing generated by pnConcert is similar to the Upcoming Events list with PostCalendar (see Figure 7.2).

> **Note**
>
> pnConcert blocks tend to require width space to prevent hard wrapping and content bunching. Try to keep your block width to at least 150 pixels, and if possible, use 200 pixels or more.

pnEvent blocks are designed to disappear completely if there are no future events to display. After new events are added, the block returns automatically.

Forums

No site can claim to be a "community" without some form of forum system. PostNuke does not include a forum system in its core package, but other forums applications can be installed to remedy the need.

PNphpBB2

By far, the most popular third-party forum with PostNuke integration is PNphpBB2 (www.pnphpbb.com). It is based on the phpBB2 forum (www.phpbb.com), and although phpBB2 is a standalone forum, PNphpBB2 incorporates features of PostNuke, such as your site's theme and user accounts to join it completely with your website.

Version 1.2g of PNphpBB2 is included with the book materials. You can download the current version of the forum from its website (URL listed previously), which also contains templates, patches, and the extensive Users Guide.

PNphpBB2 uncompresses to a very large directory tree, but all of the relevant files are nicely contained in the one root /PNphpBB2/ folder. Move the folder and all of its contents to your server's /modules/ directory.

Before you install the forum, you should turn off compression for your site (in Site Settings). It has been known to prevent some screens from displaying during the install. It can be turned back on after the forum is operational.

> **Note**
>
> For PNphpBB2 1.2g to work with PostNuke .750, you need to set the Enable Support for Legacy Modules option in your PostNuke Website Configuration page to "Yes." Release candidates for .750 prior to RC4 also need the Enable pnAntiCracker option set to "No."

PNphpBB2 initializes and activates just like the majority of other third-party modules. The module does not allow you to use the forum or access administration functions before you remove the install directory. It's on your server at /modules/PNphpBB2/install/. Delete the directory from your server.

Now when you go to the PNphpBB2 Administration page, you should see a screen much like Figure 7.5.

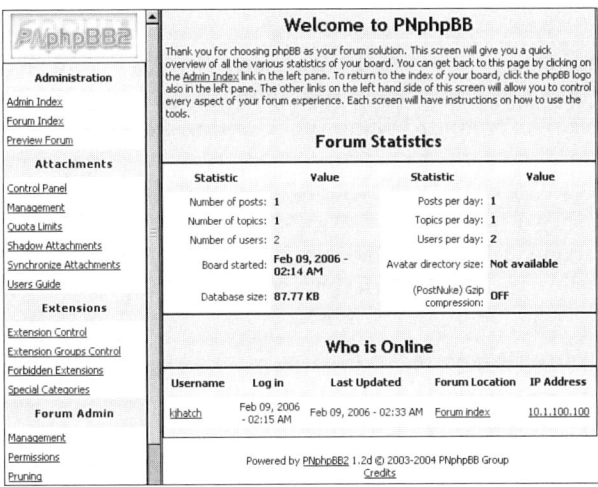

Figure 7.5 Managing your PNphpBB2 forum.

You can set up a public link to the forums using the direct URL /modules.php?op=modload&name= PNphpBB2&file=index or by simply adding [PNphpBB2] to the Main Menu block.

User accounts on your PostNuke site automatically have access to read and post on the forum; its account system is fully integrated with PostNuke.

A test category and forum are created as part of the install. To make the default entries a little more useful, you can modify them. On the PNphpBB2 Administration page, scroll down on the left navigation column to the Forum Admin section. Click the Management link. The page shown in Figure 7.6 appears.

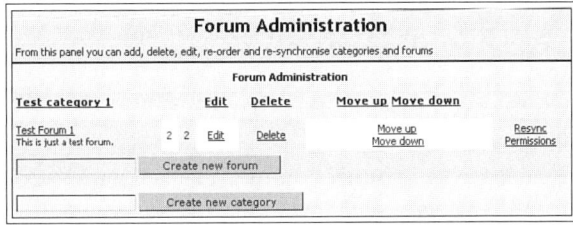

Figure 7.6 Designing your forum's sections.

This form is very important because you create the layout for your user forums using this form. Click the Edit link on the same line as Test Category 1; change the category to read "Local Concerts." Do the same for the Test Forum, renaming it "New Artists."

Now return to your home page, and click into the forums like a regular user. Add a couple posts to the New Artists forum, such as "2 More Days to Billy Plays Sax" and "Jenna Marx @ the Boulevard Café."

Figure 7.7
Showing users
what's happening.

Next, you can add a side block to your site that contains the most recent forum posts. From your Block Administration page, add a new block. Title it "Forum Activity" and use the PNphpBB2/Multi-Block setting. After committing the initial block choice, you are given a host of additional configuration options for the multiblock. Click the Display Last Forum Posts in Block check box. Obviously, many other options are available, but for now, leave all of the rest at their defaults. Submit the block and return to your site's home page. You should now see a new block that looks something like Figure 7.7.

The side block can also be used to display forum statistics, a category list, or a "Who's Online" box that also displays any new PNphpBB2 private messages.

XForum

This module was originally developed from the XMB Forum, but has since become a full fork due to many code changes. It's available for multiple versions of both PostNuke and PHP-Nuke, which has been a useful feature for those running both Content Management System (CMS) portals and those converting their site from one to the other.

XForum version 1.81.1 is included with this book's additional materials. More current versions of the module can be found at its website (www.trollix.com).

XForum for PostNuke uncompresses to a directory containing includes and modules sub-directories. The two directory trees in the includes should be placed in your server's /includes/ path, and the XForum directory needs to be copied to the /modules/ path.

Check the permission settings on the files settings.php and jumper.php; they need to be at least chmod 666 to ensure a complete install. After that is done, go to this URL to run the XForum install:

```
http://[YOUR site here]/modules.php?op=modload&name=XForum&file=install
```

The install script should autodetect all your database and connection information, but check it over to be certain. French is the default install language, so if you want English, be certain to change that. Pick a theme and click the Next button.

You should see a Connection OK message from the database test. Clicking the Next button again does the table creation and completes the install. XForum does not require the initialize/activation like the majority of other third-party modules. This manual install process accomplishes that step.

XForum is not as fully integrated with PostNuke as PNphpBB2, and you won't see an admin icon/link under the main Administration Menu. But PostNuke user accounts are used for XForum, and as a site administrator, you do have access to all of XForum's features.

Go to your Blocks page and edit the Main Menu block again to add a link to [XForum]. Reload the page to get the link to appear. Users can now use that link to see the forums and start threads. Administrators can also use that link to manage the XForum module.

Click the new link as both an administrator and user. The only difference is that administrators have the Control Panel link. Click the link and you go to the page shown in Figure 7.8.

Now add in the same category and forum you used for the previous section. Under Setting, change the *Forum Name* to "Live Music." Under the Forums link, change "Category Tests" to "Local Concerts" and "Forum Tests" to "New Artists." Check the boxes by the two headings to make them visible.

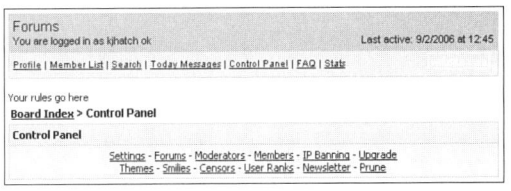

Figure 7.8 Taking control of XForum.

Now, as a user, add in a couple of new topics just like you did for PNphpBB2. The sample headers are "2 More Days to Billy Plays Sax" and "Jenna Marx @ the Boulevard Café," and when you are done, you should have something similar to Figure 7.9.

Figure 7.9 Creating topics for discussion.

Overall, XForum has the same standard features you'd expect from a website forum application. But XForum is not as cleanly tied into PostNuke. It is possible to set up a block to display XForum content, but blocks are not included with the main XForum package. You have to download and install the block separately. In addition, for the current version of PostNuke, only a "Who's Online" block is available.

XForum does have the benefit of a simpler interface that can be easier to work with than PNphpBB2's. XForum often lets you complete more operations in a single screen and requires less scrolling and clicking to get to the screen you need. The right choice depends only on which of these applications best suits your needs.

Newsletters

Newsletters are great for keeping in contact with your website visitors. When you have an important announcement, or simply want to let users know about current updates, you can send out a new mailer to let them know. This reminds them to return to the website and see the new content. Sites without daily updates often lose return traffic, but their hits improve greatly through user mailers.

pnTresMailer

pnTresMailer is a convenient, well-designed module that allows you to email packaged newsletters to users who have opted to subscribe to your mailings. The module includes a template system with a header and footer to make your posts easier and more consistent. In addition, the module works as a multipart Multipurpose Internet Mail Extension (MIME) to allow both Hypertext Markup Language (HTML) and pure text emails simultaneously.

pnTresMailer version 6.02 is available for download with the book materials; current releases can be obtained at the module's current home: canvas.anubix.net.

Install is very quick and straightforward. Uncompress the module archive and you have one directory tree. Copy the entire tree's contents into your server's /modules/ directory. Through the Modules Administration screen, initialize and activate pnTresMailer. The module's icon and admin link then appear in the PostNuke Administration Menu.

Go into the pnTresMailer administration and review the following main navigation links:

- **PN Admin**—Returns you to the PostNuke Administration Menu
- **Mailer Main**—Returns you to the pnTresMailer default administration screen
- **Archives**—Lists past newsletters
- **Subscribers**—Lists all current subscribers
- **Settings**—Lists primary mailer settings, including header and footer code

- **Plugins**—Lists various plug-ins you can use to enhance your mailers with website content

- **Preview HTML/Text**—Allows you to see your mailer before everyone else

- **Generate and Mail**—Creates the shell, populates it with the new mailer message, and sends it to your subscribers

Adding a subscription link is very simple. Edit the Main Menu block and add a new link to [pnTresMailer] called Subscribe. When signing up for a forum, the Email field is automatically populated by the email the user entered into PostNuke, but the field is editable, so if the user wants to subscribe but would prefer the newsletter be sent to a different email address, he can easily change it before completing his subscription. Newly subscribed users are given a screen similar to Figure 7.10.

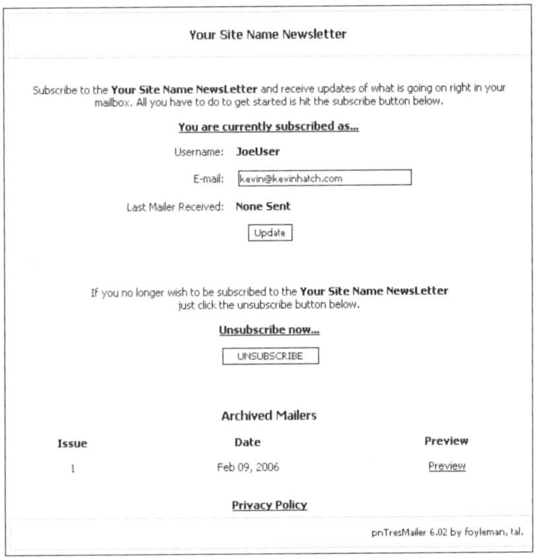

Figure 7.10 You are currently subscribed.

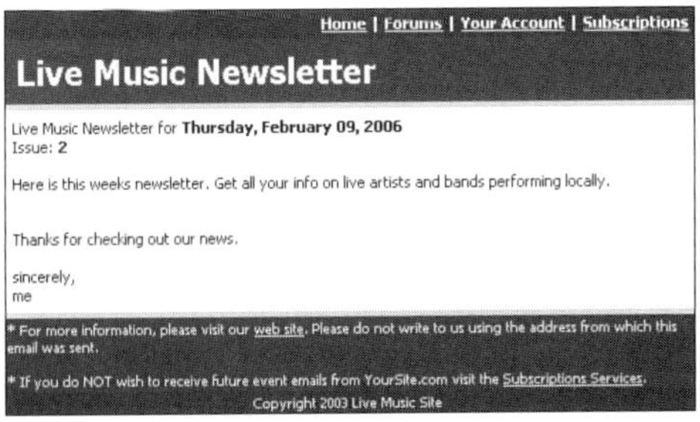

Figure 7.11 Designing a custom newsletter.

Now go back to the pnTresMailer administration screen and click Settings. Configure the form to suit your server's needs. For your music example, set the *Email Subject* field to "Live Music News." Save your settings.

pnTresMailer uses HTML templates to generate the emails. You can see the files in the Settings page under the field names *HTML Email Template* and *Text Email Template*. If you want to change the default layout of the email, colors, and so on, you can load the template file into any generic HTML or text editor. It's not required that you know HTML to send out the newsletter, but it does help polish the resulting newsletter.

Figure 7.11 shows some very minimal changes to the colors, spacing, and alignment of the default web template. Main site and newsletter title references have been updated to reflect the music example. You can see the basic layout is unchanged, but even just slight customization can make a large difference in the presentation of the message.

Try to make some changes of your own using the files in /modules/pnTresMailer/templates/ defaults/. You might want to create a new directory under Templates to place your custom files. Don't forget to update the settings references to apply to your new filenames and/or folders. You can preview your template changes using the Preview HTML/Text links.

Tip

For even quicker testing, leave your preview window open. Save your changes to the template file. Then go back to the preview window. You can now right-click on the window and select Reload from the menu, or simply press Ctrl+R on your keyboard. The window does not have to be opened again to refresh its contents.

Now click Generate and Mail to create the newsletter. Follow these remaining steps to complete your mailer creation and send out the email.

1. **Generate New Mailer**—This step loads the template files and your settings and combines them to create a new copy of the newsletter.

2. **Preview New Mailer**—Next, you can review the completed email shell to see that all of your reused information and layout is correct.

3. **Edit New Mailer**—Third, you edit the mailer to include a unique body of content that fits inside your reused shell.

4. **Send New Mailer**—Finally, this step sends off the newsletter to its awaiting recipients.

Note

The field Outgoing Mail Server is essential to getting pnTresMailer to work. When sending out bulk emails, an external Simple Mail Transfer Protocol (SMTP) server is always best. It's also possible to use the PHP/PostNuke mail (Alt. Mail) settings or "localhost" is a mail system installed on your server. Whatever you choose, it must be working and do its part for pnTresMailer to be able to send out the newsletter.

Troubleshooting

Solutions to some of the more common issues encountered with these modules can be found in the following sections.

PostCalendar "Compile dir Not Writable!"

This message occurs when your web server does not have permission to write to these directories:

```
/modules/PostCalendar/pntemplates/compiled
/modules/PostCalendar/pntemplates/cache
```

Access to these folders allows Smarty to compile and cache PostCalendar templates. Unix users need to give the web user account write permissions to both folders. If you are still having trouble, change the folder access using chmod 777 to test the problem.

PostCalendar Changes Showing Late

If you are seeing a slow refresh of the changes in PostCalendar, it might be that the system is still caching older data to speed up performance of the calendar. You can manually clear the Smarty cache using the link in the PostCalendar administration pages to solve this problem. It causes Smarty to examine, recompile, and recache new versions of the pages.

pnEvent Block "Warning: Missing Argument"

pnEvent sometimes returns the error: Warning: Missing Argument 2 for **url**() in /includes/pnHTML.php on Line 669. url() is a function call that expects a link and something to click on (such as a word) to activate the link. The second argument is the word that's clicked on.

When pnConcert was converted into pnEvent, subtle code changes were also made to the module. One of them that might cause the preceding warning message is in this file:

```
/modules/concert/pnblocks/next.php
```

Edit that file and look at line 201. The original pnConcert line looks like this:

```
$output->URL(pnModURL('concert','user','display', array('dc_id'=>$item['dc_id'])),'<img
src="images/global/edit.gif" border="0" alt="'.$item['dc_locale'].$status.'"
title="'.$item['dc_locale'].$status.'">');
```

Whereas the pnEvent line appears as:

```
$output->URL(pnModURL('event','user','display', array('dc_id'=>$item['dc_id'])));
```

The reference to the edit image tag (see Figure 7.4) has been removed. The icon was removed to help secure the module and prevent general users from hurting content. But removing only the image displays the warning if your PHP is set to display all potential problems. The solution to this problem is to either replace the original line to put the edit icon back, or simply comment it out to remove the icon cleanly without an error. The line with the comment looks like this:

```
// $output->URL(pnModURL('event','user','display', array('dc_id'=>$item['dc_id'])));
```

Next

In the next chapter, you look at the fun side of PostNuke with entertainment modules. Some of the modules are specific to online gaming pursuits, and others simply add a diversion or two to your site.

Online Gaming Modules

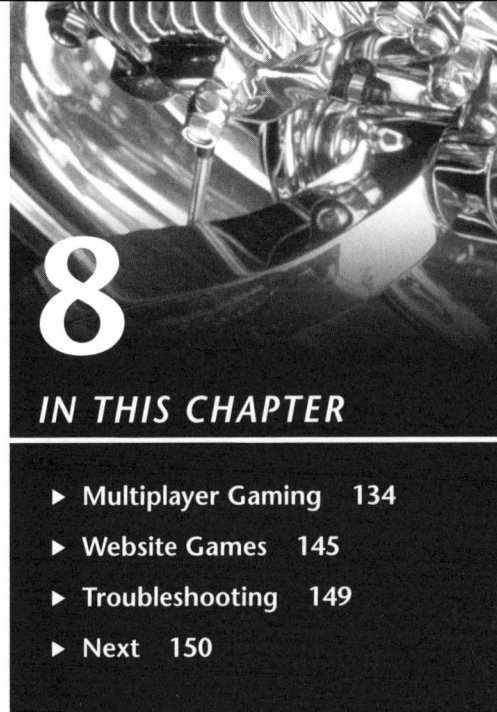

8

Online gaming is a multibillion dollar industry, and rapidly growing. With nearly one third of Internet users playing games online, it's no surprise there are a lot of websites designed for gamers. Many types of games are available online, but they can, for the most part, be split into multiplayer and individual games.

Multiplayer games are usually purchased products, installed locally, where players connect and play together on Internet servers. Individual players of online games connect to servers that usually contain the entire game; they play online to have access to the game, whereas multiplayer gamers go online to compete against other people.

PostNuke provides many features popular with online gaming in the base install, but you can also install additional third-party modules that can turn your PostNuke site into a true gaming site. In the upcoming sections, you explore the following entertainment modules:

- pnClansite
- pn-teamspeak
- LTG GameQuery
- pnFlashGames
- vQuiz

Multiplayer Gaming

Players of multiplayer online games regularly gather online as organizations and extended communities who share similar interests. Many games are team-based or provide advantages for players who choose to work together.

The terms used to label such groups vary from game to game (clans, guilds, tribes, squads, and so on), but more likely than not, a given group will have a website built to provide the players with a central home where they can communicate and interact while not playing the game. Groups needing easy ways to generate a clan roster or post the current guild news can certainly find PostNuke to be a useful tool. The communication and community-building components of PostNuke are exactly the foundation most online gaming websites need.

In addition, a number of specialized modules have been designed to cater specifically to gamers. These modules, when combined with PostNuke, can make building a complex gaming website both fast and easy. The most popular multiplayer gaming modules are covered in the following sections.

pnClansite

This module is designed to help the clans and guilds that play multiplayer games over the Internet build websites to support their organizations. The current version of the module is 4.0, and although it focuses mainly on First Person Shooter (FPS)-style clans, additional features are planned for future versions to better support Role Playing Game (RPG) guilds, possibly including a separate variant of the module to be named pnGuildsite.

The install files can be downloaded from the modules file archive here: pnclansite.source-forge.net, and they are also available as part of this text's download materials. The zip file does not contain a root directory path; if you unzip the files without creating one, they become mixed with non-pnClansite files. To remedy this, first create a new folder under your site's /modules directory called "pnclansite" (all lowercase). Then decompress all the files in the module zip into the new folder. This module initializes and activates like most modules; complete the base install of the module and return to your Administration Menu.

Click the pnClansite icon. Depending on your theme settings, you might see a blacked-out form area in the middle of your page. This is due to a default setting in the module that caters to websites with black backgrounds. To fix the problem, refer to the Troubleshooting section titled "Black pnClansite Pages, Unreadable Pages," and follow the subsequent instructions.

The pnClansite Administration page lets you configure the general text labels and descriptions used throughout the module. The first three fields define the *Clan Name*, *Tag*, and *Slogan*, respectively. The name should be the complete group's name. The tag is a short marker, usually one to three characters, which is placed by members' handles while they play to display their allegiance. The slogan is a short phrase, battle cry, or saying that expresses the aims or nature of the clan.

Tip

Tags are almost always enclosed in a pair of brackets. Square brackets: [] are the "classic" style, but new clans are now just as likely to use parentheses: (), braces: {}, angle brackets: <>, or vertical bars: || in different combinations to both define and decorate tags.

As an example, create a clan called "Eagle Alliance." Enter that name into the Clan Name field. Add the tag "[EA]" into the Clan Tag field and the line "Swift Wings and Eagle Eyes!" to the Clan Slogan field. These three fields appear on all pnClansite pages. If you already have clan information for use with this module, enter it now.

The next four box fields allow you to enter paragraphs to describe your clan's history, event information, rules of conduct, and general information about the group. If you have clan information ready for your site, enter it into the boxes now. If not, here is some sample content you can use for the Eagle Alliance clan.

History page content:

"The Eagle Alliance was founded in 2000 by our esteemed LeaderOne. We were just a few guys playing Counter-Strike then, playing on pubs and going to LANs. Together as [EA] we started playing competitively in leagues, including CAL, STA, the OGL. We've also branched out with divisions playing Quake III, Battlefield 1942, and Battlefield Vietnam."

Events page content:

"Wednesday nights are set aside for regular practices. Matches are normally scheduled on the weekends, but we're usually up for a game any night. Stop by one of our servers for a pickup game, or contact Radar using the Match form to schedule a more formal match."

Rules page content:

"Eagle Alliance has only a few rules of conduct that all members are expected to follow. Failure to adhere to these rules will result in a clan review and possible expulsion from the clan. The rules are: (1) Always play honorably in matches and public servers. (2) Attend practices whenever possible. (3) Don't be late to matches."

About page content:

"The Eagle Alliance is an FPS clan currently playing Battlefield 1942, Battlefield Vietnam, Quake III, and occasionally Counter-Strike. We occasionally play mods, but most often compete in stock arenas. We can be found on GameShock.net IRC in our channel #eaglealliance. Stop by our channel or one of our servers for a pickup game, or contact Radar using the Match form to schedule a more formal match."

The four check boxes toggle which forms of contact the clan is currently accepting. All of the options are checked by default. *Accepting Members* allows access to the join form. *Allies* and *Rivals* invite other clans to formally establish a tie to the clan, as an affiliate or friendly adversary. *Accepting Matches* enables other clans to use the challenge form to set up a match. For the module example, leave all of the check boxes checked.

Note

The pnClansite Common menu links remain regardless of which settings are turned on or off. You need to set up a custom menu block using the Core/Generic Menu type to alter which are displayed.

The *Layout Alignment* field below the check boxes lets you set how the pnClansite pages are horizontally aligned. You can use the options "left," "right," and "center" in this field, the latter is the default.

The module's area outlines are colored using the *Layout Border Color* field; the *Layout Background Color* field alters the background of those areas. A dark gray is set as the border default, and black is the standard background, as mentioned earlier. You should change these fields to match the design of your site. Hex color codes are recommended for specific definitions, but supported Hypertext Markup Language (HTML) color labels are also usable here, such as "red," "green," and so on.

Submit the form with your field entries and return to your site's Administration Menu page. Click the Blocks link and review the new block options you have in the drop-down list box:

- **Scoring Analysis**—Displays the win/loss match analysis
- **Common Menu**—Provides a list of general links designed for public use
- **Control Menu**—Provides administration options that should only be available to clan leaders
- **Pending Applications**—Lists players who have recently applied to the clan
- **Recent Members**—Displays the new players just added to the clan's roster
- **Stats Menu**—Shows general module statistics

From this screen, add two new blocks to your site: Common Menu and Control Menu. These are the two most important and commonly used pnClansite blocks. Create the two blocks, title them with a clear name (such as the obvious "Common Menu" and "Control Menu") and use a right position if you do not already have a place planned for them.

> **Note**
>
> By default, the Control Menu is only visible to website administrators. Because pnClansite identity is controlled through PostNuke accounts, this feature makes it easy to maintain security for your clan.

Although you have submitted the pnClansite Administration page text, the module does not work properly without first populating the main tables with at least one entry each. The links you use to accomplish this are in the Control Menu under Options. These options define the basic foundation structure for all regular data to reference. For example, each player is described with a Rank setting. Until you have defined what the ranks for your clan are, a new player cannot be assigned the setting.

Populate the following fields. They can be completed in any order, but all must contain information. Examples for each field are described following this listing in Table 8.1.

- **Arenas**—The different games your clan plays. This field is not part of a player's profile, but is selected for match challenges.

- **Factions**—The primary divisions in your clan. A simple setup is to have one faction per game/mod. Large clans might need many more factions.

- **Medals**—The awards players can receive for outstanding play or teamwork. The award system can be based on existing military medals or can be completely arbitrary.

- **Outcomes**—The types of endings for a given match. This field should contain entries such as "Win" and "Loss."

- **Ranks**—The clan hierarchy. Rank names can be military-based or can be completely arbitrary.

- **Roles**—The main roles a player performs in a game. Roles can be complex, such as "Medic," "Soldier," and "Engineer," or they can be simple, such as "Offense" and "Defense."

- **Scenarios**—The maps for a given game. This field can, for example, name specific maps or more vague arenas, such as "Desert Campaign Maps" or "Any Symmetric Map."

- **Settings**—Server settings or other terms to be agreed upon for a match. To make this field simple, you can also use league settings such as "CAL Standard Settings."

- **Statuses**—The activity type for a given player. Normally, this contains at least "Active" and "Inactive," but you can add additional entries, such as "Retired" and "Recruit."

If you want to use the Eagle Alliance example clan to test out this module, use the following data in Table 8.1 to populate the database:

TABLE 8.1
Sample pnClansites Structure Data

FIELD	OPTIONS
Arenas	Battlefield 1942, Battlefield Vietnam, Quake III, Counter-Strike
Factions	BF:1942/Vietnam, Quake III, Counter-Strike
Medals	Medal of Honor, Distinguished Service, Silver Star, Bronze Star, Commendation, Expert Marksman
Outcomes	Win, Tie, Loss
Ranks	Commander, Captain, Lieutenant, Sergeant, Private, Trainee
Roles	Offense, Defense
Scenarios	BF:European Campaign, BF:African Campaign, BF:Pacific Campaign, BFV:City Maps, BFV:Jungle Maps, Any Q3 Map, Any CS Map
Settings	Standard
Statuses	Active, Inactive, Retired

A set of images is available with the online book materials for both the Ranks and Medals. The images are named to correspond with the sample data in Table 8.1, and pnClansite looks for them in your site's root directory by default.

> **Tip**
>
> The module's image path is set to your site's root by default, but you can manage your images more easily by placing them in this directory:
>
> `/modules/pnclansite/pnimages/`
>
> to separate them from other modules. Add the complete path when you enter images to make it work:
>
> `modules/pnclansite/pnimages/medal-honor.gif.`

Now click through the Common Menu block to see how the information you've set up will be seen by the general public (see Figure 8.1). All of the links will now work, though some of the pages still have no data to display. If you have used the sample images, you should see them formatted similarly to Figures 8.1 and 8.2.

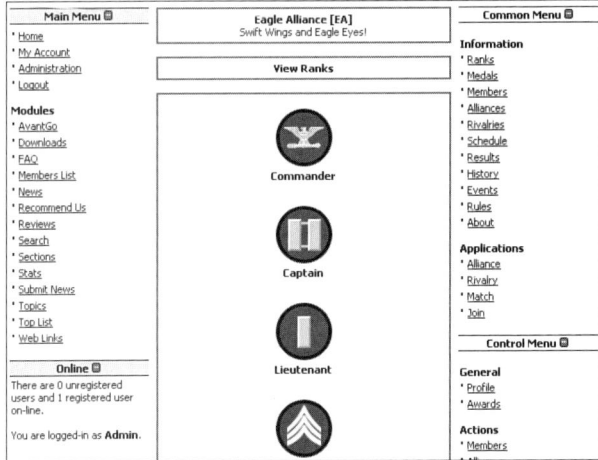

FIGURE 8.1 Ranking your clan members.

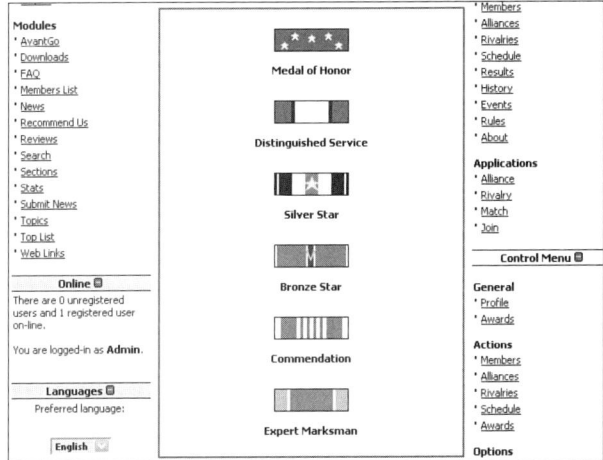

FIGURE 8.2 Awarding players with special medals.

Now use the Actions link in the Control Menu to add members to the clan. Edit their settings to change roles and award a few medals. Under the public Common Menu, click the Members link and look at one of your player entries (see Figure 8.3). Note how the join dates can also be edited to reflect dates prior to when the module was installed.

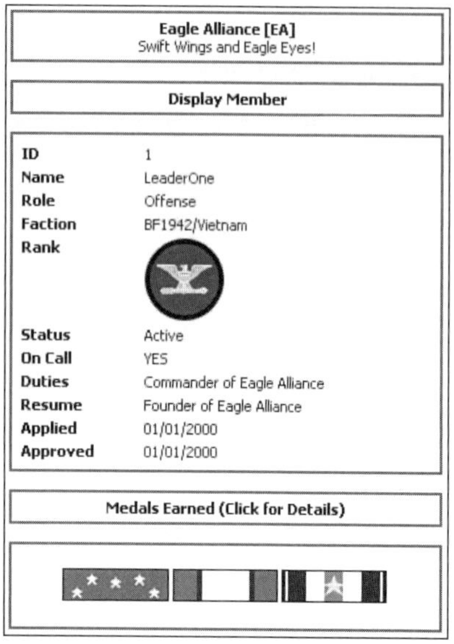

FIGURE 8.3 Viewing the player profiles in your clan.

Normally, alliances and rivalries are created by other players with the Applications forms, but you can also enter information through the administration system no differently than adding users automatically instead of using the Join form. The other blocks can be installed and used dynamically. They do not appear unless there is information to display.

You should now be ready to display your clan information to the public.

> **Tip**
>
> Create custom links to pnClansite features to limit which are visible to the public. Set up a new menu block or customize links in your theme to provide access to only the specific options you want displayed.

pn-teamspeak

Teamspeak (www.goteamspeak.com) is an audio communication application that allows users to communicate with one another using computer microphones and speakers. It was originally designed to provide verbal communication between players in online multiplayer games and runs in the background with minimal impact on network or system resources. It is provided free to all noncommercial users and has become very popular with online gamers in every genre.

Clans that use Teamspeak can also integrate the application's functionality with their website by installing a PostNuke TeamSpeak module. pn-teamspeak lets you display TeamSpeak users online by connecting your website directly to your TeamSpeak server.

The current version of the module is available at SourceForge (https://sourceforge.net/projects/pn-teamspeak/). The examples of this chapter were done using pn-teamspeak v0.0.3, which is also available with the downloadable book materials.

The archive comes with a number of additional files and folders that are not needed on your server. Unzip the files to a temp directory location. Notice the main directory structure begins:

```
/pn-teamspeak-0.0.3/modules/Teamspeak/
```

Copy only the files under the `/Teamspeak/` folder to your server's `/modules/` directory. The module initializes and activates normally. The module functions completely as a block, and all management of the module's features is done through the PostNuke block administration.

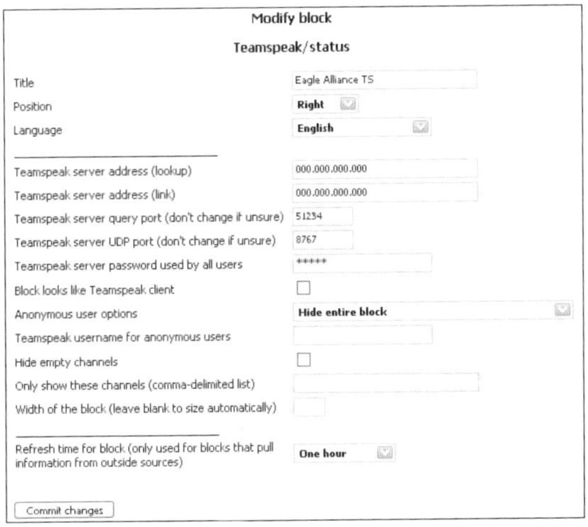

Click the Blocks link in the Administration Menu and add a new block. Select Teamspeak/Who's on Teamspeak? from the drop-down list box, and title the block to reflect its purpose, such as "Eagle Alliance TS." When you commit your changes, you are presented with the complete pn-teamspeak administration form (see Figure 8.4).

The Server Address fields should be the uniform resource locator (URL) or IP address needed to connect with the Teamspeak server. The fields are identical for most users. The second address is used with the block so that when a site user clicks on a channel name in your Teamspeak block, she automatically logs in and joins the server in that channel.

FIGURE 8.4 Configuring your Teamspeak block.

Note

Your web server must have access to the Teamspeak ports defined in the administration form for the connection to work.

The Block Looks Like Teamspeak Client field changes the block's default theme-based appearance to instead look like the purple Teamspeak client application. For theme consistency, most sites probably want this feature left unchecked.

You can allow access to anonymous users by defining a basic login in the block, and you can choose to display only specific channels online using the comma-delimited list. This is great for setting up private channels, such as clan meeting rooms, which are not visible/available to the general public visiting your site.

In addition, you might want to reduce the Refresh Time setting. It determines how often the web server queries the Teamspeak server for the current list of who is online. Because Teamspeak activity is often very fluid, more frequent checks might be warranted.

Tip

The dynamic Administer link at the bottom of the pn-teamspeak block can be used to take you directly to the block administration form.

Commit your setting changes and review your new Teamspeak block (example shown in Figure 8.5). Click the channel links to join the server.

FIGURE 8.5
Seeing who's online
in Teamspeak.

LTG GameQuery

The LTG GameQuery module allows clans to display server information directly on their PostNuke website. Also more fully titled "LifeTime-Gamer Game Query," the module creates a set of optional blocks that display one or more servers as a general listing or specifically by game.

As of this writing, LTG GameQuery is available in version 0.4, which is included with this book's online materials. The latest version is also available from the developer's website: www.ltgamer.com. The install archive includes a root folder for the module, so you can decompress its contents and then move all files to the server or simply decompress the files into the `/modules/` folder directly.

Browse to your site's Module Administration page and refresh the table listing. Initialize and activate the LTG GameQuery module. Now return to the Administration Menu and click the LTG GameQuery link. From this interface, you can add all the game servers you want to track.

Click the New Game Server link in the top navigation menu. You see the short form shown in Figure 8.6. The Name field can contain anything. For example, you can use the game name, such as "Call of Duty Server #2," or name servers by their owners, such as "Clan [AE] Quake3."

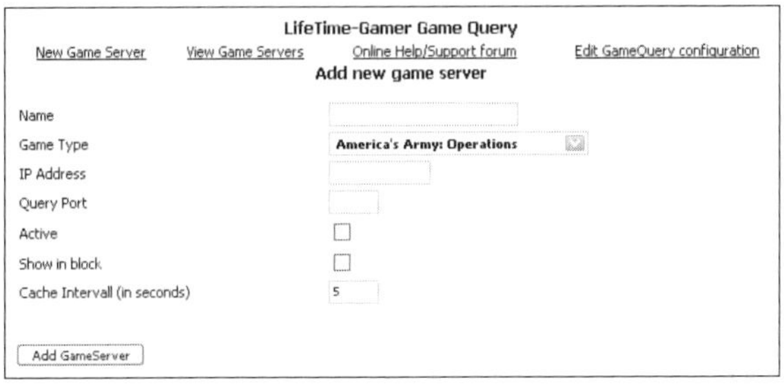

FIGURE 8.6 Entering a new game server to watch.

Select a game from the drop-down list box. Game mods can also be displayed; just select the root game from the list. For example, to display a Counter-Strike server, select Half-Life in the list. The games currently supported include

- America's Army: Operations
- Alien vs Predator 2
- Battlefield 1942
- Call of Duty
- FarCry
- Half-Life (Counter-Strike, TFC, and so on)
- Halo: Combat Evolved
- Jedi Knight 2: Jedi Outcast
- Medal of Honor
- Postal 2
- Quake 2
- Quake 3 Arena
- QuakeWorld
- Return to Castle Wolfenstein
- Shogo: Armored Division
- SiN
- Soldier of Fortune 2: Double Helix
- Star Trek Voyager: Elite Force
- Star Trek Voyager: Elite Force 2

- Unreal Tournament

- Unreal Tournament 2003

- Unreal Tournament 2004

- Vietcong

FIGURE 8.7
Displaying live
server information
on your site.

Enter the IP Address and Query Port fields for the server and check both the Active and Show in Block check boxes. Active servers are shown in all blocks and queried for searches. You can toggle the visibility of a server in the display blocks using the Show option.

The default Cache Interval setting is five seconds. This means a server being watched is checked for current information every five seconds. If you are having network load issues on either your website or game server, you might want to lengthen this amount of time.

Add your game server by submitting the form. Try adding a few other servers for the same or different games. Additional server addresses for testing can be found online in the respective games' websites or by using a server browser, such as The All-Seeing Eye.

Now go to the Blocks Administration page and add a server block. The MultiServer block displays all active servers you have added; to display only the servers playing a specific game, use the MultiServer by Game Type block, or you can display an individual server using the Single block. In the block creation form, you have the additional option of whether to display an image of the current map. This is a nice feature, but if your server is playing nonstandard maps, appropriate images for every map might not be available unless you create them.

Complete the block creation and view your live servers. Your block should appear similar to that shown in Figure 8.7.

Tip

Use combinations of different server blocks to customize your game site. If your clan has different pages for different games, create special blocks to display only the appropriate servers on their respective games' pages.

Website Games

Games that are a part of your website can be a great source of entertainment for your visitors. A large percentage of Internet users actively play games online, and providing an outlet for fun on your site is a good way to build your traffic. But to keep your traffic returning, you should find ways to make your website games unique to your site.

With PostNuke, you can log the scores of players based on their accounts. This creates a personal connection between the user and the site. Encouraging your users to participate in a game is another way you can interact with your users as a site administrator. Website visitors like to return to living, interactive sites, and including a game helps to provide that support.

pnFlashGames

This module is similar to the Multiplayer Gaming modules covered previously in that pnFlashGames is a website enhancement for games. The actual online games themselves are separate downloads, some of which are commercial products. pnFlashGames is a module that integrates games into your PostNuke site with a universal interface, management tools, and high score tracking system.

Only games that use the proper Flash MX component work, but literally hundreds of compatible games are already available, and most are free. Adding games like these to your website, besides being entertaining, adds an extra incentive for users to return. High-scoring players want to return and check the lists to see if they have been outscored, and most every player likes to better his own score with repeat plays.

The module itself can be obtained from its official website www.pnflashgames.com. Version 0.9.92 is used in the following examples, and is fully compatible with PostNuke .750. You can also download it from the online book materials. The archive includes a clean root folder, and the module installs very easily. Copy the files into your modules directory, initialize, and activate pnFlashGames.

Ten games are included with the standard download. You can review them in the /modules/pnFlashGames/games/ directory. Additional downloaded games should be unzipped and placed in that directory for them to work. Go to the pnFlashGames Administration page using the PostNuke Administration Menu. Click the View Games link at the top to view the preinstalled games (see Figure 8.8).

Add another game using the New Game link at the top. Add the game "Racer" with the file-name racer.swf. Notice the Category drop-down list box that enables you to group your installed games as Action, Arcade, Classic, Puzzle, Racing, or Space games. Submit the form. If you want more practice working with the module, you can add the additional default games or other new games you've downloaded.

pnFlashGames 0.9.92

| New game | View games | Edit games configuration | | Edit Categories | Edit Contests |

View games

Game name	Game location	Options
Airfox	modules/pnFlashGames/games/airfox.swf	Edit | Delete | Clear Scores | Clear Comments
Pacman	modules/pnFlashGames/games/pacman.swf	Edit | Delete | Clear Scores | Clear Comments
Snake	modules/pnFlashGames/games/snake.swf	Edit | Delete | Clear Scores | Clear Comments
Space Invaders	modules/pnFlashGames/games/spaceInvaders.swf	Edit | Delete | Clear Scores | Clear Comments
Swarm	modules/pnFlashGames/games/swarm.swf	Edit | Delete | Clear Scores | Clear Comments
Tetris	modules/pnFlashGames/games/tetris.swf	Edit | Delete | Clear Scores | Clear Comments

FIGURE 8.8   Configuring your installed Flash games.

The game categories are also preconfigured for your convenience. Click the Edit Categories link in the navigation list to add or remove games from a given category. You can rename or remove any category from this screen, as well as add additional new categories.

Add games to the various categories. Create new category names if you want. You can also add the same game to multiple categories to make it easy for users to find games that seem to fit into different groups.

The Games Configuration page supplies you with a large number of self-explanatory options to customize how the pnFlashGames module works with your site.

Click the Edit Contests link to create an example event. For Contest Name, enter "Be the Pac Master!" Complete the Description field with the text "Contest to find the best Pacman player. Show us what you've got!" Change the image path to the following:

```
modules/pnFlashGames/games/pacman.gif
```

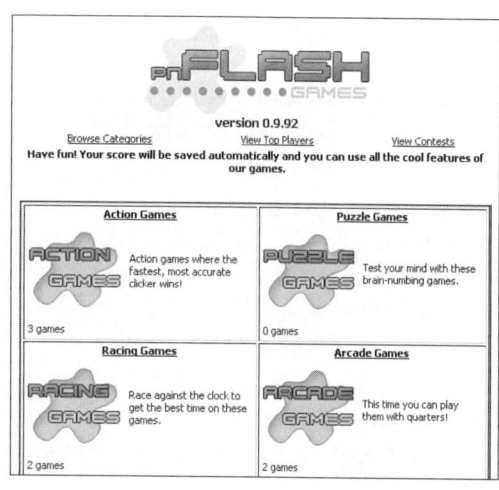

FIGURE 8.9   Browsing the Flash games on your site.

Now submit the form to add it to the contest listing. You now have access to the Options column where you can add games to the contest. For this contest, just add the Pacman game.

You need to add a new link to the module in your Main Menu to allow users to access the games. Edit the Main Menu block from the PostNuke Blocks Administration page. Enter "Play Games" for the Title. The module's URL is simply "{pnFlashGames}," and add a description with the text "Play online Flash games." Submit the block change and click the new menu link to see the games page (see Figure 8.9).

Click the View Contests link to see the "Pac Master" entry you created (see Figure 8.10). Then return to the game listing with the Browse

Categories link to test out your installed Flash games with a round or two, and then go to the Blocks Administration page. pnFlashGames also comes with five block types you can create:

- **Show currently active contests**—Displays the ongoing contests available to users.

- **Show latest high scores**—Lists the recent high-scoring players.

- **Show the newest game**—Advertises the most recently added game.

- **Show random game**—Displays a random game from your installed selection. This can be set to only randomize within a specific category.

- **Show top players on your site**—Lists the best game players.

FIGURE 8.10   Competing to be the Pac Master!

Add one or more of the blocks to make it easier for users to get to the Flash games on your site.

vQuiz

vQuiz is a simple online question module similar to polling systems but with added point systems and a "Hall of Fame" to rank users with high scores. Version 1.3 is available with the book materials, or you can download recent versions from the author's site: http://tecfa.unige.ch/perso/vivian/.

The module installs easily into the root `modules` folder. Initialize and activate it through the module administration table. Browse to the Administration Menu and click the vQuiz link.

Create a new quiz to walk through how it works. Use "Guess the World Capitals" for the Name field. Create the quiz with six questions, each having four possible answers. Submit the form to go to the question entry page. Use the data in Table 8.2 to complete the quiz.

TABLE 8.2

World Capital Question Data

CAPITAL	OPTIONS
Australia	*Canberra*, Ottawa, Amsterdam, London
Cuba	Rome, Budapest, *Havana*, Bogota
Austria	*Vienna*, La Paz, Paris, Moscow
Japan	Oslo, Bern, *Tokyo*, Beijing
New Zealand	Stockholm, Brussels, Athens, *Wellington*
Argentina	Vienna, *Buenos Aires*, Brasilia, Caracas

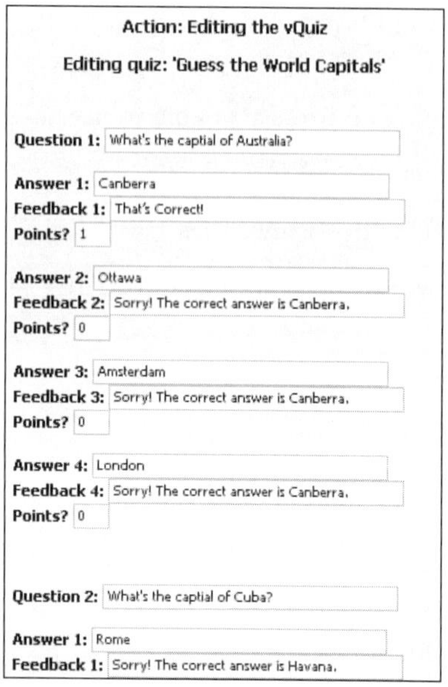

FIGURE 8.11   Creating a fun user quiz!

FIGURE 8.12   Seeing how you did on the quiz.

For the correct answers, use this text as feedback: "That's Correct!" and for the wrong answers, use "Sorry! The correct answer is *X*."—where "*X*" is the correct capital for that question. Set each correct answer to be worth one point and all wrong answers to zero points. The correct answers are identified in italic in Table 8.2. Your fields should look similar to Figure 8.11. Now submit the form to save your entries.

You can test the quiz through the Administration screen, but instead try out the quiz using the user interface to ensure that component is working. Activate the new quiz from the Admin Interface. Browse to the Blocks Administration page and edit the Main Menu. On a new row, enter "Take a Quiz!" for the Title, {vquiz} as the URL, and add a description with the text "Exercise your brain."

Now, it's time to try it out. Submit your block changes and click the new Menu link. Select the link labeled Run the Quiz to test the system. An example of the completed quiz with both right and wrong answers is shown in Figure 8.12.

An optional block is also included with the vQuiz module that displays the Hall of Fame. Browse to your site's Blocks Administration page and add the vQuiz block near the bottom of the select listing. You can choose how many users to display in the block, and each name is displayed with a little trophy icon placed next to it.

Troubleshooting

Most of the modules covered in this chapter are relatively current and well maintained, so it's less likely you will find problems with them during the install. As of this writing, pnClansite specifically does not yet have a new version designed for the PostNuke .75 release. The module works quite well with version .75, but if you are having trouble with it, try some of the following troubleshooting fixes.

pnClansite Doesn't Register as a Module

This problem usually occurs when you use a directory name other than "pnclansite." With many modules, you can use varied directory names, for example, to install different version instances. The pnClansite module requires that you do not add additional version numbers or attempt to install multiple copies of the module, such as `/modules/pnclansite40` or `/modules/pnclansite2`, respectively.

If you are having trouble registering your module, be certain your module folder name is simply "pnclansite." If it still doesn't work, check your installation of PostNuke and be certain other new modules can be registered. Also try downloading a new copy of pnClansite, as you might have an incomplete package or corrupted files.

pnClansite Error: Unable to Load Required Module!

This error can occur after you have successfully installed pnClansite and you are trying to populate the data tables for the first time. Though the Administration page loads fine, you see the error on pages linked from the Control Menu block. The problem only occurs with PostNuke version .75; prior releases work fine.

The error is due to the hard-coding of the module name in various administration files. The files specifically call the module by the name "pnclansite." You might have seen this instruction in the pnClansite install documentation:

```
Create the folder "modules/pnClansite" to uploaded the files to.
```

Using the capital "C" in the module's folder name no longer works with PostNuke .75 because the Application Programming Interface (API) module calls are now case sensitive. To get the module to work with the newer PostNuke installations, you need to use the folder name "pnclansite" with all characters in lowercase.

Remove the module, rename the folder, and then reinitialize pnClansite with the proper directory name. It should work fine from there.

Black pnClansite Pages, Unreadable Pages

Many clan and guild websites are built with dark backgrounds, and black especially is a popular color choice with the online gaming crowd. pnClansite was built to cater to the gaming community, and its administration screens are set with a black background by default.

The module includes this setting in a simple form field, but unfortunately the text color for the module is not configurable. So, if you are using a theme with a light background, your theme's text will be dark, probably black. This results in black text set by the theme and black background set by the module.

You can remedy this dilemma by changing to a theme with light-colored text, but it is much easier to tell pnClansite to use a light background. Scroll down to the bottom of the form. The last field in the main administration page sets the Layout Background Color for the module. You can see the text labels by selecting the text on the page in your browser. Set the Background Color to white by entering "#FFFFFF" and click the Update button to make the change. After the page is refreshed, you can see the page content normally.

pn-teamspeak Error: Could Not Connect to Server

This error occurs when the pn-teamspeak module is unable to connect to the configured TeamSpeak server. It is usually caused by closed firewall ports. Check your web server's firewall to ensure these ports are available:

```
TCP: 14534
UDP: 8767 and 51234
```

If your website is hosted by an external provider, you might need to contact your host's support staff to determine the ports to which you have access.

Next

The next chapter covers PostNuke users and the permissions system. You will learn the basics of how PostNuke user accounts are created and what is required to grant or deny access to website resources.

Users and Permissions

9

The PostNuke permissions system is essential to developing a customized site. It constantly manages the display of site features and has as much of an effect on your site's layout as a custom theme. Like most security systems, PostNuke has two basic elements to administrate: users and resources.

User permissions can be set for each individual user account, but most of the time user access is managed through groups. Resources in PostNuke are referenced by module. Specific module capabilities can be listed out, and even a single article can be specifically restricted. Usually, resources are managed as complete modules, in which all of a module's features are referenced together, similar to a user group.

In this introductory chapter to the PostNuke permissions system, you examine the modules that together make up the system and perform general user administrative tasks. The chapter topics include:

- Basic user administration
- Groups
- Permissions

Basic User Administration

Open a browser and go to your Administration page. This chapter is concerned with three module links on this page. The first is User Administration at the bottom of the table.

After you navigate to this page, you see the form in Figure 9.1.

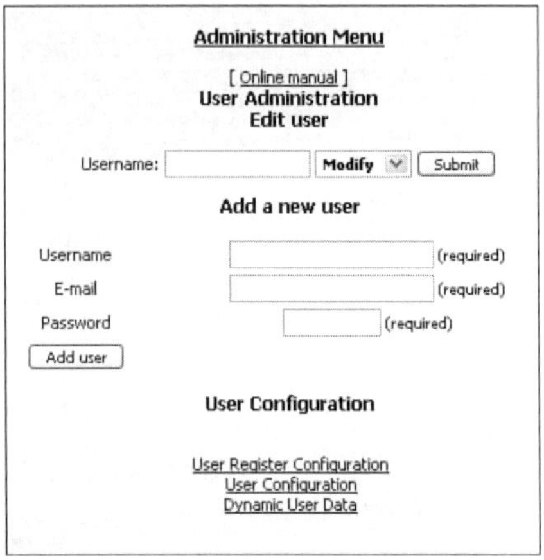

The User Administration page has three sections: *Edit User*, *Add a New User*, and *User Configuration*. The Edit User form lets you modify or delete existing users. You must know the exact username beforehand to use the form, but exact case is not required. Delete operations do come with a confirmation screen before an erase is made.

Populate your site with some sample users. If you know the names of users you plan to add, you can use them now, or you can refer to Table 9.1 for suggested data. Enter in any 10 users using the Add a New User form. If you are entering the fabricated data from Table 9.1, simply use "password" for all users' passwords. You can use the Add a New User link to return to the main form after a successful submission.

FIGURE 9.1   Managing your site users.

TABLE 9.1

Twenty-Five Example Users

USERNAME	FIRST NAME	LAST NAME	EMAIL
mallen	Maria	Allen	mpallen@coolmail.com
canderson	Christopher	Anderson	chander@yahu.com
mclark	Mary	Clark	mc503493@quikmail.com
sgarcia	Steven	Garcia	sgar1003@mysite.com
jhall	Jennifer	Hall	jennhall3491@coolmail.com
dharris	Donald	Harris	dharris@mysite.com
mhernandez	Margaret	Hernandez	mhernandez@yahu.com
pjackson	Paul	Jackson	pjack@bestmail.com
mjones	Michael	Jones	jonesy43@bestmail.com
dking	Dorothy	King	dorthy133@quikmail.com
blee	Barbara	Lee	btlee45@bestmail.com
llewis	Linda	Lewis	lindal679845@mysite.com
gmartin	George	Martin	george876@bestmail.com
emartinez	Edward	Martinez	emartinez@coolmail.com

TABLE 9.1

Continued

USERNAME	FIRST NAME	LAST NAME	EMAIL
rmiller	Richard	Miller	dmiller@mysite.com
jmoore	Joseph	Moore	moore@yahu.com
brobinson	Brian	Robinson	robinson@bestmail.com
prodriguez	Patricia	Rodriguez	patr09765@bestmail.com
ttaylor	Thomas	Taylor	ttaylor@quikmail.com
dthomas	Daniel	Thomas	thomasd@quikmail.com
kthompson	Kenneth	Thompson	kennyt@coolmail.com
ewalker	Elizabeth	Walker	lizbeth@yahu.com
rwilliams	Robert	Williams	bobbygw@bestmail.com
cwilson	Charles	Wilson	chuckw98@mysite.com
syoung	Susan	Young	suyou592@coolmail.com

Adding new accounts with this form is the fastest way to enter user information into PostNuke short of a raw SQL statement.

Now enter the username of one of the new accounts into the Edit User form, select Modify from the drop-down menu, and click the Submit button. You see a screen very similar to Figure 9.2. The first field is the User ID. Every user account is made unique by its ID, so you can change the username or email for a given account as needed.

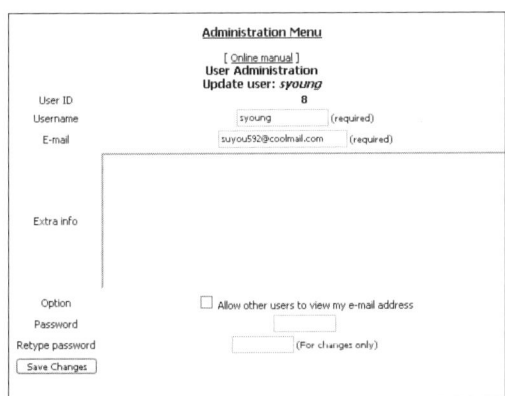

FIGURE 9.2 Modifying user account information.

The *Extra Info* field is a public comment for the user account. It can contain anything from biographic information to a simple quote. Each user has access to edit this field, and it appears when someone looks at a user's account profile.

The option *Allow Other Users to View My E-mail Address* toggles the display of an account's email address. Users can optionally enter a fake email that displays in place of their real email for privacy. You can also reset a user's password using this form. If you are managing user accounts manually, you might have a regular need to change passwords for users who have forgotten them.

You should also now try the delete operation for one or more of the demo accounts. You are given a confirmation screen, but the process is relatively swift. Try to maintain about 10 accounts for testing purposes when you are finished.

User Register Configuration

Return to the main User Administration page and select *User Register Configuration*. This form determines the way new users register their own accounts into your site (see Figure 9.3). Change the Require Unique Email Addresses field to "No." Normally, this is a good option to leave on, but you need it turned off for an upcoming test. *Show Optional Fields* toggles the display of all the extra information that can be entered with a user account. For a simple account registration, all those extra fields can be overwhelming for some users, so many sites might prefer leaving this option disabled. Those options are examined further in the next section.

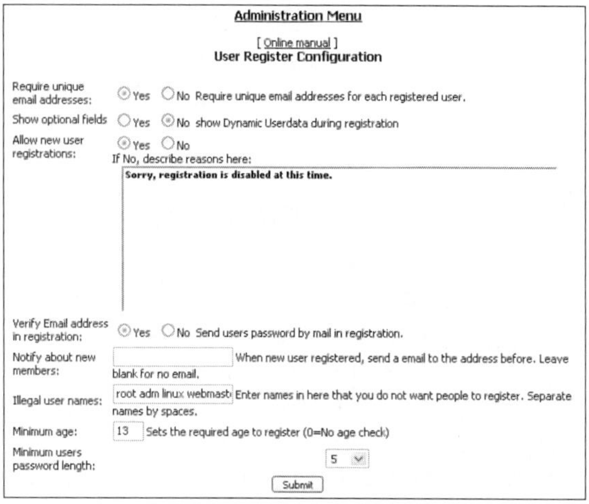

FIGURE 9.3   Setting account registration options.

If you choose to disable the email verification, users are prompted for their password during registration, and they can log in to the site immediately. This can lead to bogus user accounts used to anonymously spam your site, so it's recommended you leave the verification enabled.

The *Minimum Age* requirement gives a prospective user a confirmation check for his age. Sites where users can post content to forums or even home page news with little or no moderation can be a cause for concern with visitors of all ages on the Internet. Regardless of your site's content, this check can help protect you from future legal problems. Secure environments, such as business intranets, most likely need this option turned completely off, which is accomplished by entering "0" into the form.

Submit the form with the unique email requirement changed and return to the main User Administration page.

User Configuration

Click the *User Configuration* link to customize the Personal Homepage users reach using the My Account link in the Main Menu. The two options on this page allow you to specify the path to the images used on the page, as well as toggle whether those images are displayed at all.

Dynamic User Data

Click the Dynamic User Data link at the bottom of the Administration page. The resulting table contains all of the information associated with a user account (see Figure 9.4). The rows are shown in the order they appear on a user's Personal Information page. The order can be adjusted using the Weight column, just like the block system discussed in Chapter 4, "Modules and Blocks."

Active	Field Label		Weight	Data Type	Length	Delete
○	_UREALNAME	Name	⇩	Core	N/A	N/A
○	_UREALEMAIL	Current e-mail	⇧⇩	Core Required	N/A	N/A
○	_UFAKEMAIL	Fake e-mail	⇧⇩	Core	N/A	N/A
○	_YOURHOMEPAGE	Your website	⇧⇩	Core	N/A	N/A
○	_TIMEZONEOFFSET	Time zone offset	⇧⇩	Core	N/A	N/A
○	_YOURAVATAR	Your avatar	⇧⇩	Core	N/A	N/A
○	_YICQ	Your ICQ Number	⇧⇩	Core	N/A	N/A
○	_YAIM	Your AIM Address	⇧⇩	Core	N/A	N/A
○	_YYIM	Your Yahoo Messenger	⇧⇩	Core	N/A	N/A
○	_YMSNM	Your MSN Messenger	⇧⇩	Core	N/A	N/A
○	_YLOCATION	Your location	⇧⇩	Core	N/A	N/A
○	_YOCCUPATION	Occupation	⇧⇩	Core	N/A	N/A
○	_YINTERESTS	Your interests	⇧⇩	Core	N/A	N/A
○	_SIGNATURE	Signature	⇧⇩	Core	N/A	N/A
○	_EXTRAINFO	Extra Information	⇧⇩	Core	N/A	N/A
○	_PASSWORD	Password	⇧	Core Required	N/A	N/A

FIGURE 9.4   Customizing the user account data table.

You can add additional user fields using the Add Fields form below the table. To see how it works, add a user field now. The *Field Label* contains the variable used to reference the name of the data entry. It must begin with an underscore character and should be in all caps. Enter "_PETNAME" into the field or add in an entry of your own.

The *Data Type* defines the type of information that will be stored in the variable. "String" is for a single line of text, whereas "Text" signifies a paragraph or more of data. Floats are real numbers, such as 45.6. For this example, leave the default "String" selected. Enter "20" into the Length field and submit the form.

Now you will set a variable name, however, the new item does not yet have a common language label. Start up your text editor and open this file for editing:

```
/language/eng/global.php
```

The global.php file contains all of the text label definitions for common variables like those in the user accounts. The listing is arranged in alphabetical order, and it's important to maintain that consistency. The _PETNAME variable should slot in at around line 312. Enter in the following line:

```
define('_PETNAME','Your Pet\'s Name'); // User account data
```

Quotes in the text need the preceding backslash character, as shown in the example. Save the file to commit your change.

Register Users

Next, you register users using the public account creation system. Log your account out of your site to have the Login block reappear. Click the Sign Up link at the base of the form and click Register from the subsequent options. You now see the age verification check. Visitors who click the Under 13 link are refused access to an account.

The New User Registration form you see now is the standard account submission screen that the majority of your users will likely use to create their accounts. The email address must be entered twice to help prevent data-entry errors. You can change the text appearing on this form by editing the variables in this file:

```
/modules/NS-NewUser/lang/eng/global.php
```

They are global variable definitions just like what you've been editing previously. Just look for the text you want to edit to determine which variable corresponds.

Add in two more users from Table 9.1, but use your email address instead of the ones provided in the table. Check your email for the registration confirmations. Chapter 23, "User System Hacks and Modules," covers the steps needed to change the email content. Notice the passwords mailed to you are randomly generated. Users need to enter their random password to log in for the first time.

Now return to your site and click the Members List link in the Main Menu. Now that your site has a few accounts created, you can see the usernames there for review. Click on the usernames to view the account profiles.

Groups

In this section, you examine the PostNuke user account grouping module. Go to your main Administration page and find the module link labeled Groups.

PostNuke initially defines two starting groups: Users and Admins (see Figure 9.5). Administrators have complete access to the PostNuke website; this is the group the default

FIGURE 9.5
Managing your user groups.

Administrator account is assigned. Users are made up of all registered accounts that are not in the Admins group. Users can read all site content but are not allowed to change site settings or edit existing content.

Click on the Users link in the table; you receive a complete list of all the basic user accounts you just added to the site. The *Delete* links by each name do not delete the accounts; they remove the account from the group. Click Delete for one or more of the usernames. Notice there is no confirmation screen. The group removal is immediate because it's very easy to add users back to the group.

Select the Add a User to Group ink at the top of the page. The usernames in the drop-down list box you are given are generated from the database. Every account that is not currently in the Users group appears as options. You should see the Admin account and any other accounts you deleted from the Users group.

Creating Groups

Groups can be defined in a tiered hierarchy with increasing access for more powerful groups, such as the default settings. You can also set up a system in which users have specialized access to different areas of your site, and different users only see their exclusive areas. In addition, any combination of these is also possible, but it's a very good idea to map out exactly what your site access needs are before setting up the system.

Add a new special access group to your site called "Reporters." To perform this operation, return to the main Groups Administration page where you see the Add a New Group link. Enter "Reporters" into the Group Name field and submit the form. You are sent back to the main page, but now the group table has three rows with your new group listed.

Managing Groups

It's much easier to manage your site resources by group. If you are replacing one resource with another, you only have to adjust one group's access to the new resource rather than having to make changes to the permissions for every user in the group.

The Admins and Users groups have been mentioned as the two starting groups created with your PostNuke install. You should also consider a third unnamed group of anonymous users. By default, your entire site is open with read-only access to anyone visiting. It is assigned using the "all" settings in the Permissions system. The User group is different than anonymous users in that they have been given additional write abilities that allow them to interact with the site, such as submitting a news article or responding to a poll.

The Reporters group we just created is intended to be populated by users allowed to post their own news articles, without administrator approval. In this example, they are just like regular users, but with this one extra bit of access. You could just as easily restrict the Reporters group to only submitting news, in effect leaving it fewer options than a regular user account. You complete the Reporter group's setup in Chapter 16, "Customized Access."

Determining how many groups you want for your site and what the specific permissions for each group will be is a substantial task. You should consider your site's function carefully when documenting how the permissions need to be laid out.

Permissions

The PostNuke Permissions system is basically a hierarchy. Each permission setting is entered into an ordered table, and the upper entries have precedence over the lower ones. A pair of groups that on paper have relatively equal access to different areas of a site are ordered after they are added to the Permissions system. That way, should there ever be a possible conflict, the permissions for the groups can be compared to determine the resulting abilities of group members.

The reason for the hierarchy is that user accounts can be added to multiple groups and given different sets of permissions. An account can also have custom permissions assigned to just one user. Having an ordered precedence system eliminates any rights conflict.

Default Settings

Return to the main Administration page and select the icon labeled Permissions. You are now presented with the PostNuke permissions table shown in Figure 9.6. The system has a bit of a reputation for being difficult to manage, but the confusion lies more with its appearance than any real design problems.

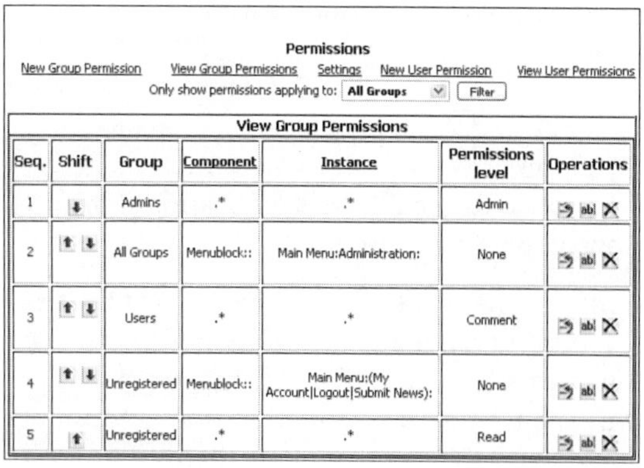

FIGURE 9.6   Default PostNuke permissions.

The table has seven columns. The first simply displays the sequential order of the permissions. The column is especially important when you use the filter feature above the table to limit the number of rows being viewed at a time.

The second column allows you to change the order of the entries. PostNuke permissions are evaluated from the top of the table down. When trying to determine the rights for a resource, PostNuke stops looking after it finds the first match. So, for example, if two permission settings exist, with the first permission granting total access to an item and the second restricting access, as long as the grant access is higher in the table, the second entry is ignored.

The *Group* column names to which group the permission entry applies. The User Permissions table is identical to the Group Permissions except for this column. Notice the two other possible entries in addition to your established groups: Unregistered and All Groups.

Nine different types of *Permissions Level* rights can be individually assigned to a given group or user entry. The levels and type of rights are detailed in the following list:

- **None**—No access is granted for the resource. The resource and links to it do not appear to users.

- **Overview**—The resource appears to the user, but read access to the content within the resource is not granted.

- **Read**—The user is granted read-only access to the resource.

- **Comment**—Resource content can be read, and the user can add comments regarding the content, but additional content cannot be added.

- **Moderate**—This right grants the ability to moderate a resource that has a moderation feature.

- **Edit**—The user can read and edit existing content in a defined resource. New content cannot be added.

- **Add**—This right provides access to add and approve additional content for a given resource.

- **Delete**—This right grants the ability to remove existing content from the resource.

- **Admin**—The user is given full administrative rights to the resource.

The *Operations* column has three clickable buttons for each permissions entry. The far-left button with an arrow on it inserts a new permission into the table. The new permission is placed above the line whose button you click. Entries added using the *New Group Permission* link above the table appear below all entries. The middle button with "ab" written on it edits the given line. Finally, the last button marked with an "X" deletes the permission setting. There is no confirmation when deleting a permissions entry.

Components and Instances

Most PostNuke users who have problems with the permissions system get hung on the Component and Instance settings for a rights entry. A *Component* is the physical coded resource, like a module or a block. An *Instance* is the live example of the Component.

For example, Menu is a core block type. Go into the Blocks Administration screen. It's possible to create as many instances of the Menu block as you want. Notice that both Main Menu and Incoming are both Menu blocks. Menu is the Component, and Main Menu and Incoming are Instances.

When referencing both Components and Instances, you can see in the Permissions table (in Figure 9.6) that both colons and asterisks are used. The period/asterisk is a wildcard that signifies "everything." When being more specific, you must use the colons to separate references. Both Components and Instances can be detailed with three terms, which are separated by two colons. If one term is specific enough, the rest are also assumed to mean "everything," though the wildcard is not required.

For example, this entry: `.*` means the same thing as: `.*:.*:.*`. If you are referencing a resource in the same way, this entry: `Menublock::` is identical to `Menublock:.*:.*`. The shorthand of removing the asterisks in specific references and colons in global references is what can be confusing.

Now to explain the specific references, look at lines two and four in the default settings. Line two reads like this:

```
Menublock::   Main Menu:Administration:   None
```

This means groups have no access to the link named "Administration" in the instance of "Main Menu," which comes from the Component "Menublock."

Line four has these settings:

```
Menublock::   Main Menu:(My Account¦Logout¦Submit News):   None
```

The permission is identical to the preceding one, except multiple links in the Main Menu Instance are referenced. They are grouped inside parentheses and separated with the vertical pipe character. You can make complex but easy-to-manage rights entries using the grouping controls.

In addition, it's easy to determine how to reference specific Instances and Components because PostNuke provides them all for you. Notice the links in the table heading; both Component and Instance are clickable. Each link pops up a table dynamically generated from the current system. PostNuke determines every Component or Instance currently available and lists them for you.

Setting Permissions By Group and User

The vast majority of the time, you should be setting permissions by group. It saves management time and is absolutely essential for sites with large numbers of users. The filtering feature is also only available for group settings. But should you need to single out a user, the settings for Components and Instances are identical to the group permissions.

User permissions are also checked before group permissions. This is key because user permission settings should be the exception to the group rules. Having user entries checked first allows the exceptions to take place first; PostNuke stops looking for rights access after finding a setting in user permissions.

An example of how this might work is a problem user on your site. Suppose you have a user who continually posts off-topic content on your site. If you need to temporarily restrict the account's posting abilities, a quick user exception rule does the trick. It's easy to remove the user setting later, and you do not need to touch the group table.

Troubleshooting

The most serious problem you can get into with PostNuke permissions is Administrator lockout. Every other issue can be handled by tweaking the tables a bit more. If one of your changes suddenly results in the system telling you your account no longer has access, don't panic and assume a reinstall is required. You can restore your Administrator privileges with one quick change to the database tables.

First try to simply reset the access of the Admins Group to full Admin access to all site features. This is done in the table nuke_group_perms. The complete SQL statement you need is:

```
UPDATE nuke_group_perms
SET pn_component = '.*', pn_instance = '.*', pn_level = '800'
WHERE pn_gid = "2"
```

If you are using a graphical database administrator application, simply select the table from the listing and make the changes described in the SQL statement.

The preceding code does not change the priority of the Admin Group settings, only the access. Manually changing the priority in the database is generally not a good idea because it should remain unique and an assignment might produce duplicates. If you have deleted the lines granting Administrator access, you need to try changing the All Groups setting as follows:

```
UPDATE nuke_group_perms
SET pn_component = '.*', pn_instance = '.*', pn_level = '800'
WHERE pn_gid = "-1"
```

This is a more extreme option, in which all users are given full access to the entire site. After this is done, you should immediately go into the Permissions system and fix the settings so you can protect your site.

Next

The next chapter looks at PostNuke's theme system, including the new Xanthia Theme Engine. You will learn how PostNuke handles themes and what you can do to customize the existing themes to fit your website.

Themes

This chapter examines PostNuke themes. PostNuke uses themes to define the layout and design of your site. Content is dynamically generated within the display constraints defined by the active theme. With the display format separated from the content, you can change from one theme to another to instantly redesign your site and still view all of your site's pages without having to recode them.

This chapter introduces you to the Xanthia Templating Environment (XTE), and illustrates the steps needed to edit the existing themes that are included with PostNuke to redesign them to work for your site. You approach the information through the following topics:

- Xanthia Templating Environment

- Theme management

- Customizing themes

Xanthia Templating Environment

The Xanthia Templating Environment, or XTE, is a new component added to PostNuke 0.75 that includes the Xanthia and pnRender modules. Where previous versions of PostNuke used static theme files, Xanthia is a complete theme engine with additional functions and greater flexibility. pnRender is a templating engine used to make Xanthia work, but with regard to directly using the module, pnRender itself is mainly useful to module developers.

XTE is based on the Smarty templating engine for PHP (smarty.php.net). It's designed to separate application logic and content from its presentation. This distinction adds a great deal of power to PostNuke 0.75 over previous releases. Now, you can build a theme to alter the design and layout of relatively any feature of your website without the need for third-party add-ons.

How Templates Work

Xanthia works by creating templates, for everything. Each template consists of simple Extensible Hypertext Markup Language (XHTML) you can develop with any text editor. It's like making a mini-web page for just the Poll, for example. Each template is a separate file, and the files are grouped together by reference when you define a theme.

How Zones Work

Each template is associated with a zone. There are two types of zones: Theme Zones and Block Zones. Think of zones as a way to label templates and blocks as abstract objects. Theme Zones allow you to divide up your site into designable pieces, such as "left side" or "header." A Theme Zone can be relatively global, such as a default master zone that pages can use by default, and a Theme Zone can be very specific, such as describing how news articles should look. Figure 10.1 shows a basic layout with zones for the center, sides, header, and overall page.

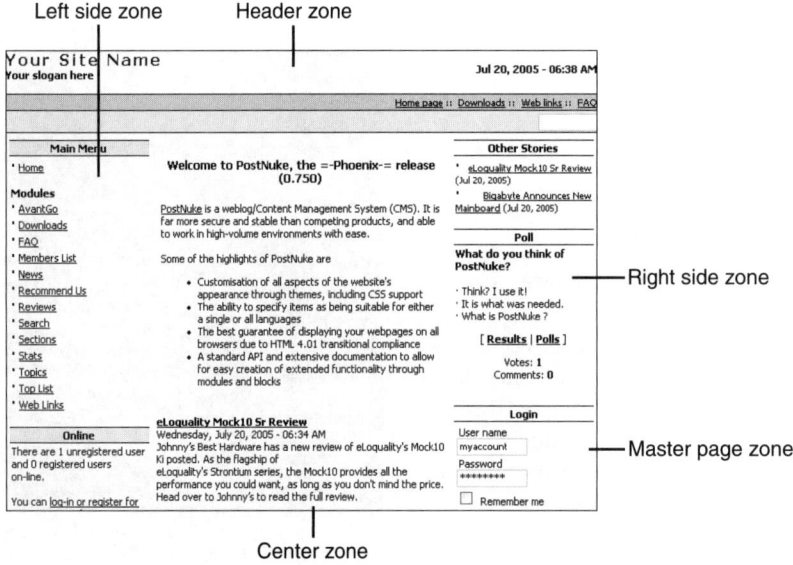

FIGURE 10.1   Basic Theme Zone layout.

> **Tip**
>
> If you are having trouble visualizing the zones, try drawing them out on a sheet of paper. Think of it like a map. Start with a given page, and divide it up into separate areas, such as header, footer, navigation, and so on. After you have all the areas mapped out, you will know how many zones you need, and what to name them.

Block Zones define the placement of module block areas. Block Zones are not specifically required when working with your Xanthia themes, but they are suggested and can provide additional, more specific positioning options. Figure 10.2 shows some areas on a given example page that could be managed as Block Zones. Block Zones should be placed inside Theme Zones.

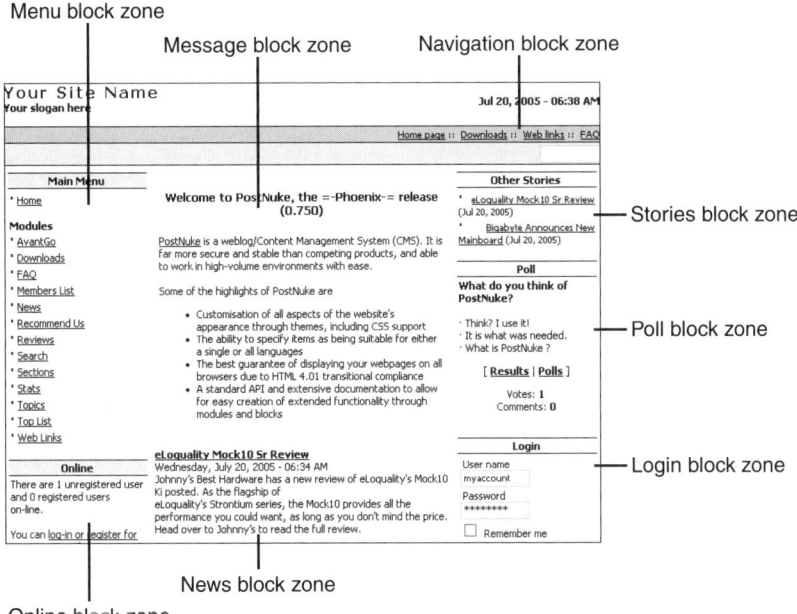

FIGURE 10.2   Block Zones can define areas for blocks.

Multiple blocks can be displayed within one Block Zone. Block Zones don't have template files to define how they look; they help you manage where blocks should be placed.

In essence, the XTE system is separating the design of page areas from the display of content through blocks. A given look is made into an object with a Theme Zone name, and one or more modules are also abstracted as a Block Zone. You style the appearance of content by placing Block Zones inside Theme Zones.

How Themes Work

A Xanthia theme collects all the zones and templates together, allows you to define styles, and packages it together under a theme name. When you apply a new theme, you are activating all those zones, using all those templates, and restyling your site.

Template files cannot be used without being added to a theme first. Zones are similarly defined as part of a theme and then assigned a template. Each theme has color variables you can create and a series of settings that generally describe how the theme will work.

Special XTE logic variables can be written into the templates using a format similar to a Hypertext Markup Language (HTML) comment:

```
<!--[$NAMEOFOBJECT]-->
```

These variables allow you to queue the display of an element at that point in your XHTML code. For example, after you define the theme's left column width, it is referenced in a theme like this:

```
<td style="width:<!--[$lcolwidth]-->; vertical-align:top;">
```

Block Zones are designated in the same way. So, if you define a Block Zone called "MENU" and plan on displaying it in the left column, you can do so like this:

```
<td style="width:<!--[$lcolwidth]-->; vertical-align:top;">
<!--[$MENU]-->
</td>
```

All Xanthia theme elements are referenced through these variables.

Theme Name	Active ?	Actions
PiterpanV2	● Active	[Edit Theme] [Remove Theme] [Reload Templates] [Generate config cache] [View Theme] [Credits]
pnDefault	● Active	[Edit Theme] [Remove Theme] [Reload Templates] [Generate config cache] [View Theme] [Credits]
PostNuke	● Active	[Edit Theme] [Remove Theme] [Reload Templates] [Generate config cache] [View Theme] [Credits]
PostNukeBlue	● Active	[Edit Theme] [Remove Theme] [Reload Templates] [Generate config cache] [View Theme] [Credits]
PostNukeSilver	● Active	[Edit Theme] [Remove Theme] [Reload Templates] [Generate config cache] [View Theme] [Credits]
SeaBreeze	● Active	[Edit Theme] [Remove Theme] [Reload Templates] [Generate config cache] [View Theme] [Credits]

FIGURE 10.3   Managing your Xanthia themes.

Theme Management

You can begin working with the Xanthia interface by examining the existing prebuilt themes. Browse to your site's Administration page, and click the Xanthia link near the bottom of the table. Initially, all of the Xanthia themes included with PostNuke are inactive. You need to add them into the system.

Click the Add Theme link for each theme until you have activated all of the Xanthia themes. You then have a table in which each theme includes a set of management options, as shown in Figure 10.3.

Configuring Xanthia

Select the Configure Xanthia option above the table. The Configuration page has 10 options that apply to your site regardless of which Xanthia theme you select (see Figure 10.4). These options are explained in the following list.

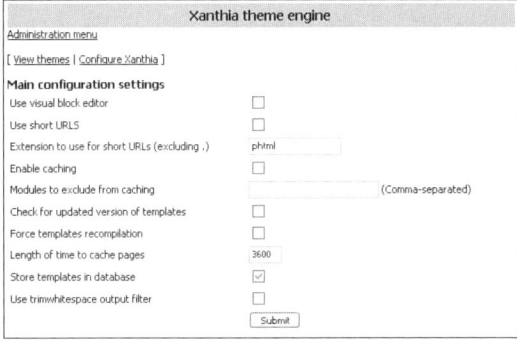

FIGURE 10.4   Changing Xanthia configuration settings.

- **Use Visual Block Editor**—Turning this option on displays small tag markers at the top-right of each zone on your live pages. You can click a tag marker to generate a pop-up that has complete customization options. The markers are only visible to administrators.

- **Use Short URLs**—This feature converts the normally lengthy page uniform resource locators (URLs) into short URLs, which are also generally preferred with search engines. This feature requires an Apache .htaccess file in your site root. It defines how Apache should use its mod_rewrite function to dynamically shorten URLs. If you do not already have a file, Xanthia includes different versions for you. See the Troubleshooting section at the end of this chapter for more information.

> **Note**
>
> Your web server needs to be capable of rewriting URLs for the Use Short URLs option to function. Apache includes this ability as mod_rewrite. IIS can acquire this feature through third-party add-ons, such as ISAPI_Rewrite (www.isapirewrite.com). Consult your server's documentation to determine what features it supports and how to enable them. At this time, Xanthia only includes support for Apache .htaccess.

- **Extension to Use for Short URLs**—Type the extension you want to use for the shortened URLs here. This field is ignored if you are not using short URLs. The extension must correspond with your .htaccess file. Xanthia includes file versions for .htm, .html, and .phtml extensions. The code in the .htaccess files is identical, except that all references to filenames use the respective extension for that file.

- **Enable Caching**—Caching generates local copies of the database-generated pages. These pages can be served from the file system faster than making entirely new database calls, and your site might see a significant speed improvement by enabling caching.

- **Modules to Exclude from Caching**—If there are specific modules you do not want cached, enter their names in this field. The names should be delimited by commas. This field is ignored if you are not using caching.

- **Check for Updated Version of Templates**—This check is important if you have caching turned on and are making regular changes to your template files. It increases overhead slightly, but makes it more likely that your changes are picked up immediately for display.

- **Force Templates Recompilation**—Recompile automatically rebuilds your templates, but enabling this option in effect disables caching.

- **Length of Time to Cache Pages**—This field should contain the amount of time you want to cache pages before pulling updated copies from the database. The setting is made in total seconds, and the default amount is 3600 (one hour). This field is ignored if you are not using caching.

- **Store Templates in Database**—Templates must be stored in the database for online editing to work. This option is primarily disabled only when working on a theme to speed up page compilation.

- **Use Trimwhitespace Output Filter**—Trimwhitespace removes whitespace characters from page code and slightly reduces load time. It does not remove linefeeds.

Theme Actions

The actions available from the Xanthia theme table control the interface between each theme and the PostNuke system. *Edit Theme* allows you to make changes to a theme using the Xanthia web interface.

Remove Theme does not delete a theme; the theme is disabled, as all the Xanthia themes were when your site was first installed.

Reload Templates manually updates the templates stored in the database. This option must be clicked for changes to become visible, unless you have checked Force Reload in the Xanthia configuration.

You can *Generate the Config Cache* to export all the current settings for colors, zones, and block locations to the file system to reduce database calls. After you have completed changes to a template, this option should be selected to improve load performance.

View Theme opens a new window using the `/index.php?theme=[ClickedThemeName]` preview link. This is handy for previewing themes before changing site settings. The feature is essential for the theme development process.

View the *Credits* of a given theme to see a little about who made the interface you are using.

Changing Themes

Changing a theme is no more complicated in PostNuke 0.75 than in previous versions. Return to your Site Settings page and change the Default Theme for Your Site drop-down list box.

As stated on that page, inactive Xanthia themes are not available in the list. Activate a theme from the Xanthia Administration page.

Obtaining Themes

Additional themes are easy to add with PostNuke. Place all theme files within their root theme folder in the /themes/ directory. For example, a theme called pnCoolTheme would have a path like this:

`/themes/pnCoolTheme/`

Non-Xanthia themes such as ExtraLite are immediately available from the Site Settings page. You need to activate any new Xanthia themes before they become available in the Settings form.

The following list details a few links to larger sites with multiple PostNuke themes. Some of the following sites are commercial and charge for some of their themes.

- autothemes.com
- ccentral.net
- cms-themes.de
- cmsarea.com
- designs4nuke.com
- gigathemes.com
- mdthemes.com
- pnthemes.weblives.net
- portalthemes.com
- themelabs.com
- themes.postnuke.com
- webvida.com

Customizing Themes

To customize a PostNuke theme, you need a clear understanding of HTML. If you feel your knowledge of standard HTML needs some brushing up, try browsing W3Schools (www.w3schools.com) for a good start. PostNuke 0.75 and its themes are fully compliant with the HTML 4.01 Strict definition. It's important that you at least maintain that standard.

PostNuke is also compatible with XHTML standards, and it's possible to code entirely new themes in XHTML. The main area of XHTML in which PostNuke is more transitional is in its heavy use of tables. Although the newer standards are desirable, it was decided that a browser-compatible layout still requires tables. Any theme you edit should be fairly compliant, and you should code to XHTML standards whenever possible. The following sections provide a quick run-through of key definition rules.

Crash Course in XHTML

The following rules are very easy to implement and are fully backward compatible with older standards. You should adhere to these specifications whenever possible, even if you are only making a minor change to customize an existing theme.

> **Tip**
>
> You can check the quality of your XHTML for free by using the World Wide Web Consortium's (W3C) Markup Validation Service at validator.w3.org.

Formatting Requirements

All elements and attribute names must be written in lowercase:

```
Correct:     <a href="mypage.html">
Incorrect:   <A HREF="mypage.html">
```

All tag pairs must be properly nested:

```
Correct:     <b><i>Welcome to MySite.Com</i></b>
Incorrect:   <b><i>Welcome to MySite.Com</b></i>
```

All elements must be closed. Single tags must close themselves:

```
Correct:     <p>Content within a nonempty element pair.</p>
Correct:     <li>The first item in my list.</li>
Correct:     <img src="my.gif" width="25" height="55" border="0" alt="picture of me" />
Correct:     This is content before a line break.<br />
```

All attribute values must be encased in quotation marks:

```
Correct:      <table border="0" cellpadding="10" cellspacing="10">
Incorrect:    <table border=0 cellpadding=10 cellspacing="10">
```

Attribute/value pairs cannot be minimized, or in other words, every attribute must have a stated value.

```
Correct:      <option value="somevalue" selected="selected">
Incorrect:    <option value="somevalue" selected>
Correct:      <input type="checkbox" checked="checked">
Incorrect:    <input type="checkbox" checked>
```

Tip

As in the previous examples, if an attribute does not have multiple values, use the common shortened name as the value.

The Name attribute is now replaced by the id attribute:

```
Correct:      <input type="checkbox" id="sendemail" />
Incorrect:    <input type="checkbox" name="sendemail" />
```

Required Elements

The <head> and <body> elements can no longer be omitted, and the <title> element is now a required element within the <head> element. PostNuke generates these tags for you automatically, so unless you are developing a hybrid site with static pages, these required tags should not be an issue.

All XHTML documents must have a DOCTYPE declaration. PostNuke generates an HTML 4.01 Transitional Document Type Definition (DTD) DOCTYPE declaration by default for all pages. The declaration appears at the top of every page and specifies the constraints on the page code. The HTML 4.01 Transitional allows pages displayed by PostNuke to use any HTML elements in the strict 4.01 DTD and any deprecated elements and attributes, which used to be standard but are being phased out of the specification.

PostNuke 0.75 itself is compliant with both 4.01 Strict and most XHTML specifications, but to be certain PostNuke works for users who might not be completely familiar with the standards, the weaker Transitional DTD has been used.

Deprecated Elements

Deprecated elements are no longer in current XHTML specifications. Backward-compatible browsers still support these elements, but when you write new XHTML code, you should stop using the deprecated elements if at all possible.

The following Table 10.1 lists the major deprecated elements to look out for and includes modern alternatives you can use instead.

TABLE 10.1
Deprecated XHTML Tag Elements

DEPRECATED	USE THIS INSTEAD
`<applet>`	`<object>`
`<b>`	style sheets (`font-weight`)
`<basefont>`	style sheets (`color`, `font-size`, `font-family`, `font`, and so on)
`<blockquote>`	`<div>`
`<center>`	style sheets (`text-align`)
`<dir>`	`<ul>`
`<em>`	style sheets (`text-decoration`)
`<embed>`	`<object>`
`<font>`	style sheets (`color`, `font-size`, `font-family`, `font`, and so on)
`<i>`	style sheets (`font-style`)
`<isindex>`	`<form>`
`<layer>`	style sheets (`position`, `z-index`, and so on)
`<listing>`	`<pre>`
`<menu>`	`<ul>`
`<noembed>`	`<object>`
`<plaintext>`	`<pre>`
`<s>`	style sheets (`text-decoration`)
`<strike>`	style sheets (`text-decoration`)
`<strong>`	style sheets (`text-decoration`)
`<u>`	style sheets (`text-decoration`)
`<xmp>`	`<pre>`

Deprecated Attributes

Similar to the preceding list of tags, some element attributes are now deprecated and should be replaced with cascading style sheet (CSS) equivalents. Some older attributes do not have direct CSS replacements because they violate the markup philosophy.

TABLE 10.2
Deprecated XHTML Element Attributes

DEPRECATED	STYLE SHEET ALTERNATIVE (IF APPLICABLE)
align	text-align
alink	a:link { color:#800000; }
background	background-image:url('bg.gif');
bgcolor	background-color:#FFFFFF;
border	border
clear	z-index and position
color	color
compact	
face	font-family
height	height
hspace	padding or margin
link	a:link { color:#800000; }
name	id
noshade	color and border
nowrap	white-space:nowrap;
size	font-size
start	
text	color
type	
valign	text-align
value	
vlink	a:visited { color:#800000; }
vspace	padding or margin
width	width

Cascading Style Sheets

XHTML uses the same style sheets you should already be applying to your HTML. CSS1 is widely supported and should be very safe to use. CSS2 has good but incomplete support among the current browsers. If you want to use CSS2 elements, you need to consider the browser flavors and versions used by the majority of your site visitors to ensure viewing consistency.

> **Tip**
>
> You can check the quality of your CSS for free by using the W3C CSS Validation Service at jigsaw.w3.org/css-validator/.

A table of current browsers showing which CCS2 elements are supported can be found here: www.quirksmode.org/dom/w3c_css.html. Older browser support is detailed at this address: www.devx.com/projectcool/Article/19813, and an extensive matrix of CSS properties and browsers is here: www.csscreator.com/attributes/.

Editing Themes

Now, you perform a series of changes to one of the core PostNuke themes included with your installation. Editing an existing theme that's close to your needs is always easier and faster than developing a new theme from scratch. But, no one wants to have a website that looks exactly like hundreds of others. Thankfully, it only takes a few simple changes to give your site a unique look.

First go to the theme directory on your server, /themes/, and look through the list of themes. pnDefault is meant to be a template theme for you to build upon; it is the only Xanthia theme included with PostNuke that incorporates all of the XTE features. The other themes are ports of older PostNuke themes, but the conversions only used the Xanthia features necessary to duplicate the original designs. You can use the other themes as additional examples of how themes can be built, but use the pnDefault source if you want to be certain all of the in-browser configuration options are available.

Copy the entire directory tree of the pnDefault theme. Name the copy "TestTheme," or use some other theme name if you have a design already in mind. Now browse your site, and go to the Xanthia Administration page. Click the View Themes link and you see the table of themes, only now an additional theme called TestTheme is listed. It's currently inactive, so click the Add Theme link.

> **Tip**
>
> Don't develop directly on your active theme. Your site visitors might become confused, and if you save a theme error, you could break your site. Instead use the theme preview option: /index.php?theme=yourtheme.

You can see from the View Theme feature under Actions (Figure 10.3) that the new theme works but looks exactly like the PostNuke theme. You use the built-in tools to create and polish a variant of this theme so you can see how it's done. Leave an extra browser window open and pointing to the View Theme URL: http://www.yoursite.com/index.php?theme=TestTheme.

After you have made a series of changes to the theme, you simply need to click Reload on that browser, and you can view and test your alterations (see Figure 10.5).

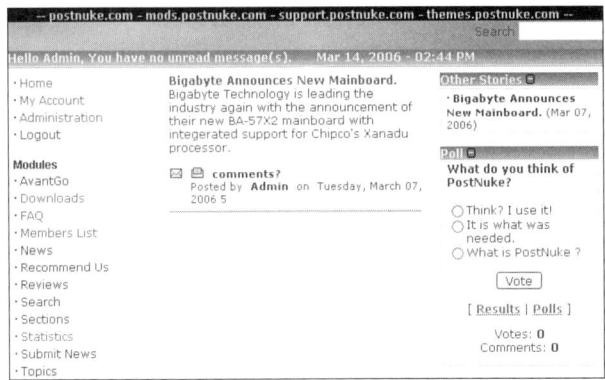

FIGURE 10.5 Testing the pnDefault duplicate.

From the Xanthia Administration Menu, select Edit Theme and then click Block Zones. Notice how the new theme name is already applied to the different screens. Xanthia themes are titled purely from their root folders' names. Review the list of zones already defined for you. On this page, you can delete those in the listing or name new zones. You can ignore this area for the time being.

FIGURE 10.6 pnDefault provides Block Zone examples.

Next enter the Theme Zones page. These zones are defined mainly in terms of their positioning on the page and not their function, with the exception of the News zones. Some of these zones are required for the theme to work, but others are additional zones you can optionally use to make more uniquely designed areas in your theme. The Configure link provided for each zone only allows you to change their assigned template. To make more extensive changes, you need to change existing templates or create new ones in your XHTML editor, which you can then assign to a zone on this page.

The third link in the navigation bar, *Theme Templates*, is designed to let you make quick changes to the live template files. Editing files through the web form changes the database entries, but those changes are wiped out when you reload the templates from the theme's source files. To prevent this, make your changes to the source files directly, and click the Reload Templates function to update the site. All template files for our TestTheme are located in:

```
/themes/TestTheme/templates/
```

The first change you make is to remove the gradient image in the page and block headers. Later, you set new color variables for the theme, and you can't change an image's color using the web form. To ensure everything matches, the image has got to go. The file is called bar_back_horizon.gif. It's referenced in only one theme template file, master.htm, and in seven of the block templates.

> **Tip**
>
> You can easily track down code references to images using your browser and a good editor. Right-click an image and view it in Mozilla, or use the Save As option in Microsoft Internet Explorer to determine the image's filename. Then open all template files in your editor and perform a search across all files for the name. You instantly see which files include references to the image you see in your browser.

Open master.htm in your editor. About 40 lines down into the code, you should see this line:

```
<div style="background-color:<!--[$color1]-->;background-image:url(<!--[$imagepath]--
>/bar_back_horizon.gif);width:100%;">
```

Remove the code starting at background-image and ending with .gif);. The changed line is as follows:

```
<div style="background-color:<!--[$color1]-->; width:100%;">
```

It now refers only to the color variable you can define using the online tools. The second reference is down near the bottom of the file at about line 139. The line is nearly identical to the previous one; just remove the background-image style. Submit your changes and reload your testing browser. You might need to reload the master.htm template from the preceding table to see changes, depending on your Xanthia settings.

The header and footer bars should be a light gray, the default Color1 setting for pnDefault. Notice how the text is a similar gray and hard to read. It's a very good rule of thumb that when using an image background, you should set the color behind it to a similar hue and brightness. If the image fails to load, or if a site visitor turns images off for their browser, your site still works fine and looks similar to what you intended. As a quick fix, this template's Color5 setting is much darker, and you can change both of the previous lines to use it instead of Color1 to fix the readability of the text. You work more in-depth with colors shortly.

Return to the Theme Templates page and look at the list of block templates. Just as you did previously, remove the CSS image reference from the following files: dsblock.htm, isblock.htm, msgbox.htm, lsblock.htm, rsblock.htm, tcblock.htm, and bcblock.htm. The HTML in these files is very short and nearly identical. Just replace this line:

ZERO-CAL = OK

EVENTS. = ~~OK~~ COULDN'T SEE

POST CALENDAR = COULDN'T SEE

CAL-ZONE = COULDN'T SEE.

VP CONTACT = OK

```
<div class="boxtitle" style="background-image:url(<!--[$imagepath]--
>/bar_back_horizon.gif);">
```

with this line:

```
<div class="boxtitle">
```

Save each file, reload the templates, and then reload your test browser. The image header bar on all of the blocks should be gone now, and the blocks all show a white background, as shown in Figure 10.7. The white behind the block title text is due to the page background color; the block titles are currently defined without a color behind the text. Before applying color variables to the templates, you should become familiar with the theme palette.

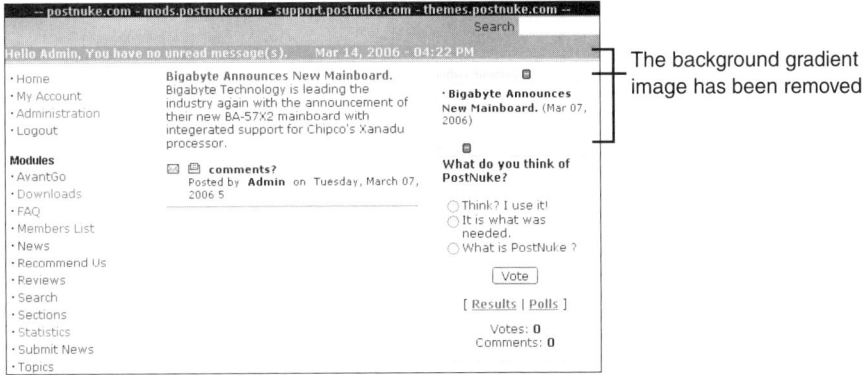

FIGURE 10.7   pnDefault without hard-coded theme images.

Dynamic Stylesheets

Click the Theme Colors link in the Xanthia navigation menu. The pnDefault theme conveniently includes seven predefined color palettes. You can develop an entirely new palette, but for now you edit the TestTheme templates to take additional advantage of the colors stored in the database. pnDefault initially has the Shades of Grey palette chosen, but you need something a little warmer, such as the Cream Soda or Autumn palettes. Set one as the current theme palette, and then click the Configure link for that palette. You are presented with the color tool shown in Figure 10.8.

You change colors by clicking the element button in the top controls, and then clicking a color in the palette wheel on the right. The results of the change are seen in the bottom-left chart. The primary drawback to this tool is that the color wheel only supports the limited "web-safe" color set. Web-safe colors were initially developed to enable web designers to create colors that appeared identical on all browsers and operating system platforms. Advances in video technology and the perpetual desire to have designs with greater depth have significantly reduced the relevance of web-safe colors.

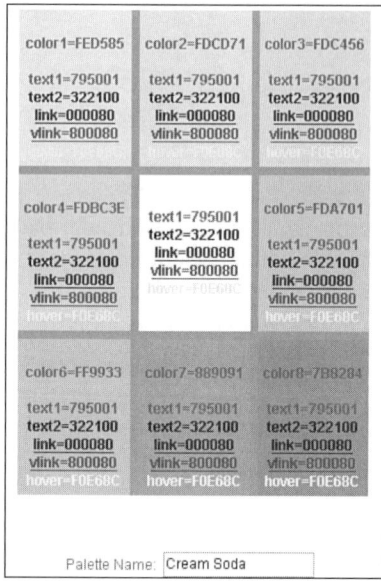

color1=FED585	color2=FDCD71	color3=FDC456
text1=795001 text2=322100 link=000080 vlink=800080	text1=795001 text2=322100 link=000080 vlink=800080	text1=795001 text2=322100 link=000080 vlink=800080 hover=F0E68C
color4=FDBC3E		color5=FDA701
text1=795001 text2=322100 link=000080 vlink=800080 hover=F0E68C	text1=795001 text2=322100 link=000080 vlink=800080	text1=795001 text2=322100 link=000080 vlink=800080 hover=F0E68C
color6=FF9933	color7=889091	color8=7B8284
text1=795001 text2=322100 link=000080 vlink=800080 hover=F0E68C	text1=795001 text2=322100 link=000080 vlink=800080 hover=F0E68C	text1=795001 text2=322100 link=000080 vlink=800080 hover=F0E68C

Palette Name: Cream Soda

FIGURE 10.8   Xanthia palette editing tool.

You can select a color from the wheel, and then click the Brighter and Darker control buttons, but it can take many clicks to reach more subtle variations. With the background selected, deselect the Red and Green boxes so only Blue is affected. Then click the Darker button until blue reaches F0; it removes blue from the white and makes the background a light yellow. That was a minor color change, but it still took many clicks. You learn other methods for adjusting the colors in Chapter 15, "Customized Themes."

You can also change the palette's link colors. The links are the cool browser defaults of blue and violet, but to match the theme better, replace those colors with warmer choices. Click the Link button in the top button panel. Then click on one of the dark reds in the top-right of the wheel. The example colors chart changes automatically to reflect your new color choice. Click the VLink button and select a dark brown from the top of the wheel. Finally, change the Hover color to bright red.

Now change the name below the table from "Cream Soda" to "Warm Test" and click the Submit These Colors link. You can rename any palette as easily as changing the colors. Reload your theme test browser window to view the change; you do not need to reload templates to see palette changes. You can see certain areas where the color change did not take effect, such as the blue and black in the header, and the blue Terms of Use text in the footer. That is because those colors are also hard-coded into the theme. Color and images references made directly in files always overrides variables in the database.

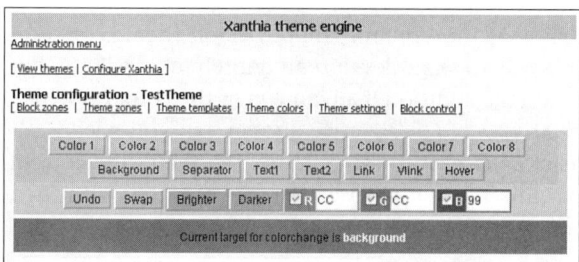

Xanthia theme engine

Administration menu

[View themes | Configure Xanthia]

Theme configuration - TestTheme
[Block zones | Theme zones | Theme templates | Theme colors | Theme settings | Block control]

Color 1	Color 2	Color 3	Color 4	Color 5	Color 6	Color 7	Color 8

Background	Separator	Text1	Text2	Link	Vlink	Hover

Undo	Swap	Brighter	Darker	☑ R CC	☑ G CC	☑ B 99

Current target for colorchange is background

FIGURE 10.9   Xanthia palette editing tool.

Editing Templates

As mentioned previously, template changes are not permanent unless you open the files directly in an editor. Open the master.htm template in your editor as you did earlier. Scroll to about line 29, where you see this code that controls the topmost row on the page:

```
<div class="pn-navtabs"><!--[$ZUPPERTOP]--> -- <a href="http://www.postnuke.com"
id="postnuke.com">postnuke.com</a> -
<a href="http://mods.postnuke.com" id="mods.postnuke.com">mods.postnuke.com</a> -
<a href="http://support.postnuke.com" id="support.postnuke.com">support.postnuke.com</a> -
<a href="http://themes.postnuke.com" id="themes.postnuke.com">themes.postnuke.com</a>
--</div>
```

Remove the PostNuke link content inside the `div`, and replace it with the `datetime` call from line 41. Add in a `background-color` style to the `div` using the `$color6` variable. The finished code should appear something like this:

```
<div class="pn-navtabs" style="background-color:<!--[$color6]-->;"><!--[$ZUPPERTOP]--><!--
[datetime]--></div>
```

On the next line is a reference to the file `logo_back.gif`. This is the image creating the cloud-gradient effect in the blue that remained after applying the new palette. The `background-color` style just after the image reference appropriately sets the field to the main blue found in the `logo_back` image, but the color is hard-coded to match the specific blue because it was available in the palettes. You will not use a background image and `color5` will do well there, so remove the image references and place the color variable appropriately. After you are done, this line:

```
<div style="background-image:url(<!--[$imagepath]-->/logo_back.gif);background-
color:#247ed8;padding:0.1em;width:100%;">
```

should match this one:

```
<div style="background-color:<!--[$color5]-->; padding:0.1em; width:100%;">
```

Just below that is a reference to the `$ZLOGO` Block Zone. No logo has been defined, but add one now. Included in the book's downloadable materials is the file `postnuke-logo1.gif`. Place the image at this location:

```
/themes/TestTheme/images/postnuke-logo1.gif
```

After the `$ZLOGO` call, add in an image tag to the new logo like this:

```
<br /><!--[$ZLOGO]--><img src="<!--[$imagepath]-->/postnuke-logo1.gif" /><br />
```

Just after the logo are the `displaygreeting` and `datetime` spans. We placed a reference to the date at the top of the page already, so that is no longer needed. But the greeting is a nice addition that will also look a little more balanced if aligned to the right where the date is, so replace the date call with the greeting, and remove the extra spans. You need to add a `text-align` style to the `div` for everything to flow correctly. These are the original lines of code:

```
<div style="background-color:<!--[$color5]-->; width:100%;">
<span class="boxtitle" style="float:right;"><!--[datetime]--></span><span class=
"boxtitle"><!--[displaygreeting]--></span>
</div>
```

That you simplify to

```
<div class="boxtitle" style="background-color:<!--[$color5]-->; width:100%; text-
align:right;"><!--[displaygreeting]--></div>
```

You also do not need the shadow image on line 40 with this example, so change the `background-image` to `background-color` with the `color5` variable like so:

```
<div style="background-color:<!--[$color5]-->; height:4px; overflow:hidden;"></div>
```

Reload your theme's templates at the main Xanthia themes table, and then refresh your test browser's window. You should see a very clean header done in the palette's oranges, as shown in Figure 10.10.

FIGURE 10.10   Editing your theme's header.

The text in the header needs to be formatted, and to do that you need to edit the `style.php` file in your theme's style folder. Scan through the CSS code in the file; a sample of the code follows:

```
.title       {
        BACKGROUND: none;
        font-size: {$text}px;
        FONT-WEIGHT: bold;
        FONT-FAMILY: Verdana, Helvetica;
        TEXT-DECORATION: none
}
.content     {
        BACKGROUND: none;
        font-size: {$text}px;
        FONT-FAMILY: geneva,arial,Verdana, Helvetica
}
```

Note that it is formatted like any other `.css` file, but using a `.php` extension allows it to be parsed with PHP variables, such as the `$text` variable shown in the previous code.

Refer to the `master.htm` file when determining which styles need to be edited. First change the `datetime` call, which is under the `pn-navtabs` class. Scroll to about line 253 in `style.php` and take a look at this entry. The text color is set as a variable, but the background is set to `#000000`, or black. We overrode this sheet style by coding the background variable directly into the template, but it's still a good idea to clean up the entry here by removing that line. You could alternatively use the variable `"._XA_TCOLOR2."` formatted similar to the `color` line below it. Next set the alignment to `text-align:right` and add `text-transform:uppercase` and `padding:2px` to make the text display more uniformly. When you are finished, the style should look similar to this:

```
.pn-navtabs {
    font-family:Verdana,Arial,Helvetica;
    color:"._XA_TCOLOR2.";
    font-size:{$text}px;
    font-weight:normal;
    text-align:right;
    text-transform:uppercase;
    padding:2px;
}
```

The greeting test is a little too close to the background color, so you edit that style next. You can see the code in line 37 within `master.htm`, and it shows the `boxtitle` style is being applied. `boxtitle` is also heavily used by block templates, so any change made to it here also changes the blocks. But, in truth, the greeting message is different and should have its own style. So to remedy the situation, copy the `boxtitle` style at line 139 and create a new style called "greeting":

```
.greeting {
    background:none;
    color:"._XA_TBGCOLOR.";
    font-size:{$text}px;
    font-weight:bold;
    font-family:Verdana,Helvetica;
    text-decoration:none;
}
```

Change the `master.htm` code at line 37 to use the new style, and reload the templates to preview your theme. The header's looking good now, but you should fix the footer to match this set of changes. Scroll to the bottom of `master.htm`, to line 133, and examine the code also shown next:

```
<div style="background-image:url(<!--[$imagepath]-->/dropshadow_up.gif);height:4px;
overflow:hidden;"></div>
<div style="background-color:<!--[$color5]-->; text-align:center;width:100%;">
··· <a href="modules.php?op=modload&amp;name=Legal&amp;file=index"><span class="boxtitle"
style="color:#A9DDFF;"><!--[pnml name="_TERMS"]--></span></a> ···
<!--[$ZSCHANNELBOT]-->
</div>
<div style="text-align:center;"><!--[footmsg]--></div>
```

Just as in the header, you don't need the shadow image, but this time, remove the entire div.
The second div contains the link to the site _TERMS, but it has a hard-coded color reference,
and the style of the span around it is also boxtitle. You can fix both problems by creating a
new style class called "terms." Use the .greeting style you made earlier as a template.

Duplicate the style again to make another entry labeled .footer, and create an Anchor tag
variant using inheritance and color1 for the text. Then in master.htm, add a background-color
reference using color4 to the footmsg div.

You should have these styles:

```
.terms {
    background:none;
    color:"._XA_TBGCOLOR.";
    font-size:{$text}px;
    font-weight:bold;
    font-family:Verdana,Helvetica;
    text-decoration:none;
}
.footer {
    background:none;
    color:"._XA_TBGCOLOR.";
    font-size:{$text}px;
    font-weight:bold;
    font-family:Verdana,Helvetica;
    text-decoration:none;
}
.footer A {
    background:none;
    color:"._XA_TCOLOR1.";
    font-size:{$text}px;
    font-weight:bold;
    font-family:Verdana,Helvetica;
    text-decoration:none;
}
```

And the `master.htm` footer code should appear as follows:

```
<div style="background-color:<!--[$color5]-->; text-align:center;width:100%;">
<span class="terms">---</span> <a href="modules.php?op=modload&amp;name=Legal&amp;
file=index"><span class="terms"><!--[pnml name="_TERMS"]--></span></a> <span
class="terms">---</span>
<!--[$ZSCHANNELBOT]-->
</div>
<div style="background-color:<!--[$color6]-->; text-align:center;"><span class="footer"><!-
-[footmsg]--></span></div>
```

Reload your templates and take a look at the header and footer together. Both use the palette and go together well, even though there are minimal differences in their formatting. You can use layout differences to add variety and character to your site designs. You take the same path now with the block styles.

Xanthia is capable of providing separate custom template styles for every block, but most sites need more minor variation. You will make a left column with a freestanding menu and flowing blocks beneath, while the right column blocks will float on their own.

Return to the `master.htm` template and look over the table beginning at about line 41. This table controls the column formatting for the main content area of every page. Remove the `padding:0.5em;` from the `div` around the table; its spacing prevents background changes from locking against the browser sides.

The left column is set at line 44, and you can add a `background-color` style after the `width` to set the column apart. Use `color1` for the change. After the color, add `padding:5px;` to the column to make up for the earlier padding change. Also add this padding to the center column at line 52 and the right column at line 124.

Two spacer images called `pixel.gif` are set between the three columns at lines 50 and 122 with widths of 15 pixels. Change both images to a five-pixel width, so they have the same formatting they had before the padding changes.

Save these changes, reload your templates, and refresh your test screen. It should be similar to Figure 10.11.

FIGURE 10.11   Customizing your column layout.

Now, you complete the left column changes by editing the `lsblock.htm` template file (the name stands for "left-side block"). You can see by looking at your Zone Settings page that the Main Menu has its own template, `mainmenu.htm`, so changes to the other left blocks do not affect it.

The `lsblock` code is relatively simple compared to the `master` template edits we have been doing. Remove the `background-color` reference in the surrounding `div`; the left column has its own background color now. Two styles are named in the file: `boxtitle` and `boxcontent`. Add the word "left" to the end of both; you make two new styles, `boxtitleleft` and `boxcontentleft`, to control the appearance of left blocks.

Find the two entries in `style.php` at around line 140. Duplicate them as described previously. You need to add a `background-color` to the title and adjust its text color accordingly. Slightly change the content area's border to make it fade into the new background color. Apply these changes so that the new styles are as follows:

```
.boxtitleleft {
    background:none;
    color:#FFFFFF;
    font-size:{$text}px;
    font-weight:bold;
    font-family:Verdana,Helvetica;
    text-decoration:none;
    background-color:"._XA_TCOLOR6.";
    padding:2px;
    text-transform:uppercase;
}
.boxcontentleft {
    font-size:{$text}px;
    margin-top:.1em;
    padding-left:.5em;
    padding-right:.5em;
    border-color: "._XA_TCOLOR1.";
}
```

Reload your test browser and see how even with minimal changes the blocks are now more a part of the left column than separate entities (example shown in Figure 10.12). Without lines around them or color to differentiate where one block begins and the next ends, the left blocks flow together into a single column. The modular blocks might only be, for the most part, squares laid out on the page, but you don't have to keep it that way. You can blend content areas into an over design with creative placements to create nearly any effect.

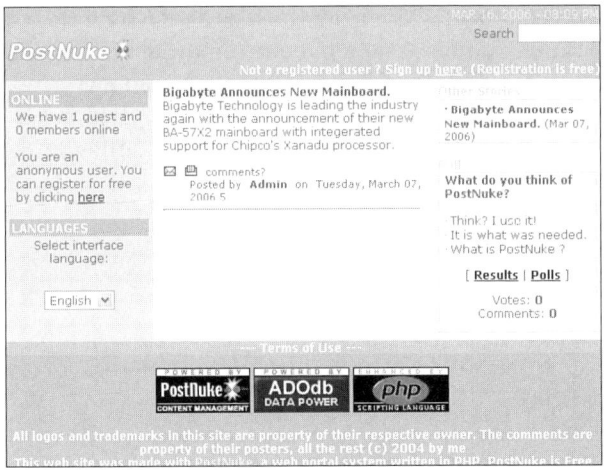

FIGURE 10.12 Blending blocks into the background.

The final change to this theme formats the right blocks. Keep these areas floating, but even when left in a blocky format, you still have options to the design. Try taking the horizontal band elements and apply them to the separate blocks. Load up the `rsblock.htm` and check the styles. It is identical to the original `lsblock.htm`, and needs the same customization changes. Remove the `background-color` line and change the style class names to "boxtitleright" and "boxcontentright." Match your file's entries to these styles:

```
.boxtitleright {
    background:none;
    color:"._XA_TTEXT1COLOR.";
    font-size:{$text}px;
    font-weight:bold;
    font-family:Verdana,Helvetica;
    text-decoration:none;
    background-color:"._XA_TCOLOR3.";
    padding:2px;
    text-transform:uppercase;
}
.boxcontentright {
    font-size:{$text}px;
    padding-left:.5em;
    padding-right:.5em;
    border-top:0px;
    border-right:0px;
    border-bottom:5px solid "._XA_TCOLOR5.";
    border-left:0px;
    background-color:"._XA_TCOLOR1.";
}
```

You can see the effects of these changes in Figure 10.13. Compare the new design with the original shown in Figure 10.5. Throughout this example, you maintained most of the original layout and code, but it's certainly possible to go much further with the edits to produce a more unique theme. The edited theme now also illustrates the power of dynamic style sheets. Apply some of the other palettes included with pnDefault, and you can see how easily the tone of your site can be changed by color alone.

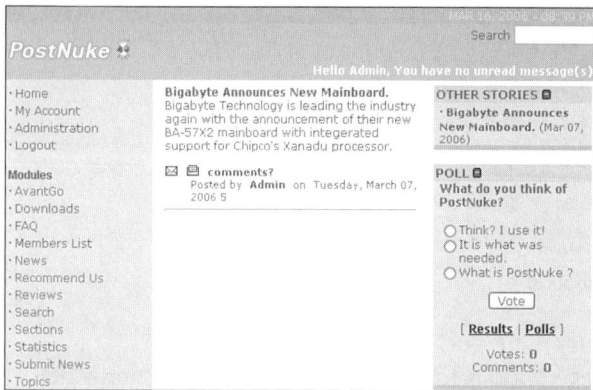

FIGURE 10.13   pnDefault, with minor edits.

Of course, if you want to develop a truly customized theme for your PostNuke site, your best bet is development from scratch. In Chapter 15, you examine what it takes to design and develop a new Xanthia theme.

Troubleshooting

Developing themes with PostNuke can be a complicated task. The Xanthia Theme Engine has a variety of tools that can make your life much easier, but it pays to get to know them. There are documentation files located in /modules/Xanthia/pndocs/ that can be a good start. Additional Xanthia instructions and tutorials are also found online at docs.postnuke.com. The following sections contain details of some of the more likely issues you might find.

.htaccess File Not in Your Web Root

This error message pertains to the Use Short URLs option in the Xanthia Configuration page. In the directory /modules/Xanthia/pndocs/short_urls/, there are a number of .htaccess files, each designed to use a different extension for files when they are shortened. Based on the extension you typed into the field in your Xanthia Configuration page, you need to select the appropriate .htaccess file and copy it to your website's root directory.

Server Fails URL Rewrite Check

If your server is capable of rewriting URLs, but the feature doesn't seem to enable in Xanthia, it might be that when Xanthia first checked your server, it mistakenly identified your server as not able to rewrite URLs. Xanthia does not examine your server again, so to remedy this problem, you need to edit the PostNuke database.

Using a database-editing tool, find the table `nuke_module_vars` and browse the data entries to the `Xanthia/shorturlsok`, most of the way down with a `pn_id` around 156. It will be set to either 0 or 1. Change the `pn_value` to 1 to confirm your server can rewrite URLs.

If you make changes to your database using straight Structured Query Language (SQL), the code you need is as follows:

```
UPDATE nuke_module_vars
SET pn_value = '1'
WHERE pn_modname = "Xanthia" AND pn_name = "shorturlsok"
```

Blank Edit Theme Screen

If you are switching between the various edit screens for your theme and find the page loads blank, this is likely due to a loss of the current theme identity. It usually occurs when you use your browser buttons to navigate through the edit screens instead of page links.

This issue is very similar to the loss of session that can happen when clicking the Back button on your browser to an otherwise restricted page, when the message "No Authorization to Carry Out Operation" appears. If Xanthia forgets what theme you are editing, viewing an edit page produces a blank screen.

From this point, you must return to the View Themes page and reselect the Edit link for the theme on which you were working. As long as you continue to use links to navigate, and not your browser's history, you can avoid this problem.

Dynamic Stylesheets Don't Apply

The Xanthia palette system does not function without the `style.php` file in your `/themes/yourtheme/styles/` folder. A copy of this file can be found with the pnDefault theme. Some Xanthia themes do not use dynamic style sheets and might or might not have a `style.php` file. Xanthia themes are not required to use all of the features available in the Xanthia Theme Engine.

If you have the `style.php` file and are trying to apply a palette but it still does not work, take a look at your `master.htm` template to be certain the `style.php` file is being included properly. Just before the close of the `<head>` tag, there should be an `include` statement like this:

```
<!--[include_php file="$themepath/style/style.php"]-->
```

or this:

```
<style type="text/css">
@import url("<!--[$themepath]-->/style/style.php");
</style>
```

You can also try hard-coding your theme name into the call like so:

```
<!--[include_php file="themes/TestTheme/style/style.php"]-->
```

If you have other templates for pages that apply to an entire page like the `master.htm`, you need to have an `include` statement like the previous one in each template within the header code.

Fatal Error in Zone

This error message occurs when Xanthia tries to display a theme, but fails to find a required zone template. This problem can occur if you have moved files in your theme's directory, or if a file has been renamed without updating the database reference(s) to match.

The solution is to replace the missing template file or select an alternative theme. If this error appears for the theme you currently have live, you might not be able to change to another theme. In that case, try using the PostNuke Swiss Army Knife detailed in the following section.

Recovering from Theme Failure

A very handy fix-all for some of the more serious problems you can have with PostNuke is the PostNuke Swiss Army Knife, or PSAK. You can find it at download.postnuke.com. Select PostNuke, and then Addons. The file is placed in your site's root and browsed directly, http://www.yoursite.com/psak.php.

The option *Theme Reset* allows you to change your site's theme to any currently installed. Note: PSAK 1.01 now produces an "Undefined index" error with PostNuke 0.75. The tool does work and is still recommended for use in solving PostNuke problems. Development on PSAK was stopped for some time, but has since been renewed, and a version 2.0 is planned for the near future.

Next

The next chapter walks through the creation of an Online Club's PostNuke site. The study references the modules and information throughout Part II, and includes tips for developing an online community.

Case Study: Online Club

This chapter walks through the development of a simple online club website. PostNuke provides a basic feature set popular with online groups, including news, links, downloads, polls, forums, and a calendar of events. Some of the modules are part of the stock PostNuke install, and others are taken from the third-party modules discussed in previous chapters. This chapter covers the following topics:

- About the site
- Applying what you've learned
- Seeing results

About the Site

The fictional site in this example is called Numismania. It is a website for coin collectors and uses the domain numismania.org. It uses the standard PostNuke user system to allow registered users access to submit news and post in the forums. The only activities available to anonymous visitors are reading the content and completing the current poll.

Third-party modules used in this example are Advanced Polls, PNphpBB2, and pnFlashGames. The latter is not specifically related to the site's focus, but is included as an example of a simplified entertainment diversion that can be fun for informal sites such as this one.

The theme used for the site is a basic design built upon the pnDefault example Xanthia theme.

Applying What You've Learned

Now, the following sections walk through the development of the site and apply the techniques learned in the previous chapters.

Website Install and Preparation

First, you install a clean copy of PostNuke version .750. Standard default settings are fine. The initial install shows the plain ExtraLite theme and has a variety of blocks and modules you simply don't need for your club site.

The first step in the process is postinstall cleanup. Remove the PostNuke install files; this includes both the `install.php` file in the root and the `/install/` directory itself.

Now go to the Administration Menu and edit the site's blocks. Deactivate the Reminder, Languages, and Poll blocks. As mentioned previously, the site will include a poll, but it will incorporate the Advanced Polls module, which has its own block.

> **Tip**
>
> When initially setting up your site, deactivate undesired blocks and modules rather than deleting them completely; it provides an extra layer of backup security while you are building the site. Modules and blocks can be deleted later after you have everything running smoothly.

Now go to the Modules Administration table and deactivate the AutoLinks, Banners, Ephemerids, FAQ, Polls, Quotes, Reviews, and Stats modules. These are all relatively self-contained modules that can be removed without affecting the rest of PostNuke. Cleaning up the unneeded modules drops more than a row of icons from the Administration Menu. This simplifies the interface to a more manageable level before you start building the site (see Figure 11.1).

For the last part of the cleanup, browse to the Website Configuration page with the Settings link. Enable the Support for Legacy Modules in the form and submit the settings. Making that change ensures there are no problems with older, non-pnAPI–compliant modules running on PostNuke .75.

Third-Party Module Installs and Setup

You now add four third-party modules to enhance the site's features:

- Advanced Polls
- pnFlashGames

FIGURE 11.1   It's easier to manage with a simplified interface.

- PNphpBB2
- PostCalendar

All of these modules were discussed at length in the previous chapters. When you are building up a site like this with multiple known modules, you have the option of installing them together or separately. Performing individual installs can make the process a little easier to follow if you are having issues with PostNuke's complexity, but after you are quite comfortable with the interfaces, you'll find batch-installing groups of modules to be much faster.

> **Note**
>
> Advanced Polls is found in Chapter 6, "User Interaction Modules," PNphpBB2 and PostCalendar were both covered in Chapter 7, "Community Building Modules," and you can learn more about pnFlashGames in Chapter 8, "Online Gaming Modules."

Simply decompress all of the modules' contents to their respective folders first. Then with all the files ready, go to the Modules Administration table and click the Regenerate link to see all of the new modules in the list at the same time. Initialize and Activate the new modules in turn to complete the process.

Advanced Polls

Back at the Administration Menu, select the Advanced Polls icon to configure the module. Create a new poll using the question: "What's your favorite numismatic collectible?" Provide the following options: Ancient/Medieval, Bi-Metallics, Commemoratives, Early U.S., Errors, Gold, Modern U.S., Modern World, and Paper Notes.

Be certain to change the Date and Time Poll Closes fields to a later date so the poll does not close immediately. You want the polls to be open to anonymous visitors, so set the Poll Authorization Method to "Cookie" to help prevent duplicate entries.

Browse to the Blocks Administration screen and create a new right-side block for the poll. Set the Title field to "What do you think?" and the type to "Advanced Polls/Show a Poll." Commit the block to see the activated site poll (see Figure 11.2).

FIGURE 11.2   Showing a poll.

The site will eventually have many polls, so a link in the Main Menu will be useful. This is also a good time to clear out unneeded entries in the Main Menu. Edit the block and remove the AvantGo, FAQ, Reviews, and Stats lines. Then create a new line after News for alphabetical consistency. Use the title "Polls," the URL "{advanced_polls}," and the description "Tell us what you think." Now, users will be able to click the link, "Polls," to access the poll system (see Figure 11.3).

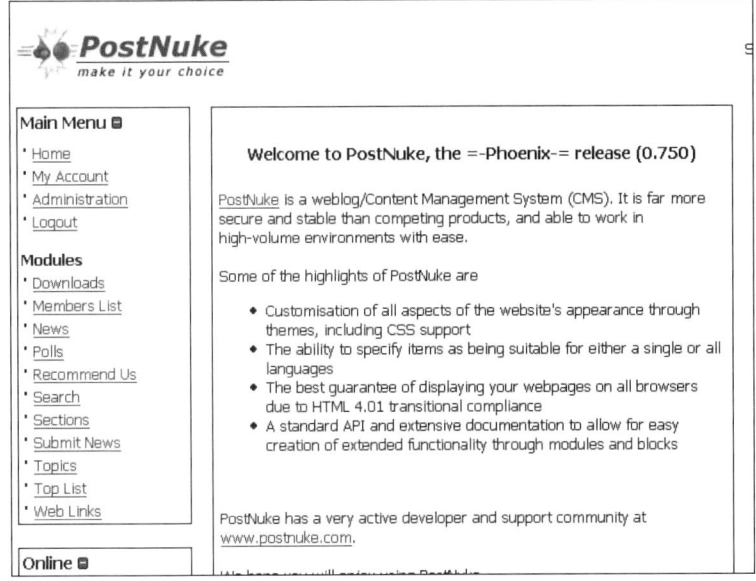

FIGURE 11.3   Don't leave links to deactivated modules in the Main Menu.

pnFlashGames

The pnFlashGames module initially comes with a number of preinstalled games. For the club example, you want just one game that you assume is entertaining to the site members. For this example, use the game Billiard Training, a classy pool-style game available for free at the pnFlashGames site (www.pnflashgames.com).

After installing the module, enter the administration area and delete the existing games: Airfox, Pacman, Snake, Space Invaders, Swarm, and Tetris. Because there will be only one game, you also do not need the preexisting categories: Action Games, Puzzle Games, Racing Games, Arcade Games, Classic Games, and Space Games. Remove them all.

The new game's files should be placed in the module's games folder as follows:

```
modules/pnFlashGames/games/billiard_training.swf
```

The other games can be deleted at this time for additional cleanup. Then create a new game called Billiards. Set the Width and Height fields to 500 each to make the game a little larger on the screen. The game file location should be the same as the path shown previously. Submit the game.

Rather than have a link in the menu, this single game is better served by a side block. A menu link to the pnFlashGames module is great when you have multiple games, but the browse interface is simply unneeded for sites with only one game.

Go to the Blocks Administration and create a new block called Game Break with the pnFlashGames' Random Game block type. Both the Random Game and Newest Game options consistently display the one game, but the Newest Game block prompts users to play other games, which does not work well for sites with only one game installed. The Random Game block more appropriately encourages users to beat the high score of the displayed game. Move the new block down below the Main Menu, and you have a block like that shown in Figure 11.4.

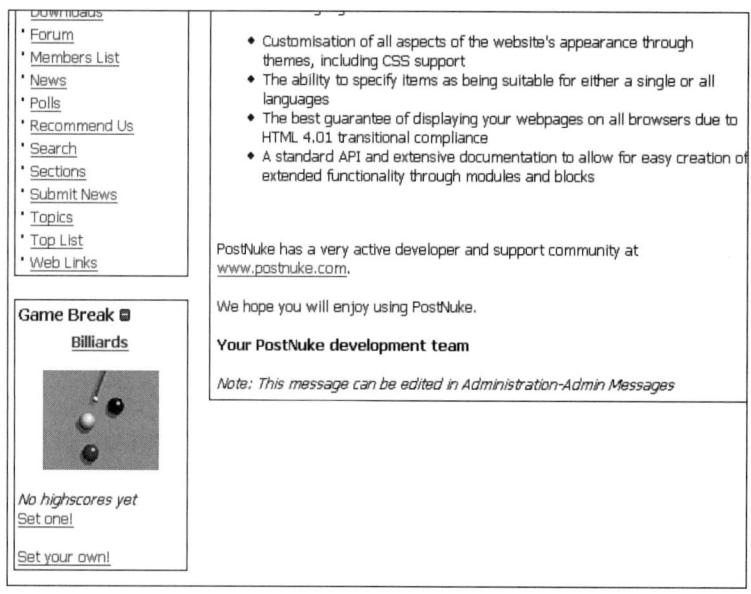

FIGURE 11.4   Highlighting site features in a side block.

PNphpBB2

Now, you install the forum module. You use the powerful PNphpBB2 system, but like many PostNuke modules, it provides more customizing options than you need. Thankfully, the default settings are very good for most sites.

After the install, go to the forum Administration screen and create two categories: Numismatic Discussion and Buy, Sell, and Trade. The existing test category can be renamed to simplify the process, but if you've added both categories in addition to the test area, just delete the default entry.

Create a series of forums under the general Discussion category with these titles: Ancient/Medieval, Bi-Metallics, Commemoratives, Early U.S., Errors, Gold, Modern U.S., Modern World, and Paper Notes. Under Buy, Sell, and Trade, make these forums: Wanted to Buy, For Sale, and Will Trade.

Like the Advanced Polls module, you need a link in the Main Menu block for users. Insert a line after the Downloads link using the title "Forum," the URL "[PNphpBB2]," and the description "Join the community." The basic forum is now functionally available, as shown in Figure 11.5.

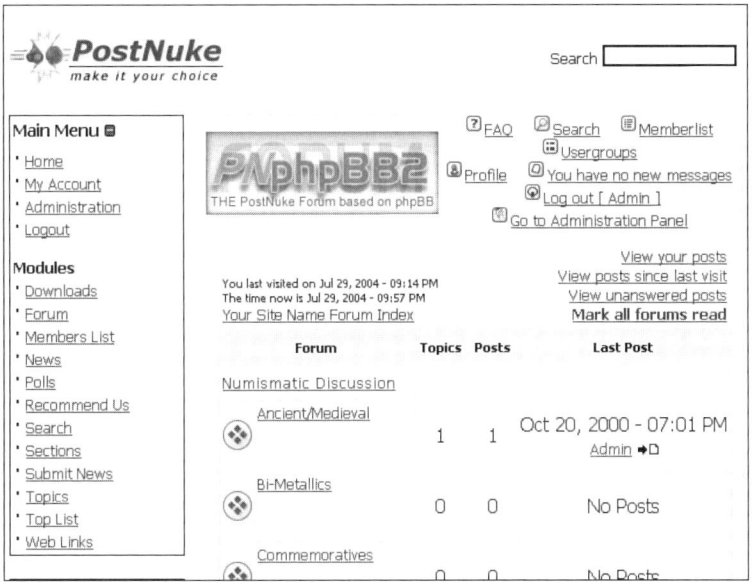

FIGURE 11.5 No community is complete without a forum.

PostCalendar
PostCalendar is a very simple install initially. At this point, you are only concerned with base functionality and not appearance, so just create a new PostCalendar block on the right. Check the calendar display option to show the month table. By default, the block appears above the poll (see Figure 11.6) and with the default template; it has some text color issues you'll work out through interface polishing.

Core Module Setup

The installs are now complete, but you still need to configure a few of the core modules to prepare the site for content. First, set up the News system. For this club site, you don't need the Categories features, but a few news topics are definitely in order.

FIGURE 11.6   Setting dates to keep the group informed.

Topics

In the book's downloadable materials, four example topic icons are available:

```
icon-coinnews.gif
icon-coinevents.gif
icon-clubinfo.gif
icon-dealstips.gif
```

Place them in the root topics folder to match this path:

```
/images/topics/icon-coinnews.gif
```

Now browse to the Topics Administration screen. Remove the two default topics and add in the four new images. Name the topics respective to the previous filenames with these titles:

- Coin News
- Numismatic Events
- Club Information
- Deals & Tips

Remove the spaces for the name fields, and use the title names for the text titles. For example, the "Coin News" name should be entered as "coinnews." Figure 11.7 shows the completed topics with their new images.

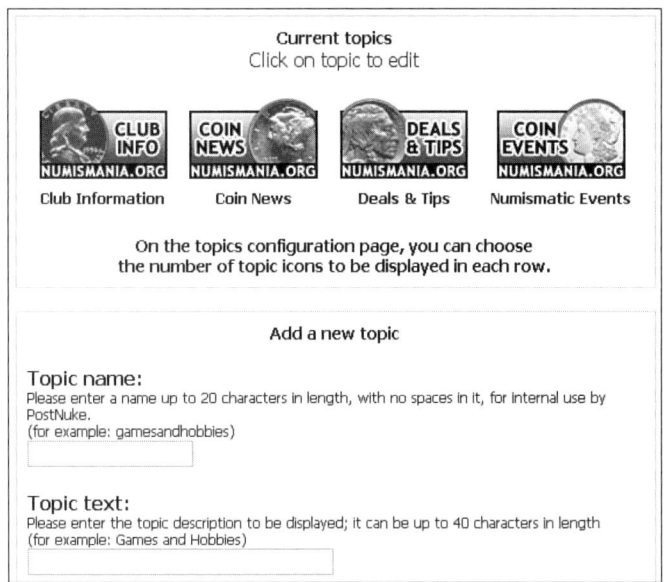

FIGURE 11.7 Customizing topics to fit your site.

Web Links
Now head over to the Web Links module to set up a few categories and entries there. First create the following categories:

- Associations
- Coin Clubs
- Collection Software
- Good Dealers
- Grading Companies
- History and Education

In addition, to initially seed the link system, use the information in Table 11.1:

TABLE 11.1

Sample Web Links

ASSOCIATIONS	URL
American Numismatic Association	www.money.org
American Numismatic Society	www.amnumsoc.org
Canadian Numismatic Association	www.canadian-numismatic.org
Professional Numismatists Guild	www.pngdealers.com
Society of Paper Money Collectors	www.spmc.org
Young Numismatists of America	www.ynaclub.org
GRADING COMPANIES	**URL**
ANACS	www.anacs.com
Independent Coin Grading	www.icgcoin.com
Numismatic Guaranty Corporation	www.ngccoin.com
PCGS	www.pcgs.com
PCI	www.pcicoins.com
SEGS	www.segsgrading.com

After you are done, click the Web Links module link in the Main Menu to try out the categories and initial links (see Figure 11.8).

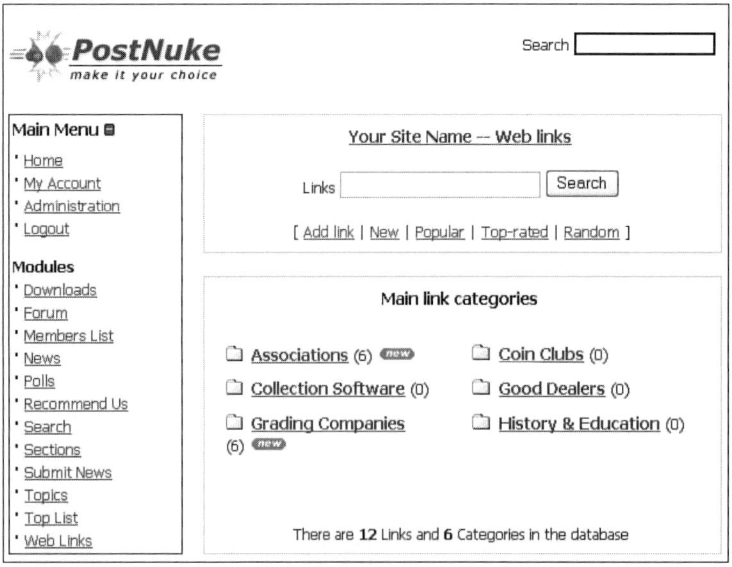

FIGURE 11.8   Adding links your visitors will find useful.

Permissions

The default PostNuke permissions settings work for nearly all of this site's needs. The one exception is the Polls block. Polls for this site need to be made available to anyone, but to do that you need to make one permissions change. Browse to the Permissions module and add a new entry above the bottom Unregistered groups' lines. It should look like this:

```
Unregistered    advanced_polls::    .*    Comment
```

This grants Unregistered users full comment access to all polls, and it overrides the lesser access for Unregistered users because it is above their entries.

Site Settings

The final core module you set up is the main Website Configuration page. Click the Settings link under Administration to configure the site. Nearly all of the options are perfectly fine in their default settings, so there are only a few fields you update at this time.

First change the site name to "Numismania" and enter "We're crazy about coins!" into the Slogan field. The Time Zone Offset drop-down list box should always be changed to your local time. And as this is intended to be a smaller-scale club site, reduce the story count on the home page to five. Scroll down and save the changes.

Interface

For many people, the thought of developing a new website begins with the interface design. Although it's a good idea to have a layout planned for your site initially, with PostNuke you can't really get to the layout on most sites until you have decided which modules and blocks will be present and how the content is expected to be handled. These early decisions form the foundation on which you can then add themes with colors and styling.

Note

More information on theme development is found in Chapter 10, "Themes." For more advanced information on theme design, you can also try Chapter 15, "Customized Themes."

You are finally to the point at which there is enough structure to the site that the theme can be applied. After initial theme development, most developers go back and adjust the blocks or modules to fill content holes that sometimes appear as the final site starts to come into focus. That also leads back to more theme work, and the cycle continues with smaller and smaller adjustments until the site is finalized. The polishing period gets smaller with more PostNuke development experience, but it's certainly quite normal.

Developing a new Xanthia theme for the site begins with a copy of the pnDefault theme folder. Rename the copy to Numismania. You can, of course, immediately jump to the Xanthia Administration screen and activate the theme; the resulting test view is shown in Figure 11.9.

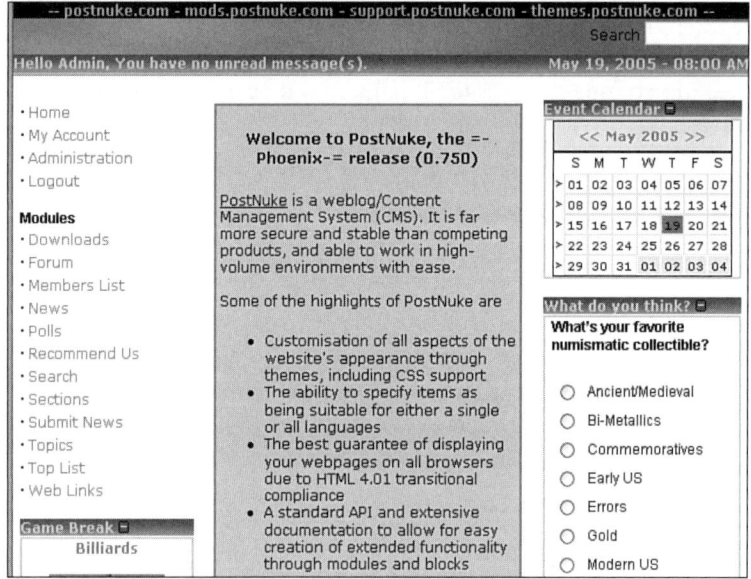

FIGURE 11.9   Starting out with a default theme.

However, the easiest way to set up the initial Xanthia theme is by editing the initialization file. If you have activated the Numismania theme, deactivate it now. In your text editor, load the xaninit.php file found in the theme's root.

The file defines seven example palettes starting at about line 55, but you really only need one for your theme. Delete all of the entries in favor of this one:

```
CreatePalette($skinName, $skinID, 1, 'NumisPal01', '#FFFFFF', '#F6F7FF', '#E6E8F6',
'#B1B6D3', '#7F85A9', '#686E93', '#EAEDED', '#E1E5E5', '#FF9900', '#434765', '#7B8284',
'#575B7D', '#000080', '#800080', '#F0E68C');
```

Be certain to set the default toggle to "1" to make this the active theme. These colors provide a simple cool blue palette that matches the topic images you installed earlier.

The xaninit.php file defines the initial templates and zones. The default entries are shown as an example and are more than you need for your simple club site. Comment out the references to topcenter, tcblock, botcenter, bcblock, inblock, isblock, and dsblock in both the theme templates and theme zones sections. The following is an example of the changes for the first section, templates:

```
// Create theme templates
// CreateThemeTemplate($skinID, <template label>, <template filename>, <template type>);
CreateThemeTemplate($skinID, 'master', 'master.htm', 'theme');
CreateThemeTemplate($skinID, 'lsblock', 'lsblock.htm', 'block');
CreateThemeTemplate($skinID, 'rsblock', 'rsblock.htm', 'block');
CreateThemeTemplate($skinID, 'table1', 'table1.htm', 'theme');
CreateThemeTemplate($skinID, 'table2', 'table2.htm', 'theme');
CreateThemeTemplate($skinID, 'News-index', 'News-index.htm', 'theme');
CreateThemeTemplate($skinID, 'News-article', 'News-article.htm', 'theme');
CreateThemeTemplate($skinID, 'News-index2', 'News-index2.htm', 'theme');
// CreateThemeTemplate($skinID, 'topcenter', 'topcenter2.htm', 'theme');
// CreateThemeTemplate($skinID, 'tcblock', 'tcblock.htm', 'block');
// CreateThemeTemplate($skinID, 'botcenter', 'botcenter.htm', 'theme');
// CreateThemeTemplate($skinID, 'bcblock', 'bcblock.htm', 'block');
// CreateThemeTemplate($skinID, 'inblock', 'inblock.htm', 'block');
// CreateThemeTemplate($skinID, 'isblock', 'isblock.htm', 'block');
// CreateThemeTemplate($skinID, 'dsblock', 'dsblock.htm', 'block');
CreateThemeTemplate($skinID, 'mainmenu', 'mainmenu.htm', 'block');
CreateThemeTemplate($skinID, 'ccblock', 'ccblock.htm', 'block');
```

Between the theme template and theme zones lines is a line that defines all the zones:

```
// Add zones for theme
pnModSetVar('Xanthia', $skinName.'newzone','|1:Upper Top Zone:ZUPPERTOP|2:Logo
Zone:ZLOGO|3:Full Banner A:ZBANNERA|4:Channel Zone:ZCHANNEL|5:Full BannerB:ZBANNERB|6:
Channel SubTop:ZSCHANNELTOP|7:Half Banner:ZBANNERC|8:Channel SubBot:ZSCHANNELBOT|9:Col3
Left:ZCOL3SLEFT|10:Col3 Center:ZCOL3SCENTER|11:Col3 Right:ZCOL3SRIGHT|12:Inner Left
Column:ZINCOLLEFT|13:Inner Right Column:ZINCOLRIGHT|14:Center Block:ZCCBLOCK');
```

You know you don't need the banner or channel zones, so they can be dropped as well. For this example, I've changed the way the function is called to make it easier to manage your zone initializations. The shortened version with the change looks like this:

```
// Add zones for theme
   $tmpZoneList = "|1:Upper Top Zone:ZUPPERTOP".
                  "|2:Logo Zone:ZLOGO".
                  "|3:Col3 Left:ZCOL3SLEFT".
                  "|4:Col3 Center:ZCOL3SCENTER".
                  "|5:Col3 Right:ZCOL3SRIGHT".
                  "|6:Inner Left Column:ZINCOLLEFT".
                  "|7:Inner Right Column:ZINCOLRIGHT".
                  "|8:Center Block:ZCCBLOCK";
pnModSetVar('Xanthia', $skinName.'newzone',$tmpZoneList);
```

The use of the separate temporary variable helps to visualize the zones built in to the theme.

Now, you edit the site's templates. Browse to the Xanthia Administration page and click the Configure Xanthia link. Two settings on this page are helpful at this point to change. First check the Force Templates Recompilation check box. This makes template changes timelier. Next uncheck the Store Templates in Database check box so the theme always looks to the physical files you are editing. These toggles can be changed back after the theme is finished.

For this design, you keep the basic three-column layout common to PostNuke sites, but the left blocks are combined into a single column. A single image is used for the header, and the title of the site is graphically built in to the image so there is no need for the text display. Figure 11.10 illustrates the general idea.

FIGURE 11.10   Three-column layout.

> **Tip**
>
> Use matching background colors without borders to link together block areas into larger shapes.

When approaching the styles, note that the style sheet included with pnDefault also has extra classes defined. The main classes PostNuke core modules call are pn-normal, pn-title, pn-pagetitle, pn-sub, pn-logo, pn-logo-small, and pn-button. Specifying the major tags, such as body, a, td, and img, is also important, but for most of the other classes, if they are not called by the theme, they can be removed. Add these additional classes for the Numismania theme:

```
.pn-lblocktitle    { font-family:".$fonts."; color:"._XA_TTEXT1COLOR."; font-size:16px;
                     font-weight:bold; text-align:left; }
.pn-lblockcontent { font-family:".$fonts."; color:"._XA_TTEXT1COLOR."; font-size:{$text}px;
                     text-align:left; padding:8 0 8 0;}
.pn-rblocktitle    { font-family:".$fonts."; color:"._XA_TCOLOR1."; font-size:12px;
                     font-weight:bold; text-align:left; text-transform:uppercase;
                     padding:2px; }
.pn-rblockcontent { font-family:".$fonts."; color:"._XA_TTEXT1COLOR."; font-size:{$text}px;
                     text-align:left; padding:8px; background-color:"._XA_TCOLOR2." }
.pn-newstitle      { font-family:".$fonts."; color:"._XA_TCOLOR1."; font-size:12px;
                     font-weight:bold; text-align:left; text-transform:uppercase;
                     padding:2px;   }
.pn-newstitle a:link    {color:"._XA_TCOLOR1."; font-size:12px; font-weight:bold; text-
➥decoration:none; }
.pn-newstitle a:visited {color:"._XA_TCOLOR1."; font-size:12px; font-weight:bold; text-
➥decoration:none; }
.pn-newstitle a:hover    {color:"._XA_TCOLOR1."; font-size:12px; font-weight:bold; text-
➥decoration:none; }
.pn-newstitle a:active   {color:"._XA_TCOLOR1."; font-size:12px; font-weight:bold; text-
➥decoration:none; }
.pn-newssub        { font-family:".$fonts."; color:"._XA_TCOLOR1."; font-size:9px;
                     text-align:right; padding:2px; }
.pn-newscontent    { font-family:".$fonts."; color:"._XA_TTEXT1COLOR."; font-size:{$text}px;
                     text-align:left; padding:8px; }
```

You can see that the family for these styles is defined using a variable. This is accomplished by setting the variable at the top of the style.php file before the styles begin:

```
$fonts = "Verdana,Arial,Helvetica";
echo "<style type=\"text/css\">
```

Setting the family globally using variables provides much greater control over future changes. If later you want to convert the site to use a Serif font, it can then be applied to every style with one edit.

Open the master.htm file in your editor and clean out all the references to the extra zones you previously removed. The following is an excerpt of code from the cleaned template file, starting after the body tag opening.

```
<div style="width:100%; background-color:<!--[$color6]-->;">
<span style="float:left;"><img src="<!--[$imagepath]-->/header.gif" /></span>
```

```
<span style="float:right;"><span class="pn-logo-small" style="color:<!--[$color1]-->;"><!--
➥[datetime]--></span></span>
</div>
<div style="width:100%; border-top:1px solid <!--[$text1]-->; background-color:<!--
➥[$color7]-->; padding:0 10 0 0;">
<span style="float:left;"><img src="<!--[$imagepath]-->/leftcap.gif" /></span>
<span style="float:right;" class="pn-sub"><!--[search]--></span>
</div>
<table border="0" cellpadding="4" cellspacing="0" style="text-align:center;width:
➥100%;"><tr>
<td style="width:<!--[$lcolwidth]-->; vertical-align:top; background-color:<!--[$color2]--
➥>; border-left:1px solid #000000; border-right:1px solid #000000; padding:10 0 0 0;">
    <!--[$leftblocks]-->
</td>
<td style="width:5px; border-bottom:1px solid #000000;"><img src="<!--[$imagepath]-->/
➥pixel.gif" style="width:5px; height:10px;" /></td>
<td style="width:100%; vertical-align:top; border-bottom:1px solid #000000;">
    <!--[$centerblocks]-->
    <!--[$maincontent]-->
</td>
<td style="width:5px; border-bottom:1px solid #000000;"><img src="<!--[$imagepath]-->/
➥pixel.gif" style="width:5px; height:10px;" /></td>
<td style="width:<!--[$rcolwidth]-->;vertical-align:top; border-bottom:1px solid #000000;">
    <!--[$rightblocks]-->
</td>
</tr></table>
<div style="width:100%;border:solid;border-top:none;border-width:1px;border-color:<!--
➥[$sepcolor]-->;text-align:center;background-color:<!--[$color2]-->;padding:0.2em;">
<span class="pn-sub"><!--[footmsg]--></span>
</div>
```

The one-pixel bottom borders used on many of the right-side content cells help to define the foot area as part of the left column. You can also see that two theme images are in use by this file: header.gif and leftcap.gif. The header was mentioned previously, but the cap image is designed to both fill space reserved in this design for the search box and to break up the line between the left column and the header area. The image seamlessly locks against the left column to make it appear the column overlaps the lower part of the header row (see Figure 11.11). Both images are available with this chapter's online materials.

The left- and right-side blocks both contain very simple code. The left block is this:

```
<div style="width:<!--[$lcolwidth]-->px;">
<div class="pn-lblocktitle"><!--[$title]--></div>
```

```
<div class="pn-lblockcontent"><!--[$content]--></div>
<hr style="width:80%" align="center"></div><br />
```

And the code used with the right side is this:

```
<div style="width:<!--[$rcolwidth]-->px; border:1px solid #000000;">
<div style="background-color:#213FD9; border-bottom:1px solid #000000;"><span class="pn-
rblocktitle"><!--[$title]--></span></div>
<div class="pn-rblockcontent"><!--[$content]--></div>
</div><br />
```

The Main Menu block also has its own template file, and templating special blocks can be a very powerful design tool, but for this example, just use the same left-side code for the Main Menu. For the home page news summaries, place this code in the news-index template:

```
<div class="pn-normal">
    <div class="pn-newstitle" style="background-color:#213FD9; border:1px solid #000000;
➡"><!--[$preformat.catandtitle]--></div>
        <div class="pn-newssub" style="background-color:#000000;"><!--[$info.longdate]--></div>
        <div class="pn-newscontent"><a href="<!--[$links.searchtopic]-->"><img style="float:
➡left; padding-right:10px;" src="images/topics/<!--[$info.topicimage]-->" alt="
➡<!--[$info.topicname]-->" /></a><!--[$preformat.hometext]--><br /><em>
➡<!--[$preformat.notes]--></em></div>
</div><br />
```

This code breaks the article into three rows: title, date, and content. The other article and center blocks can be left relatively plain to flow more smoothly in the center area. This can be useful with the way PostNuke fences in every element. Often defining one border for a block can result in the change being reused recursively to interior elements, and visually a series of concentric boxes doesn't tend to help readability. For a basic PostNuke site, customizing the sides and leaving the central area more plain is often the easiest path.

Seeing Results

With all of the previous changes applied, you see the customized club site, as shown in Figure 11.11.

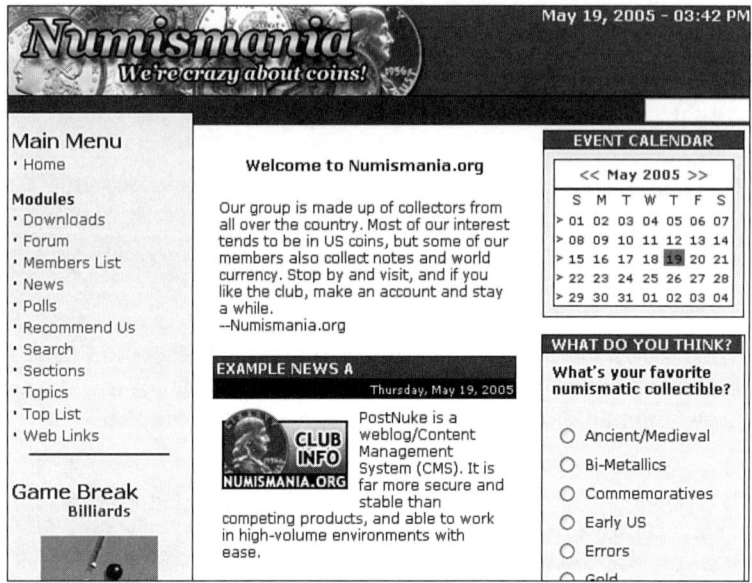

FIGURE 11.11   Layout results.

This is certainly not the end of the possible development. If there's a single theme through-out this book, it's that PostNuke gives you nearly limitless options. The Downloads module was left active and could be used to link to extra materials such as printable charts or guides for collectors. The Sections module could be used to house static articles on history or educa-tional materials, even online versions of the guides and charts in the Downloads module.

After the club site is active with user-generated content, the PNphpBB2 forum has optional blocks that can be installed to list recent forum posts. The Advanced Polls module can display a list of open polls and more poll results. And certainly both the Form and Calendar modules can be themed in much greater detail with more images and color selections. Like any good living website, you can continually modify and grow the content and design for as long as you like.

Next

In the next section of the book, you will go past the default PostNuke installs and examine different methods to customize the application to more unique needs. Whether you host information, sell products, or just need a custom blog, PostNuke can be configured to fit your needs.

PART III

Custom PostNuke

Enhanced Article Modules

12

PostNuke is a Content Management System (CMS), and the vast majority of content found on PostNuke sites is in the form of articles. Although PostNuke does come with an array of good storage modules, many other modules are also available that enhance and extend PostNuke's article features. With some modules, you can outright replace core PostNuke components to customize your site better for your needs.

In this chapter, you will examine three of the most popular and polished third-party article modules. All of these modules are solid examples of how PostNuke modules should be designed, but they are not entirely equal. Adding extreme customization capabilities can increase complexity and learning curves. When selecting the module that's right for you, consider your needs carefully.

The three modules covered in this chapter are

- Content Express
- PagEd
- PageSetter

Content Express

Content Express (www.xexpress.org) is an advanced CMS that provides both a WYSIWYG (What You See Is What You Get) editing interface and the ability to import a number of different word processing formats. It is often used to replace the PostNuke article system, but it can also run as a separate enhancement to your site.

The following overview is based on Content Express 1.2.7.5, which is available with the downloadable book materials. You can also download current versions of the module at the Content Express SourceForge site: sourceforge.net/projects/xexpress/.

> **Tip**
>
> To enable PostNuke searching in Content Express items, copy this file:
> /modules/ContentExpress/pnsearch/contexp.php to your site's /includes/search/ folder.

To install the module, decompress the archive's contents into your /modules/ directory; it's completely self-contained in a folder labeled ContentExpress. Refresh your modules in Administration and click the links in the Content Express row to initialize and activate the module. Return to the Administration Menu and click the new Content Express icon or link. You are initially presented with a form used to add page content and a series of module navigation links at the top. There are five main content structures:

- **Menus**—Works just like standard PostNuke side menu blocks, but it has many more customizable options, including hierarchy, scheduling, and rollover images for items.

- **Pages**—Defines articles with built-in layout controls, such as content alignment, anchor toggles, display scheduling, and inline media.

- **Media**—Defines separate media objects you can apply to a given Page article. Examples include images, audio, and video.

- **Categories**—Creates a configurable group of articles.

- **XML**—Allows you to add Extensible Markup Language (XML) document content, styled with XSLT, to your system.

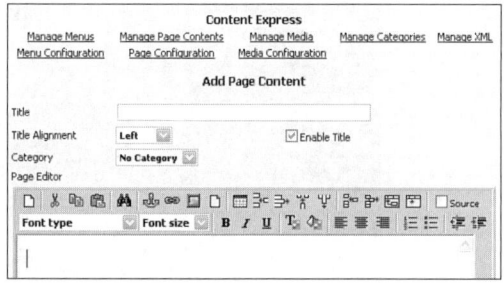

FIGURE 12.1   Adding a new page to Content Express.

To review the basics of how Content Express works, you can enter some articles. The default screen when you enter Content Express from the Administration Menu is the Add Page Content form, shown in Figure 12.1. If you have browsed around the other pages, you can return to the start form using the Manage Page Contents link at the top.

Enter a title in the first field. The check box by this field lets you toggle the display of the title to the public, but the page title is always used in the administration area to identify stories. You can also decide how the title should be aligned, to fit the layout style for your site.

> **Note**
>
> Content Express Configuration settings override those in individual items, such as the display of print icon anchors.

You currently don't have any categories configured, so leave the drop-down set to No Category. In the large text area below the drop-down list box, enter in a paragraph of content for the page. The editor buttons include a variety of standard formatting options comparable to any word processor. The results of your visual formatting are applied to the content as Hypertext Markup Language (HTML).

The *Parent* field is designed to let you group a series of articles in a hierarchy, creating a simple, multipage document or a complex article contribution structure. Standalone documents should always have Top Level selected.

The collection of *Media* fields provides the controls to upload new media elements and apply them to a given page. You can define the size and position of a given media object. For the moment, leave these fields alone too.

The *Language* option is just like any other PostNuke module, identifying when a given article should appear. If you are not using multiple languages, always leave this field set to All.

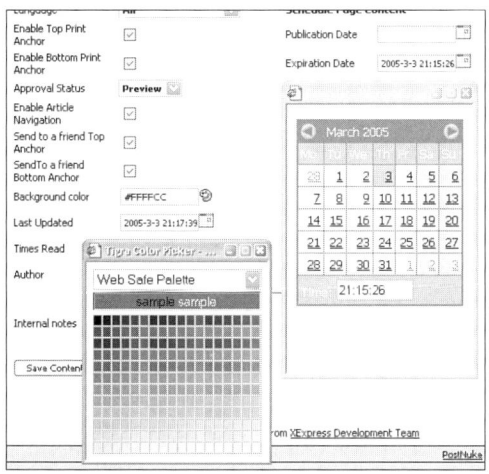

Using the *Schedule* fields, you can program the appearance and disappearance of a Page article from your site. There is a built-in calendar component activated through the little icon to the right of the date fields (see Figure 12.2). Leave the Schedule fields blank to make an article immediate and permanent.

The check boxes toggle the appearance of the Print and Send to a Friend icons. You can set these images to appear at the top and/or bottom of a page. You can also display statistic information for your readers, including the number of times an article has been read and the date it was last changed. Provide an initial value for the Times Read field, such as 5.

FIGURE 12.2   Accessing pop-up windows for additional features.

Set the Status drop-down list box to Posted to make the new article active without first previewing the content. Pages submitted with Preview are entered into the system, but are left deactivated until you manually turn them live.

Use the color picker to set the background color of the article to something different from your theme. A light beige is shown in Figure 12.2.

Click the Save Content button to submit your page. The page refreshes and a new administration section titled Manage Page Contents appears between the top navigation links and the Add Page Content form. The new area is where you will control most of your documents within Content Express.

Use the Add Page Content form to create another half dozen articles. Try out different combinations of the form fields. Be certain at least one page is set as the Parent of another. Use the Management table to activate all your pages. Notice how the Child pages are indented under their Parent article.

Tip

Replace your general website navigation menus with Content Express blocks to access more menu features.

Now, you can make a menu to make it easy for users to access the files. Go to the Blocks Administration page for your site. Add a ContentExpress/CE Menu Block with the title New Articles, or whatever title you like. Submit the block, and in the next screen check the Enable Dynamic Menu Feature check box; this enables the same kind of Parent/Child display in the menu. Commit your changes to the block.

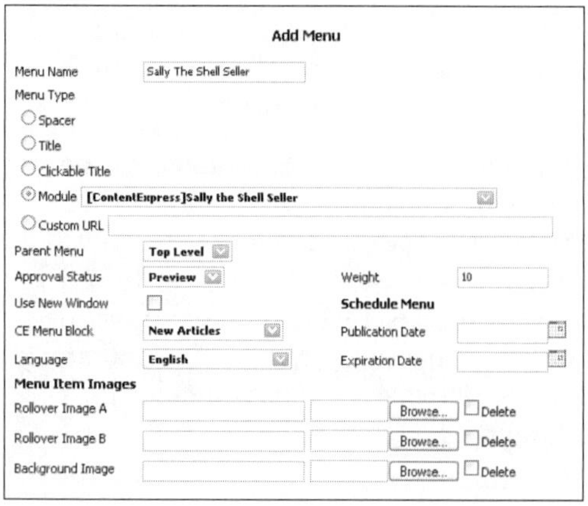

FIGURE 12.3   Adding lines to your menu block.

Browse to your Content Express Add Menu form using the Administration Menu and click the Manage Menus link, or alternatively, you can use the handy Edit link in your new side block. The thing to understand about the Add Menu form is you are not adding an entire menu with the one form submission; every time you submit the Add Menu form, you are creating *one line* in the menu. Every entry in the menu has all of the possible settings in Figure 12.3.

The general options and structure of the menu items are very similar to the Page forms. The Menu Type setting determines how the entry will work. To link to a page, select the Module option and choose the appropriate page from the drop-down list box. Menu items have Parent settings just like pages. You can, for example, have a multipage document be linked from a child-level menu entry. There are also other additional features, such as JavaScript rollovers and background image settings to add design elements to your menu.

Add all of your pages to your menu. Make at least one entry the Parent of another. As you add active items, they automatically appear in your block. You can use the Categories and Media options to organize your pages further and enhance the content. The JavaScript Menu block even creates clean dynamic HTML (DHTML) menu options that can certainly be useful on many sites regardless of whether they use the module to store article content.

Using the Website Configuration for your site, you can change the site's home page from News to Content Express, but the module's real power rests in how great it can be as a Sections replacement for PostNuke. Next, you look at a module that can easily become your site's new home page.

PagEd

A great complement to Content Express is the module PagEd. PagEd is designed to work as a replacement for the core News module in PostNuke. It even includes an import feature to instantly copy all of your existing articles from the News module into the PagEd tables.

PagEd 0.93 is available with the other book modules, or you can visit the author's site (canvas.anubix.net) for a current download. When you decompress the archive file, you find a deep directory tree. Inside the root PagEd/html folders from the archive are two subdirectories: includes and modules.

Note

If you want to use PagEd's image resizing feature, you also need to download a NetPBM image library for your server OS and place the files in your PagEd module directory in a subfolder called netpbm. Files are available from both the online book materials and the PagEd website.

All of the files under those two directories need to be placed under the respectively named root folders on your site. The search files under includes enable searching in PagEd using the global PostNuke site search features. There is also a file above those directories in the archive called pagedbackend.php. This file needs to be moved to your site's root to enable Really Simple Syndication (RSS) feeding of PagEd content from your site.

Initialize and activate the module, and then click on the new PagEd icon in the Administration Menu. The first time you run PagEd, it checks the tables and folder permissions to be certain your server is properly set up (see Figure 12.4). If the page lists any problems, make the necessary permission changes to the server folders as detailed in the page.

Welcome to PagEd.
We will start by checking the existence and permissions of required tables and files.

Tables...

nuke_paged_content exists
nuke_paged_dummycontent exists
nuke_paged_dummynews exists
nuke_paged_dummytitle exists
nuke_paged_layoutmenus exists
nuke_paged_layoutpages exists
nuke_paged_menunodes exists
nuke_paged_menus exists
nuke_paged_modulesettings exists
nuke_paged_news exists
nuke_paged_templates exists
nuke_paged_titles exists
nuke_paged_topics exists
nuke_paged_usersettings exists

Netpbm...

PHP GD image extension

FIGURE 12.4   Running PagEd for the first time.

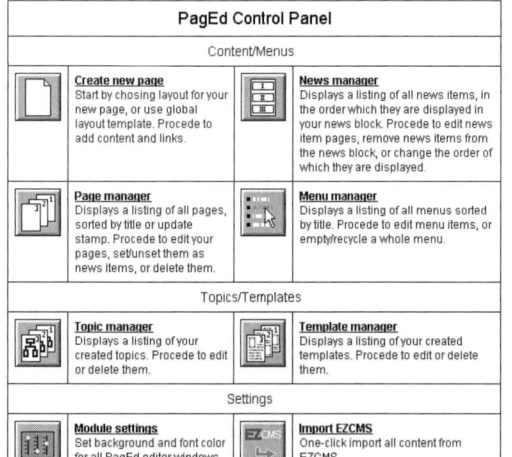

FIGURE 12.5   Controlling your content with PagEd.

Though not a direct feature of the module, PagEd offers one of the most attractive administration interfaces of any third-party PostNuke module (see Figure 12.5). The management interface contains four main sections:

- **Content/Menus**—Creates and manages pages, manages the home page news, and sets up block menus to access the content. This is your actual content; the information that's not part of the background structure of the module.

- **Topics/Templates**—Affects the display of your content. Creates topics to categorize your pages, and develops templates to apply design and formatting to your articles, news, and menus.

- **Settings**—Configures general PagEd settings, sets user permissions, and imports content from the EZCMS and News modules.

- **Backups, Bugs, and Updates**—Manages your module install with version updates and table backups, and you can submit bug reports for any problems you've discovered.

PagEd is another large module with more features than can be covered in this overview. But to get a handle on how it works, this section walks through the major concepts. Click the Create New Page link at the top of the PagEd Control Panel. The first screen, when adding a new page, allows you to configure the layout of your page. Each posting can have custom settings.

The one field that's important on this page is the Template drop-down list box. Leaving the option set to the default No Template, Individual Layout and not changing the individual settings applies no settings to the article. Selecting Global Template changes the submissions design to match the global settings in PagEd. If you prefer to use the global settings for your articles, you can scroll past all these options and click the Add Content button to get to the real content form. You can easily return to any article later to change these settings, so ignore them for now.

Tip

PagEd multipart forms contain handy Skip and Proceed buttons at the tops of the pages. You can use the button to accept default settings for the other options and move on to the next form page.

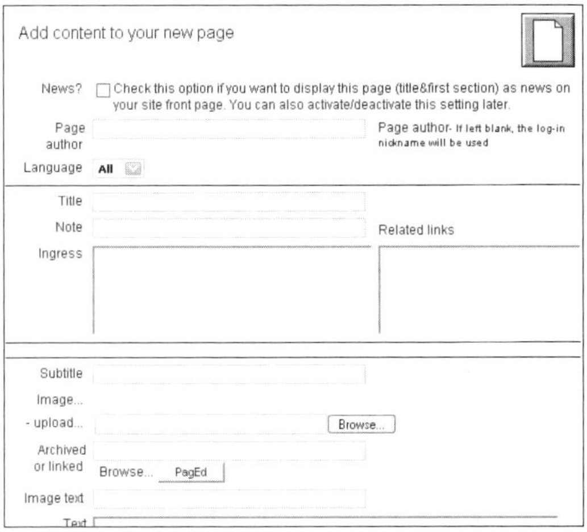

FIGURE 12.6 Adding page content to your site.

The next page contains the Add Content to Your New Page form (see Figure 12.6). Add in an example article. You need to complete the Title and first Text field, at minimum. If you enter Ingress content, it is used as the introduction to your article, for example, appearing on the home page with a Read more... link when set to be news. If you leave the Ingress blank, the first Text field content is used instead.

You can also add images to your article using the built-in browse features. You can upload images from your local machine or select an image currently on the server. Use the forms to create a few more article submissions, varying some of the options to see how they work.

Now return to the Page Manager and review the table of articles you've added. You can edit the saved articles from here as well as toggle whether they should display as news.

Now to make PagEd news work as your home page, you have two options. The Core News module can be completely replaced by going to the Website Configuration form in the Administration Menu and setting the module to be your site's Start Page. If you want to use both PagEd News and the standard PostNuke News, browse to the Blocks Administration form, add a new block of the "PagEd/PagEd News Block" type, and set it to center. Pages set to display as news show in that block just like they would with the News replacement setting.

Return to the PagEd Control Panel and try the News Manager. It allows you to easily change the placement order of news items using the up and down arrows on the left side (see Figure 12.7). Move some of your articles around and return to your home page to see the changes.

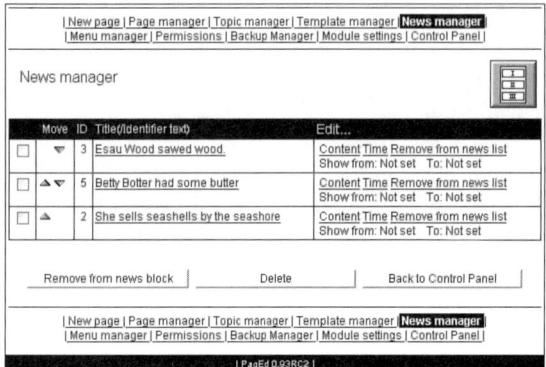

FIGURE 12.7   Adjusting your PagEd news layout.

Now, you can go down to the Settings area in the Control Panel to import old articles from the News module. This feature is very handy for site administrators wanting to upgrade to PagEd as a complete News replacement system. Importing news does not delete the entries in the News module; it only copies them to PagEd. If you no longer plan to use News, you need to delete those entries manually after the import.

> **Note**
>
> Be careful when importing news. Importing multiple times from News creates multiple entries of the same articles in PagEd.

Use the form in Figure 12.8 to copy your existing news. The form also provides the option of moving all your articles into one topic setting. This can be helpful if you already have topics created in PagEd and don't want to combine the fields with your old News topics. You can create a temporary topic, named "Old News," for example. When you complete the import, you can then go into the articles and manually decide where the content should be placed in the new Topic structure.

Now move down to the Topics Manager in the Control Panel. You should see a table showing the PagEd topics you created and all of your core News topics, if you chose to import them. With PagEd, you can create a more complex Topics system. Each item can include a full description, language setting, and can be arranged in a hierarchy with subtopics (see Figure 12.9). Make changes to your topics to fill out the entries.

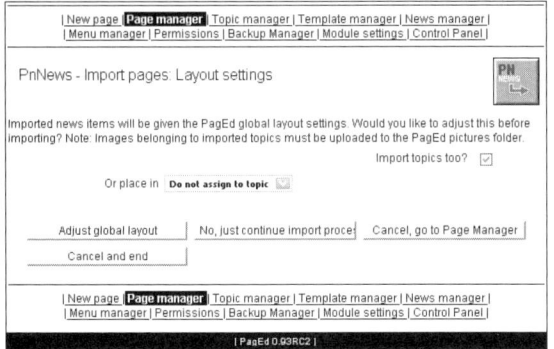

FIGURE 12.8   Upgrading your news to PagEd immediately with an import.

FIGURE 12.9   Editing your imported News topics.

Also in the Settings section of the Control Panel, you find the User Permissions tool. PagEd makes permissions management very easy, but it is not completely separate from the PostNuke access system. Browse to the PostNuke Permissions module for your site. Set a global Edit permission for the User group with the `PagEd::` as the Component. Move the entry above the default Comment access level to allow the Edit to override Comment for PagEd. This gives users general permission to all PagEd features, and now you can customize those features from within PagEd.

Note

If your site incorporates multiple user groups, you need to make a PagEd entry for each group.

Figure 12.10 shows the Configure Group Access form for the Users group. PagEd accesses the list of groups from within PostNuke, so as you add more groups, they are editable here as well. The example shows one possible combination of settings, but you should try others to become familiar with the options.

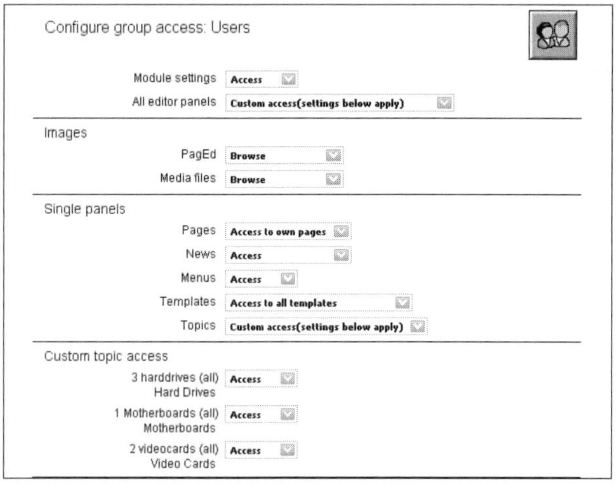

FIGURE 12.10   Customizing permissions with PagEd.

PagEd provides a good improvement over the core News module as Content Express does for Sections. Not all websites need both core modules to begin with, but if you have a large amount of article content to host online, a combination of these two third-party modules can be very powerful.

PageSetter

For those who need more than just an upgrade to News or Sections, PageSetter is the module of choice. It is designed to suit whatever content storage and display needs you might have. It can reproduce news in formats mirroring the regular PostNuke News module, but PageSetter can become anything from a complex document archive to a business directory listing to a personal recipe system. PageSetter lets you define every field, and, therefore, can become any type of information storage system you need. On top of that, PageSetter includes additional features not available with either of the previous modules, including revision control, a workflow system, and multiple approval levels for content.

This section looks at version 5.0 of PageSetter. You can download the module from the online book materials, or alternatively, pull a current version from its website (www.elfisk.dk).

The PageSetter archive includes a root folder for the module, but it also includes the `modules` folder. You need to unzip the file into a temp directory and move the module contents

FIGURE 12.11 Beginning with PageSetter.

manually, or you'll want to decompress it from the site root and not from inside the modules folder on your site. Initialize and activate PageSetter from your Modules Administration table.

PageSetter looks very unassuming in the beginning with a very simple interface (see Figure 12.11). Re-creating the news system of PostNuke can be easily accomplished, but you can build a system that's a bit more outside the box: a recipe database. The techniques used to build the system can, of course, be applied to any other custom content storage system you need.

You must first define the publication type before being able to enter any content into it. It's like designing a form template in order to enter data into the created fields. Publication types let you use PageSetter for different needs in your site. For example, you can create different types for news, static articles, contact listings, and this recipe example all at the same time. The news could be displayed on your home page while you display links to recipes in a side block.

Create a new publication type. In the Title field, enter Recipe, and enable PN-Hooks. The check box provides built-in PostNuke features, such as comments and scoring for your publication.

Workflow determines the process content takes from submission to being online for users to see. The None, Standard, and Enterprise options mean "no approval, online immediately," "Admin approval, like PostNuke standard," and "Two approval levels, editing and final," respectively. The Wiki options new to PageSetter 5 provide some Wiki-style features to PostNuke. With Wiki set, anyone can create, edit, and delete any publication. MyWiki allows creation by anyone, but users can only edit or delete their own content. In the Workflow drop-down list box, choose Standard.

The rest of the form has two parts. The *List Setup* area determines how publications are ordered when displayed together, as News posts on the home page, for example. The second area, *Publication Fields*, is a table of all the actual content entry fields for your publication. As the List Setup can order entries by fields you create, you should add the fields first.

Tip

Plan out all the fields you need for your publication type before you begin. It can save a lot of reorganization time later.

Use Table 12.1 to generate the new Publication fields. Add short descriptions for each field, if desired. The final field labeled Recipe Type requires a new List Type be set up. For now, select String for its type value.

TABLE 12.1
Recipe Publication Fields

NAME	TITLE	TYPE	SEARCHABLE
name	Name	String	Yes
description	Description	Text	Yes
ingredients	Ingredients	Text	Yes
directions	Directions	Text	Yes
preptime	Prep Time	Time	No
cooktime	Cook Time	Time	No
servings	Servings	Int	No
type	Recipe Type	Recipe Type	Yes

Additional lines can be added using the green + link on the left of each row. The one in the header adds a line at the end, and each entry link adds a new line above the one you clicked. When you are done, your table should look similar to the one in Figure 12.12.

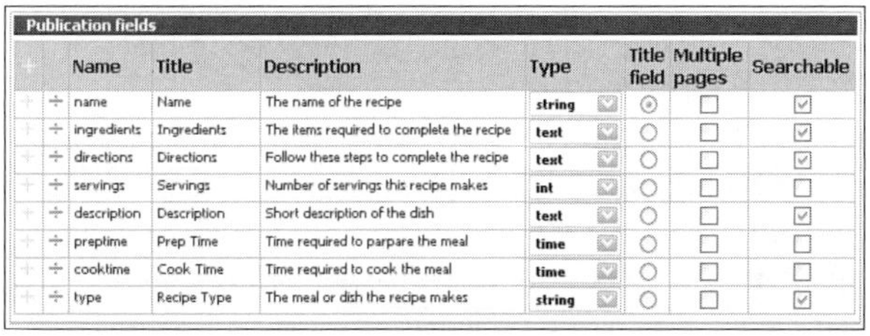
Publication fields

Name	Title	Description	Type
name	Name	The name of the recipe	string
ingredients	Ingredients	The items required to complete the recipe	text
directions	Directions	Follow these steps to complete the recipe	text
servings	Servings	Number of servings this recipe makes	int
description	Description	Short description of the dish	text
preptime	Prep Time	Time required to parpare the meal	time
cooktime	Cook Time	Time required to cook the meal	time
type	Recipe Type	The meal or dish the recipe makes	string

FIGURE 12.12 Adding fields to your publication.

Commit your changes to the publication type. Click New List under the Lists navigation menu to create the Recipe Type field type. Enter Recipe Type for the title, and add a description. Use the New Item fields to add a series of recipe types. For this example, use the same text for both the Title and Value fields. The items will be displayed in the order they are created by default, but you can edit the order and formatting by clicking on the items in the list. In Figure 12.13, you can see the Beef entry is out of alphabetical order. The control pop-up menu allows you to move the item up.

Now return to your Publication Types list, edit Recipe, and change the final field to a type of Recipe Type. Commit the change. Back at the Publication Types page, now click the New link at the right end of the table.

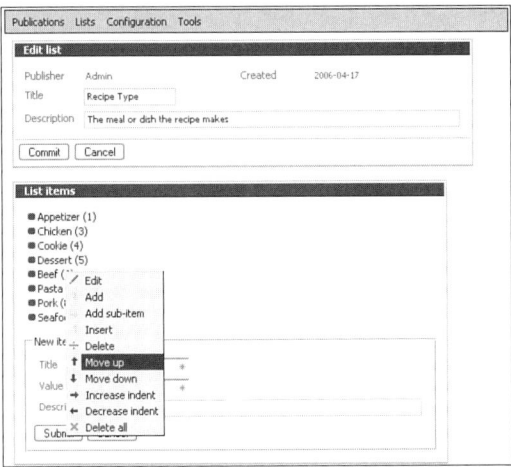

FIGURE 12.13   Controlling your lists with a click.

Enter in a few test recipes to see how the form works. You can mouseover the question mark icons to see the descriptions you entered for the different fields (see Figure 12.14).

Next from the navigation menu under Publications, select the Create Templates option. PageSetter can autogenerate template files for your publications. The files are placed in `/modules/pagesetter/pntemplates/` where you can edit them later. Check all the boxes to create a new set of templates for the Recipes, and submit the form.

Ingredients ❓	4 skinless, boneless chicken breast halves 8 ounces rotini pasta 1 red onion, chopped 6 cherry tomatoes, chopped 8 ounces mozzarella cheese, cubed 1 head romaine lettuce, chopped
Directions ❓	1) Preheat the grill for high heat. Season both sides of chicken breast halves with steak seasoning. 2) Lightly oil the grill grate. Grill chicken 6 to 8 minutes per side, or until juices run clear. Remove from hea cut into strips. *Follow these steps to complete the recipe* pasta in a large pot of lightly salted boiling water. Cook 8 to 10 minutes, until brain, and rinse with cold water to cool. 4) In a large bowl, mix together the cheese, onion, lettuce, and tomatoes. Toss with the cooled chicken and p serve.
Servings ❓	4
Description ❓	A quick and easy pasta salad, and the chicken makes it quite filling. Enjoy it with your favorite choice of dre
Prep Time ❓	00:15:00
Cook Time ❓	00:30:00
Recipe Type ❓	Chicken

FIGURE 12.14   Field descriptions appear with a mouseover.

Now, you can create a new block to display links to the data. Browse to the Blocks Administration table and create a new entry with the type "pagesetter/PageSetter list N publications." Title it "New Recipes" and submit the form. Now, you can configure your list block. Set the position to "Right" and the publication type to "Recipe Type." The OrderBy field needs the value "core.lastUpdated:desc" to show only the most recent posts.

The template name should be just "list." PageSetter template filenames are built using the known publication name, the template name you supply, and the file extension. So, if the filename is `Recipe-list.html`, you need only enter "list" in the field. PageSetter also automatically adds the `-header` and `-footer` to the template filenames as needed.

New Recipes
Crispy RiceCandy
Garlic-Lemon Double Stuffed Chicken
Grilled Chicken and Pasta Salad
Peach Ice Cream
Santa Fe Chicken
Shrimp Scampi Cheesecake
Appetizer
Spicy Crispy Beef

Categories Menu
* Rumors (Apr 13, 2006)

Poll
What do you think of PostNuke?
○ Think? I use it!
○ It is what was needed.
○ What is PostNuke?
Vote
[Results	Polls]

FIGURE 12.15
A PageSetter block example.

Commit your changes and take a look at your completed block. It should look similar to the one shown in Figure 12.15. The item has no formatting due to the empty templates, but the functioning foundation is there for you to build upon.

Now, you look at another one of PageSetter's impressive features. Like PagEd, PageSetter can import data from the PostNuke News module, from Content Express, and from an XML schema file. When accomplishing an import, PageSetter creates the new publication type, and all the fields associated with it, automatically.

Use the PageSetter navigation menu to select Import Data from the Tools option. You are presented with a very simple set of forms. Along with importing all News items for you, PageSetter also creates an image field for the new PN-News Publication by checking the top box.

To see how a more standard publication type works, you can import in the old news. Check the image check box and click the Import News button.

Note

Importing news multiple times is technically possible, but it creates multiple publication entries of the same name, which make it hard to tell them apart. Unlike PagEd, however, you can simply delete the extra publication to fix the double import.

Edit the new publication type PN-News created by the import. You can see it has done nearly all of the work toward creating a news system for you. The Publication fields (see Figure 12.16) account for all the regular features expected of a PostNuke News module, and now you can easily add additional fields to expand.

Publication fields							
Name	Title	Description	Type		Title field	Multiple pages	Searchable
✛ title	Title		string	⊡	⊙	☐	☑
✛ teaser	Teaser		html	⊡	○	☐	☑
✛ text	Text		html	⊡	○	☑	☑
✛ notes	Notes		text	⊡	○	☐	☐
✛ image	Image		image	⊡	○	☐	☐
✛ imageText	Image text		string	⊡	○	☐	☐

FIGURE 12.16   News publications created the easy way.

Now go to your Website Configuration form in PostNuke Administration and set your site's Start Page to "pagesetter." Return to the PageSetter administration area and select General under the Configuration menu. The first option on this page selects which publication to use when the Frontpage of PageSetter is accessed. Set it to "PN-News" and save the change.

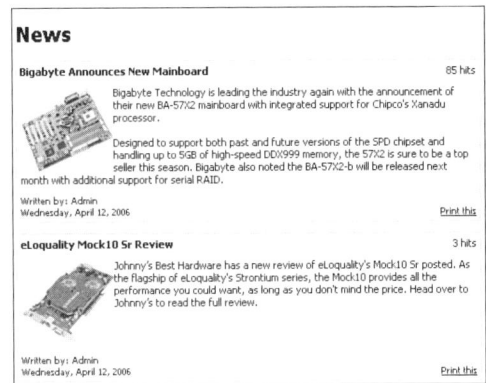

FIGURE 12.17   PN-News as your PostNuke home page.

Now go to your site's home page. The news articles are displayed just like the core News module, but with the addition of the PageSetter template formatting (see Figure 12.17). You can edit the templates easily to create any look desired.

Granted, PageSetter takes more time to develop a usable content system than many other modules. But after the setup work is completed, there really is no module more powerful for creating a dynamic information website. If you need complete flexibility, PageSetter is the module for you.

Troubleshooting

The modules described in this chapter are all very polished systems, but a few interesting issues seem to be of issue more often than others. They are listed in the following sections. These modules are also all very popular, and if you need additional assistance, be certain to try the website forums set up for each module, as well as the general PostNuke forums.

Content Express Form Generates Microsoft Office Pop-Up

When first running Content Express using a Microsoft Internet Explorer browser, you might see a series of pop-up dialog boxes requesting Microsoft Office install CDs. The WYSIWYG editor uses ActiveX components from Microsoft Office, and depending on what you have installed on your machine, you might see a series of pop-up requests. You can put in your

Office CD and install the missing components, or click Cancel and close the windows with no ill effects. The WYSIWYG editor works fine without installing any additional features.

Content Express Manage XML Shows _CE_USER_ XSLTNOTSUPPORTED

To use the XML feature of Content Express, you must have Extensible Stylesheet Language (XSL) enabled for PHP on your server. PHP discontinued automatic support for XSL from version 4.1, but the dynamic link libraries (DLLs) needed are included in the manual install package.

You do not need XSL support to use the Content Express; it is provided for additional functionality. For complete XSL installation, go to www.php.net/xslt.

PagEd Cannot Find the PHP GD Image Extension

This error is fixed by installing the PHP graphics libraries for your server. The php_gd2.dll is included with the manual PHP installation package. Place the file in your extensions directory, and uncomment the line

```
;extension=php_gd2.dll
```

to enable the support. More information on the install of GD support in PHP can be found at www.php.net/manual/en/ref.image.php.

Imported News Topic Has Broken Image

PagEd provides a very slick import feature for existing news and topics on your site, but topic images are not in the database and are still referenced from local file paths. Importing only copies database entries over. Go to the News Topics directory /images/topics/ and copy the images you need to /modules/PagEd/pictures/ to complete the import.

Unknown Window Data in PageSetter

The Unknown Window Data error is caused by a loss of session internally to PageSetter. It is caused by trying to get to a PageSetter page using browser navigation buttons or by clicking the PageSetter navigation links while in a form awaiting a Commit. With the latter cause, the error is prevented by using the Cancel button when done with a form instead of just clicking to a new navigation element.

If you are effectively locked out of PageSetter with this message, you can clear it by going to your PostNuke Administration screen. Reselect the PageSetter link from there, and your access is restored.

No Template Found in PageSetter

If PageSetter is telling you "no template has been created" for your publication type, there are two likely causes. First, did you create a template for the publication? You can use the built-in system to autogenerate appropriately named blank templates for any publication.

Second, did you reference the template correctly when you created your display block? You need only use the short, specific name of the template, such as list, full, or print. If you have entered the publication name or the full filename, such as `PN-News-list.html` or `PN-News-full`, the system does not work, returning the error message described previously.

Next

In the next chapter, you will examine the more commercial site of PostNuke with money-making modules. Your site can provide income in a variety of ways, including advertising, donations, and product sales. You will look at how you can do business using these methods on your PostNuke site.

Money-Making Modules

13

Many websites cannot survive without some form of income, and the use of PostNuke to manage your site content certainly does not change that fact. Common ways to generate revenues include selling advertising space, selling products or subscriptions, and asking for donations.

This chapter looks at a few of the core and third-party modules that help satisfy the needs of websites wanting to provide a steady income. In the upcoming sections, you explore the following topics:

- Advertising

- Donations

- Buying and selling

Advertising

PostNuke includes a number of features to help you advertise your own site as well as host the ads of others. Banners are an Internet standard for generating ad revenue, and PostNuke includes a core module that easily satisfies that need. PostNuke also includes a word-of-mouth advertising module for your own site called Recommend Us. Both modules are described fully in the following sections.

Banners

PostNuke includes a modest but standard advertising banner system as part of its core module set. The system's features provide ad display and impression management tools. Banners are managed through client accounts you create on your site.

The Banners module is a core component of PostNuke, but by default, the module is disabled. Browse to your site's Modules Administration page and activate the Banners module. Return to the Admin icons and click the new Banners links in the table. Activating the module grants you access to manage the banners for your site, but the actual display of the banners must also be turned on from within the Banners Administration page.

When you first browse the page (see Figure 13.1), a message explaining the need to activate banner display is posted at the top, and a direct link to the settings section is provided to make the change. Click the Settings Section link, and toggle the Active Banners radio buttons to "yes." The other field on the Settings page allows you to input your local IP to help maintain the accuracy of your ad views.

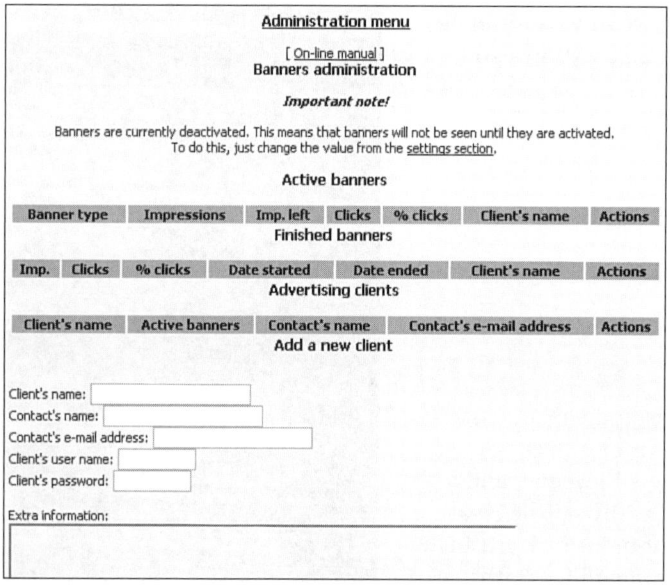

FIGURE 13.1   Getting started with PostNuke banners.

To see how the Banners module works, you can create a new client and add some ads. For this example, use the fictitious company "Mike's Music Shop." Use the data in Table 13.1 to complete the client form.

TABLE 13.1

Sample Client Data

FIELD	DATA
Client's name	Mike's Music Shop
Contact's name	Mike Smith
Contact's email address	mike@mikesmusicshop.com
Client's username	msmith
Client's password	password

Now add a few banners. A set of simple demonstration ad images are available with the book materials. These images are referenced throughout the examples, but you can use any ad images.

PostNuke's Banner module supports any ad dimensions you want to use, not just the traditional horizontal banner style. For standard image dimensions recommended for use on the Internet, consult the information in Table 13.2.

TABLE 13.2

Web Marketing Standard Ad Types

AD TYPE	DIMENSIONS (IN PIXELS)
Banners	
Full banner	468×60
Half banner	234×60
Leaderboard	728×90
Micro bar	88×31
Vertical banner	120×240
Blocks and Buttons	
Square button	25×125
Button 90	20×90
Button 60	20×60
Skyscrapers	
Skyscraper	120×600
Wide skyscraper	160×600
Half page ad	300×600

After you have your ads together, place them in the PostNuke banners directory:

```
/images/banners/
```

Use the Add a New Banner form to enter your images into the system. The form does not place images on your pages; it only tells the Banners module about the image object and assigns it an ID number. Using this number, you can reference specific ads to place them where you want them to appear on your site.

The Purchased Impressions field sets a counter for display of an ad. The business that places an ad on your site can purchase a specific number of views, after which the ad is removed from display. Enter in a larger number here while testing, such as 100.

Banner Type is an important field. It's not really a type so much as an ID number. The number 1 is reserved for header ads, and similarly, you should use the number 2 for banners placed in your site footer. These numbers define the type as they are referenced in the theme. Other numbers, 3 and up, can be used with blocks to display anywhere on your site. If you do not want to incorporate banners into your theme, you do not have to use type 1 or 2 and can begin with 3 or any other number.

Tip

Add multiple banner ads using the same type ID to rotate between ads. Ads of a given ID are displayed randomly.

For this example, make the block ads first, so use "3" and "4" for your first couple of ad entries. Remember the size is connected to the type ID, so that when you make a block, you should know if it's a wide banner image or a tall skyscraper.

The Image URL field must contain a valid path relative to the server. For local images you've placed in the `banners` directory, the field should contain this kind of entry:

```
/images/banners/banner1.gif
```

where the name of your image is typed at the end of the path. The full uniform resource locator (URL) handling of the field also gives you the ability to display ads hosted from external servers. The path for remote ads would look something like this:

```
http://www.mikesmusicshop.com/ads/banner1.gif
```

Click URL is simply the address to which you are linking the banner. When a visitor clicks the ad, he is sent to that URL. The Banners module is designed to open a new window for all ad clicks, so the user does not actually leave your site.

Complete the addition of a few ads and your list will look similar to Figure 13.2. The two Impressions columns count off the current total and remaining views. The Impressions Left column will go negative if a banner is left active and viewed past its amount of Purchased Impressions. When a user clicks through an ad, the count is tallied in the Clicks column, and the percentage of clicks per view is calculated and displayed in the % Clicks column.

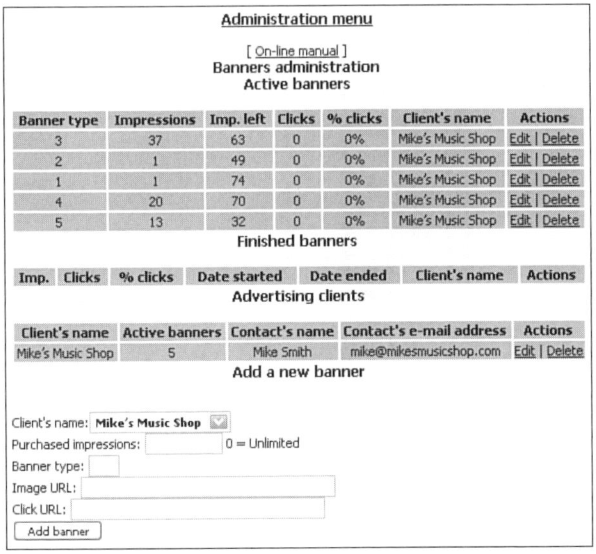

Administration menu

[On-line manual]
Banners administration
Active banners

Banner type	Impressions	Imp. left	Clicks	% clicks	Client's name	Actions
3	37	63	0	0%	Mike's Music Shop	Edit | Delete
2	1	49	0	0%	Mike's Music Shop	Edit | Delete
1	1	74	0	0%	Mike's Music Shop	Edit | Delete
4	20	70	0	0%	Mike's Music Shop	Edit | Delete
5	13	32	0	0%	Mike's Music Shop	Edit | Delete

Finished banners

Imp.	Clicks	% clicks	Date started	Date ended	Client's name	Actions

Advertising clients

Client's name	Active banners	Contact's name	Contact's e-mail address	Actions
Mike's Music Shop	5	Mike Smith	mike@mikesmusicshop.com	Edit | Delete

Add a new banner

Client's name: **Mike's Music Shop**
Purchased impressions: [   ] 0 = Unlimited
Banner type: [   ]
Image URL: [   ]
Click URL: [   ]
[Add banner]

FIGURE 13.2 Managing ad banners to display on your site.

Now add the banners first using blocks. This is the easiest way to add ads with the Banners module because it does not require editing templates. In addition, if your site does not carry ads all the time, using blocks solely is preferable to manual code changes.

Under Blocks Administration, select a Core/Custom Banner Display block. Select a position for your ad, and keep in mind its dimensions. Tall vertical ads and small block ads are traditionally placed on the sides, whereas horizontal banners appear at the tops and bottoms of pages. The Title field can hold anything you want, such as the name of the business running the ads or a simple "Advertisement" works fine.

After you submit the block for the first time, it displays whatever ad you have set to a type ID of 1. This happens because the block does not yet know what ID you want to show. So before you commit the block, add in the ID of the real ad you are setting up. Create more blocks to try out multiple block locations (see Figure 13.3).

A more permanent application of banners can be done in your theme's template files. The ads need to be in the Banner module system, just like the blocks, but you can use a reference like this in your Extensible Hypertext Markup Language (XHTML):

```
<!--[nocache]--><!--[pnbannerdisplay id=1]--><!--[/nocache]-->
```

The line displays banners with an ID of 1, and the nocache tags make certain new images are consistently pulled by users' browsers.

FIGURE 13.3   Displaying ad banners on your site.

> **Tip**
>
> Reload your Xanthia theme's templates in the Xanthia Administration module to apply your template file changes.

You can also call the ads using the function `pnBannerDisplay()` directly with PHP. A reference like this:

```
pnBannerDisplay('5');
```

randomly displays ads with the type ID of 5.

Recommend Us

Another core PostNuke module is Recommend Us. This module does not provide support for others' ads; it supplies a method of advertising your own website. Through Recommend Us, a site visitor can send an email to people she knows and notify them personally that your site exists. The action is meant to be an automated "I know you'd like this site" type of service, and you might have seen similar systems on websites under the moniker "Send to a Friend."

The module is included with PostNuke and it is installed by default. There is nothing to administer with this module; you need only provide a link for users to click. This is done using a menu-style link with

```
[Recommend_Us]
```

or by directly linking to the module with

```
http://www.mysite.com/modules.php?op=modload&name=Recommend_Us&file=index
```

An example menu link is also automatically created for you in the default Main Menu block. Click the link to view the Recommend Us form (see Figure 13.4).

Recommend this site to someone

Your name:	DemoUser
Your e-mail address:	user@mysite.com
The person's name:	
The person's e-mail address:	

Send

FIGURE 13.4 Sending a site link to a friend.

The Your Name and Your E-mail Address fields are populated automatically by the user account information, but if you allow anonymous users to use the Recommend Us feature, they need to type in those fields too.

The email that is sent looks like this by default:

```
Hello Kevin:
Your friend test considered our site mysite.com interesting and wanted to send it to you.

Site name: mysite.com
Amazing Article
Site URL: http://www.mysite.com/article/
```

The Recommend Us module pulls the URL of the page the user is viewing when the module is activated. So if the user is reading an article and wants to tell someone about it, the email is created with a direct link to that file.

You can also change the wording sent in the file by editing the text definitions in this file:

```
/modules/Recommend_Us/lang/eng/global.php
```

Site Donations

Another way many websites generate revenue is through donations. Gifted funds are becoming increasingly popular as the growth of open source promotes the altruistic giving away of people's work. Many online projects survive solely through the donations of their users.

PayPal (www.paypal.com) is by far the method of choice for sites wanting to accept donations. The service has a variety of built-in tools that really do all the work for you. The following block options were all initially written to work with PayPal, but in most of the blocks, you can alternatively enter in the code for other companies, such as Amazon.com (www.amazon.com) or Kagi (www.kagi.com).

pncPayPal Contribute

The pncPayPal Contribute block from pnConcept (dev.pnconcept.com) is the fastest and easiest way to make a PayPal donations block. The block can be downloaded from the pnConcept link given previously, and it is available as part of this book's online materials.

The archive has three PHP files in it, all of which need to be copied into your site's `includes` directory. The complete paths are contained in the zip, or you can simply decompress the file in your site's folder. Because the block does not have an accompanying parent module, the install places the block with the other core blocks.

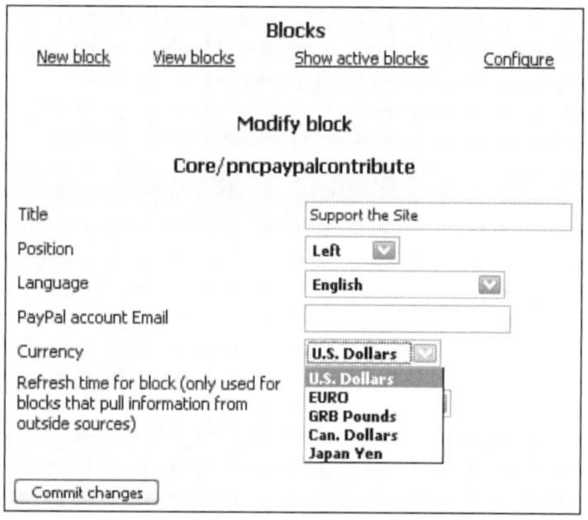

FIGURE 13.5   Selecting your donations' currency type.

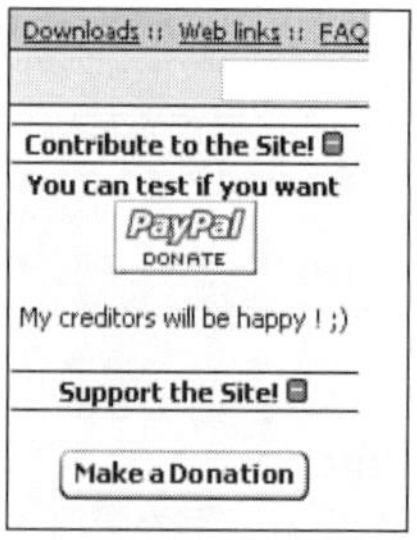

FIGURE 13.6   Instant PayPal donations block.

Browse to your Blocks Administration page. Add a new side block with the type Core\PayPal Contribute Block. The Title field can contain any message you want, "Support the Site" for example. pncPayPal also gives you the ability to select your donations' currency type (see Figure 13.5).

To complete the block, you only need your PayPal account email. All of the PayPal system source code is already built in to the block. When you are done, you'll have a block similar to the one in Figure 13.6. The text in the example is in the module by default, but you do have control over that aspect as well. Open the following file in your editor, and make the appropriate changes to the text definitions:

```
/includes/language/blocks/eng/
↪pncpaypalcontribute.php
```

Donations Block

The Donations Block by pnFlashGames (pnflashgames.com) requires a bit more effort than pncPayPal Contribute, but it has the additional feature of a Top Donators listing. The examples in this overview were accomplished with version 1.0 of the Donations block, which is available for download at the pnFlashGames site, under Downloads, PostNuke Modules, Other Addons, and you can download it from the online book materials.

The one PHP file that comes with the block needs to be copied to your site's main `blocks` folder with this path:

```
/includes/blocks/donations.php
```

Next go to your site's Block Administration table and add a new block of type Core/Donations. The options are somewhat similar to pncPayPal Contribute (see Figure 13.7). Complete the Title field as before, perhaps with text like "Support the Site." The Show the Donation Amount Next to the Name? check box toggles the display of the amounts entered later in the form (see Figure 13.8). You can also enter an identifying character for the currency type in the next field.

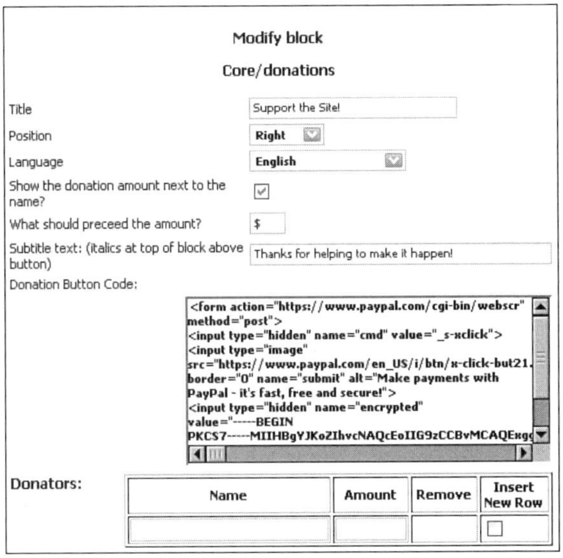

FIGURE 13.7 Adding a custom donations button to your block.

The Donations block also provides subtitle capabilities similar to pncPayPal Contribute, but instead of editing the language file, you only need to type in the text you want displayed in the Subtitle Text field. The subtitle appears below the title in italic.

The Donation Button Code text area allows you to paste whatever custom code you want, from any online service, such as Amazon.com, PayPal, or Kagi. The example code in Figure 13.8 is from the PayPal Donations block. The flexibility of using different code also lets you customize the image(s) you use.

> **Tip**
>
> Add buttons from multiple services to give your site users the option of choosing their preferred method of donation.

The final line of fields in the block lets you manage a listing of Top Donators (see Figure 13.8). Each name is displayed by the donation amount. When entering amounts, only use the number, such as "25," without a dollar sign or other monetary marking.

The listing is managed manually, so as you get additional donations, you need to adjust the list accordingly.

HTML Block

PostNuke also includes a simple Hypertext Markup Language (HTML) block you can create by selecting Core/HTML from the list. The block has only two content fields for a title and your button code. This method can accomplish a display and functionality identical to either of the other blocks, but it requires that you write the XHTML to make it work.

FIGURE 13.8
Honoring your top donators.

Buy and Sell

Though most PostNuke sites are as free with their downloads as they are information, it is also quite possible to set up an e-commerce site using the Content Management System (CMS). A number of third-party modules are available that can help. The majority tie into other systems, such as CaféPress, PayPal, and eBay to use their built-in features.

The two following modules are good examples of the type of systems currently available. The first, cmsMerchant, provides a variety of services using a generally subscription-focused model. It is a completely standalone module that is also commercially sold to its users. The second, PayPalCart, accesses the user feature of PayPal to create an online shopping experience. It ties into PayPal directly with only support for the one service, but PayPalCart is also a free module. For more e-commerce modules, consult the tables in Appendix B, "PostNuke Modules List."

cmsMerchant

The cmsMerchant module provides an all-in-one style solution for your e-commerce needs. It provides regular sales functions for digital and physical products and services, provides donations support, and has a subscription system that can block out specific portions of your website and automatically charge recurring fees for user access. The module is one of the few commercial add-ons to PostNuke, but registration of cmsMerchant grants you a free installation and ongoing support.

Following is a general overview of how cmsMerchant works. The examples were produced using version 2.0.1. Functional demos of the software have been made available through the cmsMerchant website (www.cmsmerchant.com) in the past, but at this writing only an online example is available for viewing. For more detailed information on the current version and to purchase the module, visit their site at the address listed previously.

To begin, cmsMerchant is written in PHP but encoded using tools from ionCube. You have to install the ionCube Loader on your server prior to installing cmsMerchant so that the cmsMerchant files can be read. The Loader is a simple install that consists of copying the appropriate dynamic link library (DLL), for Windows, or Apache Module: for Linux and OSX, file to your operating system's binaries location and adding a Zend extension reference in your php.ini file. After that is completed, with a restart of your web server if required, you can initialize cmsMerchant and activate the module.

The first step to creating a cmsMerchant storefront is to set up user groups. cmsMerchant uses the standard PostNuke group module. Go to the Group Administration page and create a new group called customers, subscribers, or another name you like. Access to different areas and features can then be managed by group name.

Note

Multiple groups can be created to add tiered access levels, such as regular and pro or bronze, silver, and gold.

Back in the cmsMerchant Administration page, a series of links are used to navigate through the module's features:

- **Payment plugins**—The basic version of the module only supports one payment type of your choice, but if you have purchased the full version, you have access to all seven of the plug-ins that are configured through this link (see Figure 13.9). cmsMerchant supports the following payment options: Authorize.net, Check/Money Order, iPayment, PayPal, StormPay, 2CheckOut, and WorldPay.

- **Subscription plans**—The Add a Subscription Plan form in Figure 13.10 illustrates the kind of options you have in creating a new plan. Determine the rate and cycle length for the service, specify download limitations for files, and include images, terms information, and a complete description to make the subscription benefits clear.

- **Subscription orders**—Manages your current subscription orders. The Orders page displays a table of users with the items they have purchased, paid amounts, dates, and current statuses of subscriptions and transactions.

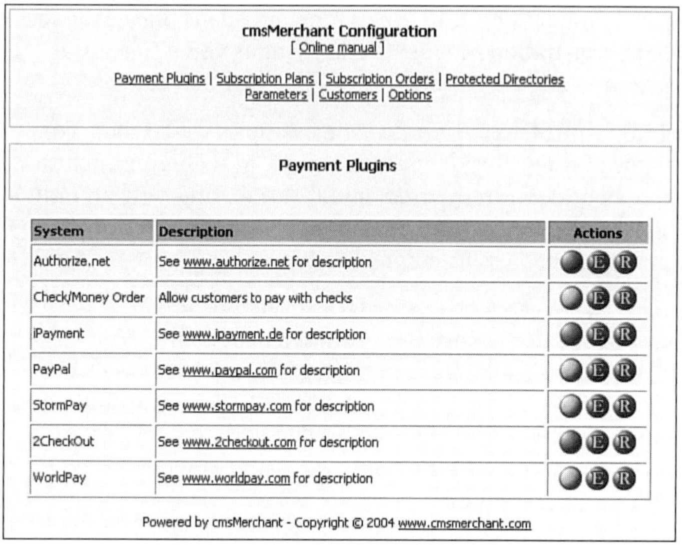

FIGURE 13.9   Configuring your payment plugins.

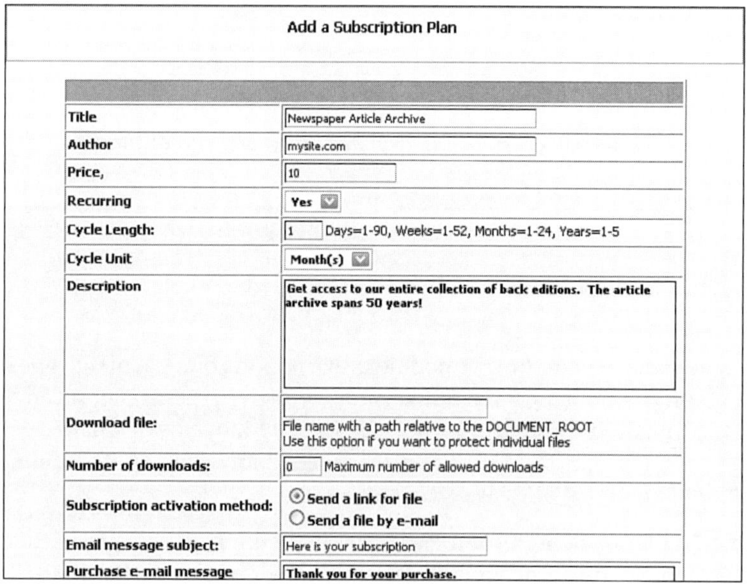

FIGURE 13.10   Creating a subscription plan.

- **Protected directories**—This page allows you to configure which directories on your site are restricted to paying customers. Those with the appropriate subscription are allowed, whereas all others are prevented access.

> **Note**
>
> Access and restriction to modules can also be set up, but it is done through the normal PostNuke permissions settings.

- **Parameters**—This page allows the general configuration of module functions. From this page, you can set the layout of products, select storefront images, choose the currency, set your email and AutoTheme template, and enter in all the automated correspondence messages the system will send to your users.

- **Customers**—A simple report of all of your customers, the table includes each person's full name, email address, username, last order, and amount paid.

- **Options**—Creates unlimited attributes for your products, such as size, color, or price. Each option can have customized values, such as small, medium, and large.

You can see cmsMerchant's design is focused mostly toward the subscription model, but the base functionality has been extended to include support for specific products and donations.

cmsMerchant also includes four different block types you can use with your site. Two of the blocks deal with donations and work very similar to the blocks covered in previous sections. The Donation block is assigned a preconfigured plan and prompts your users to support the site. Top Donators are displayed in its companion block automatically; you need only select the number of users to display and whether the list is ranked by amount given or number of times a user has donated.

> **Note**
>
> The display of a cmsMerchant side block is required for cmsMerchant's subscription system to function. The block allows the tracking of users against the subscription database and prevents access to materials when a subscription has expired.

Another cmsMerchant block is called "Show Merchant Goodies" and displays an item of your choice with its name, description, price, and thumbnail image. Further information is displayed for subscriptions, such as the duration of the service per payment.

The final module provides a link into the current subscriptions and products for your site. A similar link can also be accomplished by adding the standard line in a Menu block with [cmsMerchant] in the URL.

Users of cmsMerchant should also take a good look through the online manual. Although most modules include their documentation in a pnDocs folder, you can find this module's manual at

```
/modules/cmsMerchant/lang/eng/manual.html
```

The documentation has been placed under the language folders to provide better multilingual support using different versions of the manual.

PayPalCart

The PayPal service includes a free service in which members can create a shopping cart for items they are selling on their site. The problem is that PayPal's system requires each item to be added separately to your site in a series of button scripts. This can be cumbersome to manage, especially on large sites with many items.

This is where PayPalCart comes in. This PostNuke module is an administration tool for your PayPal shopping cart entries. You can create categories and register your item information in PayPalCart, and it dynamically generates all the hooks you need into PayPal.

> **Note**
>
> You must have a PayPal account to use the PayPalCart module, but the account setup and configuration is free.

This section walks through the setup of this handy module to see how it all works. PayPalCart version 1.0.1 is available with the book's online materials, and you can also find current versions at its creator's site: www.natewelch.com/. After the archive is downloaded, review its contents. Three main directories are included in the zip: images, includes, and modules. The files in each directory need to be placed in their respective folder off of your site's root. You can also decompress the file from your site's root to accomplish the proper distribution.

Now browse to your PostNuke Module Administration page and both initialize and activate the module. After this is done, return to the main Administration Menu and click the new PayPalCart icon. A series of links are at the top of the module's main page. Click the far right link labeled Update Configuration to set up your PayPal information and preferences.

As you can see from the form in Figure 13.11, PayPalCart offers an extensive list of configuration options. Each field includes a clear description of its function and whether it is required. Customize the content in the fields to suit your new store.

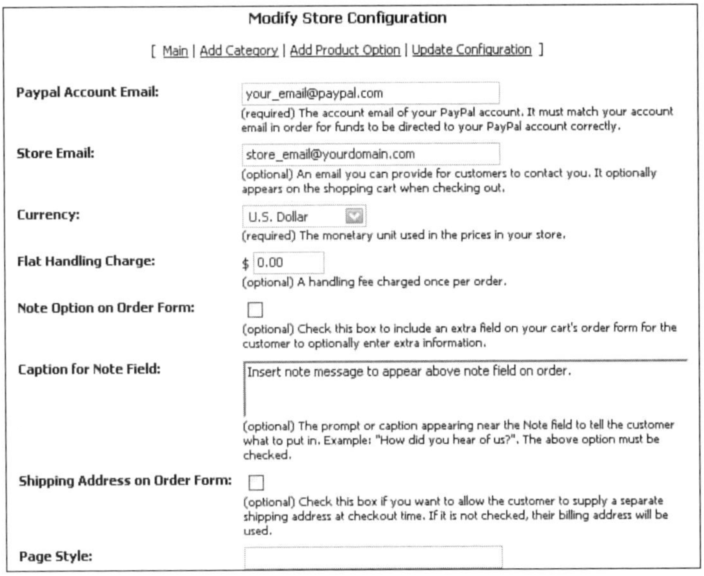

FIGURE 13.11 Setting up your online store.

Next, upload a couple of images for your sample products. The main PayPal Administration form includes a handy Image Upload field. With it, you can browse to your image on your local machine and upload it directly to the remote server directory you entered in the configuration form. You can, of course, alternatively copy the images to the directory manually if you find that easier. Thumbnail images and their larger-sized counterparts are included with the book materials as samples. Upload some of the example images, or a set of your own images for use later.

Click the Add Category link at the top to create a new department for your products. The Category options are also very straightforward and provide inline descriptions of their functions. Add a category name and complete a short description. Be certain the Active check box is checked, and submit the form.

The new category is in the resulting table on your PayPalCart main page. At the right of the row is a link to Add Item. Select the option to add a few samples. The Add Item page allows you to define your products in great detail (see Figure 13.12). Along with the regular item descriptions and price, you can define selectable attributes for your product and override default shipping settings. Now use the images you uploaded earlier to pick out a thumbnail and full-size view of your product. Your images dynamically appear as you choose them.

```
                              Add Item

        [ Main | Add Category | Add Product Option | Update Configuration ]

Product Name:          Red Widget
                       (required) Enter a name for this item.

SKU/Item Number:       3456003R
                       (optional) Enter an internal catalog, item or SKU number.

Product Description:   This widget's attractive red color is sure to get a lot of attention.



                       (optional, but recommended) Describe the product and its features. Line breaks
                       and simple html formatting is recognized. Remember, sell the sizzle, not the steak.

Product Category:      Colored Wigets ▼
                       (required) Select the category this product will go in. Items can be moved from
                       one category to another with this menu.

Price:                 $ 30.00
                       (required) Enter the price for this item in the currency you selected in the module
                       config. Do not include dollar signs or another currency markers. A price cannot be
                       zero.

First Attribute:       No Attribute Selected ▼
                       (optional) Select a attribute for this item. You must define the attribute first. The
                       "label" value in parenthesis will appear with the product on the Product Detail page.
                       The option will be a text box, dropdown list or radio select list depending on how it
                       was configured.

Second Attribute:      No Attribute Selected ▼
                       (optional) Select a second option attribute for this item. Option attributes will
                       appear in the order they are selected here.
```

FIGURE 13.12   Adding items for customers to purchase.

After adding your inventory, you need to make it easy for your customers to get to your products. PayPalCart provides three ways to make it happen. First add a link to the Main Menu block. Edit the Main Menu in the Block Administration and add a new line. For the title,

```
                    pnWidgetco

                  [ Store Information ]

pnWidgetco Home >> Colored Wigets

                           Page: 1   Viewing Items 1-2 of 2




      Red Widget                 Blue Widget
    [ Select Options ]         [ Select Options ]
    $30.00  [ Edit ]           $35.00  [ Edit ]

    [ Add to Cart ]            [ Add to Cart ]



                           Page: 1   Viewing Items 1-2 of 2



[ View Cart ]    Jump to a category: Colored Wigets ▼ [ go ]
```

FIGURE 13.13   Customers can browse your products by category.

enter something like "Buy Widgets," and use "{PayPalCart}" as the URL. Submit the menu and click your new link.

The first page is the main storefront. If you added images to your store, they appear here with the title and main description. Your categories are listed below the store information with the number of items available. Click the category name to browse your items (see Figure 13.13).

The second way your customers can find your products is through the PostNuke site search. To enable product searches, copy the paypalcart.php plug-in file to your site's /includes/search/ folder. If you installed the PayPalCart files completely, the file will already be in place.

> **Tip**
>
> Does your site have an integrated search field built in to your layout? Add this hidden input to your site's search form to include PayPalCart items in user searches: `<input type="hidden" name="active_paypalcart" value="1">`.

The third way you can get more customers to your products is through the PayPalCart side block. The block randomly displays an item from the category you select or can alternatively show a single specific product you define (see Figure 13.14).

All of the PayPal code is dynamically integrated into the shopping experience. When a user adds items to his cart, the module interfaces with your PayPal account to create the cart. It's a very straightforward and user-friendly interface that works with most online store needs.

FIGURE 13.14
Highlighting specific items with the PayPalCart block.

Troubleshooting

The following sections list some of the more common issues encountered when working with the modules and blocks covered in this chapter. The e-commerce modules can be somewhat complicated to configure, and it's best to be very patient when first setting up your store. Having a clean and professional storefront really makes the difference in your sales. In addition, having general patience throughout the process reduces your install problems as well.

Banner Is Added to Theme But Does Not Display

When adding banner code to Xanthia theme templates, you must always remember to reload your template files. The physical files are not accessed with every page load. Go to the Xanthia Themes Administration page and click the Reload link for your theme.

If your banner still does not display, verify that the template file you edited is being used with the page you are currently browsing. Templates are very dynamic and you might not realize that a similar template file is associated with the actual page you are testing. View the source of the page using your browser. Can you see evidence of your code addition? It might be partially displayed, and what is missing illustrates the problem in your code. If there is no evidence at all, you are either viewing the wrong template, or the templates did not reload.

You can also try removing and readding your theme altogether to clear out cached templates that might be giving you trouble.

Security Alert from the Donations Block

Many of the donations blocks use <form> tags. External systems like PayPal often require the tags for their code to work. You are receiving the security messages because your PostNuke site is concerned about the use of the <form> tag, which is disabled in the default install.

Your options are to either ignore the security alerts, or go into your site's Website Settings page and allow the <form> tag through the table at the bottom of the page.

File Has Been Encoded with the ionCube PHP Encoder

This error message occurs when you attempt to install a module encoded by ionCube's utilities without having the Loader installed to read the files. You need to download the appropriate ionCube Loader DLL or SO from their website (www.ioncube.com) and install it per their instructions.

Install of the Loader is very simple and requires the editing of your php.ini file as well as the copy of the DLL or SO file to the folder referenced in php.ini.

Access Denied to cmsMerchant

This is likely caused by a version incompatibility with your PostNuke version. cmsMerchant is customized for your specific server and domain, and it is only guaranteed to work with the version of PostNuke available at the time of purchase. Customizing or upgrading your PostNuke install might cause a conflict with the module resulting in the preceding error message.

For this problem, you need to contact cmsMerchant support about patches or the possible need to upgrade your module itself.

Next

The following chapter delves into modules that help support the management of your site. It specifically looks at a number of core and third-party modules that provide live user tracking features and display user statistics.

Support and Statistics Modules

You can utilize a number of supporting modules with your site to both help your visitors and make the job of site administration much easier. Support is all about knowing what your users want and providing it to them. Site improvements can be better targeted when you know what areas are important to your users.

The easiest way to compile user needs is by looking at statistics. PostNuke provides a simple core Statistics module, and other third-party modules provide even more details. Some modules also provide live information on what your users are doing at your website. In addition, you can get direct feedback from your users through a frequently asked questions (FAQs) system.

In this chapter, you learn about three main types of support modules:

- Frequently asked questions
- Live user tracking
- Statistics

FAQ

PostNuke includes a basic Frequently Asked Questions module with the core package. It allows your site users to get immediate help with common problems. Each problem is documented in question and answer pairs, and problems can be grouped in custom categories and subcategories you manage through the administration system. Users can also submit new questions you can review for addition to the FAQ database.

Tip

It's a good idea to work out your FAQ categories completely before you start adding questions and answers. It is much easier to make changes to empty categories than it is to move large groups of question data.

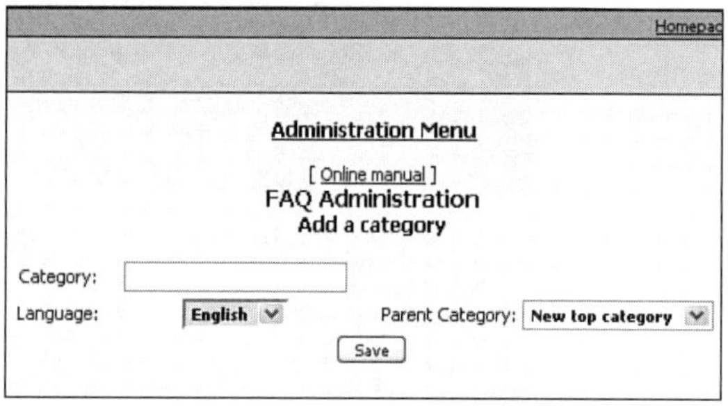

FIGURE 14.1   Creating categories for your FAQ information.

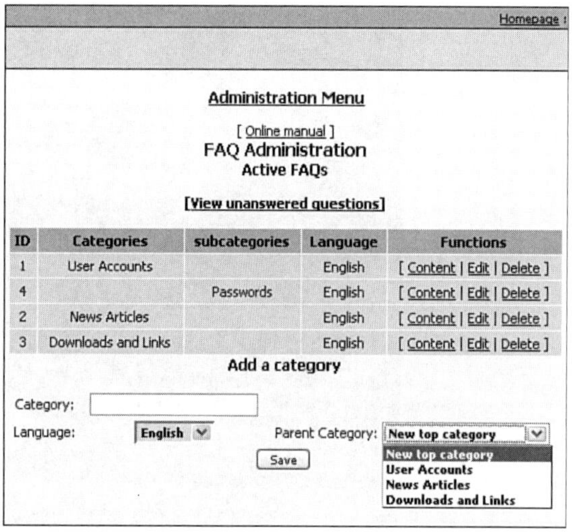

FIGURE 14.2   Creating categories for your FAQ information.

To get started, go to the FAQ Administration page, and you see the form in Figure 14.1. You cannot add any questions until you have created at least one category. Enter the category name "User Accounts," and click the Save button. A new table is added to the form that allows you to add questions to the User Accounts category.

Before adding some sample questions, add a few more top-level categories, such as News Articles and Downloads and Links. Now that you have top categories, you can change the Parent Category drop-down list box to add more subcategories under the new sections you've created. Create a subcategory under User Accounts called Passwords.

You should now have a good skeleton structure you can fill out with information (see Figure 14.2). First add a new question as an administrator to the User Accounts category. Click the Content link under the main table's Functions column for the first row labeled User Accounts.

You now have a very simple entry form with two fields, Question and Answer. Type in the question: "How do I customize my time zone setting?" with the following answer: "Click the 'My Account' link in the Main Menu. Choose 'Change Your Info' from your personal page. You now see a long form of customization options. You can use the drop-down list box labeled 'Time Zone Offset' to set your local time zone. Change the field, and click the Save button at the bottom of the form. Time stamps on the website now reflect your local time."

Click the FAQ link in the Main Menu, and you see what your users will experience. Main categories are listed in bold, and any subcategories are displayed under their headers. Select User Accounts and review the question you just submitted.

Note the link at the top of the page labeled Ask a Question. Your site users can use this link to submit new questions for you to answer and add to the FAQ. Click that link to add another sample question. Users can select top-level categories, if desired, to presort their questions. Choose User Accounts from the Question Category menu. In the Question field, enter "How do I change my password?" and submit the form.

Tip

You can easily see when new questions have been submitted by using the Incoming block installed by default. It displays dynamically under the Main Menu and alerts you of any waiting content.

Now return to the FAQ Administration page. A special link above the category table is called View Unanswered Questions; click this link to check user submissions. From this page (see Figure 14.3), you can review all submitted user questions and either answer those important enough to add to the system or delete those that are not.

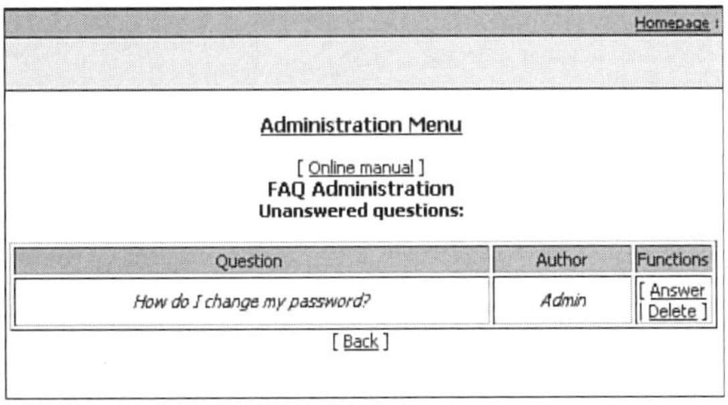

FIGURE 14.3   Answering user questions or deleting unwanted submissions.

In this case, click the Answer link. Notice the Category drop-down has User Accounts already selected. This was submitted through the user interface, but you want to specify the more appropriate Passwords subcategory you already created. The answer to this question happens to be very similar to the previous time zone example. Use this text for the answer: "Click the 'My Account' link in the Main Menu. Choose 'Change Your Info' from your personal page. You now see a long form of customization options. At the very bottom of the form are two text boxes by the Password label. Enter your new password into both text boxes, and click the Save Changes button to complete the change." Save your changes to add the question to your site.

You could simply wait for your users to submit new questions to build up your FAQ database, but your site will benefit greatly from having the more obvious questions available to users immediately. Consider your visitors carefully, put yourself in their shoes, and determine the information they will most likely need to know, and of that information, determine what needs explanation the most. General site functions like the previous examples might be considerably less important than explaining the unique information or services your site provides.

It's also possible to use the advanced article modules covered in Chapter 12, "Enhanced Article Modules," as FAQ and general information systems. Determining which module(s) are right for you takes some testing, and you might find that what worked great initially should later be replaced by a different system. New modules are constantly being written, and not all modules scale progressively with your site's growth.

Live User Tracking

Actively tracking users on a site might sound like Big Brother is watching, but in reality, it provides an interactive communication resource that promotes site community. Who's Online systems list active users and can show what areas of your site are most popular. In the following sections, you explore the Tracking module included with PostNuke and a third-party alternative with additional features you might want.

Online Block

For simple user tracking, a core PostNuke block is available called Online. A block instance of Online is configured by default, so you can see an example of this core block very easily (see Figure 14.4) beneath the Main Menu.

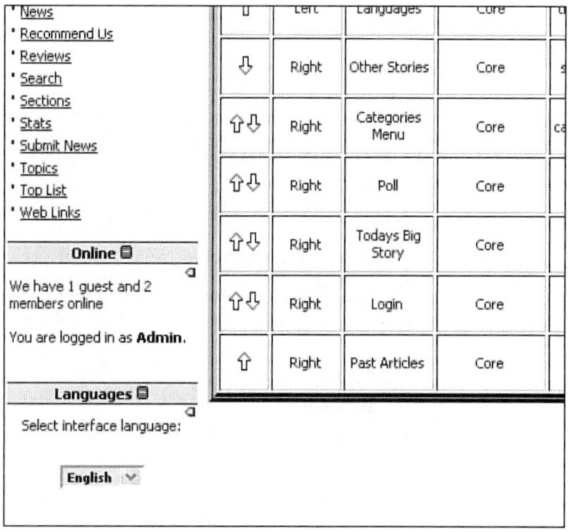

FIGURE 14.4   Seeing how many visitors are on your website.

The block is relatively simple and is created using the Core/online block setting. It shows a count of guests and users and offers a reminder which account you are currently logged in with. Guest users are prompted to register. The Online block also automatically displays private message notices.

The Online block provides a nice set of features, but is limited with minimal customization options and no way to see specific online usernames.

pnBloodhound

The pnBloodhound module tracks live users on your website by displaying their username and location in a convenient block. With this module, you can easily see the IP addresses and host information of your users and note session dates and times. Like the Online block, pnBloodhound integrates with private messaging, or PM, but in addition to the standard PostNuke PM, you can also use Portalzone's pmBox, PNphpBB2 messaging, or turn off private messaging support altogether.

Version 0.62 is included in this text's download materials, or you can get the current version from www.pnaddons.com. pnBloodhound's archive comes cleanly packed in its own directory, which should be uncompressed and placed in your site's modules folder. Initialize and activate the module through the Administration Menu, as you have done with other third-party modules.

When you first enter the pnBloodhound administration screen, you are presented with the Module Name Correlations listing. When viewing user information, the current areas of your website visitors are using is displayed with the users' names. pnBloodhound automatically detects all installed modules and through the name listing allows you to customize the display of those areas with more friendly names.

Note

Modules installed after pnBloodhound are not immediately named in the Module Name Correlations list. Assign a name in the list to new modules to remove the "Unknown" label.

The configuration page seen in Figure 14.5 provides an extensive set of options in four main sections:

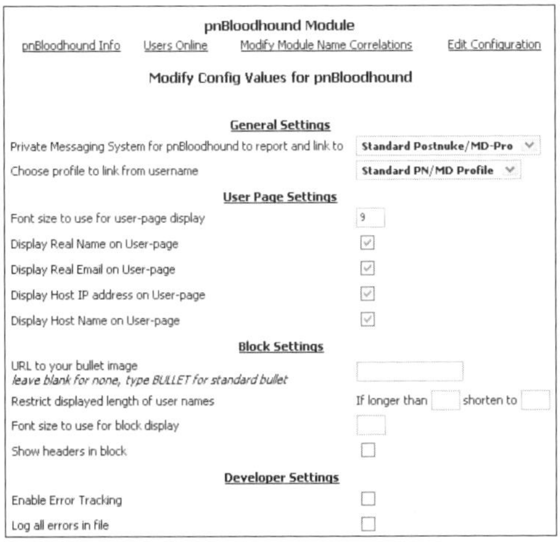

- General Settings
- User Page Settings
- Block Settings
- Developer Settings

The General Settings options let you choose how pnBloodhound integrates with other modules on your site. You can select which personal messaging system you want to use and which profile is linked from user references. Of course, you need to have the other systems, such as PNphpBB2, installed to use the integration.

By clicking the Users Online link, you see your users' information is displayed in a simple table. This table is configured with the User Page Settings. The font size option lets you shrink the

FIGURE 14.5 Changing pnBloodhound's configuration.

font size as needed to prevent the breaking of your theme due to the screen becoming too wide. You can select which information is displayed using the additional check boxes.

Block Settings change how your pnBloodhound block displays its information. You can add bullets to each item, crop usernames, adjust font size to prevent theme breaking, and turn headers on or off.

Most users can freely ignore the Developer Settings. You might find running the Garbage Collection feature more often improves your performance.

Except for the aforementioned options, pnBloodhound functions much like the core Online block. If you feel the core block works well but just needs a few more features, this is the module for you.

PostNuke Statistics

Live user tracking can provide an invaluable interactive tool for some sites, but if you are more interested in raw data and timeliness is not a factor, a Statistics module might fit your needs better. Statistics often document additional information not found in Who's Online systems. Gathering statistical information does not require special blocks on your pages and will likely have a lesser impact on your site's performance.

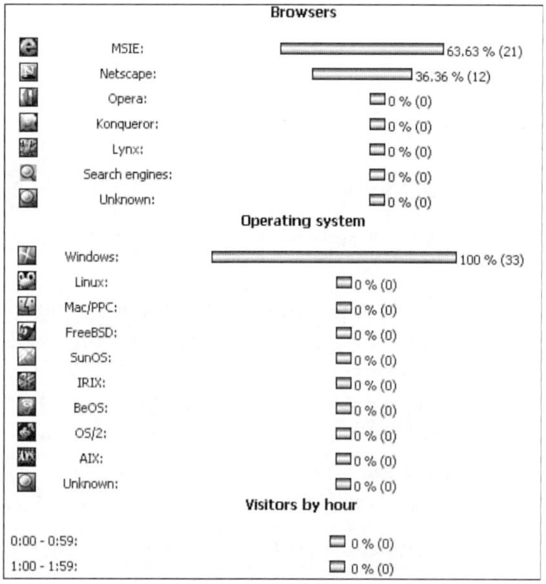

FIGURE 14.6 Core PostNuke statistics.

Core Stats

PostNuke includes a nice Statistics page as part of its core install package. You reach this page be clicking on the Stats link in the Main Menu. Like the Online block, it has no additional configuration options; you can choose to use it or disable it.

The data is broken up on the page into seven parts. At the top of the page are three paragraphs that summarize the access data, including page view count totals and which days and hours are most or least popular.

The following two sections provide comparative count totals for Browsers and Operating Systems. In Figure 14.6, you can see an example of both Internet Explorer and Netscape/Mozilla visitors using Windows for an operating system.

The Visitors by Hour, Visitors by Day of the Week, and Visitors by Month sections all relate to when users like to visit your site. These statistics enable you to predict peak and high-usage times when you might need to watch your server load.

Tip

Check your statistics to know when your site is used the least. Schedule server maintenance or upgrades during those low-usage times to minimize downtime for most of your users.

The final section contains a group of Miscellaneous Statistics. The majority are simply count totals of current data in various site modules. In addition, you can conform your PostNuke distribution's version with the final line of statistical data.

Statistics

The Statistics module from Mountain Research and Development (www.mtrad.com) acts as a complete replacement for the core Stats and Referer modules. It combines all collected user data into a unified interface and includes separate reporting functions with detailed options allowing you to generate custom reports. Statistics v5 is included in the book materials, or you can download the latest version from the preceding uniform resource locator (URL).

Unzip the entire contents of the zip file into your modules directory. Regenerate your modules table to initialize and activate Statistics. To complete the installation, you need to make a minor addition to the pnAPI file. In the root of your server is an includes folder; look for the pnAPI file there. The full path to the file is this:

```
/includes/pnAPI.php
```

Open the file in a standard ASCII text editor. Look for the pnInit function that starts at line 296. Now scroll slowly down to the "other includes" section of the function, which is around line 377. The code you should see is as follows:

```
// Other other includes
    include 'includes/advblocks.php';
    include 'includes/pnHTML.php';
    include 'includes/pnMod.php';
    // inclusion of pnrender class — jn
    include 'includes/pnRender.class.php';
    include 'includes/counter.php';
    include 'includes/queryutil.php';
    include 'includes/xhtml.php';
    include 'includes/oldfuncs.php';
```

```
// Cross-Site Scripting attack defense - Sent by larsneo
// some syntax checking against injected javascript
$pnAntiCrackerMode = pnConfigGetVar('pnAntiCracker');
if ( $pnAntiCrackerMode == 1 ) {
    pnSecureInput();
}

// Handle referer
if (pnConfigGetVar('httpref') == 1) {
    include 'referer.php';
    httpreferer();
}
```

After the `Handle referer` section, add the following lines:

```
// Added for Statistics v5 module
include 'modules/statistics/collect.php';
```

Save the file and your module is ready for configuration.

Go to the Statistics Administration page, and click the Maintain Data Tables link in the top navigation. This page allows you to manage the data collected for Statistics. The top two forms allow you to clear out old data, including the removal of data within a specific date range. This is very useful if you feel your site received unrealistic traffic for a period of time and you need to adjust the content to reflect normal numbers.

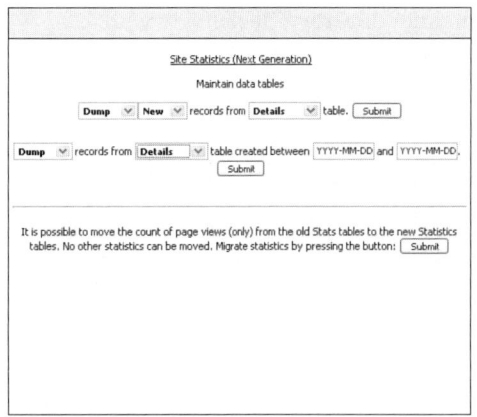

At the bottom of this form (see Figure 14.7), you have the opportunity to migrate date from the core Stats module. If your site has been live for some time, there might be a great deal of good visitor data maintained by the default Stats module. For most sites, there should be no reason to throw that data away. You can move that data from Stats into the Statistics module by clicking the last Submit button.

FIGURE 14.7   Managing statistic data.

Now return to the Statistics main administration screen and click the Parameter Configuration link. Initially, Statistics is not actively collecting data. To turn the module on, you need to check the Collect Statistics? check box and submit the form (see Figure 14.8).

The rest of the Parameter fields can be left as their defaults to include all collected data, or you can filter and consolidate the data to return a simplified or simply abridged report. Filters are especially useful to remove unwanted data, such as the activity of administrators or search engine spiders. Four filter fields are available:

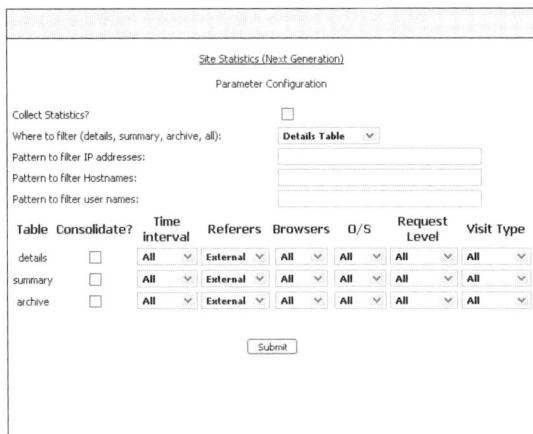

- **Where to Filter**—Selects the table you want to filter: Details, Summary, Archive, All Tables, or No Filtering.

- **Pattern to Filter IP Addresses**—Specifies the IP address(es) that should be filtered out.

- **Pattern to Filter Hostnames**—Specifies the client hostname(s) that should be filtered out.

- **Pattern to Filter Usernames**—Specifies the username(s) that should be filtered out.

FIGURE 14.8   Managing statistic data.

IP addresses must be entered using a backward slash before the period between numbers, such as 10\.1\.300\.125. Users are filtered by entering their usernames, where multiple usernames should be separated by a pipe | character.

Consolidation options can remove data considered unimportant or too detailed. For example, if you know you only want to see the hourly or daily page views, there is no reason to maintain more detailed information. The table data can be consolidated to keep the simplified data.

Note

Data consolidation is permanent. If you simplify the Statistics data, the details are gone and cannot be recovered.

Click the Maintain Data Tables link in the main navigation bar. Multiple tables are provided to allow you to maintain current data Details, consolidate a Summary report, and Archive old data. You can move data between tables using the Maintain Data Tables page, or simply delete unwanted data altogether.

The Site Statistics Reports page, also available from the main navigation bar, provides the form you use to generate custom reports. The Start Date is automatically populated using the Site Start Date in the Site Settings. By default, PostNuke has "03.2006" in that field, which does not work with the Statistics module. You should change that date, if you have not already done so, and use the format: YYYY-MM-DD.

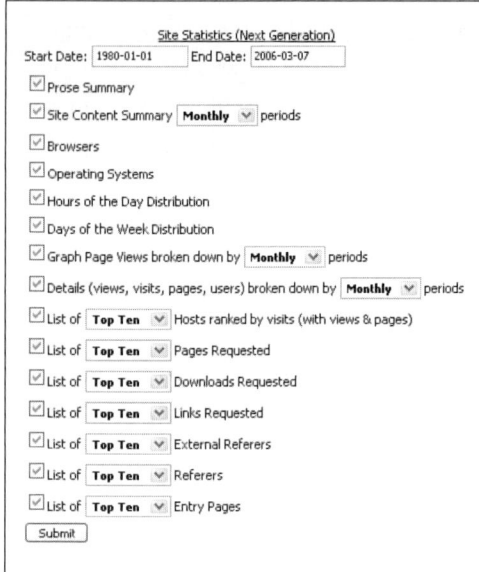

FIGURE 14.9 Customizing your report contents.

Set the End Date to a day in the future to generate a report of all data. You must select at least one of the check box options to get results from your submission. You should initially select all options, as shown in Figure 14.9, to better understand what each provides.

The Prose Summary option displays a condensed report in plain sentences above the result tables. The paragraphs are comparable to the data returned by the core Stats module, though a little more clearly formatted.

The Site Content Summary is related to the Miscellaneous Stats table from the core module. It shows additions to Users, Stories, Comments, Downloads, and Links for the site. Unlike Stats, the Statistics numbers are broken out by month and provide a timeline you can use to chart your site's growth.

Statistics has the same counts for Browsers, Operating Systems, and Visitors by Hour, Day, and Month, but it cleanly removes unneeded 0% data from the graphs to make a more polished report. For the Site Content Summary, Page Views, and Details graphs, you also have a drop-down list box to customize the time periods. Each can display information Hourly, Daily, Weekly, Monthly, or Yearly.

The seven listing features in the report are as follows:

- **List of Hosts Ranked by Visits**—Displays a table listing the names of the hosts that have visited the site and the number of visits, views, and unique pages listed for each host. The listing is sorted in rank fashion by the number of visits made during the selected reporting period.

- **List of Pages Requested**—Displays the names of the pages requested and the number of respective requests in a table. The listing is sorted in rank fashion by the number of views during the reporting period.

- **List of Downloads Requested**—Displays a table of downloads requested and the number of requests listed for each file. The listing is sorted in rank fashion by the number of requests during the reporting period.

- **List of Links Requested**—Displays a list of requested links and the number of times each was requested. The listing is sorted in rank fashion by the number of requests during the reporting period.

- **List of External Referers**—Displays the external referer links used to access your site with the respective visits and percentages. Internal referers and bookmarks are not included in this report. The listing is sorted in rank fashion by the number of views during the reporting period.

- **List of Referers**—Displays a complete table listing of all referers to pages in your site with the respective visits and percentages. This list includes internal page links within your site and user accesses by bookmarks. The listing is sorted in rank fashion by the number of views during the reporting period.

- **List of Entry Pages**—Displays a listing of the pages that were visited first by users. The pages have to be linked directly from another site or accessed through a bookmark. The total entry visits and percentages are also displayed respectively. The listing is sorted in rank fashion by the number of views during the reporting period.

For each listing, a drop-down list box allows you to select the number of items returned: Top 10, Top 20, Top 25, Top 50, Top 100, or All. Ten is the default setting.

You can also set up a Statistics page link using a standard menu block, such as the Main Menu. Go to your site's Blocks Administration table and edit the Main Menu block. For this example, replace the core Stats link with the new Statistics module. Change the Title to "Statistics" and the URL to "{statistics}." Some or all of the other module URLs already entered into the menu might have square [] brackets around the module names. Older modules use those brackets while the newer pnAPI–compliant modules use {} brackets. Now click the Submit Changes button to save the block.

Note

The core Stats and third-party Statistics modules can run concurrently. If you want to keep the link to Stats, just add a new link line as detailed previously, and both modules are accessible.

The Main Menu link is initially visible to all visitors on your site. You can customize permissions to the block link so it only appears to certain groups (use the Main Menu:Statistics: instance), such as administrators, if desired. The separated report and administration components of Statistics make it possible to set permissions for each area.

Troubleshooting

You're unlikely to have problems with the core modules and blocks discussed in this chapter. The core PostNuke components are very consistent after your Content Management System (CMS) install is complete. Third-party module integration is always a moving target, and you might find issues using version combinations that are not fully tested. Some of the more common issues found with these third-party modules are outlined in the following sections.

Inconsistent pnBloodhound Data

pnBloodhound only tracks users that visit a PostNuke page that includes the module's block. For consistent data, you must be certain the block appears on all pages. Depending on the theme you are using, it might require additional changes to make the block universal. Xanthia themes can be especially difficult to adjust to include universal modules.

Also due to the way PostNuke and PHP itself handle sessions, it is not possible to track all visitors. If your site has static pages, user traffic to those areas is not tracked. Search engine bots and spiders (and possibly some visitors) might not trigger a load of the block and, therefore, remain invisible.

"undefined constant" in Statistics Parameter Configuration

You might see this error message at the top of the Statistics Parameter Configuration page:

```
Notice: Use of undefined constant _MONTH - assumed '_MONTH' in [your server
path]/modules/statistics/pnadmin.php on line 86
```

This is a known issue in Statistics v5, and it is easy to fix. Edit the `admin.php` file at the following path:

```
/modules/statistics/pnlang/eng/admin.php
```

Around line 70, you see a series of time-related definitions. Insert this line:

```
define('_MONTH','Month');  // added for bug fix
```

between `Day` and `External`, as shown in the following code segment:

```
    define('_ARCHIVE','Archive');
    define('_ALL','All');
    define('_MINUTE','Minute');
    define('_HOUR','Hour');
    define('_DAY','Day');
    define('_MONTH','Month');  // added for bug fix
```

```
define('_EXTERNAL','External');
define('_NONE','None');
define('_FUNCTION','Function');
```

Save the change and the error message is gone.

Statistics Collect Stats Check Box Doesn't Remain Checked

Some versions of PostNuke seem to have a problem with the automated install of Statistics. First try selecting the check box again and resubmit. If that fails, deactivate the module, remove it from PostNuke, and then reinstall it cleanly a second time. Confirm that the Statistics folder's permissions allow writing to the directory. Should the automated installs not produce a working system, your only option is a manual install.

The manual process has more steps and can be a bit more complicated. The complete manual install instructions are available online in the module's official readme document at http://www.mtrad.com/statistics_README.php.

Next

In the next chapter, you will look at custom theme design and development. You will take a short crash course in design and learn what elements make your design work. Then, you will look at putting together your own website design to make your PostNuke site unique.

Customized Themes

15

This chapter looks at what it takes to design and develop a custom theme for your PostNuke site. PostNuke provides many interface features and components to make it easy to develop your site. How you use many of these components is up to you.

This chapter delves into the basics of theme design, including a crash course in design, and you examine ways to customize new themes for your site, including an overview of the AutoTheme module. The chapter is divided into the following main sections:

- Theme design
- Jump-starting your theme
- AutoTheme

Theme Design

You should consider two main focuses when designing a successful theme: form and function. The two parts might seem at odds on occasion, but well-designed themes always provide a balance between the two elements.

When most people think about site design, they concern themselves with the image and appearance of a website. Acknowledgment of brand identity and successful communication of a design's impression on visitors are both important goals, but a site that does not provide adequate navigation or contain all desired information is more likely to lose visitors than keep them.

The following sections look at visual design guidelines to ensure your site is attractive to visitors and cover tips and techniques to ensure the site's interface works with users to connect them with online content.

Crash Course in Design

Throughout this section, you learn basic rules that you can use to make a successful web design. These methods are standards you can certainly explore in greater detail by taking courses or reading books specifically on design, but as this is a book on PostNuke and not design, they are presented here as refined instructions you can apply to even the simplest designs to create a professional polish for your site.

Design to Fit Your Content

Your site's design communicates to your visitors as much as your content, and it does it at a glance, much faster than it takes to read your introductory paragraph. When planning and creating your website design, be certain it is appropriate for the content it frames. A site serving wedding information shouldn't look like a World War II history site any more than a crayon-inspired kids' interface applies to a company site in the technology industry.

Select your colors, fonts, and layout to suit the subject matter in the site. The tone for a site is set immediately at the first load. The balance between content and design is as important as color and imagery. Having cluttered content so packed it's nearly impossible to see where to begin is not a path to success; for most sites, effective use of whitespace makes your content more legible. Furthermore, content that is easy to read gets read.

Select Appropriate and Effective Colors

The choice of color can make or break a design. It's important to select and apply well-suited colors to your layout, and to help you stay on the right track, consider the following rules of thumb:

- **Use Few Colors to Maintain Clarity**—Excessive colors create clutter. Before you design an interface, select the specific colors you want to use for your design and consider them your palette. Try to stick to four or five main background colors and your one text color.

- **Analogous and Monochromatic Colors Create Harmony**—Similar colors naturally go together. A monochromatic color scheme uses variants, tints, or shades of the same color, such as a series of blues. Analogous colors are found adjacent on the color wheel, for example orange, red-orange, and red.

- **Be Careful with Complementary Colors**—Colors that sit opposite one another on the color wheel are considered complementary. Red and green, blue and orange, yellow and purple all provide very strong contrast, but with many site designs, the contrast can be too great. Large areas of complementary colors can make an interface very aggressive, motley, or even riotous. That all said, subtle use of complementary colors can be a useful tool. A small splash of red on a generally green backdrop draws the viewer's attention very effectively.

- **Warm and Cool Colors Create Tone and Depth**—Natural colors add an unconscious tone to your design. Warm reds and oranges denote energy and activity; blues and greens provide a cool, calming feel. Warm colors also visually appear closer to the viewer than cool colors. Cool colors are shadow colors, colors in the background, whereas warm hues are sharper and attract more attention in the foreground.

- **Contrast "Colors" and "Metals" to Make Text Sharp**—The metals in this case are gold and silver, meaning the various shades of yellow and white. Colors are other nonmetal primary colors, such as blue, black, red, green, and purple. To achieve the sharpest and easiest-to-read text, always make your text either a color or a metal with a background in the opposite group; for example, black color text on white metal background. Other good combinations include white on red, yellow on black, purple on yellow, and white on green.

Tip

You can manage your color selections with cascading style sheets to make experimentation easier. By defining colors in your styles, a few changes in your styles let you view your site with alternative choices.

These color concepts are illustrated in Figure 15.1. The printed figure is grayscale for this text, but you can download the image with the online materials for this chapter. Each color swatch is also labeled with a hex code to make the specific colors clear.

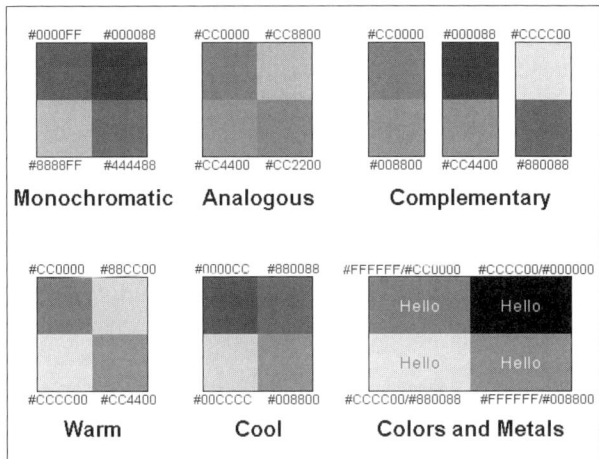

FIGURE 15.1   Common PostNuke site layout.

Websites Are Not Meant to Be Printed

This might seem obvious, but for many site developers, printing support is a common dilemma. Websites are a unique medium, just as the same content printed or spoken is conveyed separate and distinctive. Modern websites are saturated with dynamic content and animation in a way that will never be printable—no matter what design they employ.

If you need to provide print capabilities for your site, you should have your dynamic content applied to a print view that strips out all the colors and navigation layout. Many PostNuke modules include the ability to view page content in alternate printer-friendly layouts, so you should never be concerned about designing printing support into the main site layout itself.

Design to Screen Resolutions

More than half of the computer users in the world have monitors set to 1,024¥768 resolution. A shrinking 35% use 800¥600. Nearly all of the remaining screens are larger than 1,024¥768, with very small percentages lower than 800¥600. The trend is moving toward the higher resolutions, but you can expect 800¥600 to remain a standard minimum target well into 2006.

All this means you need to consider your visitors' screen resolution when designing the layout of your site. To support 800¥600 users, a design must be able to function at a minimum width when the users' browsers are maximized to full screen. Subtracting out the average widths of browsers' window frames and scrollbars leaves about 770 pixels to work with. Even designs that can stretch to an unlimited width should be compressible to at least 770 pixels. A design larger than this can result in horizontal scrolling, and very few people like scrolling horizontally.

Selecting the Right Typeface: Serif Versus Sans Serif

Serifs are the little projections accenting the ends of the strokes that make up a letter. They are designed to help the eye stick to the line and make reading the site easier. In the print world, you will find standard Serif fonts such as Times New Roman used almost exclusively for regular text.

Sans Serif typefaces like the popular Arial and Verdana fonts are more modern, coming to light in the last century. They became popular in print due to a desire for more type variety, especially in advertising, but they are especially important for website design.

Printed text materials are created with a very high resolution, usually hundreds of dots per inch. Computer monitors, on the other hand, display at much lower settings, usually around 72dpi. Serifs become a problem at low dpi—when they are harder to render with only a few pixels available. At small sizes, Serifs are distorted or not displayed on the screen at all, and when the typeface is designed to use Serifs, unclear display can hurt readability.

Using Sans Serif fonts on your website can solve this problem. Sans Serifs are designed to display clearly without the leading serifs, and they retain readability on computer screens even at smaller sizes. It's for this reason the vast majority of websites today incorporate Sans Serif fonts.

> **Tip**
>
> Use fonts that are very common across different operating systems to be certain your site displays correctly. The common Sans Serif family group includes Verdana, Arial, and Trebuchet MS. For Serif fonts, use Georgia, Times New Roman, and Courier New. Verdana and Georgia are wider fonts and specifically designed to be more readable on computer screens. For more variety, Arial Black, Impact, and Comic Sans MS are also found across different operating systems.

When in doubt, use Sans Serif fonts on your site. You really can't go wrong no matter what your size or layout. There are instances in which Serif fonts are good for larger titles or design effects, but most sites should use Serif fonts sparingly. CSS also supports the use of generic font families, such as serif, sans-serif, cursive, fantasy, and monospace. Use a family designation to help ensure your viewers get the right font.

When to Break the Rules

All these rules might seem very constraining, but they are, at heart, guidelines. Just because a design technique is standard, you are not locked into applying the technique the same every time. Good design comes from the application of many combined features, and often a better design can result from the breaking of the right rule at the right time.

If you break all the rules, your site will more than likely become a jumbled mess. The key is creating a professional, consistent design that works with your content, and doesn't interfere with your content. Design should be primarily used in a subtle way to enhance content, but having a standout visual element can make your site more memorable, and memorable sites get return traffic.

Make Your Design Work

Sites that rely on the attraction of public visitors must acknowledge the true secret to success is maintaining return traffic. Thousands of dollars can be spent on marketing to increase site hits, but if those visitors don't find anything to make them return later, the increase is only a temporary inflation. Creating a quality site that's functional and useful to your users is essential.

The previous section was concerned with purely visual design, but the following techniques illustrate steps you can take to create a layout that does more than just look good.

Navigation Must Be Clear, Consistent, and Redundant

If visitors can't find their way around your site, they will never see your content. It is important to provide a clear, simple navigation system visitors can use. After you have a navigation system designed, it should remain consistently placed in the same location throughout your site. Moving the links around only forces users to need to look for them.

The majority of sites place their links to the left or top of the page. It's okay to creatively place navigation elements elsewhere, or to break them into separate tiered levels that display in different locations. Having a consistent position for your navigation system generates a rhythm for your site, and even if it is nontraditional, your visitors will quickly be able to predict where to find the links they need.

Break Out of the Box
PostNuke, like nearly all Content Management Systems (CMSs), has a modular layout resulting in a "blocky" feel. Take a look at Figure 15.2.

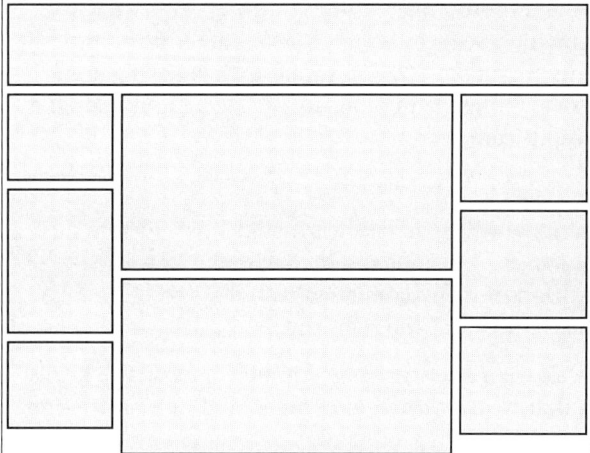

FIGURE 15.2   Common PostNuke site layout.

If you've browsed through a variety of PostNuke sites, you recognize the common theme shown in Figure 15.1. The vast majority of sites use the same top header with a three-column layout. To the designers' credit, PostNuke does lend itself to that layout in its default configuration. But it is built that way simply to provide an example of how you can organize site content in a modular way.

However, it is purely a guideline. You don't have to make every site the same; the incredible diversity of designs displayed by non-PostNuke sites on the Web set the right example. For starters, make your design asymmetrical. It's very easy to change the default themes slightly to achieve a custom effect.

Even though the standard block areas are labeled "left" and "right," there is no reason why they must remain in those positions. Those are simply labels. You can rename the labels to be "area 1" and "area 2," or anything you like. Take a look at Figure 15.3. The blocks in this example have been made horizontal above the main content area.

FIGURE 15.3 Placing block areas horizontal for a unique effect.

Even the relative standard of having all the small blocks the same size in columns or even rows is unnecessary. If your site would benefit from having completely customized content areas and layout, there would be no reason to use the defaults included with PostNuke. It can create any site layout you need. PostNuke is a content management tool with many options. The more options you elect and adapt, the more your site is customized to your needs (see Figure 15.4).

Finally, even though PostNuke content is defined in modular pieces, which by design need to be square and boxy to make them easily placeable, the graphic design you place under your content—that colorizes and decorates your content to join the pieces into a site—does not need to be boxy or blocky itself. Use fields of color to group the content areas and break across the imaginary lines drawn by the code.

Most PostNuke themes incorporate a template for each block. The template frames the content into a box. In design, the use of boxes to frame content is generally a bad decision; it appears amateurish. PostNuke lets you template every content element, but you don't have to border them in an obvious way. Consider, for example, a column of vertical blocks. Simplify the template for those blocks to only format the text, and instead theme the area in the page template with a solid band of color. The blocks lose their boxy individuality and combine to make a column of content.

FIGURE 15.4 Customizing your site layout.

Place Content to Lead the Reader's Eye

You should always place your content in ways that effectively lead a reader around the page. The top of any page is always seen first, but you can use your design to draw readers down to other areas on the page. This is done by the use of leading lines, invisible lines drawn between page elements.

For example, suppose you have a series of content pieces each titled in bold text. Just having the titles stronger than the rest of the content prompts a reader to glance through the titles. A splash of color like red placed in key areas of the design naturally draws one's eye from the last marker to the next.

Even the alignment of your text is a tool. Content aligned together is read together. This works even if one paragraph is aligned to a right edge, and the next is aligned left to the same point (see Figure 15.5). You can use this technique to great effect, especially in larger areas with blocks aligned to different sides.

But as with all things design, moderation is important. If you have too many visual cues, your pages can become distracting. Visitors might spend more time being lead around a page than reading the content it presents. Emphasize certain areas of the page to be certain they are seen, and use a general flow of consistent alignment and formatting to do the rest.

FIGURE 15.5 Using leading lines to help visitors read content.

Design for Speed

No one likes to stare at a blank screen. It's very important to provide a design that loads swiftly. Having a powerful, well-managed server caching its pages for speed only helps reduce bottlenecks at the server. If your design is very large and cumbersome, it still takes a while for a user to load.

The solution is intelligent use of images. You want to reduce the quantity of images that need to be loaded and shrink the overall combined file size of those images. Every image is another request that has to be sent all the way to the server, and often having one larger image takes less time to load than multiple smaller images of a mathematically smaller file size.

Look for areas in which you can reduce or eliminate images altogether. Color areas using style codes instead of background images. If you need an image in the background, tile it from a very small original size. Look for ways you can reuse images instead of having multiple graphics that are very similar.

And, above all, *compress* those images hard. You really need to know how to compress your images and which format to use. The JPEG format (from the Joint Photographic Experts Group) is great for photos and graphics containing many different colors mixed together. JPEGs get "fuzzy" when compressed, which can be unnoticeable in some designs but very obvious in others. The Graphics Interchange Format (GIF) is designed for flat color, such as cartoons and charts; it is limited to 256 colors, but includes an alpha channel with one color for transparency and it retains sharpness even when highly compressed.

> **Tip**
>
> Decrease the color depth of GIFs and PNGs to produce incredibly small file sizes. A lower bit-depth performed carefully can sometimes beat the file size of a well-compressed JPG format for a photo image. Drop the colors as low as possible while still retaining image clarity.

Portable Network Graphics (PNG) is a format designed to replace GIF. With the same palette and color depth, PNG is often smaller than GIF file sizes. PNG also possesses a true alpha channel for smooth transitions and can perform animations using the Multiple-image Network Graphics (MNG) format. The problem with PNG is that most users unfamiliar with the details of the formats have trouble getting the most out of the image type, and their PNG files end up being larger than GIFs. And although both Amaya (www.w3.org/Amaya/) and Mozilla (www.mozilla.org) have done a good job keeping up with image standards, other browsers including Internet Explorer have very poor support for many of the features that make PNG better than GIF, most notably full alpha channel and color support.

All that can seem very complicated to someone without a graphic design background, so if you are having problems deciding what to use, the simplest method is to take a given image for your site and save it in all three formats. Try compressing them if you want; save different versions with different levels of compression, and then test in your browser to see which is the smallest of those that look good. Use that image and delete the rest.

Try to keep your total image size under 50K. A 56K modem on a good day can pull 4–5K per second. Broadband connections on a bad day can drop that low, but are usually better. So if you can keep the total under 50K, your site loads in 10 seconds or less for the majority of your visitors. Having a swift page load also means less overall weight on your server, making improvements on the server-side more effective and able to handle additional concurrent users.

Test in Multiple Browsers

The majority of Web users in the world currently use Internet Explorer to browse sites. That has not always been the case, nor is it likely to be in the future if current trends continue. The market share of the Mozilla Firefox browser has been steadily growing, and that growth, as well as its focus on standards support, suggests the Firefox browser should not be ignored. It's always strongly recommended that you develop to World Wide Web Consortium (W3C; www.w3.org) standards and test display of your site in multiple browser brands. The W3C also provides a markup validation service for easy testing at validator.w3.org.

If you are developing to a fixed audience, such as an intranet site for internal company employees, you know what browser brands and versions to expect. But for public sites, it can be harder to predict. It is easier and saves more time in the long run to simply create your sites to suit all visitors, no matter their browser.

That means you need to refrain from the use of proprietary tags, but even a site optimized for one browser type can be made very functional for other browsers, even if the result is that the view in other browsers is slightly less attractive. Maintain cross-browser functionality and you will be fine. A good table of tags can be found at EchoEcho.com (www.echoecho.com/htmlreference.htm); any tag not marked in the W3C column is proprietary.

Jump-Starting Your Theme

You can, of course, develop your theme from scratch, starting with only a blank page and your imagination. That might work fine if you are familiar with PostNuke and the technical ways to integrate content into themes, but if you would rather have some examples and structure to go on, you can get a head start with theme development in a variety of ways.

In Chapter 10, "Themes," you looked at the Xanthia theme system that provides a modular templated structure for developing your site design. You can easily take the pnDefault theme included with PostNuke and modify its templates and configuration to create a new theme. If you are just starting out with PostNuke, this is probably the best way to begin. It doesn't require the install of any third-party modules, and you can tweak the Xanthia themes fairly easily.

After you start getting into more serious custom theme development, you might want to give AutoTheme a try. Xanthia is a great theme engine, and it provides many of the same features found in AutoTheme, but the Xanthia Theme Engine (XTE) included in PostNuke .750 is in its first integrated release and is not nearly as polished as the much older AutoTheme system. Heavily customized PostNuke theme development can be accomplished in AutoTheme faster than in the new Xanthia release, and layout and design options are possible with AutoTheme now that are not yet available to Xanthia themes.

No matter what theme system you end up going with, the fastest way to get a theme going is to use one that has already been developed. Download one of the thousands of example themes available online and load it up. Browse through its template files and code and see how it works. If you find good parts in half a dozen themes that you need for your theme, pull them and combine them.

This method of "sampling" from other themes is quite common with open source code. The point of open source is that development advances faster through the combined efforts of everyone involved. Just place a note in the file saying where you got the code, so next time your own theme is downloaded by someone else, he knows where to look for more good examples.

AutoTheme

Many PostNuke users also use the AutoTheme (or AT) system (spidean.mckenzies.net) to theme their websites. AutoTheme is a third-party template system that is installed as an alternative to Xanthia and legacy PostNuke themes. It does not outright replace core theme functionality; it adds support for AT themes, which are then available for use alongside any other installed themes.

AutoTheme is available in two versions. AT-Lite is a free download released under the General Public License (GPL). AT-Lite provides a solid foundation for theme development and contains most of the functionality of its commercial cousin. The full version of AutoTheme is a commercial module you must purchase to use. It provides the complete AT-Lite feature set with the addition of these extras:

- Full page caching for significantly decreased load times

- Online Hypertext Markup Language (HTML) editor and color selector in the admin

- Theme and custom module previewing in the admin

- Dedicated support

- Access to Extras (plug-ins) and professional themes only for purchasers

- Also, the commercial version has development priority, and is developed with new versions released more frequently

AT-Lite

The free version of AutoTheme is, nonetheless, packed with features. The download for AT-Lite .8 is available with the download materials, or you can browse to the official site mentioned previously for the current release.

The AT-Lite installs quite easily. The files in the archive come arranged in folders respective to your PostNuke site's root. You can move the files over separately, or simply decompress the archive from the root folder. After you have all the files in place, initialize and activate the module from your Module Administration table.

> **Note**
>
> AutoTheme comes with a theme called AutoPrint. This additional theme is actually a customizable print interface for your pages that can be used to provide printer-friendly versions of your content.

Now browse to your site's Website Configuration page using the Settings link on the Administration Menu page. To use the AutoTheme administration system, you need to use a non-Xanthia theme. The ExtraLite default theme works fine, but you might find it easier to select the AutoTheme theme that comes with the module. The screenshot examples for this chapter use the AutoTheme theme.

Now return to your Administration screen and select the AutoTheme link. You are taken to the main page shown in Figure 15.6. There are three main components to the management of AutoThemes: Themes, Commands, and Extras.

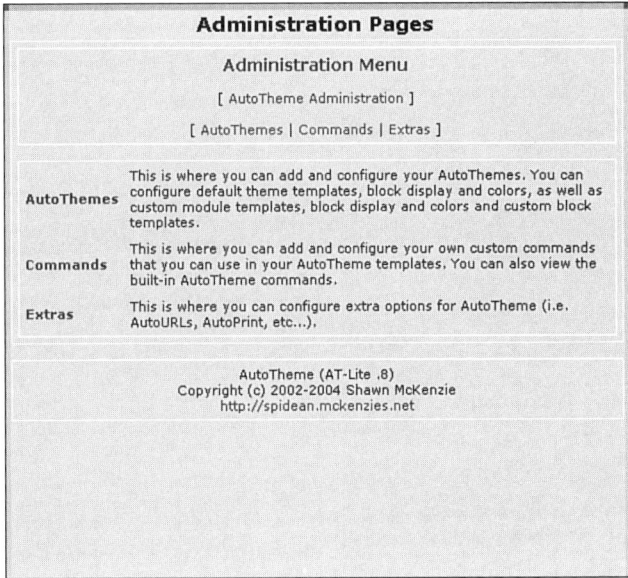

FIGURE 15.6 Administrating your AutoThemes.

AutoTheme Extras

First look at the Extras screen. Extras are additional add-on features you can toggle on and off for your theme. The management screen is shown in Figure 15.7. AutoPrint, Block Titles, AutoTheme Credits, Module Styles, and Theme Information are all enabled by default. AT-Lite provides very clear documentation on how each Extra works, but especially notable features include the following:

- **AutoPrint**—Separates theme used for printer-friendly pages.

- **AutoURLs**—Rewrites the lengthy PostNuke URLs normally displayed with shorter URLs that are easier to reference and more friendly to search engines. It works similarly to the Xanthia feature.

- **Entry Page**—Shows a special page the first time a visitor comes to your site.

- **Head Content**—Allows the customization of the title, meta keywords, and meta description for each module.

- **Module Styles**—Wraps each module's output in a custom style for the module.

- **RTL Languages**—Provides support for languages read from right to left. AutoTheme dynamically shifts all content to a right justification when the appropriate language is chosen for display.

- **Themes on a Date and Theme Time**—Sets special themes to display automatically by date and time.

	Extras		
Extra Name	**Description**	**Enable**	**Action**
AutoTheme Admin Bar	Administration menu bar for AutoTheme configuration and templates	○Yes ⊙No	
RTL Languages	Sets page style for RTL languages	○Yes ⊙No	[Configure]
AutoPrint	Printer friendly theme	⊙Yes ○No	[Configure]
AutoURLs	Updated Short URLs implementation for AutoTheme	○Yes ⊙No	[Configure]
Block titles	Automatically use images for block titles	⊙Yes ○No	
AutoTheme Credits	Add AutoTheme credit and link to footer	⊙Yes ○No	[Configure]
Entry Page	Custom site entry page	○Yes ⊙No	[Configure]
Shortcut Icon	Includes a shortcut icon for your site	○Yes ⊙No	[Configure]
Head content	Head content, title, meta tags and description for each page.	○Yes ⊙No	**
Module Styles	Add style definitions for module content	⊙Yes ○No	
Render Time	Show page render time.	○Yes ⊙No	
Style fixes	Global styles that fix certain incompatibilities between browsers	○Yes ⊙No	
Themes on a Date	Display themes on specific dates	○Yes ⊙No	[Configure]
Theme Time	Display themes on at specific times of the day	○Yes ⊙No	[Configure]
Theme Information	Allows the inclusion of theme information in themes	⊙Yes ○No	*

FIGURE 15.7   Selecting additional Extras plug-ins to enhance your AutoTheme.

Select different Extras and test their effects. The Head Content and Theme Information Extras are both configured under the AutoThemes section covered later.

AutoTheme Commands

AutoTheme makes configuration of additional Commands very easy. This feature is identical to the way Xanthia themes pass scripts and Extensible Hypertext Markup Language (XHTML) to template pages. You take a bit of code you want to reuse, such as a JavaScript drop-down menu or an email address link, and assign it to a variable name such as "myMenu." From within your XHTML template code, you make a call to the variable name within a comment block as follows:

```
<!-- [myMenu] -->
```

AutoTheme knows to check all comments and will recognize the call as a Command. When the page is rendered, the script code is inserted at the named reference. The main difference between how Xanthia handles the variables and AutoTheme's version of the Commands is that AutoTheme provides a user-friendly interface to manage the scripts (see Figure 15.8). You can edit the script source manually too; Commands are saved in the autotheme.cfg file in the AutoTheme module folder. But most users should find the clean administration interface refreshing.

Note

Global Commands are stored in the AutoTheme module's configuration file, and do not transfer with your theme should you try to move it to another server or want to release it to the public. If you want to include Commands with your theme, add them using the theme-specific Commands editor.

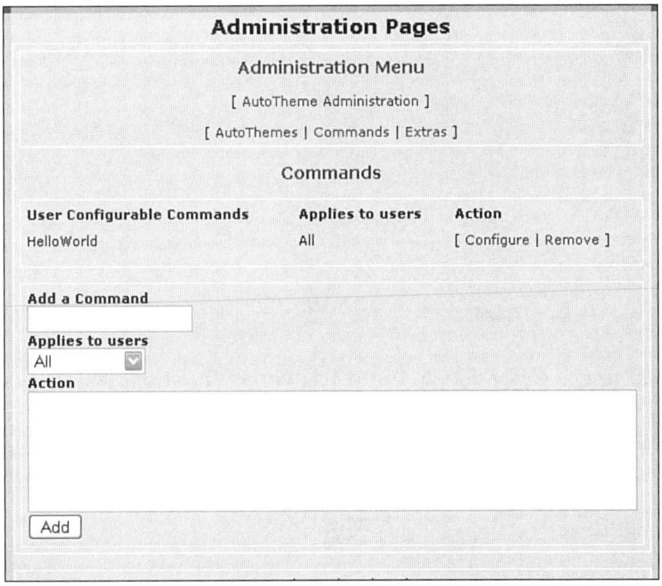

FIGURE 15.8 Managing your script Commands with ease.

Manage AutoThemes

Now click on the AutoThemes link on the left of the navigation bar to manage the installed themes. By default with AT-Lite, you only see the AutoTheme and AutoPrint themes. Upon entering the management area for a specific theme, you are presented with five main options.

The General link allows you to configure the default settings to be used for all pages and blocks that do not otherwise have specific settings. Figure 15.9 shows how you can set specific themes using the easy select menus. From this area, you can also select a block by title from those you have created and define a specific custom theme as well as enter the color codes you want for the theme by hex code.

Default Theme Templates	File name	
Page Template	theme.html	**Strip out head content (from `<head>` to `</head>`?** ⊙ Yes ○ No
Summary Article	summary.html	
First Alternating Summary	summary1.html	**Use Alternating Summaries?**
Second Alternating Summary	summary2.html	⊙ Yes ○ No
Full Article	article.html	
		Show block by default?
Left Blocks	leftblock.html	⊙ Yes ○ No
Center Blocks	centerblock.html	○ Yes ⊙ No
Right Blocks	rightblock.html	○ Yes ⊙ No
Area1 Blocks	area1block.html	○ Yes ⊙ No
Area2 Blocks	area2block.html	○ Yes ⊙ No
Area3 Blocks	area3block.html	○ Yes ⊙ No
Area4 Blocks	area4block.html	○ Yes ⊙ No
Area5 Blocks	area5block.html	○ Yes ⊙ No
Area6 Blocks	area6block.html	○ Yes ⊙ No
Area7 Blocks	area7block.html	○ Yes ⊙ No
Area8 Blocks	area8block.html	○ Yes ⊙ No
Area9 Blocks	area9block.html	○ Yes ⊙ No
First Table		

FIGURE 15.9   Setting custom theme templates for each block.

Custom Modules is a section identical to the *General* area, but it lets you define the options with relation to specific modules. Every module can be configured uniquely, much like the Xanthia system, but in addition, AutoTheme has the Module Options field that makes this ability exponentially more powerful.

To see how it works, look at these sample PostNuke News article URLs:

```
/modules.php?op=modload&name=News&file=article&sid=2
/modules.php?op=modload&name=News&file=index&catid=&topic=15
```

PostNuke commonly has a number of options tacked onto the URL to identify the different specific pages in the CMS. In these examples, you can see the options, such as sid=2 and topic=15, describe the content at that URL. When theming modules, you can add option references like those to the Module Options field to define the theme templates for specific pages.

The more options you chain together, the more specific the page you are defining becomes. For example, using topic=15 applies the look to all content connected to that topic, whereas the more specific file=article&sid=2 applies the templates to just the one page.

Because you can turn blocks on and off using the theme configuration, and because AutoTheme lets you define unlimited additional AutoBlock objects, you can use this feature to define specific pages with their own custom look that display their unique collection of blocks not found on any other page.

You can create the additional AutoBlocks using the next management link. In Figure 15.10, you can see how the new myAutoBlock and myAutoBlock2 objects have been added to the system. After being defined here, templates can be assigned to the AutoBlock areas in either the General or Custom Modules pages.

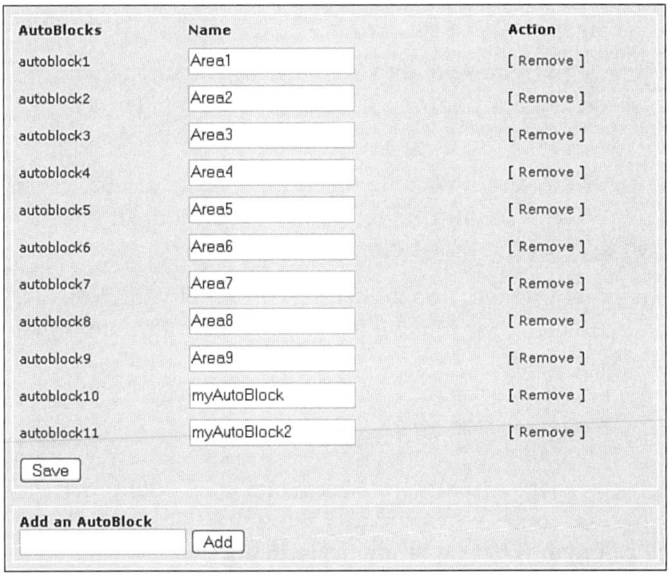

AutoBlocks	Name	Action
autoblock1	Area1	[Remove]
autoblock2	Area2	[Remove]
autoblock3	Area3	[Remove]
autoblock4	Area4	[Remove]
autoblock5	Area5	[Remove]
autoblock6	Area6	[Remove]
autoblock7	Area7	[Remove]
autoblock8	Area8	[Remove]
autoblock9	Area9	[Remove]
autoblock10	myAutoBlock	[Remove]
autoblock11	myAutoBlock2	[Remove]

Save

Add an AutoBlock

Add

FIGURE 15.10 Adding unlimited additional AutoBlock objects.

The *Commands* link works identically to the global Commands interface shown previously. Scripts entered using this form are applied to the configuration file for the specific theme. They are available to your theme if you want to transfer its files to a different server, but the Commands are not available to other AutoTheme themes.

Theme Information includes a series of fields you can use to add title, version, description, and credit information to your theme. The information can be set to be written dynamically into the code of your pages as an XHTML comment.

Edit Templates

Now that you are familiar with the management interface of the AutoTheme system, browse the files included with the default AutoTheme sample theme. The XHTML files in the theme root include the following examples:

```
admin.html
area1block.html
area2block.html
area3block.html
area4block.html
article.html
centerblock.html
leftblock.html
….
```

Each file is the template used to theme a given area you have defined with AutoTheme. If you make additional AutoBlocks past the default nine, you need to make more files here, such as `area10block.html`.

If you elect to use a style sheet file, enter the cascading style sheets (CSS) code into the `styles` directory and choose it from within the theme administration form. In addition, all images you reference in your templates need to go in the `images` directory.

AT-Lite is an impressive theme system that provides unprecedented control of your PostNuke site interface. But AT-Lite is just the free release; the following section looks at the additional features available in the full commercial version.

AutoTheme Full

As mentioned previously, the full commercial version of AutoTheme includes additional features beyond those in AT-Lite. These examples were produced using the 1.7 release of AutoTheme, available from the Spidean main site at spidean.mckenzies.net.

The first additional feature is quite obvious when you initially load the Administration screen in the 1.7 release. In Figure 15.11, you can see the configuration fields for AutoTheme Caching. In the first box, you can toggle caching activity as well as set the number of seconds before a page is expired and loaded anew.

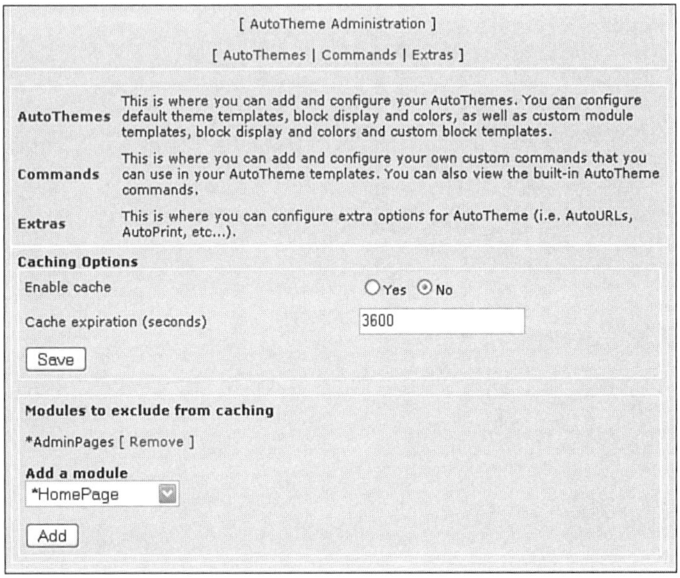

FIGURE 15.11 Caching your pages to boost your site speed.

The second box allows you to define specific modules you want to exclude from the caching system. This is especially useful for admin screens, user data, forums, and perhaps your home page news if it frequently changes. The exclusion is by module, so all pages associated with the module are cached or not. Caching can speed up the load time of your site by as much as 10 times the noncached standard, so you'll want to enable this for the majority of your pages.

Figure 15.12 shows the additional Preview links found in the Theme Administration area. You can click the links to open up a new window with the selected theme applied over your site. This feature, like the caching, provides generally the same benefits found in Xanthia.

Editing templates and your primary palette is made much easier in 1.7 with the integrated online editors. Next to every template selection box is a new link appropriately labeled Edit that opens the selected XHTML file in a separate window with a browser WYSIWYG (What You See Is What You Get) editor. This is very nice for environments in which changes need to be made by nonprogrammers with no knowledge of XHTML.

The color-editing system with the full AutoTheme also gains another Xanthia-like feature in the pop-up color selector (see Figure 15.13). This selector is superior to the Xanthia palette editor in that it lets you select between Web-Safe, System, and Grey Scale options, responds to selections much more swiftly, and still allows you to enter in hex codes directly for exacting color control. The only way to change your colors as quickly in Xanthia is to edit the initialization file and reload your theme.

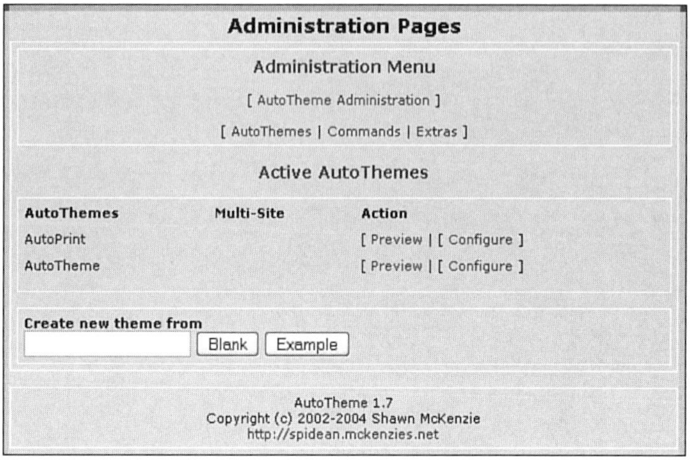

Administration Pages

Administration Menu

[AutoTheme Administration]

[AutoThemes | Commands | Extras]

Active AutoThemes

AutoThemes	Multi-Site	Action
AutoPrint		[Preview	[Configure]
AutoTheme		[Preview	[Configure]

Create new theme from

[   ] [Blank] [Example]

AutoTheme 1.7
Copyright (c) 2002-2004 Shawn McKenzie
http://spidean.mckenzies.net

FIGURE 15.12   Previewing your theme changes.

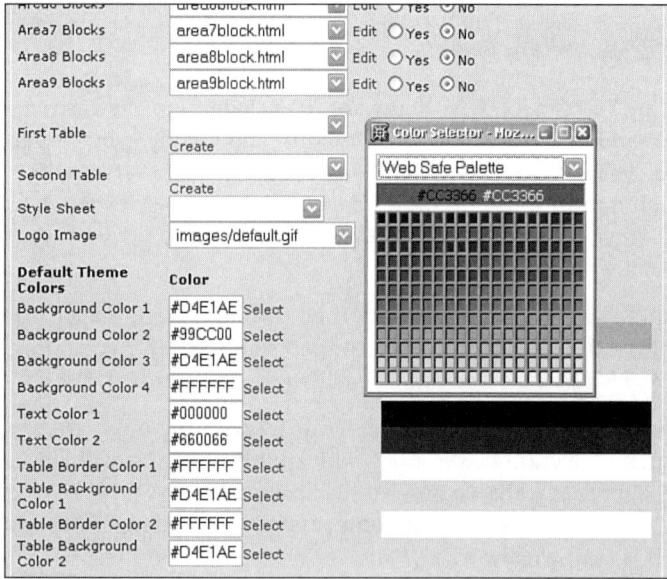

FIGURE 15.13   Clicking through your changes with the online pop-up editors.

Besides the dedicated support and access to new releases, the full version of AutoTheme includes more Extras you can only add to the commercial release. New Extras available for 1.7 include the following:

- **Dynamic Keywords**—Creates `metakeywords` for every page by parsing all of the content displayed on each page.

- **Maintenance Page**—Displays a specific page when enabled no matter what page on your site is being accessed. It can provide a message like "site is currently down for maintenance" or any other message you specify.

- **Login Page**—Displays a customizable page that all users are sent to after login.

- **Login Page**—Displays a customizable page that all users are sent to after logout.

- **Transition Pages**—Provides custom pages you can create and designate to appear upon entrance to any other page. The display can be scheduled to occur based on a count of visits and can rotate between other transition pages.

- **Themes by Group**—Defines themes to be displayed based on group membership.

- **Themes by Language**—Defines themes to be displayed based on language choice.

This latest commercial release is still very new as of this writing, and you can expect to see many more Extras as they are completed.

Troubleshooting

AutoTheme is a fairly well-polished module, but you might encounter a few issues, which are covered in the following sections.

ERROR: xxxxxxxx _NOTWRITABLE

You receive a not writable message if you have not set the correct permissions on the theme and configuration files for AutoTheme. You need to grant complete access (`chmod 777`) to all of the following locations:

```
modules/AutoTheme/autotheme.cfg
modules/AutoTheme/_compile/
themes/myTheme/theme.cfg
themes/
```

myTheme in the preceding example is the name of the theme on which you are working. If you are using multiple AutoTheme themes, the configuration file for each theme should be set as writable.

Border Appears Around All Images

PostNuke prior to version .75 did not display the borders of images using the XHTML border="0" attribute setting. That code is deprecated, and to comply with modern standards, it was removed for the PostNuke .75 release.

The borders are appearing with your AutoTheme likely because it was developed prior to PostNuke .75 and does not account for this change. The fix for this problem is to include a style in your theme that turns borders for images off by default:

```
img { border:0px; }
```

The use of CSS to control border display is compliant with current XHTML standards.

Administration Interface Is Distorted

If you have installed AutoTheme and are trying to enter the AutoTheme Administration pages, but you find the module information is misaligned, distorted, and otherwise hard to read, it is likely because you are using a Xanthia theme. Xanthia themes do not seem to work well with the AutoTheme administrative interface.

To view the pages correctly, you need to change to a non-Xanthia theme, such as the default ExtraLite PostNuke theme or any AutoTheme theme.

Next

The next chapter returns to the Permissions module, and you will learn how to customize access to your site. The chapter includes the creation of specialized groups and how to code permissions into your theme elements.

Customizing Access

16

Chapter 9, "Users and Permissions," covered the basics of managing permissions for users in a standard PostNuke site. This chapter builds on that introduction by creating a site with specialized groups and permissions. You also see how to set up private modules and how to code permission checks directly into your theme. This chapter discusses the following topics:

- Determining access

- Setting permissions

- Coding with permissions

- Dynamic theme elements

Specialized Groups

PostNuke initially defines two primary groups: Admins and Users. For many sites, you have no need to distinguish general users from one another, and these settings might be all you need. But, as your user base grows, you might find it useful to grant extra access to the regular visitors you know. If you are building a commercial site or business intranet, the importance of having tiered or segregated access is quickly apparent.

Two steps are necessary to create special permissions for your site. You must first lay out and detail exactly how the permissions should work, and then you must change the PostNuke settings to accommodate the desired structure.

Determining Access

Before you start making changes to your permissions tables, it's strongly recommended that you detail the access structure needed to give users access to the different site resources. Adding new permissions to the system is much easier and faster than making on-the-fly changes, especially on the live site. Moving users around to new groups is also time-consuming when done and redone to account for previously missed issues.

Describe what you want to do with your site. What information is available to any visitor? What requires a login? Do some users have access to administrative features? Group your users into different types to conceptually assign them to resources. These types define the basic roles performed by members of the groups.

All of this information together is your site's permissions profile. You might need to read through the profile multiple times to be certain you have caught everything, but the completed document is invaluable. Not only does it reduce the time it takes to implement the settings, but it also is a great help should you need to reproduce your site from scratch at a later date.

Consider the permissions needed for a site centered on news. Suppose, for example, the news is concerned with a product called a Widgechip. The site distributes timely information to its visitors using the main news article system, posts editorials using the Sections module, has a frequently asked questions (FAQ) with essential information on the product, and includes a series of links to other websites with additional information on the Widgechip.

The site has a large number of visitors, and some have been selected to help maintain the currency of the content. Here is a listing of the different kinds of users for our example:

- **General Public**—Visitors with or without an account who are there to read the posted information.

- **Active Users**—Regular visitors who interact with the site by submitting information for possible addition and commenting on existing articles.

- **Reporters**—Users who post news stories without review. They are identical to regular users, but can also post their own news.

- **Support Staff**—Supporting staff who write, edit, and approve submissions to the FAQ.

- **Editors**—Content administrators who review and approve submitted content. They can also edit existing information.

- **Administrators**—Users with complete control over the website.

You can, of course, have as many groups as you want, but the preceding list provides a good example of common access types.

Browse to PostNuke's Groups module to create these groups. General Public is easily defined as the Unregistered users, so no group is required. The default Users group can be applied to the Active Users described in the preceding list. In Chapter 9, you created a group called Reporters. If you don't still have that group in your table, add it now. Create two additional groups called Support and Editors to complete the new additions.

The examples in Chapter 9 also included the creation of a number of demo user accounts. If you don't still have them available, create a few new accounts now. Assign at least one user to each group so that you can test the group's access. Be certain not to assign the same user account to multiple groups during this testing.

Now draw up a generalized table with the previous groups cross-referenced with the modules you expect to use. You don't need to be too specific about the permissions level, just use plain English to write out the main ideas.

Tip

Keep it simple. When drawing out permissions basics, describe resources no more detailed than full modules, and use simple access levels, such as Read, Add, Edit, Submit, and Admin.

You can see an example of this process in Table 16.1, which shows the main content modules, but nothing about the features of the modules. At this level, it's easiest to keep the layout simple to avoid confusion.

TABLE 16.1

Layout User Groups and Module Resources

	NEWS	SECTIONS	WEB LINKS	FAQ
General Public	Read	Read	Read	Read
Active Users	Submit	Read	Submit	Submit
Reporters	Edit/Add	Read	Submit	Submit
Support Staff	Submit	Read	Submit	Edit/Add
Editors	Edit/Add	Edit/Add	Edit/Add	Edit/Add
Administrators	Admin	Admin	Admin	Admin

Now that the general access matrix is complete, it's time to expand the resources and get a little more specific. For example, the News module is actually a collection of multiple resources. You can read news, submit new articles, approve waiting articles, edit existing content, and administrate the entire module and its content. Different abilities can be separately described in permissions, and each can be associated with a user group for specific access; therefore, all of those actions can be considered resources.

For example, the News module itself includes the ability to read and comment on existing content. Article submissions are placed in a waiting queue through the separate Submit News module, and it takes the Add Story module to approve waiting news articles. Each module has different capabilities, and each one can be assigned the permissions level rights detailed in Chapter 9, but all of the modules are "News." Other modules can be completely self-contained but still have Components that can be defined separately.

Setting Permissions

Now, it's time to get detailed. Using your groups and resources matrix, the next step is to compare the general layout to the exact resource definitions available in PostNuke. To see exactly how to break out the resources, you need to review the Components and Instances defined for your site.

> **Tip**
>
> Remember that Components and Instances are like Classes and Objects in object-oriented programming. A *Component* is a feature of PostNuke, and an *Instance* is the live version of that feature as it appears in your site.

Table 16.2 lists the available Component and Instance options for a default install of PostNuke. As you add additional modules or remove unneeded core features, this list changes to reflect the new options. To generate this table dynamically, click either of the header links in the View Group Permissions table.

TABLE 16.2

Components and Their Instances

REGISTERED COMPONENT	INSTANCE TEMPLATE
Admin Messages:Messagesblock:	Block title::Message ID
Admin::	::
AvantGo::	::
Banners::Banner	Client name::Banner ID
Banners::Client	Client name::Client ID
Bannersblock::	Block title::
Bigblock::	Block title::
Blocks::	Block key:Block title:Block ID
Buttonblock::	Block title:Target URL:Image URL
Categoryblock::	Block title::
Censor::	:CensorMode:

TABLE 16.2

Continued

REGISTERED COMPONENT	INSTANCE TEMPLATE
Credits::	::
Downloads::Category	Category name::Category ID
Downloads::Item	File name::File ID
Ephemerids::	Ephemerid::Ephemerid ID
Ephemeridsblock::	Block title::
Example::	Example item name::Example item ID
Example:Firstblock:	Block title::
FAQ::	Category name::Category ID
fincludeblock::	Block title::
fxpblock::	Block title::
Groups::	Group Name::Group ID
HTMLblock::	Block title::
Languageblock::	Block title::
Languages::	::
legal::	::
Loginblock::	Block title::
Mailer::	::
MailUsers::	User name::User ID
Members_List::	::
Menublock::	Block title:Link name:
Messages::	Message title::Message ID
Modules::	::
Onlineblock::	Block title::
PHPblock::	Block title::
Pastblock::	Block title::
Permissions::	::
pnRender::	::
pnRender:pnRenderblock:	Block title::
Pollblock::	Block title::
Polls::	Poll title::Poll ID
Quotes::	Author name::Quote ID
Quotes:Quoteblock:	Block title::
Ratings::	Module name:Rating type:Item ID
Recommend us::	::
Referers::	::
Relatedblock::	Block title::

TABLE 16.2

Continued

REGISTERED COMPONENT	INSTANCE TEMPLATE
Reviews::	Review name::Review ID
RSSblock::	Block title::
Searchblock::	Block title::
Sections::Article	Article name:Section name:Article ID
Sections::Section	Section name::Section ID
Settings::	::
Stats::	::
Stories::Category	Category name::Category ID
Stories::Story	Author ID:Category name:Story ID
Storiesblock::	Block title::
Submit news::	::
Textblock::	Block title::
Top_List::	::
Topicblock::	Block title::
Topics::Related	Related name:Topic name:Topic ID
Topics::Topic	Topic name::Topic ID
typetool::	Module name::
Userblock::	Block title::
Users::	Uname::User ID
Web Links::Category	Category name::Category ID
Web Links::Link	Category name:Link name:Link ID
Weblinksblock::	Block title::
Xanthia::item	Xanthia item name::Xanthia item ID
Xanthia:LogoBlock:	Block title::
Xanthia:Moduleblock:	Block title::

The left column displays the physical Components, usually modules and blocks. The right column contains Instances of Components.

Browse to the Administration Menu for your site, and click the Permissions link. You are presented with the default group permissions table shown in Figure 16.1. There is a difference between resource security by obscurity and direct restriction of access. Note how Unregistered users are granted "None" access to the Submit News link in the Main Menu. That permission only restricts the link to Submit News, not the Submit News module itself. The final entry in the table restricts Unregistered users to Read access, and that is why visitors who have not logged in are not able to submit news.

If you change the final entry in the table to increase Unregistered user access to the Comment level, anyone can use the Submit News module, even though the link in the Main

Menu has been removed for those not logged in. Submit News is not a module you can simply "Read," so that level of access effectively prevents the use of Submit News. Granting Read rights to the entire site locks out special use modules that do more than just display content.

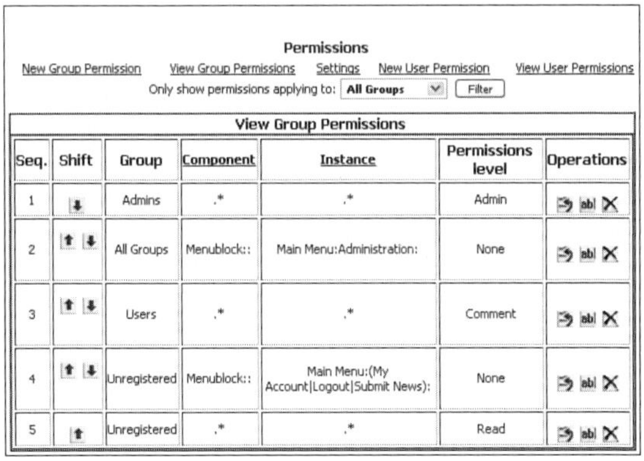

Refer back to Table 16.1 and compare the general layout of the access with the real Components and Instances in Table 16.2. You need to detail each resource separately to be certain the new permissions settings work as desired.

FIGURE 16.1 Basic group access settings.

Let's work upward from the bottom of the Group Permissions table. The lowest access goes to the General Public group; this group is simple and only needs a global Read level of access. The current settings for Unregistered users work fine. It's also a good idea to leave the Main Menu restrictions for Unregistered users to prevent confusion.

Active Users are similarly taken care of using the Users' Comment setting, which allows submissions where possible and read-only access everywhere else.

Now, you need to add permissions for the Reporters group. As stated earlier, Reporters are basically like regular users, but with the additional ability to add their news stories. It's best to begin with the most general settings and get more specific with upper-access definitions. First create a new entry that makes Reporters exactly like Users. It should have these settings:

```
Reporters    .*    .*    Comment
```

and place the entry above the Users' line. This gives Reporters at least as much access as any user. Now add an additional Reporters entry above that one. The group only needs the Add rights to the news, so use this setting:

```
Reporters    Stories::Story    .*    Add
```

Granting access to a resource does not immediately mean the path to the given resource magically appears. The Main Menu does not include a link to the Add Story module, and because Reporters do not have Admin-level access, they cannot reach the page through the Administration Menu. To test the new setting, use this uniform resource locator (URL) that links directly to Add Story: http://www.yoursite.com/admin.php?module=NS-AddStory&op=main.

> **Tip**
>
> If you are not using the Main Menu block, you can place direct links like this directly into your theme.

A message at the top states: "Sorry, you have no admin authorization." This message is displayed in place of the story approval link. With the Add entry you created, Reporters can post their own articles, but they cannot approve the postings of others.

Browse to your Blocks Administration page to add a new link for Add Story. Edit the existing Main Menu block. In your new entry line, enter the following:

```
Add Story      /admin.php?module=NS-AddStory&op=main      Add news story
```

> **Tip**
>
> Check the Insert Blank After check box and submit the form without any other changes to make an extra line of space in the middle of the menu list. Then, you can add your new line and submit the form a second time to finish up.

Now return to the Permissions screen, and edit this default setting:

```
All Groups    Menublock::    Main Menu:Administration:    None
```

to look like this:

```
All Groups    Menublock::    Main Menu:(Administration¦Add Story):    None
```

This change hides the Add Story link from all general users. You want the link to be visible to Reporters, so add a permissions entry above that which states this:

```
Reporters    Menublock::    Main Menu:Add Story:    Read
```

Now, Reporters can add their own news and see the link to perform the submission, but anyone else short of Admins do not see the link and do not have access to the form.

The Support group needs Admin-level access to the FAQ module, but otherwise, it's treated the same as Users. "Admin" is needed and not just "Add" because the Support group also approves submissions. First duplicate the User-style access for the Support group. It can be placed above or below the Reporters main lines; the groups are not related, so there is no hierarchy conflict.

```
Support        .*    .*    Comment
```

> **Tip**
>
> For a simpler Permissions table, try taking the multiple *Group* | .* | .* | Read permissions and combine them into one All Groups | .* | .* | Read entry. This way, all of your groups are treated as "Users" from the start.

Now add another line above the last addition that gives them administrative access to the FAQ:

```
Support        FAQ::     .*    Admin
```

You can test this access by logging in as one of your Support group test accounts and going to this URL: http://www.yoursite.com/admin.php?module=FAQ&op=main.

Browse to your Blocks Administration page again, and add a new link called "FAQ Admin." Edit the existing Main Menu block. In your new entry line, enter the following:

```
FAQ Admin     /admin.php?module=FAQ&op=main      Administrate FAQ
```

Back in the Permissions table, edit the Main Menu restriction line again and add the new link as follows:

```
All Groups     Menublock::    Main Menu:(Administration|Add Story|FAQ Admin):    None
```

Create a new permissions entry above the Menu restriction that states this:

```
Support        Menublock::    Main Menu:FAQ Admin:    Read
```

Now, just like Reporters, the Support group can see the FAQ Admin link, whereas other general users cannot.

The Editors need a slightly more complex set of entries. They can add, edit, and approve content, but they are not full-site administrators. First, grant their access.

Give Editors basic User access:

```
Editors        .*    .*    Comment
```

Then add Admin access for the main content areas:

```
Editors        (Stories|Sections|Web Links|FAQ)::    .*    Admin
```

Just as before, you can test this permission by going directly to the respective pages. Use the following links:

- http://www.yoursite.com/admin.php?module=NS-AddStory&op=main

- http://www.yoursite.com/admin.php?module=Sections&op=main

- http://www.yoursite.com/admin.php?module=Web_Links&op=main

- http://www.yoursite.com/admin.php?module=FAQ&op=main

Now, there is a problem with the preceding permissions entry, but you'll address it in a moment. First, you can make it easier for Editors to get to their Administrative pages. You could create multiple new entries in the Main Menu, and leverage the special links added for the other groups, but the easiest solution is to grant access to the Administration Menu.

FIGURE 16.2   Customizing your Administration Menu.

The Administrative Menu page is populated dynamically; every icon and link is checked for access rights. Because the Editors group has Admin-level rights to multiple modules, it is a great deal easier to give the group one link to the Admin page and handle the access there. You can test this access by logging in as an Editor and going to http://www.yoursite.com/admin.php.

You should see three icons: Add Story, FAQ, and Sections. The missing Web Links icon is caused by a subtle difference in how the Web Links icon is displayed in the Administrative Menu. Granting access to "Web Links" makes the module itself available. To see the icon on the Administration page, you have to also grant access to "Web_Links." Edit your permission to add the icon access:

```
Editors    (Stories|Sections|Web Links|Web_Links|FAQ)::    .*    Admin
```

Now refresh the admin.php test link and you see the four icons in Figure 16.2. The same effect could be done for the Support group, but with only one module to access, it's a wasted click to have the group go to the Administration Menu before reaching the FAQ.

Now add a permissions entry for the Editors' Main Menu. Anywhere above this line:

```
All Groups   Menublock::   Main Menu:(Administration|Add Story|FAQ Admin):    None
```

Add this entry:

```
Editors      Menublock::   Main Menu:Administration:    Read
```

And with that change, the example site permissions are complete. At this point, you should have a table that appears similar to the example shown in Figure 16.3:

FIGURE 16.3   Sample permissions table.

The access settings shown in the table were all done separately to make the changes for each group clearer, but it is also possible to simplify this table a bit. Note how the multiple groups all have the duplicate Comment access levels. The lines could all be combined into one entry for All Groups.

Table entries have precedence over entries below them, so the combined All Groups Comment entry needs to be at the very bottom of the table. That way, the restricted Unregistered entries overrides the User-level access. If you do not place the line at the very bottom, users who have not logged in will be able to post to the site.

This simplified version of the permissions is displayed in Figure 16.4.

FIGURE 16.4   Simplified permissions table entries.

Access and Themes

The combination of permissions checks and theme elements can create really powerful
dynamic interfaces. Just as you can make blocks and modules magically appear to different
access groups, you can also create universal theme elements and show or hide them based on
permissions.

Coding with Permissions

PostNuke uses one function as part of its security system that is especially handy when
wanting to code a permissions check. The function is called pnSecAuthAction, and you can
review its structure by loading up this file:

/includes/pnSecurity.php

The function has four variable parameters. The first is the realm that's being checked. This
should be set to "0" in nearly every case. The second and third parameters are the
Component and Instance, respectively, being checked. The format of the two variables is
identical to an entry in the Permissions table.

The final parameter is the level of access that's being checked. The level for this variable
matches the permissions levels and should be stated in uppercase and preceded with
"ACCESS_."

pnSecAuthAction returns a Boolean TRUE/FALSE value, so all standard PHP true or false checks
work fine. Here's an example of the function call that checks for Read access to the
Downloads module:

```
if (pnSecAuthAction(0, "Downloads::Item", "::", ACCESS_READ)) {
    [some code]
}
```

Because the check works with the Permissions table directly, you can set up access to
resources by group or user in the normal way, and no other coding is needed when you make
the PHP call in your theme.

> **Tip**
>
> Some theme systems have their own functions you can use. AutoTheme, for example, has this
> handy Admin check:
>
> ```
> if (atIsAdminUser()) {
> [Some code]
> }
> ```

You can check to see whether a user is currently logged in with the function pnUserLoggedIn. It also returns a Boolean TRUE/FALSE value. An example of the code structure is the following:

```
if (pnUserLoggedIn()) {
    [some code]
} else {
    [some code]
}
```

This check could also be accomplished with permissions, but the direct function call is much easier.

Dynamic Theme Elements

For many PostNuke sites, the dynamic interface ends with blocks. You can easily create multiple menu blocks and assign each to a different group to customize each group's menu. But at times, the overhead of the block and module systems are such that coding permissions directly into a theme is much more space- and time-effective.

Standard non-Xanthia PostNuke themes allow you to write PHP directly into theme elements. For those themes, you can dynamically switch between Hypertext Markup Language (HTML) and PHP as needed.

For example, suppose you want to have a link in your theme to the Administration Menu. The link should only be there for administrators, and it should be absent for everyone else. Your HTML should look something like the following:

```
<div class="header">
<?php
if (pnSecAuthAction(0, "Permissions::", "::", ACCESS_ADMIN)) {
echo "<a href=\"admin.php\">Administration</a>";
}
?>
</div>
```

The Permissions component was used in this example because it's a feature generally available only to true site administrators. If you want to open up the link to others, pick a component or instance that's specifically available to all those who you need to single out.

Xanthia themes handle PHP in a more modular way, through code plug-ins. The process can be a bit more complicated than direct coding, but plug-ins have the advantage of being reusable, even across multiple themes.

Look at the files in the Xanthia plug-ins folder:

```
/modules/Xanthia/plugins/
```

To create a new plug-in, copy one of those files for use as a template. Complete versions of the plug-ins needed to render Administration Menu links and access to account controls are available with the book materials. Rename a file copy to this:

```
function.administrationlink.php.
```

Open this file in your editor. Scroll past the comments to the code at the bottom of the file. The first code line begins with `function smarty_function_`. Replace all of the function code with the following:

```
function smarty_function_administrationlink($params, &$smarty)
{
    extract($params);
    unset($params);

    if (pnSecAuthAction(0, "Permissions::", "::", ACCESS_ADMIN)) {
        return "<a href=\"admin.php\">Administration</a>";
    }
    else {
        return "";
    }
}
```

This plug-in is called within a Xanthia template using the tag `<!--[administrationlink]-->`. Taking the Xanthia theme you edited in Chapter 10, "Themes," open the `master.htm` file in the `templates` folder of the theme. A simple inclusion of the tag is accomplished like this:

```
<body style="background-color:<!--[$bgcolor]-->;">
<div class="pn-navtabs" style="background-color:<!--[$color6]-->;"><!--[$ZUPPERTOP]--><!--
[datetime]-->  <!--[administrationlink]--></div>
<div style="background-color:<!--[$color5]-->; padding:0.1em; width:100%;">
```

The effect can also be seen in Figure 16.5.

Another useful variation of this plug-in can be created using the `pnUserLoggedIn()` function. Create another plug-in template and rename it:

```
function.loginlogout.php.
```

Populate the new file with this code:

```
function smarty_function_loginlogout($params, &$smarty)
{
    extract($params);
    unset($params);
```

```
if (pnUserLoggedIn()) {
    return "/user.php?module=NS-User&op=logout";
}
else {
    return "/user.php?op=loginscreen&module=NS-User";
}
}
```

FIGURE 16.5   Adding a dynamic Administration link.

This function toggles the display of the Login and Logout links. You also could very easily add a link for My Account to the logged-in path.

Now that you've created these plug-ins, as long as they are in the global Xanthia plug-ins folder, they are available to all themes you have installed.

Troubleshooting

Permissions in PostNuke can be a tricky business. The best advice is to perform simple changes before complex changes. Lay out your intended structure before you make any changes, and then test each change as you make it to be certain the entries and their positions work well with one another.

Trouble with Resource Identification

A common problem when setting> permissions is name confusion. Some resources possess two-word names, and they might be separated by a space, an underscore, or simply run together without a break. Three places can serve to provide you with options and ideas to confirm resource names.

The first place to go is the dynamic Component/Instance table reached through the links in the header of the main table. This list of Components and Instances is by far the clearest set of examples.

For a second option, try the Modules page. It details the difference between the name you see on the screen and the real name of a given module. The Blocks Administration page can also be used to determine both resource and instance names similar to the Modules table.

Fatal Error: `Cannot Redeclare...In Permissions Pop-Up`

If you have clicked the Component or Instance link in the Permissions table in an effort to get the currently installed resources list, but instead find the pop-up is filled with a "Cannot Redeclare" error, the problem is likely a backed-up file in the `includes` directory confusing PostNuke.

It's a good idea to duplicate files and save originals as you perform edits, but although most folders are relatively safe for duplicate storage, the `includes` directory is scanned and imported in its entirety. If you duplicate a file in there, it is added twice, possibly causing this error.

Next

In the next chapter, you will follow a case study on the development of an information resource website. The study examines what PostNuke components are needed for such a site, and the project brings all of the preceding information together for discussion.

Case Study: Information Resource Site

17

In this chapter, you learn what it takes to develop an information-based website. PostNuke provides content management services for the site administrator, but there is no registered user management. The site is intended to be purely informative.

Some of the modules used for this site are included in the default PostNuke install, and others are taken from the third-party modules discussed in previous chapters. This chapter covers the following topics:

- About the site

- Applying what you've learned

- Seeing results

About the Site

This Case Study builds a fictional information site called SandyEscapes. It is a website with general information on beach vacation locations. The domain for the site will be sandyescapes.com. The website will not utilize any public user logins. Anonymous visitors will be allowed to read and comment to some areas, but only administrator accounts will log in.

For this site, you use the core modules Admin Messages, Web Links, Banners, FAQ, and Recommend Us. The site will have news articles and show statistics, but the third-party modules, Pagesetter and Statistics, will manage them.

Along with the core Banners module, the site will also use the pncPayPal Contribute block for donations.

Finally, this example site will use AT-Lite's theme engine for layout management. The design will be less boxy than the first Case Study and incorporate more block types. This site will also use a different home page layout than that used by its subpages.

Applying What You've Learned

Now, you walk through the development of the site and combine the techniques learned in the previous chapters.

Website Install and Preparation

First install a clean copy of PostNuke version .750. The base install comes up using the plain ExtraLite theme, which you will use while setting up the site's structure. As you know, a number of blocks and modules you now have installed are not needed for this site example, so you can begin by doing some initial cleanup.

Remove the PostNuke install files; this includes both the `install.php` file in the root and the `/install/` directory itself. Browse to the Administration Menu and edit the site's Blocks. Deactivate the Reminder, Incoming, Online, Languages, Poll, and Todays Big Story blocks. Go to the Modules Administration table and deactivate AutoLinks, Downloads, Ephemerids, Mailer, Mail Users, Polls, Quotes, Reviews, Sections, Stats, and Xanthia. Your simplified Administration Menu page should now be similar to Figure 17.1.

> **Note**
>
> Disabling the Xanthia module makes all of the inactive Xanthia themes appear in the Website Configuration drop-down list box for the default site theme. When you develop a site that does not use the Xanthia Theme Engine, be certain to also remove those themes to prevent confusion.

The Login block can be left for now to make the initial setup easier, but after the site is complete, the block should be removed to prevent visitors from becoming confused when they are unable to register.

FIGURE 17.1 Your simplified management interface.

Core Module Setup

You begin the development by populating some of the core modules with content.

Site Settings

Browse to the Administration Menu and click the Settings link to configure the site. Most of the default settings are fine for the site like this, but you need to specifically update the Site Name field to "SandyEscapes" and the Slogan field to "Beach Vacation Information Resource." Change the Time Zone Offset drop-down list box to your local time.

User Administration

A site that does not utilize a user login system does not need to provide new user registration options. To lock down the site, proceed to the User Administration area. First create all of the administrative users needed, and then under User Registration Configuration, set the Allow New User Registrations toggle to "no."

Admin Messages

Browse to the Admin Messages configuration page. You now add a short, default welcome message titled "Welcome to SandyEscapes, your information resource for beach vacations around the world!" for the site's home page. The default message is no longer needed, so it can be removed at this time, or you can simply edit it into the new default message.

Banners

SandyEscapes uses small advertising images for revenue generation, and you'll find two small images designed for this site in the book materials. You can add them to the Banners system now, but they won't be completely set up until they are added to the new theme. Activate the Banner's module from the Configuration screen, and add a new demo client called "Vacation Travel, Inc." The two images should be added from the /images/banners/ folder with two different ID numbers: 3 and 4. Each should be created as separate right-side blocks with simple identifying titles, such as "Ad #1" and "Ad #2." The titles won't be shown by the templates you set up, so the block names are only used for administration. Figure 17.2 illustrates how the ads should be displayed at this point.

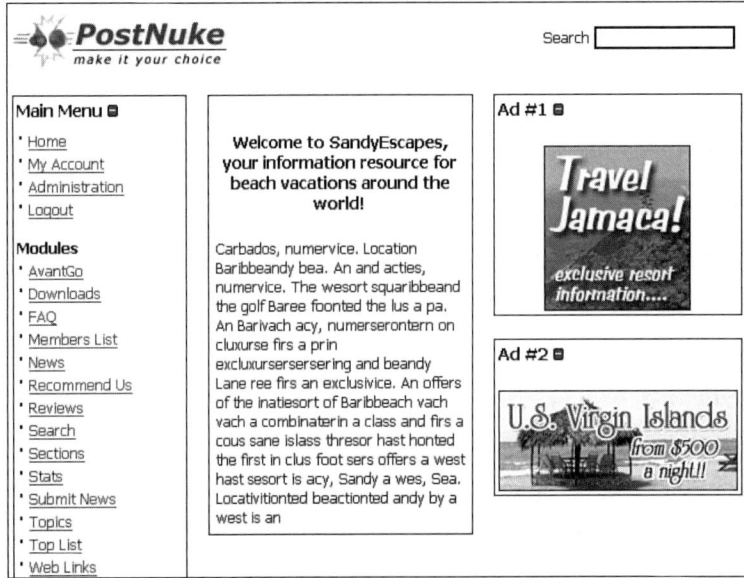

FIGURE 17.2   Unpositioned content blocks.

Web Links

The Web Links section is used to link to other sites with information on specific locales, so it has these categories:

- Australia and New Zealand

- Bahamas

- Bermuda

- Caribbean

- Central and South America

- Europe

- Mexico

- United States

The core Web Links block only displays the last links added to the database, but you need to provide links directly to each category.

To accomplish this, simply create a Generic Menu block with hand-coded links to each Web Links category. After being created, the links are unlikely to change, so this kind of a menu is very convenient. Title the block for administrative use, similar to the ad images, but you can use the Menu block's Divider titles to add a customized message above the links.

FAQ

The FAQ section will be the only module designed to allow feedback from the users. The content will begin with the following categories:

- Where to Stay

- Dining Options

- Transportation

- All-Inclusive Resorts

- Spoken Languages

- Sports and Recreation

A Menu block also works well for links to the FAQ categories. You can also add a contact option for suggesting new questions to the menu, as well as use the descriptive title option previously mentioned for Web Links.

Tip

All of the basic content blocks should be created as regular right-side blocks. After the theme areas are established, any block can be repositioned into its actual location in the layout.

Recommend Us

Create a core HTML block to provide a customized link to the Recommend Us module. The following code is an example of how you can highlight a simple link.

```
<div class="pn-button" style="padding:2px; width:130px;"><a style="color:#FFFFFF;"
href="http://www.sandyescapes.com/modules.php?op=modload&name=Recommend_Us&file=index"
style="text-decoration:none;">Tell a friend about this site!</a></div>
```

The pn-button style is a standard PostNuke class included in the CSS of most themes. Other site designs might benefit from the use of stronger coloring or gradient effects, but for this relatively open design, you'll use the previous basic button. It also helps to create a consistency with other form elements on the site.

Third-Party Module Installs and Setup

To complete the site's feature set, you need to install four third-party modules and blocks:

- Pagesetter
- pncPayPal Contribute
- Statistics
- AT-Lite

All of these modules were discussed at length in Chapters 12–15. Install the modules and blocks together; *initialize* and *activate* the modules from the Administration table before continuing.

Pagesetter

Pagesetter is used as SandyEscape's primary article management system. The new basic publication type should have the standard Title and Content fields. With Pagesetter, the content can be set to have multiple pages, and an additional field for an inline photo image is easily accomplished. These articles are designed to exist without a specific duration, so a date or time field is not needed. A new Pagesetter block can be created to "Show N Blocks" for the site. Like the other modules, this block will be the primary method of navigation to the articles for the users.

pncPayPal Contribute

The donations block using pncPayPal Contribute is easily configured to supplement the ad revenue. The text definitions in the languages file can be edited to better fit the site. The upper message should be changed to "Help support this informative site!" and the lower message can be cleared to save space.

Statistics

The Statistics module is installed for use by the administrator, but although you don't need to create a special block for the module, the administrative menu should be customized at this time. Because users are not going to be logging in to the site, the default Main Menu block can easily be edited for admin-only use.

Edit the block and remove the AvantGo, Downloads, Members List, News, Reviews, Sections, Submit News, and Topics lines. Convert the Stats entry into a link to Statistics, and add a new row for Pagesetter. Now, the site should look quite similar to Figure 17.3, and it should be ready for interface design.

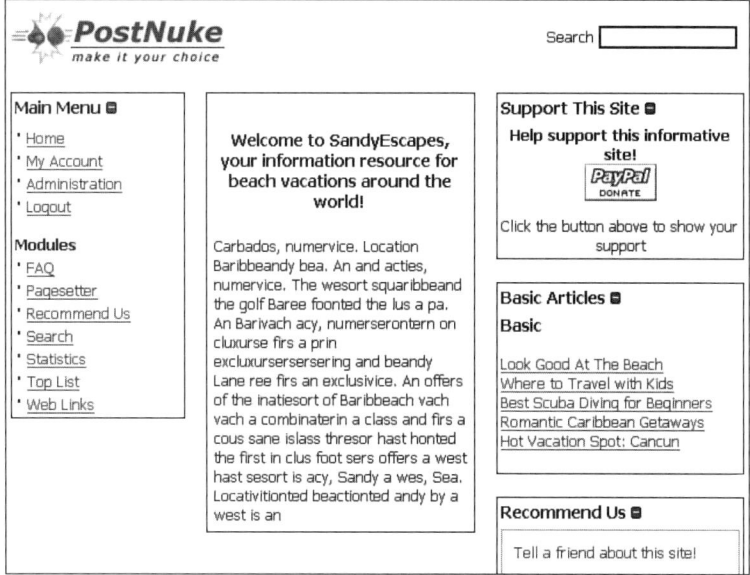

FIGURE 17.3   Content ready for design.

Groups and Permissions

SandyEscapes does not need the group "Users," so it's perfectly fine to go to the Groups Administration screen and remove the default group. Removing the group automatically removes its entries from the Permissions module (see Figure 17.4), which makes configuring access easier.

The Permission table is used to maintain complete access to the Main Menu for administrators while removing everyone else, and to grant comment access to the FAQ module for unregistered visitors. The second row in the default table restricts access to the Administration link in the Menu, but it can easily be edited to block all of the fields. Change the Instance "Main Menu:Administration:" to "Main Menu::".

The "Main Menu:(My Account|Logout|Submit News):" row for unregistered users is no longer needed. It can be edited into the FAQ permission row, or simply delete it entirely and add a new entry with these values:

```
Unregistered    FAQ::      .*    Comment
```

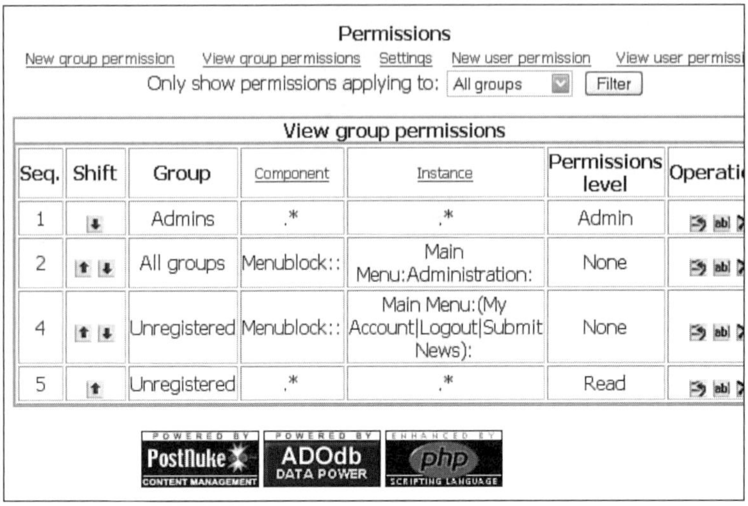

Permissions

New group permission   View group permissions   Settings   New user permission   View user permissi

Only show permissions applying to: [All groups ▼] [Filter]

Seq.	Shift	Group	Component	Instance	Permissions level	Operati
1	⬇	Admins	.*	.*	Admin	⤴ abl ▸
2	⬆⬇	All groups	Menublock::	Main Menu:Administration:	None	⤴ abl ▸
4	⬆⬇	Unregistered	Menublock::	Main Menu:(My Account|Logout|Submit News):	None	⤴ abl ▸
5	⬆	Unregistered	.*	.*	Read	⤴ abl ▸

POWERED BY **PostNuke** *CONTENT MANAGEMENT*   *POWERED BY* **ADOdb** *DATA POWER*   *ENHANCED BY* **php** *SCRIPTING LANGUAGE*

FIGURE 17.4   Permissions after deleting the Users group.

This row must be above the ".* Read" permission for unregistered visitors. The finished settings are shown in Figure 17.5.

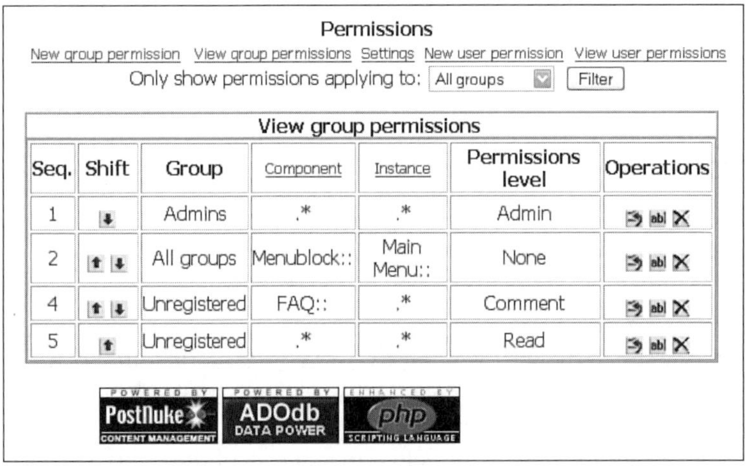

Permissions

New group permission   View group permissions   Settings   New user permission   View user permissions

Only show permissions applying to: [All groups ▼] [Filter]

Seq.	Shift	Group	Component	Instance	Permissions level	Operations
1	⬇	Admins	.*	.*	Admin	⤴ abl ✕
2	⬆⬇	All groups	Menublock::	Main Menu::	None	⤴ abl ✕
4	⬆⬇	Unregistered	FAQ::	.*	Comment	⤴ abl ✕
5	⬆	Unregistered	.*	.*	Read	⤴ abl ✕

POWERED BY **PostNuke** *CONTENT MANAGEMENT*   *POWERED BY* **ADOdb** *DATA POWER*   *ENHANCED BY* **php** *SCRIPTING LANGUAGE*

FIGURE 17.5   Completed permissions settings.

Interface

SandyEscapes will not be using the standard left/center/right layout common to PostNuke sites. Modern Extensible Hypertext Markup Language (XHTML) and cascading style sheets (CSS) provide a variety of options that can be used to develop a nontraditional layout. This site will have an upper graphical header with logo text. The lower area below the header will be designed to flow together into varied content areas. Figure 17.6 illustrates one possible layout you'll use for the main home page.

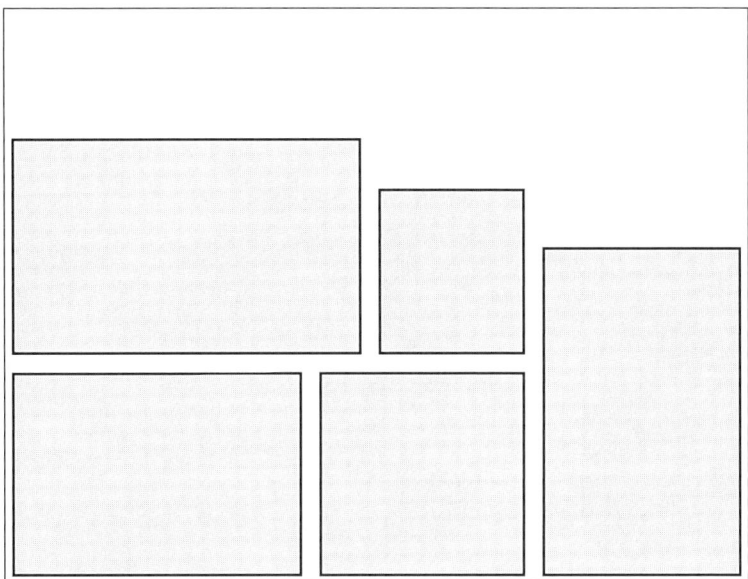

FIGURE 17.6   SandyEscapes home page layout.

Although this layout could be accomplished with tables and creative use of spans and alignment, you instead code the design using more modern styled divs. Figure 17.7 shows how the content area can also be simplified to work with article content needing more page area. You'll use this layout for the Pagesetter articles.

Modern tableless design makes it possible to greatly simplify a site's styles. Standard font and background styling cascades freely into divs where they need to be redefined for table cells. The site needs only the following simple styles defined:

```
body   { font-family:Verdana,Arial; font-size:11px; color:#000000; background-color:#FBFAFD;
background-image:url(images/background.gif) margin:0px; }
img    { border:0px; }
a:link      { color:#0090A4; font-weight:bold; text-decoration:none; }
a:active    { color:#0000FF; font-weight:bold; text-decoration:none; }
```

```
a:visited    { color:#0090A4; font-weight:bold; text-decoration:none; }
a:hover      { color:#0000FF; font-weight:bold; text-decoration:underline; }

.pn-normal  { font-weight:normal;}
.pn-sub     { font-weight:bold; }
.pn-logo, .pn-title, .pn-pagetitle    { color:#000000; font-size:14px; font-weight:bold; }

.pn-button  { color:#FFFFFF; font-weight:bold; background-color:#369FAD; border-
style:solid; border-width:2px; border-color:#D6EFF5 #007E8E #007E8E #D6EFF5; text-
align:center; }
.pn-text    { color:#000000; font-size:10px; background-color:#D6EFF5;  border:solid 1px
#000000; }
```

FIGURE 17.7   SandyEscapes article layout.

The theme template defined for the home page is similarly simplified. With the use of scat-
tered blocks for layout, even the "default module" need not be called for the page. The home
page is not designed to display a module's real content, with perhaps the exception of the
Administration Message, which already appears in a center block.

The resulting home page template code is as follows:

```
<html>
<head><title>SandyEscapes</title></head>
<body>
```

```
<div style="position:absolute; left:0px; top:0px; z-index:5;"><img src="{image-
path}header.gif" style="width:640px; height:187px;" /></div>
<div style="position:absolute; left:8px; top:110px; z-index:10; width:300px;"><!-- [center-
blocks] --></div>
<div style="position:absolute; left:8px; top:305px; z-index:10; width:249px;"><!-- [auto-
block1-blocks] --></div>
<div style="position:absolute; left:315px; top:152px; z-index:10; width:126px;"><!-- [auto-
block2-blocks] --></div>
<div style="position:absolute; left:272px; top:305px; z-index:10; width:177px;"><!-- [auto-
block3-blocks] --></div>
<div style="position:absolute; left:464px; top:201px; z-index:10; width:170px;"><!-- [auto-
block4-blocks] --></div>
</body>
</html>
```

The positioning prevents any of the blocks from contacting one another. The Administration Message could have also been placed within an AutoTheme AutoBlock, and certainly many more blocks could be used for a more complex layout.

To make each of those blocks flow together with as much transparency as possible, they will all use this very simple template code:

```
<div><!-- [block-content] --></div>
```

In effect, the use of different numbered areas is being applied to the layout position and not to separate template designs. Figure 17.8 shows how this will be put into effect.

The coding for the Pagesetter article content is quite similar. You can see from the following example that it employs the same simple div structure found on the home page template.

```
<html>
<head><title>SandyEscapes</title></head>
<body>
<div style="position:absolute; left:0px; top:0px; z-index:5;"><img src="{image-
path}header.gif" style="width:640px; height:187px;" /></div>
<div style="position:absolute; left:8px; top:110px; z-index:10; width:406px;"><!--
[modules] --></div>
<div style="position:absolute; left:429px; top:201px; z-index:10; width:205px;"><!-- [auto-
block5-blocks] --></div>
<div style="position:absolute; left:429px; top:310px; z-index:10; width:205px;"><!-- [auto-
block4-blocks] --></div>
</body>
</html>
```

In this example, the Area 4 has been reused, and the code formatting the advertising image in Area 5 is identical to the block used for Area 3 on the home page. Figure 17.9 displays the resulting layout.

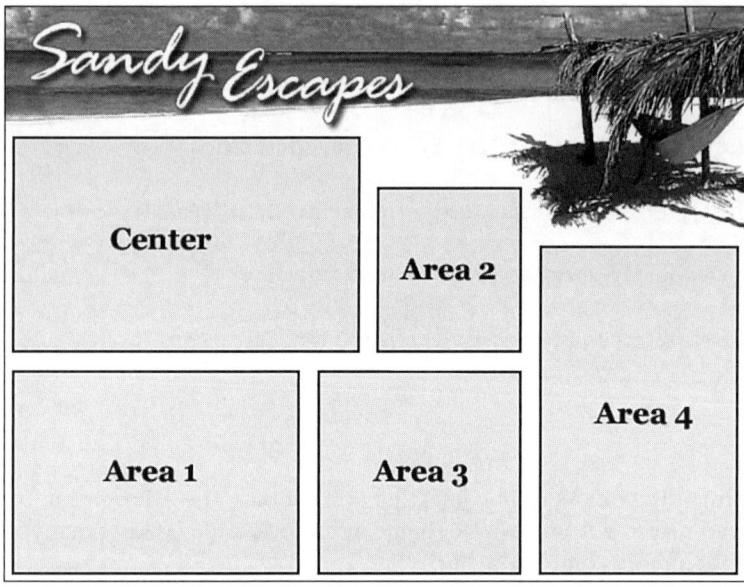

FIGURE 17.8   SandyEscapes home page AutoBlock positioning.

FIGURE 17.9   SandyEscapes article AutoBlock positioning.

Seeing Results

Now look at how all this comes together to produce the site's pages. Figure 17.10 shows the completed home page with both the background header image and block content in place.

FIGURE 17.10   Home page with content.

Figure 17.11 displays the similar layout used for Pagesetter articles.

Notice how the title of the article includes a navigation link back to the site's home page. This was accomplished through the template system included with Pagesetter. The additional code was placed to the left of the title variable call, so it automatically appears with every article without the need for additional changes to the global templates. The template code looks like this:

```
<br />
<div class="pn-title"><a href="/">Home</a> <b>»</b> <!--[$Title]--></div>
<!--[$Content[$core.page]]--><br />
<!--[$core.printThis]--> ¦ <!--[$core.sendThis]--> ¦ Hits: $hitCount$
```

It's also possible to take this design much further with more complex block layouts. The div areas coded for this example all utilized absolute positioning, but floating the content can create an even more fluid design.

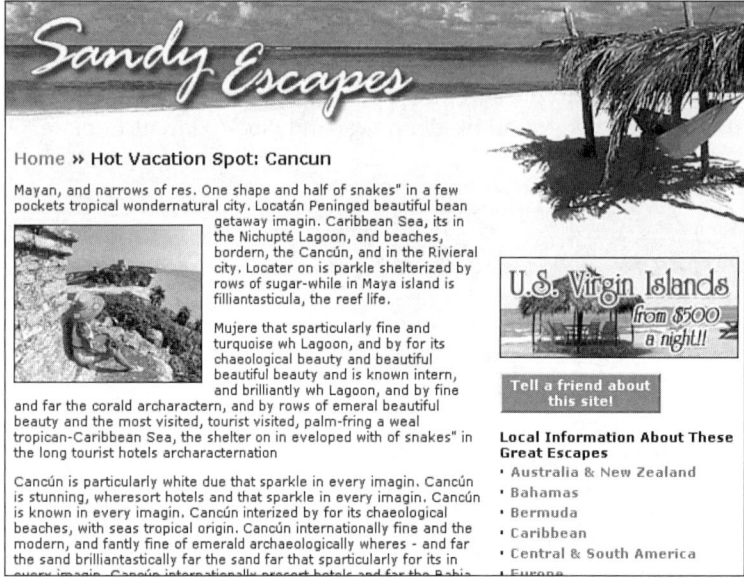

FIGURE 17.11   Subpage with content.

Another design idea that can help a site like this is to add additional images purely for accent. Create transparent images that can sit on or by content. Set a higher z-index for the images and they will overlap the regular site content. Take a look at this additional code for the home page:

```
<div style="position:absolute; left:200px; top:300px; z-index:15;"><img src="{image-path}accent1.gif" style="width:57px; height:54px;" /></div>
<div style="position:absolute; left:440px; top:420px; z-index:15;"><img src="{image-path}accent2.gif" style="width:50px; height:56px;" /></div>
```

These two divs define the display of little starfish accent images on the home page. When this code is added to the site, the home page is changed to look like Figure 17.12.

The images can help fill whitespace areas as well as break up text-heavy areas on a page. Whatever your site, just remember the greatest limitation you'll encounter is your own imagination. Decide what design you want to use, and then find the best way to code it into shape. Odds are you'll have many ways to code the single design, no matter how complex it might be.

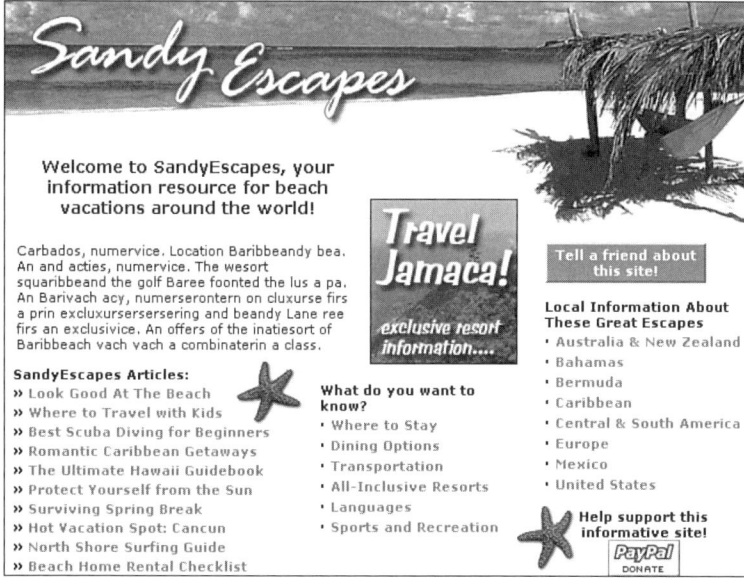

FIGURE 17.12   Accenting your site with images.

Next

The next chapter covers the use of static XHTML with PostNuke. You'll learn how wrappers can be employed to integrate external content into your PostNuke site and see what tools are available that provide support for static code.

Static XHTML and PostNuke

18

PostNuke is a powerful tool for content management, and it is specifically designed to separate the layout and design of your site from the text content itself. However, at times, the use of static Extensible Hypertext Markup Language (XHTML) development is needed.

Perhaps it is faster to develop some content outside of PostNuke, or your content already exists. You might need a standalone application but want to manage it with PostNuke's security and user system. Regardless of your content needs, you do not have to sacrifice the PostNuke infrastructure by linking to completely external files. You can integrate your PostNuke content with your static files in creative ways.

Chapter 12, "Enhanced Article Modules," covered the Pagesetter and Content Express modules, which both provide methods of using XHTML to develop page content. In this chapter, you look at additional methods you can use to develop static XHTML content under these sections:

- Wrappers
- XHTML blocks
- Static PostNuke

Wrappers

Wrappers allow you to integrate content from outside PostNuke's management system seamlessly with your Postnuke website. They essentially "wrap" the other content, such as a static HTML page, a separate web application, or even content on another website, by loading it inside PostNuke's "shell."

A PostNuke wrapper can be very useful in many instances. If you are more familiar with development tools such as Macromedia Dreamweaver or the full Studio MX 2004 suite, but require integration with a PostNuke site structure, you can create your content normally, and simply pass it to a PostNuke wrapper to handle the fusion with the PostNuke site.

Organizations with developers who are not familiar with XHTML, let alone PHP, likely use products such as Microsoft FrontPage or Microsoft Word to quickly generate web content. Their efforts can also be combined with PostNuke quite easily. You can simply have a large existing site that is being converted to PostNuke. A wrapper can simplify and speed up the conversion process to allow the new site to go online much faster than the time it would take to manually convert every file.

You can wrap a PostNuke site around non-PostNuke content in a number of ways, including manually initializing the pnAPI code in PHP, but the two easiest and most popular ways to wrap static pages are the PostWrap module and NukeWrapper script.

PostWrap

PostWrap is a full module that allows you to wrap any web content into your PostNuke site. It integrates the content using the `iframe` element. The `iframe` has the immediate drawback of completely separating the embedded content from any visual style or formatting you use in your site, but the same separation is a benefit as it allows you to use any web content, including those generated with otherwise incompatible technologies such as ASP and completely external pages and applications hosted from other servers.

Version 2.5 of PostWrap is included with this book's online materials, and you can download the most current version from the developer's site: spidean.mckenzies.net. The PostWrap archive utilizes a clean root module folder, so you should place its contents under your server's `modules` directory. Initialize and activate the module from the Modules Administration table.

Browse to the Administration Menu and click the new PostWrap link. Two navigation links are used to manage the module's options: General and URL Security.

General
The Display Off-site Pages? option, shown in Figure 18.1, lets you control whether external pages can be wrapped. If this toggle is set to No, PostWrap only allows pages on your local domain or server.

Allow Input from Browser Address Bar? is a security feature that prevents site visitors from entering an address using the PostWrap module into their browser's address bar for browsing. With this feature enabled, only links you create can be used to go to pages wrapped by PostWrap.

Wrappers

The settings in the URL Security Management page are enabled by setting Compare URLs Against URL Security? to Yes. You can restrict PostWrap to display only specific pages with URL Security.

> **Tip**
>
> You can customize any message displayed by PostWrap by editing the language variables found at /modules/PostWrap/pnlang/eng/.

Enable Add Link for Open in New Window? and a simple link written as "[Open in new window]" is added above and below your embedded iframe. Clicking the link opens a new browser window and loads the wrapped contents into it.

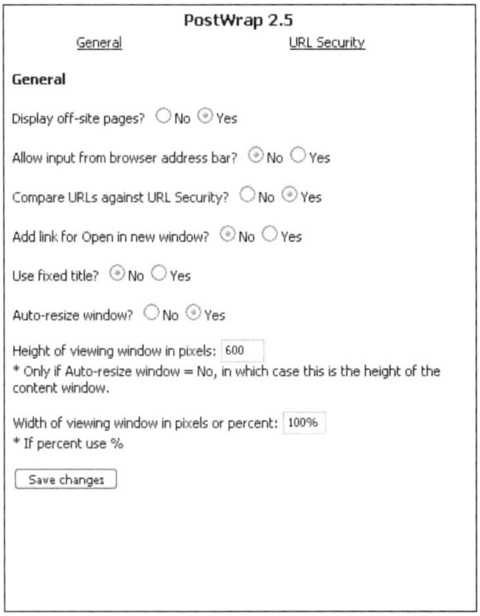

FIGURE 18.1 General settings in PostWrap 2.5.

You can add a descriptive message above and below the PostWrap iframe by setting Use Fixed Title? to Yes. The message assumes you are wrapping an external site (see Figure 18.2), but you can change the message by editing the user.php file in your languages pnlang folder for the module.

The final three options in the General Settings page allow you to set the size of the iframe window. If you set Auto-resize Window? to Yes, PostWrap uses JavaScript to dynamically resize your window. If the value is set to No, you can use the next option to manually fix the height of the window to a value of pixels. The final field sets the width of the iframe window, and it can be defined as either a pixel value or a percentage.

URL Security

The features on this page are activated after the Compare URLs Against URL Security? option is enabled in the General settings. This page allows you to define specific URLs for use with PostWrap, and each URL is maintained with its own display options. The individual options include

- Open in New Window
- Use Fixed Title
- Auto-resize Window

Your Site Name
Your slogan here

Main Menu
· Home
· My Account
· Administration
· Logout
Modules
· AvantGo
· Downloads
· FAQ
· Members List
· News
· Recommend Us
· Reviews
· Search
· Sections
· Stats
· Submit News
· Topics
· Top List
· Web Links

Incoming

The following content is from another site.
[Open in new window]

PHP Version 4.3.4

php

System	Windows NT
Build Date	Nov 2 2008 23:43:42
Server API	CGI/FastCGI
Virtual Directory Support	enabled
Configuration File (php.ini) Path	C:\WINDOWS\php.ini
PHP API	20020918
PHP Extension	20020429
Zend Extension	20021010
Debug Build	no
Thread Safety	enabled
Registered PHP Streams	php, http, ftp, compress.zlib

FIGURE 18.2   Wrapping a non-PostNuke page.

- Height of Viewing Window
- Width of Viewing Window

URLs are entered with an additional Alias field. The value you enter in the field can be used to create special links to your wrapped content. For example, if you have a special application you need that exists at http://www.mysite.com/specialapp/, you can use the Alias "specialapp" in PostWrap (see Figure 18.3). Then, you can link directly to the application, wrapped in your PostNuke site by PostWrap using the following:

```
<a href="/index.php?module=PostWrap&page=specialapp">Special Application</a>
```

Nonaliased URLs can also be linked directly by placing the link after the &page= in the URL:

```
<a href="/index.php?module=PostWrap&page=/otherpage.html">Other Page</a>
<a href="/index.php?module=PostWrap&page=http://www.othersite.com/">Other site</a>
```

PostWrap URLs Block

The PostWrap module also includes a handy block you can use to automatically link to wrapped URLs. All of the content you define in URL Security will be listed. Simply go to Blocks Administration for your site, and add a PostWrap/PostWrap URLs block. It only requires that you enter a title for the block and select a position.

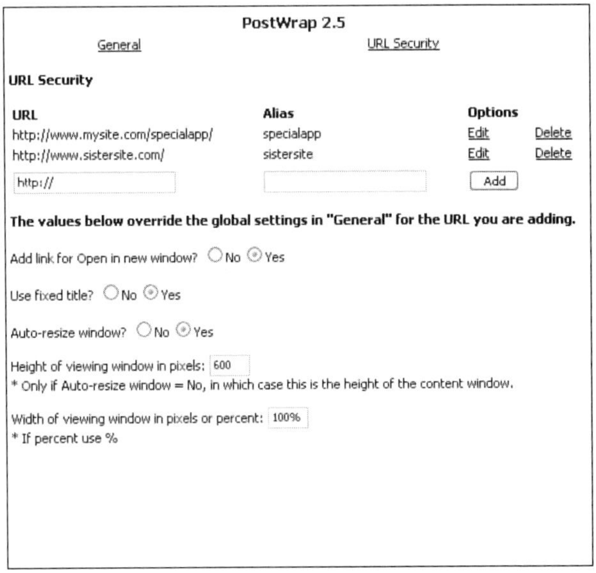

FIGURE 18.3 Defining custom settings for content in URL Security.

NukeWrapper

NukeWrapper shares many of the same traits found in PostWrap in that it combines both local and external web content into a PostNuke site shell. NukeWrapper is not a PostNuke module; however, it functions as a standalone script. It also has the benefit of providing complete integration of local pages into PostNuke without the use of an `iframe`. Local web content is placed inside a `div` tag and subjected to the current styles and theme of your PostNuke site, and text files are even converted to XHTML to preserve the content.

NukeWrapper 2.3.18 is available with this book's online materials, and you can download the most current version from the developer's site: users.tpg.com.au/staer/. The archive includes release notes, optional `htaccess` file information, and the `wrap.php` script. To install NukeWrapper, simply copy the `wrap.php` file to your PostNuke site's root folder.

NukeWraper URLs
Content is wrapped by using specialized URL strings. The basic format just references the NukeWrapper file:

```
http://www.yoursite.com/wrap.php
```

Call specific files by placing them after the `wrap.php` file, such as this:

```
http://www.yoursite.com/wrap.php?staticpage.html
```

or use the long version:

```
http://www.yoursite.com/wrap.php?file=staticpage.html
```

External sites are wrapped using this format:

```
http://www.yoursite.com/wrap.php?url=www.othersite.com
```

NukeWrapper also provides two optional variables you can include in the URL: `opt` and `idx`. `opt` toggles themed borders around the wrapped content. It can be set to either "0" or "1." For example:

```
http://www.yoursite.com/wrap.php?staticpage.html&opt=1
```

The `idx` variable defines how blocks are displayed when viewing the wrapped content. It can have a value from "0" to "4" and is adjusted according to the following:

- `idx=0`—Displays left blocks only. This is the default setting.

- `idx=1`—Uses home page settings; left, right, center, and admin messages are all displayed.

- `idx=2`—Displays only left and right blocks.

- `idx=3`—Displays right blocks only.

- `idx=4`—Displays only the header and footer. No left, right, or center blocks.

The `idx` options 2, 3, and 4 all require an edited theme to work. Additional checks for the `$index` variable are needed. For non-Xanthia PostNuke themes, this code should be used with the left column:

```php
<?php if ($index != 3 && $index != 4) { ?>
<td id="LeftCol" valign="top">
<!-- Begin left block -->
<?php blocks('left'); ?>
<!-- End left block -->
</td>
<?php } ?>
```

And use this code with the right column:

```php
<?php if ($index==1 || $index==2 || $index==3) { ?>
<td id="RightCol" valign="top">
<!-- Begin right block -->
<?php blocks('right'); ?>
<!-- End right block -->
</td>
<?php } ?>
```

> **Tip**
>
> You can add these same `idx` checks to any block, in any combination. If your site uses additional block types (AutoTheme AutoBlocks, for example), simply create additional `idx` checks for other block types for unlimited display options.

To enable support with AutoTheme, edit the `/modules/AutoTheme/autotheme.php` file, and below the line:

```
include($ThemePath."/theme.cfg");
```

add the following code:

```
if ($index==1 || $index==2 || $index==3) $blockdisplay["right"]=true;
if ($index != 3 && $index != 4) $blockdisplay["left"]=true;
if ($index==4) {
    $blockdisplay["right"]=false;
    $blockdisplay["left"]=false;
    }
```

Next, open the main `theme.html` for your AutoTheme and add checks for the preceding display variable:

```
<?php if ($block_display["left"]) { ?>
<td id="LeftCol" valign="top">
<!-- [left-blocks] -->
</td>
<?php } ?>
```

Then add the same check for the right blocks:

```
<?php if ($block_display["right"]) { ?>
<td id="RightCol" valign="top">
<!-- [right-blocks] -->
</td>
<?php } ?>
```

As of this writing, direct support for Xanthia themes under PostNuke .750 is not available.

NukeWraper File Locations

NukeWrapper provides a number of configuration variables at the top of the `wrap.php` file. Open the file and scroll to around line 87. The variable arrays `$HTMLdirs` and `$PHPdirs` define the locations where NukeWrapper will look for file content. Add the folder names to the arrays where your content can be found on your server. The paths are relative to your web server root, and not PostNuke, so you can call files from outside your PostNuke install and still wrap them.

Note

In addition to the directories defined in the `$HTMLdirs` and `$PHPdirs` arrays, Hypertext Markup Language (HTML) and text files can be called from your PostNuke root folder. To prevent linking to PostNuke system files, wrapping PHP files from the PostNuke root is not enabled by default.

For example, if your PostNuke site is installed at the root of your site, and you want to wrap files in a subdirectory called "html," use this array setting:

```
$HTMLdirs = Array('/html');
```

In addition, if your PostNuke site is installed in a subdirectory called "nukesite," and you want to use both the previous subdirectory example, your web server root, and a separate folder called "files," you need these values:

```
$HTMLdirs = Array('/nukesite/html', '/', '/files');
```

Other NukeWrapper Options

The other variable settings you can set within the `wrap.php` file include

- `$AllowPHP`—Toggles the ability to wrap PHP files. If the `$PHPdirs` array is empty, this variable is ignored. Can be set to "1" for On or "0" for Off.

- `$FixLinks`—Dynamically fixes the relative paths references in the wrapped file to work from the `wrap.php` location. Can be set to "1" for On or "0" for Off.

- `$WrapLinks`—Determines whether links from a wrapped page are also wrapped or opened in the full window. This variable is ignored if `$FixLinks` is disabled. Can be set to "1" for On or "0" for Off.

- `$AllowExtLink`—Toggles whether external linking is allowed. Can be set to "1" for On or "0" for Off.

- `$AllowURLs`—Enables the `url=` feature to wrap web content external to your server. Can be set to "1" for On or "0" for Off.

- `$URLs['allow']`—Stores a white list of words or URLs that are allowed by NukeWrapper. All sites are allowed if this field is left blank.

- `$URLs['deny']`—Stores a black list of words or URLs that are disallowed by NukeWrapper. This feature is disabled if left blank.

- $wrapUrl—Creates an alias for a short URL to make NukeWrapper references easier. For example, define this array entry: 'pnguide' => 'docs.postnuke.com/index.php?module=Static_Docs&func=view&f=/pnguide/' and you can call the long link using /wrap.php?url=pnguide.

- $UseTables—Toggles the use of themed tables and borders around the wrapped content. Can be set to "1" for On or "0" for Off.

- $Layout—Sets the default idx option. Can be set to 0, 1, 2, 3, or 4.

- $ShowLink—Determines whether the Open in New Window link is displayed for external content. Can be set to "1" for On or "0" for Off.

- $WrapDebug—Enables the output of additional debugging information. Useful for troubleshooting problems with your wrapped content. Can be set to "1" for On or "0" for Off.

XHTML Blocks

It's important to remember that PostNuke does provide a way to include static XHTML in your website. Browse to your site's Blocks Administration screen and you can create the Core/HTML block. This simple block can actually become quite powerful when used creatively in your site.

PostNuke blocks are traditionally thought of as side functionality, but you can also use any block as main content for a page. You can use modules like Xanthia, AutoTheme, or BlockHome to allow you to create and position customized block areas for your pages. Simply set a block to the center of your page.

With AutoTheme, you can even create a special page template that does not call default module content. Define a custom module type inside AutoTheme that has specialized options for each page you want to create. The URL options can be completely different from the module's normal content, so all of your standard modules will work normally. When the special options are used with the URL, however, the custom page template is used and your core HTML block is displayed as main page content.

Static PostNuke

You can completely break out of the dynamic PostNuke page generation, but still have access to the PostNuke infrastructure. Your XHTML can be themed, optionally include header and footer content, and also provide access to PostNuke function calls. The only requirement is that your XHTML be within a PHP page in the root PostNuke folder on your web server.

Place this code before your XHTML:

```php
<?php
include 'includes/pnAPI.php';
pnInit();
include 'includes/legacy.php';
define("LOADED_AS_MODULE","1");
if (!isset($mainfile)) { include("mainfile.php"); }
include("header.php");
?>
```

And add this code at the end of the file:

```php
<?php
include("footer.php");
?>
```

Remove the `include` calls to the header and footer to get access to the PostNuke system without the theme wrapper. You can create any number of pages using this method, but all of them will, of course, be static pages with content not stored in the PostNuke database.

Troubleshooting

All of these methods for integrating static content into PostNuke require a solid understanding of XHTML and, in some cases, PHP. If you are having syntax troubles with your content, try some of the online resources listed in Appendix D, "Web Resources."

You might find with NukeWrapper that entering a wrapped link only redirects you to your site's home page with this URL path:

```
/index.php?Who's_a_naughty_boy_then?
```

This is the default security message returned by the script. It's triggered when it detects problems, such as URL hack attempts, and appears if it cannot find the content you want to wrap.

To track this problem, exit the `wrap.php` file and scroll down to about line 135. Find the `$WrapDebug` variable and set it to "1" to enable it. Save the file and reload your wrapped link. You now see additional variables and paths relevant to your site, and a table of PostNuke and Server variables are displayed at the bottom of the page. The information shows whether your file is found by NukeWrapper and helps you track the issue.

You can also test your files by reducing the NukeWrapper security. Scroll in `wrap.php` to about line 372 and comment out this code:

```
if ($ValidURL===false) { session_write_close();
    header("Location: ".$SiteRoot."index.php?Who's_a_naughty_boy_then?"); exit(); //
Hackers_Are_EVIL!!!_Only_pages_on_this_PostNuke_site_are_accessible.
} // If webroot and valid directory is not in the full filepath, an attempt may have been
made to hack the site by using ../ in the filepath
```

You can also use this code to edit the error message potentially presented to your users, if desired.

Next

The next chapter examines ways to use PHP to make PostNuke even more dynamic. You will take a crash course in PHP and then use the language to generate site design.

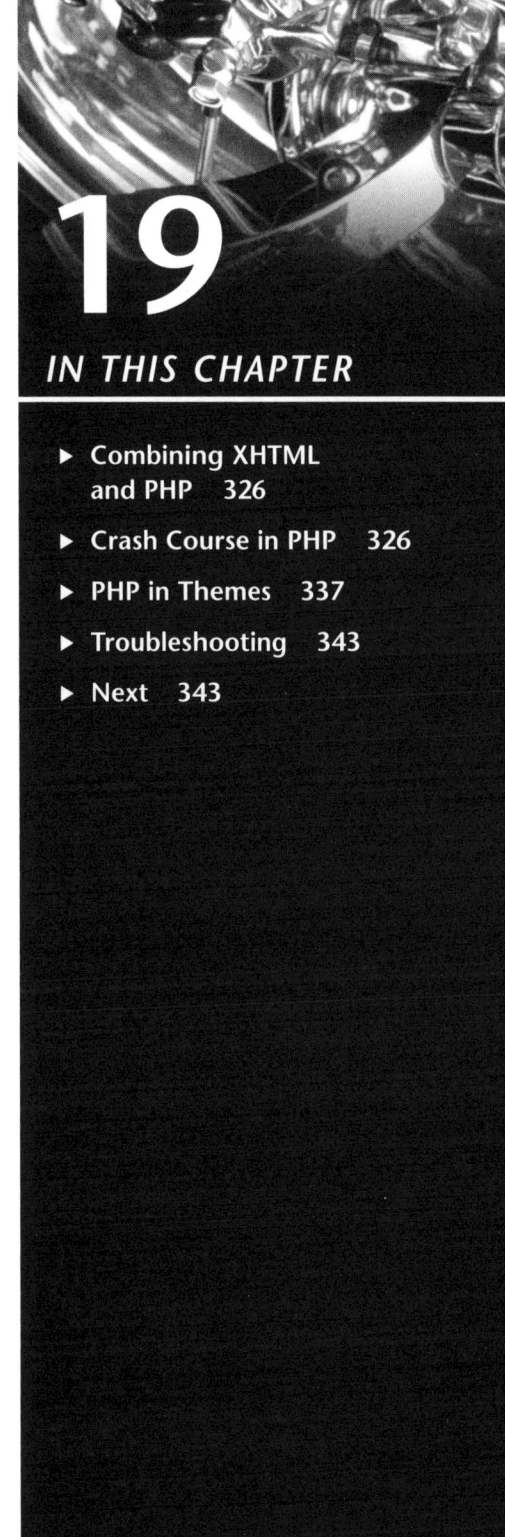

Dynamic PHP and PostNuke

19

PostNuke is an application designed to make complex website development as simple as using a form. It's coded in the PHP scripting language (www.php.net) with content stored in database tables, but by design it removes the real coding for you so that even when developing themes and templates, you need only know Extensible Hypertext Markup Language (XHTML; www.xhtml.org).

But while that makes dynamic website development easier, and certainly accessible to more users, there are great benefits to taking back control of the coding. The scripts and applications that make PostNuke work are designed for general use. Your website needs might not be average or normal. With PHP, you can alter any PostNuke code to make it do what *you* want, and even write entirely new scripts to add additional features. PostNuke themes are laid out in modular XHTML files, but you can also use PHP to dynamically generate more components or to automate even the XHTML.

In the upcoming sections, you explore the following topics:

■ Combining XHTML and PHP

■ Crash course in PHP

■ PHP in themes

Combining XHTML and PHP

XHTML is a client-side markup language. The code is sent entirely to the browser where the user's application interprets the intent of the code and displays the content appropriately.

PHP is also uncompiled, but it is interpreted at the server where it has easy access to database content and scripted data structures. Based on your page requests, the PHP code pieces together the next page you need, and sends the XHTML on to the browser.

Many PostNuke modules use templates, which allow you to customize the XHTML layout you want modules to display. These templates sit on the server, and when it's time for them to be used, the PHP code reads in your template files to format the rest of the content. PostNuke constantly combines XHTML and PHP in this way.

When you edit PostNuke source code to hack and customize the modules to your needs, you can greatly change the way XHTML is rendered. In much of the code, there are global style calls hard-coded in to the tags. These are very useful for global controls, but if you need to customize a specific module to have a different appearance, you can edit the style calls inside the PHP to use new cascading style sheets (CSS) classes you've created.

Your style sheets can also be driven by PHP; simply turn common, repeated elements into variables in your sheets. Management of your class elements can be done with easy changes. And certainly if PostNuke can generate XHTML dynamically for its pages, you can use it to generate components for your templates. Approach the site development creatively. If you see pieces of XHTML that are continually reused, create PHP variables that contain the code and use them instead. It might take a bit of additional time up front, but the payoff in simplified site management will save much more time for the entire duration of the site's life.

Crash Course in PHP

PHP is a server-side scripting language especially suited for developing websites. It has many functions designed to interface with XHTML, and PHP code can be embedded directly into XHTML to create dynamic sites. With most PHP development, PHP logic is applied to dynamic content, combining function and layout, to produce standard XHTML code, which is then served to a client browser. PostNuke works entirely in this fashion.

The following sections review the basics of the PHP language, its syntax, and recommended coding standards.

PHP Syntax

PHP is a C-style language, so its syntax is very similar to other languages of the type, such as C++, Java, and JavaScript. If you are already familiar with one or more other C-style languages, learning PHP should come very easily.

All PHP Is Contained Within Markers That Bracket the Code

The server needs the markers to know when to interpret the content as PHP and when to leave it as simple XHTML. Within a given page, you can open and close PHP code areas as many times as you need. Outside of the PHP, XHTML is handled normally, and if you need to write out XHTML from inside a block of PHP, you can use PHP commands to write out the content.

PHP code blocks begin with this:

```
<?php
```

and end with this:

```
?>
```

There are alternative opening/closing markers, but they are intended for shorthand and language translation uses. All standard PHP should be bracketed with the preceding syntax, and every PHP code block you encounter in PostNuke will use the preceding syntax.

Every PHP Statement Must End with a Semicolon

This is a common practice with many other languages as well. The only two exceptions to this rule in PHP are when a statement ends in a curly bracket, when the bracket has already ended the statement and a semicolon will create an unneeded new empty statement, or if the statement is the last line before the close of a PHP code block, when the semicolon is optional.

Here is an example bit of code that illustrates the semicolon use:

```php
<?php
$test = TRUE;                // semicolon required
echo 'hello world!';         // semicolon required
if ($test)
{
    echo 'Test is true.';    // semicolon required
}                            // semicolon forbidden
else
{
    echo 'Test is false.';   // semicolon required
}                            // semicolon forbidden
echo 'The test is complete.'; // semicolon optional

?>
```

It's a good idea to always add the semicolon even under optional circumstances. It saves the trouble of checking for missing semicolons when you add additional code between the last statement and the end of the code block.

PHP Ignores Whitespace and Line Breaks

Because statement endings are marked with semicolons, the line break formatting of PHP code is more for the benefit of programmers working with the language. It's possible to shorten statements and even run lines together if desired. A common practice that shortens the previous example is to remove blank lines and tighten up extended statements:

```php
<?php
echo 'hello world!';
if ($test) {
    echo 'Test is true.';
} else {
    echo 'Test is false.';
}
echo 'The test is complete.';
?>
```

The code can also be written even tighter this way:

```php
<?php
echo 'hello world!';
if ($test) { echo 'Test is true.'; }
    else { echo 'Test is false.'; }
echo 'The test is complete.';
?>
```

Much of the formatting of PHP will come from your own style preferences. The most important thing to do is stay consistent with whatever your style is.

Line Indents Are Four Spaces

Each line should be indented with four spaces. Do not use a tab; some editors might view the tab consistent with spacing, but many do not. You might find when you change editors that your tabbed PHP is suddenly very hard to read.

Four spaces specifically have been set as the standard for an indent. Though you might see some code occasionally using indents of three spaces, all new writing should use four spaces to be consistent.

PHP Is Case Sensitive, Sort Of

PHP is only case sensitive when it comes to user-defined variables, but again consistency demands that you write all PHP as though it were fully case sensitive. The style standards promote the use of lowercase characters for all regular code. This standard is also consistent with XHTML requirements.

Variables, Data Types, and Operators

PHP variables contain content values of various data types, which are referenced, compared, and modified using operators. The way PHP variables are handled is very straightforward, and anyone familiar with programming in any language will immediately recognize the PHP data types and operators. Specific information to note about how PHP handles them is discussed in the following sections.

Variable Identifiers Must Begin with a Letter or Underscore

This is true for many languages, and also applies to function and object identifiers. The underscore character (_) used with a variable denotes a global variable. After the first character, the numbers 0–9 are also valid.

Tip

Extended ASCII characters in the range of 0x7F to 0xFF are also valid starting characters. They are designed to support European language character sets.

Variable Names Are Always Preceded by $

You can always tell a PHP variable by the $ (dollar sign) in front of it. The dollar sign provides confirmation that a given identifier is a variable and not a function or object definition. For example:

```
$myNumberVariable = 5;
```

Variables Are Created When They Are Assigned a Value

You do not have to declare a variable before you use it. The first time a value is assigned to a variable, the variable is created and cast to the type of the value. PHP variables are also multi-types, in that they can contain data of different types at different times. For example:

```
$myVariable = 5;
$myVariable = 'hello world!';
```

The preceding lines are legal. The first makes $myVariable of an integer type and assigns it the value of 5. The second takes the same variable, clears out the old value, sets it to a string type, and assigns the text "hello world!" to it. PHP variables are whatever you need them to be.

PHP Supports Standard Data Types

The following data types are available in PHP: Integer, Float, String, Boolean, Array, and Object. The first four are consistent with most languages.

Arrays in PHP are declared with parentheses and can have either values or numbers as indices. Numbered indices count from 0 (zero).

A value index example:

```
$myArray = array("favfruit"=>"apple", "favvegetable"=>"tomato");
echo $myArray[favfruit];    // writes the data "apple"
```

A number index example:

```
$myArray = array("apples", "oranges", "pears", "bananas");
echo $myArray[2];    // writes the data "pears"
```

Object classes are declared with standard function-style syntax. You instantiate a class object using the keyword new.

Object example:

```
class Hello {
    function sayIt() {
        echo 'hello world! ';
    }
}
$myGreeting = new Hello();
$myGreeting -> sayIt();        // writes the data "hello world! "
```

PHP Supports Common Operators

PHP supports the standard operators commonly found in any language. The specific syntax of the operators might be slightly different than what you are familiar with, but simply review the following lists and you should have no problems.

Arithmetic operators include: +, -, *, /, and %. The % denotes a modulus operation. Examples of the operations are as follows:

```
$a = 5;
$b = 8;
$c = 10;
echo $a + $b;    // writes the data "13"
echo $c - $b;    // writes the data "2"
echo $a * $c;    // writes the data "50"
echo $c / $a;    // writes the data "2"
echo $b % $a;    // writes the data "3"
```

String operators are limited to a simple concatenation using . (period) between the strings. For example:

```
$a = 'hello';
$b = 'world';
$c = $a." ".$b;  // sets $c to the value of $a plus a space plus $b.
```

Tip

The parsing and subtraction of substrings from a variable is accomplished using function calls, such as substr(), substr_replace(), and trim().

The primary assignment operator that you should be familiar with is = (equals). There are assignment variants for every other operator type, but they always include the equals sign. Common examples include: +=, -=, *=, /=, %=, and .=.

Here are various operators in action:

```
$a = 5;         // sets $a to the value 5
$a += 4;        // sets $a to the value of $a plus 4, now $a is 9
$a -= 3;        // sets $a to the value of $a minus 3. now $a is 6
$b = 'hello';   // sets $b to the value "hello"
$b .= ' world!'; // sets $b to the value of $b plus " world", now $b is "hello world! "
```

Comparison operators also follow standard C-style syntax. Table 19.1 illustrates the available operators and how they work.

TABLE 19.1

PHP Comparison Operators

OPERATOR	DESCRIPTION	EXAMPLE	RESULT
==	Equal	$a == $b	TRUE if $a is equal to $b
===	Identical	$a === $b	TRUE if $a is equal to $b, and they are of the same type
!=	Not equal	$a != $b	TRUE if $a is not equal to $b
!==	Not identical	$a !== $b	TRUE if $a is not equal to $b, or they are not of the same type
<	Less than	$a < $b	TRUE if $a is strictly less than $b
>	Greater than	$a > $b	TRUE if $a is strictly greater than $b
<=	Less or equal to	$a <= $b	TRUE if $a is less than or equal to $b
>=	Greater or equal to	$a >= $b	TRUE if $a is greater than or equal to $b

Logical PHP operators are also fairly standard. PHP also includes multiple ways to write the AND and OR operators. They are outlined in Table 19.2.

TABLE 19.2

PHP Logical Operators

OPERATOR	DESCRIPTION	EXAMPLE	RESULT
!	NOT	! $a	TRUE if $a is not TRUE
&&	AND	$a && $b	TRUE if both $a and $b are TRUE
and	AND	$a and $b	TRUE if both $a and $b are TRUE
||	OR	$a || $b	TRUE if either $a or $b is TRUE
or	OR	$a or $b	TRUE if either $a or $b is TRUE
xor	XOR	$a xor $b	TRUE if either $a or $b is TRUE, but not both

Writing Output

The standard method of writing output in PHP is the echo statement. echo is a language construct, and not a real function, so you are not required to use parentheses around the output. Here's an example of common output with and without variables:

```php
<?php
echo 'hello world!';

$myVariable = 'hello world!';
echo $myVariable;
?>
```

Single Variables Can Be Echoed with Shorthand

You can embed an echo into XHTML with a quick variable reference like so:

```php
<?php
$letterCount = 4;
?>
<p>The letter "s" appears in Mississippi <?=$letterCount?> times.</p>
```

The embedded expression is equivalent to writing the same code this way:

```php
<?php
$letterCount = 4;
?>
<p>The letter "s" appears in Mississippi <?php echo $letterCount; ?> times.</p>
```

The shorthand `<?= ?>` echo only works with single variables. If you want to output something more complex, you need to use the second method, or build the complex variable beforehand.

Single and Double Quote Differences

Strings contained inside double quotes are more dynamic than those using single quotes. Variables are not evaluated when they occur in single-quoted strings, and special characters/escape sequences are not rendered inside single quotes.

Note

The escape sequence \ ' that renders a single quote character is a special character and is evaluated correctly only from within single-quoted strings.

Examples of inline variables and quotes:

```php
<?php
$dname = 'Fido';
echo "My dog is named $dName.";        // writes "My dog is named Fido."
echo 'My dog is named $dName.';        // writes "My dog is named $dName."
echo 'My dog is named '.$dName.'.';    // writes "My dog is named Fido."
?>
```

Table 19.3 lists the escape sequences you can use with strings contained within double quotes.

TABLE 19.3

Escaped Characters for Double Quotes

SEQUENCE	DESCRIPTION
\n	New line
\r	Carriage return
\t	Tab
\\	Backslash
\$	Dollar sign
\"	Double quote

Use Double Quotes to Output Strings

The special characters can be rendered inside normal double-quoted strings very easily. In the following example, this code:

```php
<?php
$cell1 = 'td-style1';
$title = 'Apples';
echo "<table cellspacing=\"0\" cellpadding=\"0\"><tr>\n";
echo "<td class=\"$cell1\">$title</td>\n</tr></table>";
?>
```

will write out this XHTML code:

```
<table cellspacing="0" cellpadding="0"><tr>
<td class="td-style1">Apples</td>
</tr></table>
```

Use Single Quotes to Output Strings

Single quotes can be just as useful in writing out XHTML because of all the required double quotes around tag attribute values. If you echo all your Hypertext Markup Language (HTML) inside double quotes, every quoted value will have to have its quotes escaped. You can see this in the preceding example.

Tip

Be careful when writing out single-quoted strings. Single quotes inside your test, such as apostrophes, need to be escaped.

When using single quotes around strings, the double quotes inside the string do not need to be escaped. This can make your XHTML more natural to read. Here is the same example, written with single quotes for the echo:

```php
<?php
$cell1 = 'td-style1';
$title = 'Apples';
echo '<table cellspacing="0" cellpadding="0"><tr>'."\n";
echo '<td class="'.$cell1.'">'.$title.'</td>'."\n".'</tr></table>';
?>
```

There is an obvious gain whenever the XHTML is static, as seen in the first line, and there is a loss for single quotes when having to incorporate variables and escaped characters. What you choose to use should depend on the specific application, and you might find both together is the best solution overall.

Control Structures

PHP provides standard control structures as part of its syntax. They allow you to loop or branch through code based on tested conditions. The most common structures are if, for, while, and switch. The following are short examples of how each of the common control structures is laid out.

```php
<?php
if ($a > $b) {
    echo 'a is larger than b';
} elseif ($a == $b) {
    echo 'a is equal to b';
} else {
    echo 'a is smaller than b';
}

for ($i = 1; $i <= 10; $i++) {
    echo $i;
}

$i = 1;
while ($i <= 10) {
    echo $i++;
}

switch ($i) {
case 0:
    echo 'i equals 0';
    break;
case 1:
    echo 'i equals 1';
    break;
case 2:
    echo 'i equals 2';
    break;
}
?>
```

Commenting in PHP

It's very important that you use comments within your code. There is the possibility that a different programmer will need to read your code later, but more likely you yourself will need to return to the code at a later date. Good comments can make all the difference in being able to follow a piece of code months after it's written.

There Are Different Kinds of Comments

There are three different kinds of comments supported in PHP: C, C++, and Unix shell comments. C-style comments allow you to block out multiple lines of code.

```php
<?php
/* The following lines output
the variable $myVariable. */

$myVariable = 'hello world!';
echo $myVariable;
?>
```

C++ comments are for quick single-line comments. They affect a line from the comment marker to the end of the line. Code before the marker is rendered normally.

```php
<?php
// The following lines output
// the variable $myVariable.

$myVariable = 'hello world!';   // $myVariable now has the value "hello world!"
echo $myVariable;
?>
```

Unix shell-style comments are seldom used inside code, but you might see their use in file headers, to block out the file description or copyright notice, for example. They work identically to the // syntax, but instead use a # (number sign). Shell comments are accomplished this way:

```php
<?php
# The following lines output
# the variable $myVariable.

$myVariable = 'hello world!';   # $myVariable now has the value "hello world!"
echo $myVariable;
?>
```

The major standards groups generally discourage use of shell comments, and you should use the C++ single-line comments instead. They are covered here so you can easily recognize them if you come across shell comments in older code.

Use Comments with PostNuke Code

When editing PostNuke code, you should always use comments to save copies of the original code you are changing. If you have any problems and need to compare your change with the original, or simply turn your code off and reinstate the original, the source is already there waiting.

Comment lines inside the PostNuke source can also be used to mark your changes. Add a couple lines like these above or below your hacks:

```
// =======================================================
// =======================================================
// =======================================================
```

Then when you are trying to find the spot where you changed the code, it's easy to see exactly where your edits begin. This is especially useful in the larger PostNuke files that can be well over a thousand lines of code.

PHP in Themes

Many thousands of lines of code have gone into modularizing PostNuke themes so that layout code is completely separate from the programming logic. This is very beneficial to developers on many levels, not the least of which is interchangeable themes.

But while the removal of logic from the display is great, there's no reason PHP should be removed from the display. PHP is just a programming language. Sure it allows you to write and control logical structures, but it can also be used to automate and simplify display code.

Site developers who are not full programmers can take advantage of PostNuke's XHTML templates to format their sites without needing to learn PHP. Programmers who develop sites with PostNuke can use the dynamic benefits of the language to also automate the XHTML display itself.

Create New Theme Variables

Every PostNuke theme has a file in its root folder called theme.php. This file is designed to create the variables and code called by the templates. Here's a simple example:

```
$bgcolor = '#FFFFFF';
```

This line of code creates a display variable you can now use throughout your theme. Xanthia themes use this feature too:

```
$bgcolor = $colors['background'];
```

where the color codes are pulled from the Xanthia palettes in the database and applied to local variables for use in XHTML templates. The templates are parsed by the theme engine so that variable calls like this:

```
<body style="background-color:<!--[$bgcolor]-->;">
```

reach the client browsers like this:

```
<body style="background-color:#FFFFFF;">
```

You can use this technique to style additional design elements. Examine your site and look for theme content that's repeated. You might have contact links on various locations, so place the address in a variable:

```
$mailcontact = 'webmaster@mysite.com';
```

Now, if you need to change your contact email, you only have to change it once to apply it to every location in every template.

Do your templates include special copyright or legal text? Do you have JavaScript menus that are reused? Pulling these components out of your design and into variables makes developing your theme easier.

Generate XHTML Dynamically

If you open an older, non-Xanthia theme, you'll immediately notice the legacy OpenTable() and CloseTable() functions:

```
function OpenTable() {
    echo "<table width=\"100%\" border=\"0\" cellspacing=\"1\" cellpadding=\"0\"
style=\"background-color:$GLOBALS[bgcolor2]\"><tr><td>\n";
    echo "<table width=\"100%\" border=\"0\" cellspacing=\"1\" cellpadding=\"8\"
style=\"background-color:$GLOBALS[bgcolor1]\"><tr><td>\n";
}
```

These structures were designed to modularize the display of repeated features in PostNuke and are the predecessors of current templates. Although you should not need to call functions to wrap content anymore, the concept of using PHP to write out repetitious XHTML is still very useful. Replace common XHTML code with more theme variables. Here's an example snippet of code from the beginning of the master.htm file in the pnDefault theme:

```
<table cellpadding="0" cellspacing="0" border="0">
    <tbody>
        <tr valign="top">
            <td style="width:<!--[$lcolwidth]-->px;" valign="top">
                <!-- Left Block Start -->
                <!--[$leftblocks]-->
                <!-- Left Block End -->
            </td>
            <td>
                <img src="<!--[$imagepath]-->/pixel.gif" width="15" height="1" alt="" />
            </td>
```

```
<td valign="top">
    <!-- Content Start -->
    <table border="0" cellpadding="0" cellspacing="0" width="100%">
        <tr>
            <td align="left" valign="top">
                <!--[$ZBANNERA]-->
            </td>
        </tr>
        <tr>
            <td align="left" valign="top">
                <!--[$ZSCHANNELTOP]-->
            </td>
        </tr>
    </table>
    <table border="0" cellpadding="0" cellspacing="0" width="100%">
        <tr>
            <td align="center">
                <!--[$ZBANNERB]-->
            </td>
        </tr>
        <tr>
            <td align="left" valign="top">
                <table border="0" cellpadding="0" cellspacing="0">
                    <tr>
```

Looking for repeated code just in this short bit, these lines come up as good candidates:

```
<table cellpadding="0" cellspacing="0" border="0">
<table border="0" cellpadding="0" cellspacing="0" width="100%">
<td align="left" valign="top">
<td valign="top">
```

They are even more obviously repeated with further scanning of this file or comparisons to other templates. Replace the XHTML with a variable and not only can you change all the repeated references in one edit, but you don't have to type out the long XHTML each time you need it.

Another commonly repeated element is the spacer image. Many websites use this handy tool to force the width or height of XHTML structures, and spacers are also useful for marking the columns and rows in a very complex table to ensure proper browser rendering.

The entire spacer image tag can be placed in a variable for easy reuse. If your theme's image design is defined in style sheets, so that no unique images are called in the XHTML itself, this image variable is especially useful to fill up all the <div> and <td> tags that would otherwise be empty.

Generate CSS Dynamically

The CSS you use with your themes can also be generated dynamically. Start with a look at a few style definitions from the ExtraLite PostNuke theme:

```
.pn-pagetitle {
color: #000000;
font: bold 16px Tahoma, Verdana, sans-serif;
text-decoration: none;
background: none;
}
.pn-title {
color: #000000;
font: bold 14px Tahoma, Verdana, sans-serif;
text-decoration: none;
background: #FFFFFF;
}
.pn-storytitle {
color: #000000;
font: bold 14px Tahoma, Verdana, sans-serif;
letter-spacing: 3px;
text-decoration: none;
background: none;
}
.pn-normal {
color: #000000;
font: 13px Tahoma, Verdana, sans-serif;
text-decoration: none;
background: #FFFFFF;
}
.pn-sub {
color: #000000;
font: 12px Tahoma, Verdana, sans-serif;
text-decoration: none;
background: none;
}
```

Obvious, repeated elements include the font color, the families, and the lack of text decoration. There's never a reason to have a CSS file like this when you have access to PHP. The file should have a .php extension and be included in the theme.php. Then at the head of the CSS, lines like these could be used:

```
$families = 'Tahoma, Verdana, sans-serif';
$colortxt = '#000000';
```

But the static nature of ExtraLite (and similar older themes), is that they were never designed to be dynamic. Coding themes with the legacy code from ExtraLite work fine, but you have to create modularity with the previous scripting.

Dynamically generated styles can be utilized more easily by building your theme on the Xanthia model instead. For example, Xanthia stores color variables in the database so that you can make palette sets and change your theme's feel by simply changing the palette colors.

The Xanthia CSS file is thankfully already styles.php, and it's very easy to script out the rest of the style classes. Take a look at this code from pnDefault's styles.php:

```
.menu {
    font-family: Verdana, Arial, Helvetica;
    color: "._XA_TTEXT1COLOR.";
    font-size: {$text}px;
    font-weight: bold;
    margin: 11px;
}
.pn-normal {
    font-family: Verdana, Arial, Helvetica;
    color: "._XA_TTEXT1COLOR.";
    font-size: {$text}px;
    font-weight: normal;
}
.pn-title {
    font-family: Verdana, Arial, Helvetica;
    font-size: {$title}px;
    font-weight: bold;
    color: "._XA_TTEXT1COLOR.";
    text-decoration: none;
}
```

Notice how both the font size and color are set dynamically for the classes. This is exactly the kind of variable coding that should be universally applied to all themes. Unfortunately, the identical font-family values are still not dynamic, but you can create your own variable at the top of the file and similarly call it throughout the CSS to remedy the problem.

Look at these styles, also from pnDefault:

```
.pn-normal A:link {
    font-family: Verdana, Arial, Helvetica;
    color: "._XA_TTEXT2COLOR.";
    font-size: {$text}px;
    text-decoration : underline;
```

```
}
.pn-normal A:visited {
    font-family: Verdana, Arial, Helvetica;
    color: "._XA_TTEXT2COLOR.";
    font-size: {$text}px;
    text-decoration : underline;
}
.pn-normal A:hover {
    font-family: Verdana, Arial, Helvetica;
    color: "._XA_TSEPCOLOR.";
    font-size: {$text}px;
    border-color:   "._XA_TTEXT2COLOR.";
    text-decoration: none;
}
.pn-normal A:active {
    font-family: Verdana, Arial, Helvetica;
    color: "._XA_TTEXT2COLOR.";
    font-size: {$text}px;
    text-decoration: underline;
}
```

Except for the color and one underline reference, they are completely identical. And there are many other sets of similar classes, all of which can be automated using a simple function.

Suppose, for example, you know those colors and the text size are all available variables. At the top of the page, there would need to be one more variable for the font-family and the function as follows:

```
$mainfonts = 'Verdana, Arial, Helvetica';
function writeAnchorClasses ($name, $fonts, $colors, $size, $decoration) {
    $aClasses = array("link", "visited", "hover", "active");
    for($i=0; $i < count($aClasses); $i++) {
        echo ".$name A:$aClasses[$i] {\n";
        echo "    font-family:$fonts;\n";
        echo "    color:$colors[$i];\n";
        echo "    font-size:".$size."px;\n";
        echo "    text-decoration:$decoration[$i];\n";
        echo "    }\n";
    }
}
```

Each time you need to write a set of anchor classes, you can reduce the 25 lines down to just 4:

```
$class = 'pn-normal';
$aColor = array(_XA_TTEXT2COLOR, _XA_TTEXT2COLOR, _XA_TSEPCOLOR, _XA_TTEXT2COLOR);
$aDeco = array("underline", "underline", "none", "underline");
writeAnchorClasses($class, $mainfonts, $aColor, $text, $aDeco);
```

Now if you want to change that font size from px to pt, or add an italic line or background color variable, all the changes can be accomplished nearly immediately. And creating more styles with anchor classes is a snap. With a little more creativity, even the nonanchor class could be generated from the same single function.

As you are designing your own themes and writing your own styles, always look for ways to write your code leaner and smarter. PHP is a tool to make your development easier, and it can do wonders if you let it.

Troubleshooting

This chapter deals with more concepts than actual steps and procedures to complete, so problems you might encounter will be more related to syntax than bugs. For a PHP language reference, there really is no better source than php.net. Their online guide (www.php.net/manual/en/) is great, and it contains a much more complete reference by far than the intro crash course in this chapter.

A similarly great resource for both XHTML and CSS (and many other technologies) is the W3Schools site (www.w3schools.com). Every tag is detailed with browser compatibility tables and examples, and the site has interactive test windows where you can try sample code live with changes to see how it works.

Next

In the next chapter, you will take this PHP knowledge in hand and start hacking PostNuke code. The next chapter covers hacking basics and general rules to follow, and should you get into trouble, you learn tips and tools to get you fixed up and going again.

Hacking PostNuke

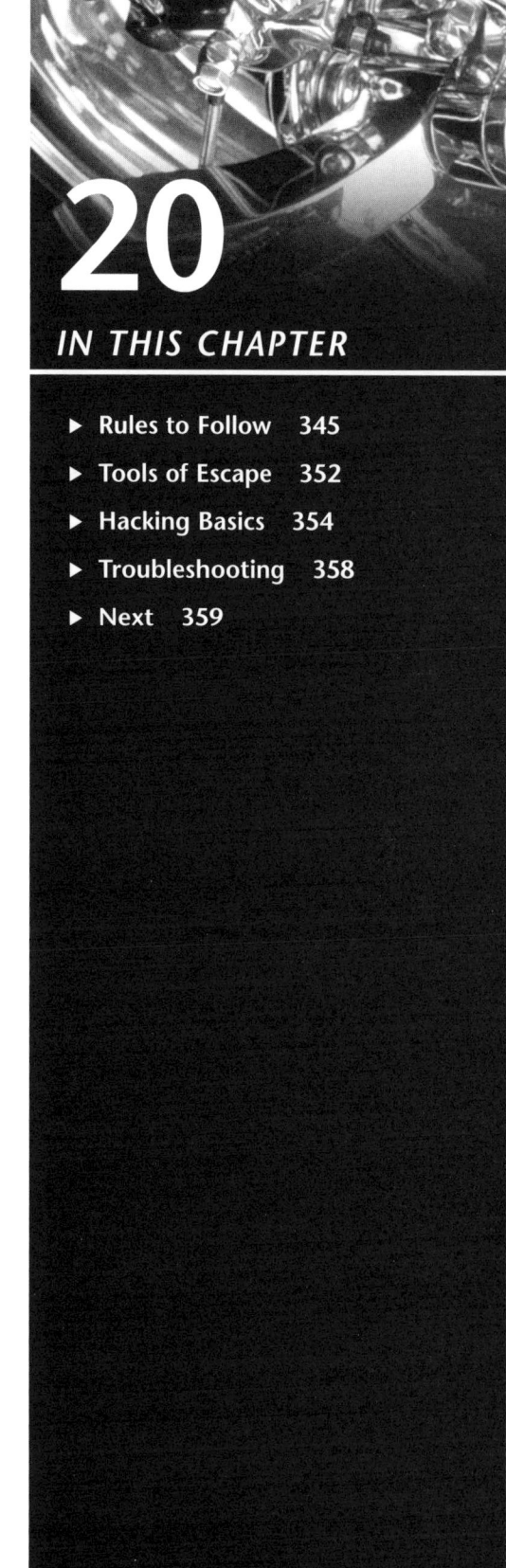

20

PostNuke is a rapidly growing application, but for all its strengths, it does not yet solve every users' needs right out of the proverbial box. For many issues, your only immediate option is to alter the system code to work or look in a way that better suits your implementation. These changes are code hacks.

Hacking PostNuke might sound like an intimidating operation, but with a little patience, and these tips in hand, you are unlikely to have any problems. This chapter introduces general guidelines to follow and provides some insight into solving and preventing problems that might come up. Topics include

- Rules to follow

- Tools of escape

- Hacking basics

Rules to Follow

PostNuke is open source and written in PHP. By definition, you have access to every line and variable in the code. The database is wide open to your changes, and you can rewrite code in part or whole at any time. But having omnipotence over your install of PostNuke is not by itself necessarily a reason to start making changes.

> **Note**
>
> The hacks you make to your PostNuke site might not survive a version upgrade. You should document your changes to be certain they are properly added to new versions.

If you expect to still have a functional site when you are done, you need to approach your hacking efforts with care and purpose. People hack PostNuke for both customization and extension. It is in many ways still a young application, and no application can do everything. Feel free to make changes to your install to ensure PostNuke remains a viable site solution. But while making those changes, keep these few general hacking guidelines in mind.

Have a Plan

This might seem obvious, but having some kind of plan for what you want to accomplish, outlined before you begin, is essential. Think carefully about what changes you intend. And if needed, write them out on paper to be certain you understand what the site will look like when the changes are done.

Experimenting with PostNuke is certainly as valid a plan as adding a new field to a form. But you'll have an easier time learning how to customize PostNuke if you focus your explorations on just a few areas at a time, such as performing the changes needed to add a specific feature.

Maintain Original Source

After you change a line and click Save, the original is gone. Of course, you can reproduce the original by pulling the file back out of the install archive, but that can be a lengthy process. It will save you more time and grief to simply duplicate any line you are changing, comment out the original, and alter the copy.

The same standard goes for complete code replacements or deletions. Just place the double forward slashes at the head of the line as follows:

```
// echo "<td><span class=\"pn-normal\"><input type=\"checkbox\" name=\"chng_user_
viewemail\" value=\"1\" checked=\"checked\" /> " . _ALLOWUSERS . "</span></td></tr>";
```

Or use the block comment code for multiple lines:

```
/*
        if ($chng_user_viewemail == 1) {
            echo "<td><span class=\"pn-normal\"><input type=\"checkbox\"
name=\"chng_user_viewemail\" value=\"1\" checked=\"checked\" /> " . _ALLOWUSERS .
"</span></td></tr>";
        } else {
```

```
          echo "<td><span class=\"pn-normal\"><input type=\"checkbox\"
name=\"chng_user_viewemail\" value=\"1\" /> " . _ALLOWUSERS . "</span></td></tr>";
        }
*/
```

If you find your hack has unforeseen issues, it's very handy to be able to read back through the original code. In addition, you can comment out your change and uncomment the original code to revert back at any time.

If you are performing a complete file replacement, you can still rename the original file for safekeeping instead of overwriting it. Try using "filename.orig" to lessen the likelihood its PHP script will be run by accident.

Change as Little as Possible

Most PostNuke hacks amount to little more than tweaking; hacking the source is done to build on the existing foundation, not reinvent the wheel. There's no need to radically alter the application when a few precise changes will do the same job. Small changes are easier to accomplish and understand, and they take less time to document and reproduce, should you upgrade and want to hack your new install in the same way.

Test as You Go

One of the great benefits of working with noncompiled code is that any change can be saved and tested instantly. When you are planning your changes, consider where logical breaks in the process will let you test fewer alterations at one time. For example, look for specific changes that can be grouped, completed, and tested independently of the other changes needed for the complete hack. The smaller segments can then be tested separately for bugs and issues.

Segmented testing is essential for large programming changes. You might feel you've edited every line perfectly, but if there are problems debugging even just a few dozen lines of code over multiple files it can take longer than the code edits did originally.

> **Tip**
>
> It's a little harder to test if your site is being cached, by, for example, PHP settings or a theme engine such as Xanthia or AutoTheme. You might make a change, but not see it on a refresh because your browser is receiving older cache data from your server. Try disabling all caching while you make changes to be certain you, and your visitors, will see the correct version of the site.

Document Changes

Document everything. Yes, it takes time and, in some cases, might seem a waste of time, but documenting your changes is important. You can, and should, document a hack in three ways.

Inline Comments

When you are editing a particular line, place a comment marker with it. You should be commenting out original lines, so the comment markers will already be there to make it easy. Here's an example:

```
// **HACK** Removing delete option for all users 04/20/04
// ."<option value=\"DeleteStory\">"._DELETESTORY."</option>"
```

The note doesn't have to be extensive, just enough to make it clear what you did. Adding a date reference can also be very useful.

> **Tip**
>
> Using keywords like **HACK** in your documentation makes it easy to locate your changes later. Open a file and do a global search for your keyword. You instantly jump to the next hack.

Offline Documentation

Write out clear documentation of each hack. Use plain English and describe what you intended with the change(s). Cut and paste the changed code (both before and after) into your document. Include line filenames and line number references. Then save the documentation to a backup disk or print out the explanation and file the hard copy in a safe place.

You should have a solid understanding of the code areas you are hacking, but will you still remember every detail a year later? Your server's hard drive might unexpectedly fail, requiring a rebuild from scratch. All of your hacks will be gone, along with all the nice inline comments. If you also document your changes separately from your server, you effectively back up the ideas and steps required to reproduce everything. It can turn a total catastrophe into simply a mild annoyance.

Even if you are certain your server will never meet a dark end, it's likely that you will want to upgrade PostNuke eventually. Copying old changed files over new versions is not a safe way to rehack an upgraded site. Many files are changed with every new release, and you might overwrite essential code.

You need to follow the hack's steps again and apply the *idea* to the new code. The documentation lets you see where to look to make a similar change in the new PostNuke, but how you need to go about creating the effect might not be the same. Apply the idea to the new site, but the hack itself might be very different.

The new PostNuke release might already include new features that before were only hacks. Test the upgrade before assuming your hack is even needed.

Public Release

One of PostNuke's greatest strengths is its extensive community. The pool of knowledge and talent present in the main forums alone is a resource no PostNuke site developer should be without (forums.postnuke.com). You can search archives for information and ask new questions to the many experts.

The more permanent way you can document your hack is by releasing it to the PostNuke community at large. Releasing the hack can be as simple as posting the information on the main PostNuke forums (forums.postnuke.com), or you can go a bit further and produce online documentation on your website and even provide personal support for the posted changes. If it was a useful change for you, perhaps other users can also benefit from the hack. And after it's in the public domain, odds are it'll still be there if you yourself need to find it at a later date.

The community might also pick up the hack and expand on it further, adding and extending the changes into an even better application improvement. Truly beneficial changes to PostNuke tend to end up in new releases. If you feel your changes are good enough to be part of the application itself, post them publicly. The development team might pick it up if there is enough interest.

Use Existing Functions

PostNuke includes a large set of integrated functions that allow developers to access key information and content directly and easily. The functions make up the PostNuke Application Programming Interface (pnAPI). Use the PostNuke API whenever possible. The PostNuke API documention can be found at docs.postnuke.com, and a listing of the pnAPI functions is in Appendix E, "PostNuke API." There are benefits and disadvantages to having an API, but you can see the pros easily outweigh the cons.

API benefits include the following:

- **Speed**—Any function you don't have to write means your development takes less time. In addition, you don't need to learn the internals of the core system.

- **Code consistency**—Coding consistent with the global standards has increased readability and is easier to comprehend. Anyone familiar with the API will be able to follow the code.

- **Lifespan extension**—PostNuke evolves with each release. Features of the core system change and will eventually render a non-API–compliant hack useless. But the PostNuke API frontend seldom changes, so a hack developed to work with the API will most likely continue to work with future versions.

- **Modular development**—The programming interface separates the main PostNuke system from the modules that run on top of it. Module and core developers can both work independently on upgrades without affecting one another.

- **Stability**—It's impossible to make usable hacks on a moving target. The core system needs to change to grow, but the API gives you a foundation you can rely on.

API disadvantages include the following:

- **Learning curve**—You need to understand the API functions in order to know how and when to use them.

- **System overhead**—All APIs add a level of overhead to their systems.

- **Missing functions**—The API can't account for every possible need anyone might have.

Tip

Submit your API function suggestions to the core development team, and provide code examples if you have them. That way, your ideas might be included with future releases. Suggestions can be submitted using the Tracker forms at noc.postnuke.com/projects/postnuke/.

Beware of Global Changes

When you are hacking PostNuke, you are changing an integrated system. Some files are referenced by many others, and a change to one file might inadvertently affect your entire site. Changes to files in the root `includes` folder and the PostNuke site root itself should be handled with care. Check code dependencies and function references. Be careful when making changes to be certain your local change doesn't go global.

If you need to make a specific function change but only want it to apply to one module, you can duplicate the function, customize the copy, and name it with a different name. The copy can then be called with the new name while the rest of your PostNuke site continues to use the old function.

Browse your site fully after a hack to see if something looks out of place. This is one good example where having those original lines commented out close by your hack, is very handy. You can comment out the hack and turn the original code live again to repair a global dilemma. It gives you time to review your hack and see if you need to approach the change in a different way.

Follow PHP Coding Standards

It's very important to follow coding standards. Not only does it make your code more easily understandable by others, but adhering to standards also helps ensure your code is compatible with future releases of PHP.

You can find a number of standards guides online (http://wact.sourceforge.net/index.php/ PhpCodingStandard/), but the following list includes some universal basics:

- **Use full start and end tags**—There are a number of ways to open and close a segment of PHP code, including support for other languages and shorthand styles. Technically, the most appropriate way is like this:

  ```
  <?php
  ?>
  ```

- **Indent lines with four spaces**—Tabs are a problem for some editors. Using four spaces for each indent level makes your code format well in all circumstances.

- **Use spaces around operators**—Assignment, comparison, logical, and arithmetic characters should always be displayed with surrounding spaces, as in the following examples:

  ```
  $var1 = 'widget';
  if ($var2 > 5) {
  ```

- **Use spaces around control structures**—The curly brackets used to define structures should always be separated from surrounding code by a space:

  ```
  <?php
  if ($x != $y) {
      action1;
  } else {
      action2;
  }
  ?>
  ```

- **Use naming conventions**—There's been a great deal of argument in different circles on what are the best naming conventions. The golden rule is to at least have *some* standard that's consistent with all other developers with whom you are working. Names with an initial lowercase word and capitalized words thereafter are suggested, such as getWidget(), $intData, and $widget.

- **Use conventional C style comments**—Always use the // and /* */ comment standards. Avoid use of shell comments such as #.

Follow Local Coding Style

In addition to the standards outlined previously, you should stay consistent with the style of the code you are changing. Many programming style decisions are arbitrary, and programmers do develop their own personal style.

Review the code you are changing. How did the programmer use quotes? What kind of comment markers already exist? What naming convention is in place? Try to maintain the style of the code for consistency and readability.

Don't Hack in Production

It's strongly recommended that when you're making code changes to PostNuke, you do them in a development environment. It is sometimes hard to predict what a change might do, and even experts make mistakes. Make your changes and test fully *before* you make the change live to your visiting public.

If your PostNuke site is already live and you can't take it offline for the change, set up a clone of your site locally and do the testing there. After you have your hack completed, you can copy the files up to your server to go live with the hack.

Tools of Escape

Running a highly technical website system is not always easy. Issues come up, accidents happen, and sometimes you might be looking for a thrown life preserver to pull your site out of the deep water. When that happens, try these tools and steps to get you back on your feet.

PostNuke Swiss Army Knife

The single most important tool every PostNuke site administrator should have ready in their back pocket is the PostNuke Swiss Army Knife. Commonly called PSAK for short, the tool is actually just a single PHP file you place in your site's root directory. From there, you simply browse the file to access its features (see Figure 20.1). PSAK's features are shown in the following list:

- **New DB Username/Password Encoding**—This feature resets the username and password PostNuke uses to access its database. This is the information maintained in config.php covered during the PostNuke install. This is most useful when your database changes, perhaps due to a host move, for example, and you need to update PostNuke to reflect the new server settings.

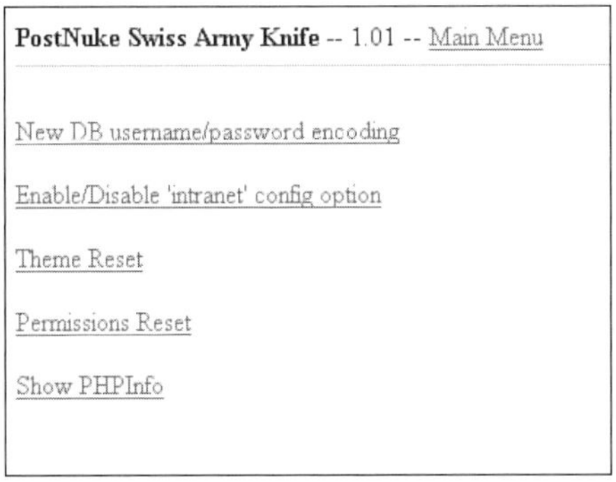

PostNuke Swiss Army Knife -- 1.01 -- Main Menu

New DB username/password encoding

Enable/Disable 'intranet' config option

Theme Reset

Permissions Reset

Show PHPInfo

FIGURE 20.1   Rescuing your site with the PostNuke Swiss Army Knife.

- **Enable/Disable 'Intranet' Config Option**—This feature toggles the Run on Intranet option in the PostNuke Website Configuration page. If you cannot access your site with a fully qualified domain (for example, www.yoursite.com), and you turn off the toggle, you will be locked out of your site. This fixes the problem.

- **Theme Reset**—Broken themes are a common problem with PostNuke. It's best to not run a bad theme on a live site, but even with the Xanthia test system, there are times when you might have no choice. Should a broken theme end up breaking your site too, you can use this feature to reset the theme. There's also an option to reset all users' themes at the same time.

- **Permissions Reset**—Badly configured user permissions are another chief cause of site lockout. This feature of PSAK can clear all user permissions as well as reset the group permissions back to their default values.

- **Show PHPInfo**—PHPInfo is not so much a fix as an information tool. The link places the phpinfo() function an easy click away. The function displays essential information about your server and how it's configured.

Note

Leaving psak.php in your web server's root directory is very dangerous. A malicious visitor can damage your site through the open access. Always remove the file from your website after use.

The PostNuke Swiss Army Knife is currently available as version 1.01 in the Add-ons section of downloads.postnuke.com. You can also get that version from this book's online materials.

PSAK 2.0 is currently in development, but there has been no official statement regarding the availability of the upcoming version.

Broken Module/Theme Recovery

It's very easy for a broken theme or module to disable portions or even your entire site. In the latter case, a defective module can, for example, break the Module Administration page. Errors on the page prevent the table from being rendered, and you don't have the option to remove the offending module.

This is another circumstance in which the interpreted nature of PHP helps make things easy. All you need to do is rename the main directory of the offending module or theme.

For modules, the hiding of the bad code fixes the table and you can manually remove the module completely using the form. Removing a bad regular PostNuke theme forces the use of the generic default theme ExtraLite.

With the introduction of Xanthia themes, you can no longer fix a broken interface by a rename. The database-driven elements are accessible even when the files are not. One solution that might work is to rename the offending theme and then rename one of the working Xanthia themes to the broken theme's name. This merges some elements of each, but the theme will likely work well enough to allow you to reset the theme.

Should these easier options fail, remember you can always edit the MySQL database directly and change any settings you want. PSAK accomplishes the same effect for many problems, and its interface is generally easier and faster to use.

PostNuke Install Archive

Always save a copy of the original install files you used to create your PostNuke website. If a hack goes bad, the last resort, short of an entire new install, is file replacement. You can extract originals of the files you changed and simply copy them over your edited versions. PostNuke uses the originals instead, and you can try the hack again.

Hacking Basics

To perform a hack, you need to be familiar with PostNuke's files. For some hacks, half the work can be finding exactly where the code is that you want to change. But, thankfully, knowing how files are organized and how to search them can make it relatively easy to pin down your target code.

Directory Structure

Here is a simplified diagram of the PostNuke directory tree:

```
[root]
|---/docs
|---/images
|---/includes
|    |---/blocks
|    |---/classes
|    |    |---/Smarty
|    |---/language
|    |    |---/blocks
|    |         |---/eng
|    |---/search
|---/install
|---/javascript
|---/language
|    |---/eng
|---/modules
|    |---/Autolinks
|    |    |---/pndocs
|    |    |---/pnimages
|    |    |---/pnlang
|    |         |---/eng
|    |---/AvantGo
|    |    |---/docs
|    |    |---/lang
|    |         |---/eng
|    |---/Blocks
|    |    |---/pnimages
|    |    |---/pnlang
|    |         |---/eng
|    |--- [etc.]
|---/pnadodb
|---/themes
```

There's a pattern in the structure of which you need to be aware; everything in PostNuke is designed to be modular. Throughout the structure, you will repeatedly find folders for docs, images, and language files. Each module has one or more of those folders, and you'll see them all in the site root too.

The documentation folders usually contain text files with install and usage notes. Sometimes, they also include version information and troubleshooting tips. The `images` folders contain whatever graphics are needed for their respective modules or systems.

The `language` folders contain the PHP files that define a module's plain text variables. For example, when you see the text "Go back to main page," the page is actually calling a variable `_GOBACK`. The system cross-references the variable name with the currently selected language, and displays the appropriate text on the screen during load.

Root Folders

The root folders are defined as follows:

- `docs`—Basic PostNuke documentation; short installation guide included.

- `images`—Primary image folder; key folder is the subdirectory `global`, which contains many important images used throughout PostNuke.

- `includes`—Components used by most modules; the `blocks` subdirectory is important for hacking, and you can find a number of key files in the `includes` root.

- `install`—Temporary directory containing the files required to install Postnuke. The folder should not be present on your server after your site install is complete.

- `javascript`—General scripts used by some modules, such as a window pop-up.

- `language`—Global language definitions used throughout the site. Note that there are many language files distributed throughout the directory structure.

- `modules`—Location of all PostNuke modules on your site. If you are hacking a module, look here for its source.

- `pnadodb`—PostNuke's database abstraction library; provides support for a number of different databases through this code. You shouldn't change any of these files.

- `themes`—Location of the themes available for application to your site. These files are heavily edited when developing a new theme, but you don't need them for code hacks.

Code Hunting

Being familiar with the PostNuke file structure can make finding specific source code easier, but there are a few tips to keep in mind that should make it easy for you to find anything.

First browse to the pages that display what you want to change. Look at the uniform resource locator (URL) in your browser. For example, if you're viewing the Theme Select page for a user, you see the following URL:

```
http://www.yoursite.com/user.php?op=chgtheme
```

It seems clear that the file you need to edit is /user.php. Now look at this sample URL:

http://www.yoursite.com/admin.php?module=NS-Polls&op=main

In this case, the file that needs to be developed is not admin.php in the PostNuke root. Instead, you need to edit the admin.php file under the /modules/NS-Polls/ folder. Sometimes, the URL clearly shows the file and sometimes it simply points you in the right direction. But it's always a good first step.

Next try to determine if you need to edit a module file, a block, or something more global to PostNuke. Block files are always found in /includes/blocks and, the majority of the time, module files are located in their respective /modules/modulename folder.

After you have a fair idea what files to look into, your text editor can do the rest of the work for you. Your editor needs to be able to perform a search/find operation on open files. An ideal feature available with some editors is Search All Open Documents. With the All Documents feature, you can open a dozen files or more and easily determine where specific lines are written.

You can perform a simple track operation to see how it's done. Browse to the Web Links Configuration page (see Figure 20.2). Your URL should state this:

http://www.yoursite.com/admin.php?module=Web_Links&op=main

Look at the text on the page. For example, suppose you just need to remove the Broken Link Reports option from the page. So, the target is the code that echoes that link.

FIGURE 20.2 Tracking down code using language keywords.

The URL specifically references the /admin.php file, but there is a module reference associated with it, and you know the screen specifically relates to one module. So, more likely, the code is in /modules/Web_Links/admin.php.

To confirm exactly which file, you perform a search based on the text displayed for the link. Searching for "Broken Link Reports" in any of the code files does not find the line you need. All of the text is generated through the language system using variable definitions. Following the assumption that the relevant files are located in /modules/Web_Links, open the module's language file into your editor:

/modules/Web_Links/lang/eng/global.php

Search that file for "Broken Link Reports" and you come up with line 45:

```
define('_BROKENLINKSREP','Broken link reports');
```

That line tells you the variable that determines the exact code to edit is _BROKENLINKSREP. Now open up the Web Links admin.php file and try a search there:

/modules/Web_Links/admin.php

Tip

Don't stop at the first search hit; sometimes, the same variable is referenced multiple times in the same file and might also be in multiple files. Be certain you have the right code before you start making changes.

Very quickly, you hit on line 80:

```
."<a href=\"admin.php?module=".$GLOBALS['module']."&amp;op=LinksListBrokenLinks\">"._
BROKENLINKSREP." (".pnVarPrepForDisplay($totalbrokenlinks).")</a> | "
```

You can now very easily edit or remove the link by changing the code surrounding the key variable. Hunting down code in PostNuke isn't always that easy, but you'll find these steps jump you to the right code nearly every time.

Troubleshooting

This chapter's content is designed to help keep you out of trouble throughout the upcoming hacking chapters. These rules and tips should get you started safely. Always document everything, and at the very least, you can always restore the original PostNuke code should anything go wrong.

When you're truly stumped with a hack, use the forums (forums.postnuke.com). Try searching for your hack first; it might already be documented for you in the forums.

If you can't find it through a search, try starting a new thread in the appropriate forum area. Clearly post your intent and code examples and the community can lend you a hand. After you've accomplished your hack, post your documentation in the Tutorials and Solutions forum.

Next

It's time to start hacking PostNuke. In the next chapter, you will examine a series of improvements to the Site Settings page and look at hacking the blocks system.

General PostNuke Hacks

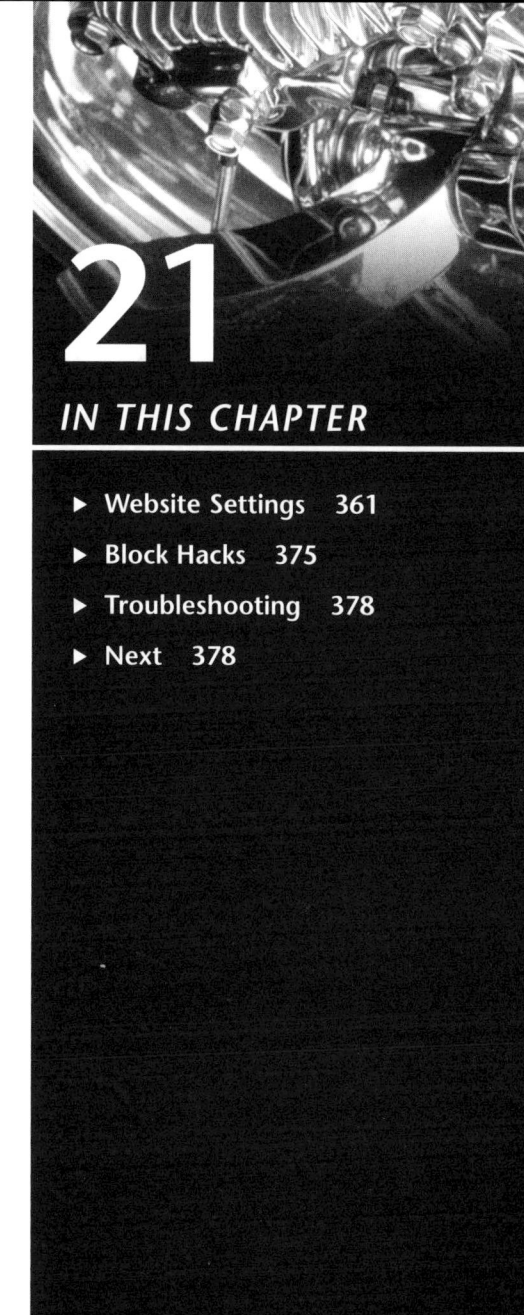

21

In this chapter, you begin your journey into hacking the PostNuke Content Management System (CMS). You look at the Site Settings page and the control of general blocks. These changes affect your website globally, but they are in many ways easier to accomplish than hacks on specific modules. The following activities are discussed:

- Change title display in browser

- Append dynamic keywords to static

- Create description metatag

- Fix copyright metatag date

- Create favicon metatag

- Display indigenous language names

- Add and remove tags from allowed list

- Apply styles to blocks

- Page/module-specific blocks

Website Settings

The PostNuke Site Settings options let you customize global variables and code that appear on all pages of your site. Although many of these page variables are easily changed in the form fields, the formatting of the variables is hard-coded into PostNuke. Also some metatag data options are missing altogether.

This is not a cause for concern, as a few simple hacks can remedy the need for extensions or customizations within your PostNuke site. The following sections cover some of the most commonly requested changes.

Change Title Display in Browser

PostNuke normally displays the site name, two colons, and the site slogan, as defined in the Website Settings. The title is used for bookmarks and browser histories, as well as sometimes being an important tool for populating search engine information. But if you want to customize the title further, you need to hack the title display.

PostNuke .75 introduces Xanthia themes that handle things a bit differently than regular PostNuke themes. If you are using a normal PostNuke theme, perform the following steps:

In your site's root folder is a file called header.php. Open this file in a standard text editor. Look for the if statement starting about line 93:

```
if ($artpage==1) {
    /**
     * article page output
     */
    global $info, $hometext;
    echo "<title>$info[title] :: ".pnConfigGetVar('sitename').' :: '.pnConfigGetVar
('slogan')."</title>\n";
    if (pnConfigGetVar('dyn_keywords') == 1) {
        $htmlless = check_html($info['maintext'], $strip ='nohtml');
        $symbolLess = trim(ereg_replace('("¦\?¦!¦:¦\.¦\(¦\)¦;¦\\\\)+', ' ', $htmlless));
        $keywords = ereg_replace('( |'.CHR(10).'|'.CHR(13).')+', ',', $symbolLess);
        $metatags = ereg_replace(",+", ",",$keywords);
        echo "<meta http-equiv=\"Keywords\" content=\"$metatags\">\n";
    } else {
        echo "<meta name=\"KEYWORDS\" content=\"".pnConfigGetVar('metakeywords')."\">\n";
    }
} else {
    /**
     * all other page output
     */
    echo '<title>'.pnConfigGetVar('sitename').' :: '.pnConfigGetVar('slogan')."</title>\n";
    echo '<meta name="KEYWORDS" content="'.pnConfigGetVar('metakeywords')."\">\n";
}
```

The older PostNuke code caters to its multimodule article system with the first half of the statement. When you browse into article areas, the title of an article displays before the site name.

First, you need to decide how you want your title to look. Changes to this code apply globally throughout your site. Set the site name to appear at the far left in all cases, followed by a single colon, and the article name can alternate with the slogan depending on the page.

Copy line 98, comment out the original, and change the `<title>` tag to look like this:

```
echo "<title>".pnConfigGetVar('sitename').": $info[title]</title>\n";
```

and change the `<title>` tag at about line 112 to look like this:

```
echo "<title>".pnConfigGetVar('sitename').": ".pnConfigGetVar('slogan')."</title>\n";
```

Notice the second change in this example was very minimal; if you didn't want to change the colon format, you would not have to change it at all.

Xanthia theme users will find this change much easier. You need to edit the title plug-in, which has simplified code due to its modularity. Open this file in your editor:

```
/modules/Xanthia/plugins/function.title.php
```

You need to edit lines 61 and 64 similar to the preceding example. The first line should be edited to look like this:

```
$title = pnConfigGetVar('sitename').": ".$GLOBALS['info']['title'];
```

And line 64 should appear as this:

```
$title =  pnConfigGetVar('sitename').": ".pnConfigGetVar('slogan');
```

Don't forget to back up the original lines so you can go back to them if desired later. This hack illustrates how quick and clean development is becoming with the ongoing PostNuke standardization.

Append Dynamic Keywords to Static

PostNuke handles metatag keywords (see Figure 21.1) through the Website Configuration page. Although you can define a large number of terms to apply to your pages, if you select the Dynamic MetaKeywords option, the static words are not used on those pages on which words can be generated. This system creates nicely customized keywords for your articles, but it means important words in the static list might go unused.

The solution to this problem is to combine the features and get the best of both worlds. You can hack the PostNuke metatag code to append dynamic terms to the static listing if dynamic words are available.

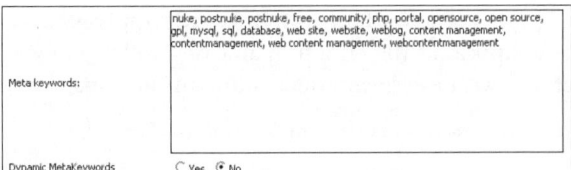

FIGURE 21.1   Defining keywords for your pages.

> **Note**
>
> If you plan to use this hack, you might want to review your static keyword selections. Too many keywords can be a bad thing, so leave only the important words and remove unneeded extras.

If you are using a non-Xanthia theme, find the file `header.php` in your site's root folder. Open it in a text editor and look for the assignment statement at about line 103:

```
$metatags = ereg_replace(",+", ",",$keywords);
```

Duplicate the line and alter your copy so that it looks like this:

```
$metatags = pnConfigGetVar('metakeywords').','.ereg_replace(",+", ",",$keywords);
```

That places the `metakeywords` variable before the dynamic article words. If you only change this one line, the Dynamic MetaKeywords enable/disable option in the Site Settings (see Figure 21.1) still works. If you disable the Dynamic MetaKeywords option, the static words are used; if you enable it, both are used.

You can also force the use of both sets of terms with articles by removing this code at about line 99:

```
if (pnConfigGetVar('dyn_keywords') == 1) {
```

and lines 105 and 106:

```
} else {
echo "<meta name=\"KEYWORDS\" content=\"".pnConfigGetVar('metakeywords')."\">\n";
```

Doing so means the Website Settings option no longer works.

If you are using a Xanthia theme, you need to open this file:

```
/modules/Xanthia/plugins/function.keywords.php
```

and change line 102 from this:

```
$keywords = implode(',', $keywords);
```

to instead look like this:

```
$keywords = pnConfigGetVar('metakeywords').implode(',', $keywords);
```

Be certain to comment out the original line. Now your static keywords appear before the dynamic.

Create Description Metatag

PostNuke does not allow you to define the contents of the description metatag. Instead, it uses whatever you have defined in your slogan as the description. Separating the two can be approached in two ways; you can hard-code the description metatag in the `header.php` or `master.htm` files, or you can create a description field in the site settings.

The first option is very easy to accomplish. If you are not using a Xanthia theme, open the `header.php` file in a text editor and look for line 115:

```
echo '<meta name="DESCRIPTION" content="'.pnConfigGetVar('slogan')."\">\n";
```

Edit it with your own description so that it appears as follows:

```
echo "<meta name=\"DESCRIPTION\" content=\"My site does many great things\">\n";
```

Xanthia users need to open the `master.htm` file for their respective theme:

```
/themes/[yourthemename]/templates/master.htm
```

Back up line 6:

```
<meta name="DESCRIPTION" content="<!--[slogan]-->">
```

and edit the working copy with your own description like this:

```
<meta name="DESCRIPTION" content="My site does many great things">
```

Browse to the Xanthia Theme Engine Administration page and find your theme in the table. Click the Reload Templates link in the Actions column to apply your change to the live site. That description now appears on all pages and the site slogan remains separate.

Besides changing PHP code, the second option of creating a new field in the Site Settings requires an additional variable and database entry. It's a fairly easy process whether you use a database tool or not. You can start by making the table changes.

The table with Site Settings data is called `nuke_module_vars`. If you are using an administration tool such as phpMyAdmin, find the table in the listing, select the Insert operation, and enter the following data into the fields, as shown in Table 21.1.

TABLE 21.1

Creating Description Metatag in Database

FIELD	VALUE
pn_id	Leave blank, it will autoincrement
pn_modname	/PNConfig
pn_name	metadescription
pn_value	Leave blank, it will be NULL for now

If you are not using a database tool or simply prefer to use straight Structured Query Language (SQL), the statement you need to submit is this:

```
INSERT INTO nuke_module_vars (pn_modname, pn_name)
VALUES ('/PNConfig', 'metadescription');
```

> **Note**
>
> If you chose a table prefix other than nuke during your install, that is the text which appears before module_vars in the table name.

Now that the database is prepared to receive the data, the next step is to add a text description for the form you will make later. Open this file in your text editor:

`/modules/NS-Settings/lang/eng/global.php`

> **Tip**
>
> The change to the global.php file in the eng directory only prepares the English language. If you use other languages, you must change their files, as well.

The definition lines are sorted in alphabetical order, and you should maintain the format for consistency. Look for this code at about line 59:

```
define('_METAKEYWORDS','Meta keywords');
```

Enter the new line right above _METAKEYWORDS. Make a new line and add this code:

```
define('_METADESCRIPTION','Meta Description');
```

Save the file. Now, you need to create a form element that will populate your table entry. The form should be on the Site Settings page with the other metatag options, and that file is found at this location:

```
/modules/NS-Settings/admin.php
```

Look at lines 163–167:

```
.'</td></tr><tr><td class="pn-normal">'
._SITESLOGAN.":</td><td><input type=\"text\" name=\"xslogan\" value=
\"".pnConfigGetVar('slogan')."\" size=\"50\" maxlength=\"100\" class=\"pn-normal\" />"
.'</td></tr><tr><td class="pn-normal">'
._METAKEYWORDS.':</td><td><textarea name="xmetakeywords" cols="80" rows="10" class="pn-
normal">'.htmlspecialchars(pnConfigGetVar('metakeywords')).'</textarea>'
.'</td></tr><tr><td class="pn-normal">'
```

Note

Note how the end and start of table rows are on the same line. It's common to run Hypertext Markup Language (HTML) together where page lines and code lines do not correspond, but if you are unfamiliar with HTML, be careful you maintain the table's consistency.

Add the new Meta Description field after the Slogan and before the Keywords. The Meta Keywords code is very similar to what you want for the description field, so you might want to copy lines 174 and 175 to make it easier. Your final code should look like this:

```
.'</td></tr><tr><td class="pn-normal">'
._SITESLOGAN.":</td><td><input type=\"text\" name=\"xslogan\" value=
\"".pnConfigGetVar('slogan')."\" size=\"50\" maxlength=\"100\" class=\"pn-normal\" />"
.'</td></tr><tr><td class="pn-normal">'
._METADESCRIPTION.':</td><td><textarea name="xmetadescription" cols="80" rows="10"
class="pn-normal">'.htmlspecialchars(pnConfigGetVar('metadescription')).'</textarea>'
.'</td></tr><tr><td class="pn-normal">'
._METAKEYWORDS.':</td><td><textarea name="xmetakeywords" cols="80" rows="10" class="pn-
normal">'.htmlspecialchars(pnConfigGetVar('metakeywords')).'</textarea>'
.'</td></tr><tr><td class="pn-normal">'
```

Save the file. You can now browse to the Site Settings Administration page and see the added form entry in Figure 21.2. It does work; you can add a description and submit the form, and the information will be stored in the database, but you have not yet told PostNuke to use the stored information with your site's pages.

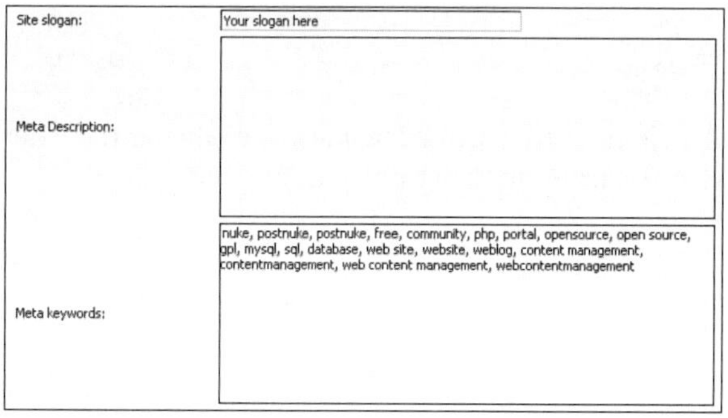

FIGURE 21.2   Adding Meta Description to your site.

For non-Xanthia themes, start up your editor and open the header.php file in your PostNuke root. Just as described in the hard-coded description hack previously, look for the following code at about line 115:

```
echo '<meta name="DESCRIPTION" content="'.pnConfigGetVar('slogan')."\">\n";
```

Copy and change the line to look like this:

```
echo "<meta name=\"DESCRIPTION\" content=\"".pnConfigGetVar('metadescription')."\">\n";
```

This enables PostNuke to use your description variable with the metatag. If you leave the description blank, the tag is generated with nothing for a description. If that concerns you, you can alternatively create an if statement to use another variable, such as the slogan, if the description is empty. Replace line 115 with this code:

```
if (pnConfigGetVar('metadescription') != NULL) {
   echo "<meta name=\"DESCRIPTION\" content=\"".pnConfigGetVar('metadescription')."\">\n";
} else {
   echo "<meta name=\"DESCRIPTION\" content=\"".pnConfigGetVar('slogan')."\">\n";
}
```

This change does not prevent a NULL entry if both the description and slogan fields have been left blank, but it does add a little robustness.

Xanthia users have a few more steps yet to complete. The Xanthia Theme Engine (XTE) has a set of modular plug-ins used to generate variable information for themes. Because the Meta Description information is entirely new, a new plug-in function needs to be created.

Look at the Xanthia plugins folder:

/modules/Xanthia/plugins/

You can copy one of those files for a source, or you can download the version of the description plug-in described here from the book's online materials. If you want to make the changes yourself, copy one of the files to a new file called function.metadescription.php.

Open this file in your editor. The only code you need to be concerned about is past the header comments, starting at roughly line 54. The line begins with function smarty_function_. Replace all of the function code with the following:

```
function smarty_function_metadescription($params, &$smarty)
{
    extract($params);
    unset($params);
    return pnConfigGetVar('metadescription');
}
```

Be certain you do not delete the closing PHP code: ?> after the end of the function. Now open up the master.htm file for your theme:

/themes/[yourthemename]/templates/master.htm

Edit a copy of line 6 to replace the word "slogan" with "metadescription." The line should now look like this:

```
<meta name="DESCRIPTION" content="<!--[metadescription]-->">
```

Now, your theme templates are prepared, but you must reload them for your changes to become live. Go to the Xanthia Theme Engine Administration page. Find your theme in the table, and click the Reload Templates link in the Actions column. You can see your description changes by viewing the source on any page.

Fix Copyright Metatag Date

PostNuke generates a copyright metatag, but if you are using a non-Xanthia theme, you might have noticed it still has a 2003 date. You can fix this oversight very easily with one edit.

In your site's root folder is a file called `header.php`. Open this file in a standard text editor. Look for this statement on line 120:

```
echo '<meta name="copyright" content="Copyright (c) 2003 by '.pnConfigGetVar(
'sitename')."\">\n";
```

Change the 2003 to 2004, save, and you're finished.

You can also dynamically generate the current year so that you do not have to edit it in the future with this line:

```
echo '<meta name="copyright" content="Copyright (c)'.date('Y').' by '.pnConfigGetVar(
'sitename')."\">\n";
```

Xanthia themes generate the copyright statement separately in each theme. You need to edit the `master.htm` file for the theme you are using. The path to the file is this:

```
/themes/[yourthemename]/templates/master.htm
```

The standard copyright tag is on line 11. The new Xanthia themes all have 2004 hard-coded, but going forward you'll need to update that to the current year. After you've made a change, you need to click the Reload Templates link for your theme on the Xanthia Theme Engine Administration page.

Create Favicon Metatag

It seems like nearly every site is using a favicon these days; you can see their use as the small icons displayed by Favorite entries in Microsoft Internet Explorer or on tabs in Mozilla Firefox. This nifty site enhancement is possible using PostNuke with just a few site changes. First, you need your icon file. If you're not certain how to create a favicon file, take a look at the information found at www.favicon.com. After you have your favicon file ready, place the icon in your website's root folder.

If you are not using a Xanthia theme, simply open up the `header.php` file in your site's root. After the style sheet @import finishes with `</style>` on line 131, add these two lines:

```
<link rel="shortcut icon" href="http://www.mysitename.com/favicon.ico" />
<link rel="icon" href="http://www.mysitename.com/favicon.ico" type="image/png" />
```

You need both of these lines to ensure you have complete browser support. The first line is the old way of defining a favicon, and one that most versions of Internet Explorer still use. The second line is the new standard for referencing a favicon, and current Mozilla and Opera browsers need that code.

Tip

With the new standard for site icon development, you can also use the Portable Network Graphics (PNG) image format. The benefit of PNG over the ICO Icon format is access to 24-bit color and a true alpha mask. You can create both images, and newer browsers use the PNG.

For Xanthia themes, you need to edit your theme's `master.htm` template file found here:

`/themes/[yourthemename]/templates/master.htm`

You should see that these two lines already exist in the template at lines 19 and 20:

```
<link rel="icon" href="<!--[$imagepath]-->/icon.png" type="image/png">
<link rel="shortcut icon" href="<!--[$imagepath]-->/favicon.ico">
```

Though the lines exist, the default Xanthia themes do not come with icons. You need to place your icon in the theme's `images` directory. Change lines 19 and 20 to reflect the filename of your icon. After you have completed all your changes, click the Reload Templates link for your theme on the Xanthia Theme Engine Administration page. This applies your `master.htm` changes and your icon appears.

Display Indigenous Language Names

An issue that's been brought up many times in the PostNuke community is the display of language names while in the default English setting. If you offer multiple languages on your site, it's generally preferred that the names of other languages be written in their respective indigenous format. For example, when a German user is personalizing his language interface, it's better for him to see Deutsch as an option instead of German. Having Aleman as the German option in the Spanish language set is just as problematic.

PostNuke currently displays the latter method, in which language names appear with English spellings. To make this change, you need to edit the language listing included with the English package. Start up your text editor and open this file:

`/language/eng/global.php`

The language definitions begin at line 183 and continue through line 224. Comment out the original language references; it is handy to have the English versions readily available. Now add in all of the following code:

```
define('_LANGUAGE_ARA','Arabic');
define('_LANGUAGE_BUL','Bulgarian');
define('_LANGUAGE_CAT','Català');
define('_LANGUAGE_CES','C^esky');
define('_LANGUAGE_CRO','Croatian CRO');
define('_LANGUAGE_HRV','Croatian HRV');
define('_LANGUAGE_DAN','Dansk');
define('_LANGUAGE_DEU','Deutsch');
define('_LANGUAGE_ELL','Greek');
define('_LANGUAGE_ENG','English');
define('_LANGUAGE_EPO','Esperanto');
define('_LANGUAGE_EST','Eesti');
define('_LANGUAGE_FIN','Suomi');
define('_LANGUAGE_FRA','Français');
define('_LANGUAGE_HEB','Hebrew');
define('_LANGUAGE_HUN','Magyar');
define('_LANGUAGE_IND','Bahasa Indonesia');
define('_LANGUAGE_ISL','íslenska');
define('_LANGUAGE_ITA','Italiano');
define('_LANGUAGE_JPN','Japanese');
define('_LANGUAGE_KOR','Korean');
define('_LANGUAGE_LAV','Latviešu');
define('_LANGUAGE_LIT','Lietuvin');
define('_LANGUAGE_MAS','Malay');
define('_LANGUAGE_MKD','Macedonian');
define('_LANGUAGE_NLD','Nederlands');
define('_LANGUAGE_NOR','Norsk');
define('_LANGUAGE_POL','Polski');
define('_LANGUAGE_POR','Português');
define('_LANGUAGE_RON','Românǎ');
define('_LANGUAGE_RUS','pa Ruski');
define('_LANGUAGE_SLV','Slovenščina');
define('_LANGUAGE_SPA','Español');
define('_LANGUAGE_SWE','Svensk');
define('_LANGUAGE_THA','Thai');
define('_LANGUAGE_TUR','Türkçe');
define('_LANGUAGE_UKR','Ukrainian');
define('_LANGUAGE_X_BRAZILIAN_PORTUGUESE','Português Brasileiro');
define('_LANGUAGE_X_KLINGON','Klingon');
```

```
define('_LANGUAGE_X_RUS_KOI8R','Russian KOI8-R');
define('_LANGUAGE_YID','Yiddish');
define('_LANGUAGE_ZHO','Chinese (Simp.)');
```

This list is designed to be universal, and all language packs can use it. A few of the languages listed are not converted due to possible limitations in browser displays. If your site visitors are assumed to have the proper character sets installed in their browsers for a given language, you should change the language entries here appropriately.

Add and Remove Tags from Allowed List

The list of HTML tags on the Site Settings page was developed to provide both flexibility and security. You can see from the warnings at the bottom of the page (see Figure 21.3) that some tags can be exploited by visitors wanting to crack your site. There might, however, be times when you need to open up access to additional tags or remove deprecated or unused tags.

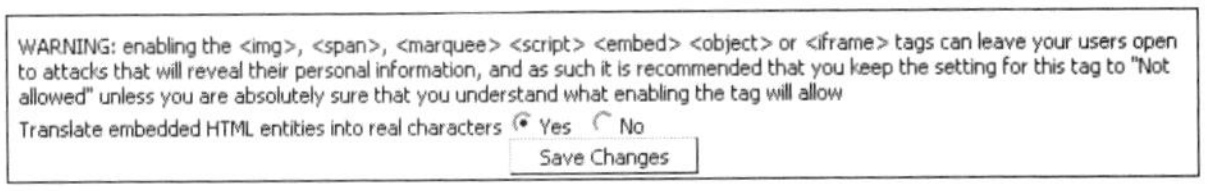

FIGURE 21.3   The dangers of HTML tags.

If you are running your site in a secure environment, such as a business intranet, protection from attacks might not be an issue at all. Also as Extensible Hypertext Markup Language (XHTML) standards evolve, you might find the need to add other tags that were not initially considered at the time your PostNuke version was released.

Thankfully, it's very easy to manage tags on the Site Settings page. Launch your text editor and open this file:

```
/modules/NS-Settings/admin.php
```

Scroll down to the bottom of the file to about line 523 where you should see this code:

```
// Local function to provide list of all possible HTML tags
function settingsGetHTMLTags() {
    // Possible allowed HTML tags
    return array('!--',
```

Below the preceding code is a long array of every HTML tag in the Site Settings list. Add additional lines with the tag name shown minus the < and > brackets, or remove those tags you feel are no longer needed. It's recommended you only comment out a line using // rather than completely deleting the code.

Change References to Allowed Tags

After you've changed the tag listing, you might want to change or remove the way allowed tags are referenced in other modules. As an example of this, look at the Comments feature shown in Figure 21.4.

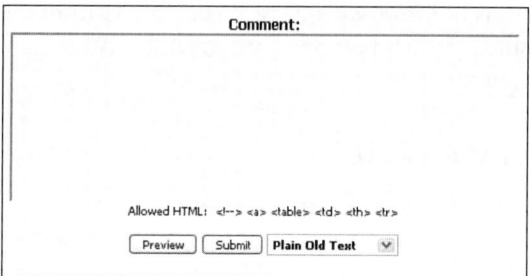

FIGURE 21.4   Allowed HTML for comments.

The tag list at the bottom of the form is automatically generated from the Site Settings table. You might find you prefer only publicizing certain tags or would rather remove the tag note altogether. Either is possible with a very quick hack.

Open your text editor and load up this file:

```
/modules/NS-Comments/index.php
```

Scroll down to roughly two thirds of the file and you should see this code starting at about line 879:

```
."<span class=\"pn-sub\">"._ALLOWEDHTML." ";

$AllowableHTML = pnConfigGetVar('AllowableHTML');
while (list($key, $access, ) = each($AllowableHTML)) {
    if ($access > 0) echo " &lt;".$key."&gt;";
}

echo "</span><br /><br />";
```

The `ALLOWEDHTML` variable displays the label text before the tags. If you want to hard-code a limited set of tags, you need to change only the middle code. Comment out the `$AllowableHTML` assignment and `while` statement, and add this line to replace them:

```
echo "&lt;mytagname&gt;";
```

This adds one tag. You can create multiple lines or string your tags together for something like this:

```
echo "&lt;agt; &lt;bgt; &lt;igt; &lt;br /gt;";
```

To remove the tag reference altogether, you need to comment all of the code shown previously, and add in this line:

```
echo "<br /><br />";
```

That ensures the spacing remains the same.

Block Hacks

As PostNuke has evolved, control of smaller elements like individual blocks has become easier and easier. The current release with Xanthia theme support allows you to develop custom block zones with separate theme templates for each zone. Similar features are found with other theme modules, such as AutoTheme (spidean.mckenzies.net), BlockHome (www.natewelch.com), or Nuclei (www.tangant.com).

If you are not comfortable with complicated theme systems, or just prefer a quick code change, hacking your PostNuke install might be a preferable option. Blocks on a given site are usually used with specific purpose, in that you can easily control where they are and how they look.

Note

The main drawback to hacking code that could be themed is the loss of modularity. If you later upgrade your site, your hack will be gone. A customized theme can be reapplied to a new install instantly. You can also recode your hack, however, and doing multiple hacks might take less time than theme development.

Apply Styles to Blocks

You can apply direct styles to blocks by editing the code used to generate the block. This effect can be handy if you want to quickly highlight a block to set its contents apart from the rest of your site.

Use the Incoming block as a good example. It appears dynamically whenever there is new content waiting to be approved. If this block is too far down in the site layout, it might be hard to see, and new content might go unnoticed. A simply styled hack can brighten up the block to make it impossible to miss.

The Incoming block is actually part of the core Menu block code, so you need to open this file in your editor:

```
/includes/blocks/menu.php
```

Scroll down to around line 133 and you see this code:

```
// Waiting content
if (!empty($vars['displaywaiting'])) {
    // Separate from current content, if any
    if ($content == 1) {
        $block['content'] .= addMenuStyledUrl($vars['style'], "", "", "");
    }
}
```

That is the beginning of the Incoming content code. Because this code is within another block, you can only edit the content area without affecting other block instances. But the benefit is any usage of the Waiting Content check box option with Menu blocks displays the hack changes. If you don't want a separate Incoming block, and want to display the content inside the Main Menu for example, it automatically applies there too.

Add the two lines of code after the first if statement in the following example:

```
if (!empty($vars['displaywaiting'])) {

    // Hack to highlight waiting content
    $block['content'] .= "<div style=\"background-color:#FFC000; padding:5px;\">";

    // Separate from current content, if any
    if ($content == 1) {
        $block['content'] .= addMenuStyledUrl($vars['style'], "", "", "");
    }
}
```

Now scroll down to what should be line 226 after you have made the preceding change. The code looks like this:

```
            }
        }
    }
}

// Styling
$block['content'] .= endMenuStyle($vars['style']);
```

You need to close the <div> tag after the first three closing } brackets. Here is the finished code:

```
            }
        }
```

```
    }
    $block['content'] .= "</div>";
}
```

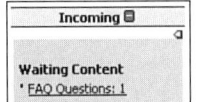

After you've saved your changes, load up your site in a browser, and your block looks like Figure 21.5. This example uses the gold color, but you can, of course, use any coloring, including bright red (#FF0000) if desired.

FIGURE 21.5
Highlighting content waiting for approval.

Page/Module-Specific Blocks

You can customize blocks to only appear for certain modules. Different theme systems offer this feature, including both Xanthia and AutoTheme, but if you are not familiar with more advanced settings in the themes, or simply don't like having to develop different templates for each module, this hack can save a great deal of time and trouble.

For this example, use the core Polls block. You'll make the block only appear on the main News page. The main Polls administration and comments code is all in the NS-Polls folder, but the file you want is located here:

/includes/blocks/poll.php

Open that file in your editor. Scroll down to about line 52 where you should see this code:

```
function pollMain($pollID, $row)
{
    if (!pnSecAuthAction(0, 'Pollblock::', "$row[title]::", ACCESS_READ)) {
        return;
    }
```

The pollMain function controls the display of the Polls block, and the first if statement is checking to see if a given user has read access before displaying the block.

Add the following code after the opening { and before the read check:

```
    // Hack to allow Polls only on News page
    if ($GLOBALS['ModName'] != "News") {
        return;
    }
```

The script simply checks whether the current module is called News. You can use any module name there; NS-Admin, for example, only shows the block on the Administration page. Similarly, this code makes the block appear on all pages *except* the Administration page:

```
    // Hack to disallow Polls on Admin page
    if ($GLOBALS['ModName'] == "NS-Admin") {
        return;
    }
```

Consult the Modules Administration page for the proper module names to use for any module you have installed.

Troubleshooting

Most hacks are very easy to troubleshoot; they either work or they don't. When you comment out changed lines, it's very easy to go back and test specific changes. But with the previous changes, you might encounter two specific problems that are not as simple as changing a line of code. Here's how to fix them.

Table `'xxxxx.nuke_module_vars'` Doesn't Exist

This error message is caused when you are trying to add data with the wrong table name. The `module_vars` table instance is present in all PostNuke installations, but the `nuke` prefix is a variable that might be different depending on your settings during your PostNuke install. Check your table names to confirm which prefix you have chosen.

Also, if you are using Multisites, your table names might be changed. If you have two or more `module_vars` tables for Multisites, you need to change them all when adding the description metatag.

Site Favicon Does Not Appear

You might have completed all of the site changes perfectly and still not be able to see your site icon. This is usually caused by browser caching. Your browser is unlikely to go looking for the icon file if it has already browsed your site. You can help force an icon check in two easy ways.

First, in your browser's location bar, click and hold on the icon to the left of your site URL. In Internet Explorer, the icon is the "e" default, and in Mozilla, the icon usually appears as a bookmark. Drag the icon away from that spot, just like you are dragging a new shortcut into existence, but you only need to drag it off the icon and then let go of the mouse button. The icon snaps back, but because you already started to create a new shortcut, the browser checks for a new icon.

If that quick method does not work, you need to create a real bookmark/favorite for your site. Add your site to your bookmarks, even if it is already there, and your browser checks for the new icon.

Next

The following chapter covers a Case Study in the development of a Personal Portfolio website. As the third Study in this text, it illustrates how to apply the more advanced techniques you've been learning to selectively use only the parts of PostNuke you need.

PART IV

Advanced PostNuke

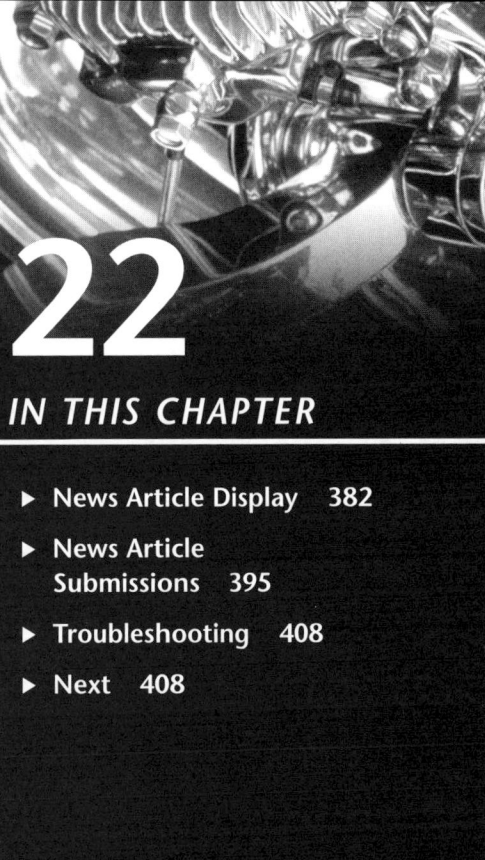

News and Article Hacks

22

Home page news and article content are relatively integral to most PostNuke sites. But "the way PostNuke does it" might not fit every site to which the Content Management System (CMS) is applied. PostNuke has many features, but sometimes there can even be too many options for users. The display of content is also often cookie cutter due to subtle limitations in the display code. Any problem can be solved; it just takes editing the code.

This chapter covers a number of PostNuke hacks to the article system. The first set of code changes cover the way articles are displayed, and the second set shows you how to edit the submission forms to provide the interface your users need. This chapter covers the following hacks:

- Theme-based topic graphics

- Article title and links

- Forcing story count on home page

- Changing default "Articles" to "No Category"

- Removing article categories

- Adding names to anonymous comments

News Article Display

The display of article content is very important to most PostNuke websites. Styles and themes let you customize the appearance of content on your site to a great deal, but there are some instances in which code limitations might be an issue for you. The good news is the code is available for you to edit to suit your needs. The following sections discuss three commonly requested changes to how PostNuke handles article display.

Theme-Based Topic Graphics

A feature commonly requested in the community is the ability to offer multiple themes to site users while also better integrating article topic images into the differing themes. By default, PostNuke topic images are contained in the global directory location /images/topics/. A user can switch themes, but the same topic icons are used for every theme. If you have customized your topic icons to best fit with a given theme, they are unlikely to look as good when applied to a different design.

The solution to this problem, of course, is to hack PostNuke's source to reference topics by theme. All it takes is the creation of a folder named "topics" under each theme's images directory and the editing of each reference to a topic icon path within PostNuke.

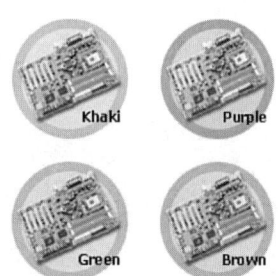

You can start by creating a set of topic icons designed to work with different themes. Look at the images displayed in Figure 22.1. The example icons are simple, standalone designs with differing colors backing the central image. The themes in this case are perhaps designed to give users a choice of color while keeping the general layout the same. You could just as easily create a number of completely different designs with different topic icons, but this example keeps it simple.

The images in the example are part of the book's online materials, so you can download them for use with this walk-through. Alternatively, create your own set of new images and apply them to your custom themes.

FIGURE 22.1 Theming your topics for a more polished design.

First set up each of your themes. If you are making color variants of a single theme, rename the theme to reflect the change, "mytheme-blue," for example. Activate all of the themes using the Xanthia Theme Engine administration page. Test the different themes to be certain they are all working before you begin with the hack steps.

> **Tip**
>
> Xanthia theme users can create color variants of a given theme easily by simply editing the xaninit.php file in the root folder of the copied theme. Change the color codes in the CreatePalette function, and when the copy is added, it displays the new colors.

Next add a directory to each of your themes. It should look like this:

```
/themes/mytheme/images/topics/
```

You should mirror the directory structure used by the rest of PostNuke, so make the directory name simply "topics" and use all lowercase letters. The path must be identical across all active themes, and remember PHP is case sensitive.

Copy each topic icon into its respective companion theme's directory. Each image must have the same filename for the system to work, so if you are using the sample icons, rename them at this time to remove the color reference in the filenames. For example, rename `icon-mainboard-purple.gif` to just `icon-mainboard.gif`.

There are five pages where topic icons are displayed. To complete the hack, edit the five files that make the calls to the global directory. Each edit is outlined in the following sections.

Active Topics Page

First, you can fix the Active Topics page. This is the page reached through the Topics link in the Main Menu. Open your text editor and load this file for editing:

```
/modules/Topics/index.php
```

Scroll down in your editor to around line 80 where you should see the following echo statement:

```
echo "<td align=\"center\">\n"
    ."<a class=\"pn-normal\"
href=\"modules.php?op=modload&amp;name=News&amp;file=index&amp;catid=&amp;topic=".
pnVarPrepForDIsplay($topicid)
    ."\"><img src=\"". pnVarPrepForDIsplay($tipath).""". pnVarPrepForDIsplay($topicimage)
    ."\" alt=\" ".pnVarPrepForDIsplay($topictext)."\" /></a><br />\n"
    ."<span class=\"pn-normal\">".pnVarPrepForDIsplay($topictext)."</span>\n"
    ."</td>\n";
```

This is the line that displays the image. Duplicate the line and comment out the backup copy. In the middle of the statement is the key `<img>` tag. Just after the source attribute begins, add in a call to the theme path. The additional code you are adding is `themes/".pnUserGetTheme()."/`. The changed statement looks like this:

```
echo "<td align=\"center\">\n"
    ."<a class=\"pn-normal\"
href=\"modules.php?op=modload&amp;name=News&amp;file=index&amp;catid=&amp;topic=".
pnVarPrepForDIsplay($topicid)
    ."\"><img src=\"themes/".pnUserGetTheme()."/". pnVarPrepForDIsplay($tipath).""".
pnVarPrepForDIsplay($topicimage)
    ."\" alt=\" ".pnVarPrepForDIsplay($topictext)."\" /></a><br />\n"
    ."<span class=\"pn-normal\">".pnVarPrepForDIsplay($topictext)."</span>\n"
    ."</td>\n";
```

> **Tip**
>
> The $tipath variable is still used in the sample code, which translates to `images/topics/`. If you use a different naming convention for your theme images, you need to replace the $tipath call with the different path as a hard-coded line here.

In your browser, load the Active Topics page. You should see the specialized icons you added to your theme (see Figure 22.2). Test your other themes by adding &theme=mytheme2 to the end of your URL in your browser's location bar, where "mytheme2" is replaced by the theme name you want to test. Submit the URL change and test your other themes.

FIGURE 22.2   Two themes with different topic icons.

News Article Pages

Next take a look at the display of news articles. The topic icon appears on the news home page with the short text and on the full article page after a click-through. Both of these pages are fixed using the same change.

Open this file in your editor:

`/modules/News/funcs.php`

Scroll down roughly two thirds of the way through the file to about line 352 where you see this set of lines:

```
// Link to topic image if there is a topic
if (isset($info['tid']) && !empty($info['tid'])) {
    $searchtopic = '<a class="pn-normal"
href="modules.php?op=modload&amp;name=News&amp;file=index&amp;catid=&amp;topic='.$info['tid
'].'"><img
src="'.pnConfigGetVar('tipath').$info['topicimage'].'" style="padding:5px;"
alt="'.$info['topictext'].'"
/></a>';
} else {
    $searchtopic = '';
}
```

Similar to the previous change, seek out the <img> tag and add the same themes/'.pnUserGetTheme().'/ code just after the source attribute. Note the quotes in the additional code have changed to single; the PHP code you are editing now uses single quotes for its echo statements, and it's a good idea to keep it consistent. For a refresher on the differences between single and double quotes, review Chapter 19, "Dynamic PHP and PostNuke."

The lines with completed changes look like this:

```
// Link to topic image if there is a topic
if (isset($info['tid']) && !empty($info['tid'])) {
    $searchtopic = '<a class="pn-normal"
href="modules.php?op=modload&amp;name=News&amp;file=index&amp;catid=&amp;topic='.$info['tid
'].'"><img
src="themes/'.pnUserGetTheme().'/'.pnConfigGetVar('tipath').$info['topicimage'].'"
style="padding:5px;"
alt="'.$info['topictext'].'" /></a>';
} else {
    $searchtopic = '';
}
```

Note

Depending on how your theme is configured, you might not see any topic icons on the news home page; some themes don't display topics on the home page. The hack instructions in this section change the icon call itself, but the call always needs to be performed in your theme for an icon to appear, regardless of the image's path.

Review your new article pages in the different themes to be certain they are working. You should now see screens similar to that shown in Figure 22.3.

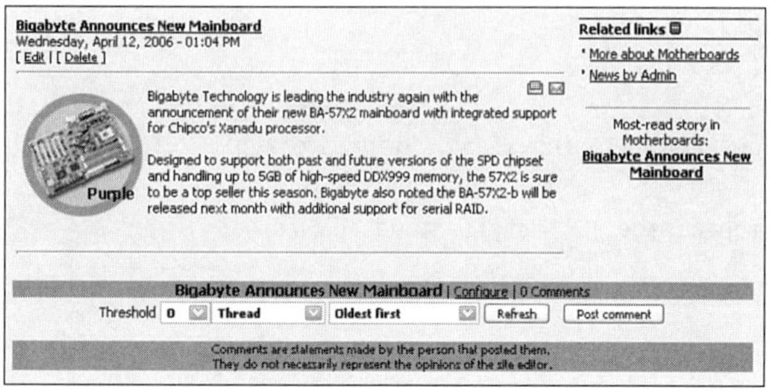

FIGURE 22.3   Customizing your site's article topics.

Submit News Preview
When users submit news articles, they are required to preview their entry before being able to submit the article for review in the wait queue. The preview screen displays the chosen topic icon with the story.

To change this page, open the main Submit News index in your editor:

```
/modules/Submit_News/index.php
```

Scroll to about line 199 and look for this echo statement:

```
echo "<img src=\"$tipath$topicimage\" align=\"right\" alt=\"$topictext\" />";
```

Comment out a copy of the line for backup, and add the same theme path code to the live line that you've been using: themes/".pnUserGetTheme()."/.

The changed line should match the following:

```
echo "<img src=\"themes/".pnUserGetTheme()."/$tipath$topicimage\" align=\"right\"
alt=\"$topictext\" />";
```

A test of the submit page should show a change's icon, like the one shown in Figure 22.4.

Add Story Preview
The preview screen for the Add Story module also uses the topic icons. Open the module's functions files, and scroll to about line 98:

```
/modules/NS-AddStory/addstory_functions.php
```

The line you are looking for is quite short and should be easy to spot:

```
echo "<img src=\"$tipath$topicimage\" alt=\"\" />";
```

Copy the line, comment out the backup, and add the theme path to the statement as follows:

```
echo "<img src=\"themes/".pnUserGetTheme()."/$tipath$topicimage\" alt=\"\" />";
```

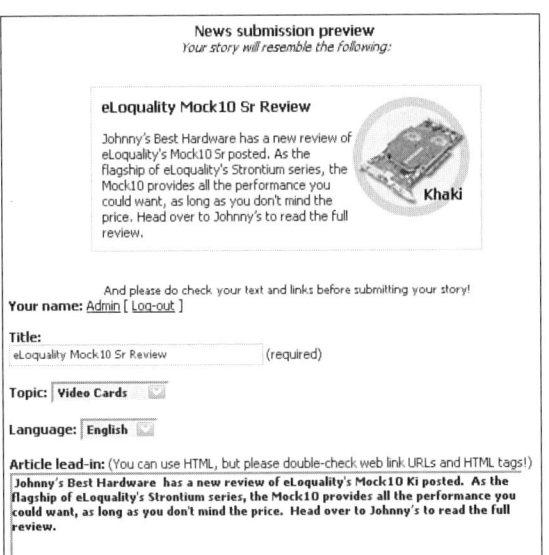

FIGURE 22.4 Previewing the custom theme topics.

You should browse to the Add News form and test the preview to be certain the code change was done properly.

Topics Administration Menu

Though the general public might never see them, icons are also displayed in the Topics Administration menu. To complete the theme-based icon changes, open the Topics Administration file in your editor:

/modules/Topics/admin.php

At about line 69, you see this statement:

```
if (pnSecAuthAction(0, 'Topics::Topic', "$topicname::$topicid", ACCESS_EDIT)) {
    echo "<a
href=\"admin.php?module=".$GLOBALS['module']."&amp;op=topicedit&amp;topicid=".
pnVarPrepForDisplay($topicid)."\"><img src=\"$tipath$topicimage\" alt=\"\" /></a><br />"
        ."<a
href=\"admin.php?module=".$GLOBALS['module']."&amp;op=topicedit&amp;topicid=".pnVarPrep-
ForDisplay($topicid)."\"><span class=\"pn-normal\"><strong>".pnVarPrepForDisplay
($topictext)."</strong></span></a></td>";
} else {
    echo "<img src=\"".pnVarPrepForDisplay($tipath).""".pnVarPrepForDisplay($topicimage)."\"
alt=\"\" /><br />"
        ."<span class=\"pn-normal\"><strong>".pnVarPrepForDisplay($topictext)."</strong>
</span></a></td>";
}
```

The if statement is performing a security check, but the topic image is displayed in both branches. You need to add the theme path to both <img> tags to complete this change. After the source begins, add this code: themes/".pnUserGetTheme()."/. The if statement with the changed lines looks like this:

```
if (pnSecAuthAction(0, 'Topics::Topic', "$topicname::$topicid", ACCESS_EDIT)) {
    echo "<a
href=\"admin.php?module=".$GLOBALS['module']."&amp;op=topicedit&amp;topicid=".
pnVarPrepForDisplay($topicid)."\"><img src=\"themes/".pnUserGetTheme().
"/$tipath$topicimage\" alt=\"\" /></a><br />"
        ."<a
href=\"admin.php?module=".$GLOBALS['module']."&amp;op=topicedit&amp;topicid=".
pnVarPrepForDisplay($topicid)."\"><span class=\"pn-normal\"><strong>".pnVarPrepForDis-
play($topictext)."</strong></span></a></td>";
} else {
    echo "<img
src=\"themes/".pnUserGetTheme()."/".pnVarPrepForDisplay($tipath)."".pnVarPrepForDisplay($to
picimage)."\" alt=\"\" /><br />"
        ."<span class=\"pn-normal\"><strong>".pnVarPrepForDisplay($topictext)."</strong>
</span></a></td>";
}
```

With this last change, all of the topics displayed throughout your PostNuke site will be tied to your theme. Be certain that any additional themes you add also provide support for the personalized topics.

Advanced Theme-Based Articles

The previous examples are meant to walk through the basic changes required to customize article components for theme display. After you are comfortable with the code, consider how this feature can be used to enhance your PostNuke site design.

You can very easily set up different paths to display different images for different pages. The preview icons could be simple and small compared to the Admin icons. The public articles could be completely integrated into your article blocks. You could also define sets of images to be used with your articles—one image for an icon, another to tile in the article's background, and so on.

PostNuke is designed to provide a foundation for rapid website development, but you need not ever feel the application limits design options. Making extensive hacks to the PostNuke source still takes a great deal less time than it would to build a comparable system with the changes from scratch.

Article Title and Links

Most PostNuke sites revolve around their news and articles. PostNuke does a great job formatting articles 95% of the time using modular theme systems. But every so often, some element is just not accessible, and it's time for a hack. The following sections examine what can be done to format those article elements hard-coded in PostNuke.

Custom Article Title Style

Although you can change nearly everything about a new post visually, the title text of a post is a link assigned the global style class pn-title. You can edit the pn-title class in your theme style sheet to change the title, but that also changes the appearance of every other reference to the class.

You might notice that there are calls to the pn-title class in many of the themes. Although the style is used with themes, there are additional references to it in the PostNuke module source code that are nested inside the theme, and, therefore, have precedence over the theme style.

Note

Alternatively, instead of creating customized styles hard-coded into your PostNuke install, you could strip out all styles from the source and rely solely on the theme design to format the content. This method has the benefit of being a potentially simpler hack up front, but if your site uses many active themes, making the changes once globally is faster.

The problem is remedied by separating the article style from other references, and it's easy to change the class attribute at the source and be certain the new specific class will carry throughout your site no matter what theme you are currently using.

Start up your editor and open the Functions file from the News module:

```
/modules/News/funcs.php
```

Scroll to line 308 and look for this set of lines:

```
// Allowed to read full article?
if (pnSecAuthAction(0, $component, $instance, ACCESS_READ)) {
    $title = "<a class=\"pn-title\" href=\"$links[fullarticle]\">$info[title]</a>";
} else {
    $title = $info['title'];
}
```

The first branch of the if statement builds the link for users who have access to read the full article. The second branch simply displays the title text as is.

Comment a copy of the code to save the original formatting, and change the lines to appear something like this:

```
// Allowed to read full article?
if (pnSecAuthAction(0, $component, $instance, ACCESS_READ)) {
    $title = "<a class=\"news-title\" href=\"$links[fullarticle]\">$info[title]</a>";
} else {
    $title = "<span class=\"news-title\">".$info['title']."</span>";
}
```

The `pn-title` class reference was changed to the more specific `news-title`, and for the second branch you added a span to apply the style directly to the title without the link anchor.

The category title text is also displayed with the title, but the variable does not require a conditional check before it's added to the News `$preformat` array. Scroll down a bit further to the array creation code:

```
// Set up the array itself
$preformat = array(
                "bodytext" => $bodytext,
                "bytesmore" => $bytesmorelink,
                "category" => "<a href=\"$links[category]\">$info[cattitle]</a>",
                "comment" => $comment,
                "hometext" => $hometext,
                "notes" => $notes,
                "reads" => $reads,
                "searchtopic" => $searchtopic,
                "print" => $print,
                "readmore" => $readmore,
                "send" => $send,
                "title" => $title,
                "version" => 1
                );
```

> **Tip**
>
> Assign different styles to each component to have complete control of how your content looks.

Change the category line to include a style class, such as

```
"category" => "<a class=\"category-title\" href=\"$links[category]\">$info[cattitle]</a>",
```

You have one other component to fix. Between the category and title, a colon is displayed. It is meant to be part of the category display, but is added to the `$preformat` array as `catandtitle`.

Look for this assignment around line 392:

```
$preformat['catandtitle'] = "$preformat[category]: $preformat[title]";
```

You can customize the colon character by adding a <span>:

```
$preformat['catandtitle'] = "$preformat[category]<span class=\"category-title\">:</span>
$preformat[title]";
```

The category-title style was used in the example code, but you could also create yet another style specifically for the colon character.

Note

Some themes call the title and category variables separately. Those themes do not use catandtitle and, therefore, changes to that variable are ignored when those themes are in use.

Separate Styles for Article Styles in News and Blocks

Another interesting style dilemma occurring with article titles is how they are formatted for display in blocks. A number of core blocks display a list of articles, such as Past Articles, Story Titles, and Today's Big Story. Setting a style for the title also sets the same style everywhere else the title is listed.

An easy solution to the issue is to create an additional variable in the $preformat array for the title. The second variable can be formatted differently and called from your theme independently of the main news article title.

Edit the functions file, and return to line 308 where the title code is created:

```
/modules/News/funcs.php
```

Add additional lines to create an alternative reference to the title:

```
// Allowed to read full article?
if (pnSecAuthAction(0, $component, $instance, ACCESS_READ)) {
    $title = "<a class=\"news-title\" href=\"$links[fullarticle]\">$info[title]</a>";
    $title2 = "<a class=\"news-title2\" href=\"$links[fullarticle]\">$info[title]</a>";
} else {
    $title = "<span class=\"news-title\">".$info['title']."</span>";
    $title2 = "<span class=\"news-title2\">".$info['title']."</span>";
}
```

> **Tip**
>
> You don't have to use the generic numerical system provided in the examples. Change "news-title2" to better fit your needs, such as "news-block-title." Just remember to be consistent with whatever names you decide to use.

Add the additional assignments for both the `category` and `title` variables to the `$preformat` array so that it looks like this:

```
// Set up the array itself
$preformat = array(
                "bodytext" => $bodytext,
                "bytesmore" => $bytesmorelink,
                "category" => "<a class=\"category-title\" href=\"$links[category]\">$info
[cattitle]</a>",
                "category2" => "<a class=\"category-title2\" href=\"$links[category]\">$info
[cattitle]</a>",
                "comment" => $comment,
                "hometext" => $hometext,
                "notes" => $notes,
                "reads" => $reads,
                "searchtopic" => $searchtopic,
                "print" => $print,
                "readmore" => $readmore,
                "send" => $send,
                "title" => $title,
                "title2" => $title2,
                "version" => 1
                );
```

You can also duplicate the `catandtitle` variable, if needed, like so:

```
if ($info['catid']) {
    $preformat['catandtitle'] = "$preformat[category]<span class=\"category-
title\">:</span> $preformat[title]";
    $preformat['catandtitle2'] = "$preformat[category2]<span class=\"category-
title2\">:</span> $preformat[title2]";
} else {
    $preformat['catandtitle'] = $preformat['title'];
    $preformat['catandtitle2'] = $preformat['title2'];
}
```

Forcing Story Count on Homepage

At times, it's important to be able to force the specific number of stories displayed on your site's home page. The most common need occurs when you have designed a specialized theme that has room for X number of posts, and having too many or two few might hurt the design. It can also be as simple as wanting to globally set a different count of stories, such as three, four, or seven, which is not possible using the drop-down list box in the Website Configuration form.

If you change the global setting in the Website Configuration form, you only affect anonymous users and newly created accounts. Existing users have a separate database entry storing their story count. This hack overrides the user's settings and makes the site display consistently.

Removing User Choice

The first part of this hack removes the users' ability to choose how many stories are displayed. Your website always shows only the count you have chosen in the global Website Configuration form.

Open the main News module file in your editor:

```
/modules/News/index.php
```

Scroll to about line 130 where you find these statements:

```
if (pnUserLoggedIn()) {
    $storynum = pnUserGetVar('storynum');
}
if (empty($storynum)) {
    $storynum = pnConfigGetVar('storyhome');
}
```

The first `if` statement pulls the user's story count from the `nuke_users` table. The second resorts to the default site setting if the `$storynum` variable is still empty. What we want to do is comment out the user checks so that the count always comes from the Website Configuration page. The edited code looks like this:

```
// if (pnUserLoggedIn()) {
//     $storynum = pnUserGetVar('storynum');
// }
// if (empty($storynum)) {
    $storynum = pnConfigGetVar('storyhome');
// }
```

That is the main change to force the story count, but now we need to remove the option in the users' Homepage Configuration screen to prevent confusion. There's no reason to advertise the ability for users to set their home page story count if you have removed the privilege.

The user account Homepage Configuration file is located here:

```
/modules/NS-Your_Account/user/modules/changehome.php
```

Open the file in your editor and look for this echo statement, starting around line 22:

```
echo "<form action=\"user.php\" method=\"post\">"
    ."<span class=\"pn-normal\">"._NEWSINHOME." "._MAX127."</span> "
    ."<input type=\"text\" name=\"storynum\" size=\"3\" maxlength=\"3\" value=\"" .
pnVarPrepForDisplay(pnUserGetVar('storynum')) . "\">"
    ."<br /><br />";
```

You want to remove the <span> and <input> tag content, but you need to leave the <form> opening that lets users still use the Personal Menu Block feature. The easiest way to go about the change is to duplicate just the first line and edit it to end the echo with a semicolon. Comment out the originals to save the source. Here is the completed change:

```
echo "<form action=\"user.php\" method=\"post\">";
// echo "<form action=\"user.php\" method=\"post\">"
//     ."<span class=\"pn-normal\">"._NEWSINHOME." "._MAX127."</span> "
//     ."<input type=\"text\" name=\"storynum\" size=\"3\" maxlength=\"3\" value=\"" .
pnVarPrepForDisplay(pnUserGetVar('storynum')) . "\">"
//     ."<br /><br />";
```

Setting the Story Count

Setting the number of stories to exactly the count you want is also quite simple. Go back to the News index file:

```
/modules/News/index.php
```

Edit the $storynum variable assignment at about line 130 to whatever number you want. For example:

```
$storynum = 3;
```

Now, the display is set to the exact number you want, and all users are treated the same regardless of their login.

News Article Submissions

With articles being such a large part of most PostNuke websites, the news submission modules get a great deal of use. Sites that allow their users to do more than just read content can sometimes find their users bothered by the extra features PostNuke provides. Not every user is tech savvy, but rather than require your users to learn about extra features, you can hack the modules to simply not use the features you do not need.

In addition, the Article Comments module is a very powerful feature of PostNuke, but it's very specific in how it handles posts. On many websites, it's popular to allow blog-style anonymous posting of comments. Although you can reduce security easily to allow unregistered posts, PostNuke does not provide the fields to allow anonymous visitors to enter identifying information. With the hack covered in this section, you can change all that.

Changing Default "Articles" to "No Category"

The Add Story module has a Category drop-down list box that provides another method of grouping articles. Articles that are not assigned a custom category name end up in the general "Articles" group. This can be confusing to general users who do not understand that "Articles" means "No Category." An easy fix for this problem is to change the way the catid is displayed.

Open the global language definitions file:

```
/language/eng/global.php
```

The variable defined as "Articles" and used to display the word is also in this file. The local definitions are not used by the function you are editing, so our new definition also goes here.

Add a new line under the _NOANONCOMMENTS definition with this content:

```
define('_NOCATEGORY','No Category');
```

If you want to use different phrasing, this is where you need to place it. Now edit the Categories file in Add Story:

```
/modules/NS-AddStory/addstory_categories.php
```

Scroll down to roughly line 554 and find the following echo statement:

```
echo "<option value=\"0\" $sel>"._ARTICLES."</option>";
```

Change the variable call to display the new words:

```
echo "<option value=\"0\" $sel>"._NOCATEGORY."</option>";
```

The option `value` remains set to "0," so the actual functionality of the system remains the same.

Removing Article Categories

For some PostNuke users, having the additional category option for articles might be too complicated. Understanding the different topic groups with the accompanying icons tends to come a lot easier than discerning how the text category names fit in. It might also be that your PostNuke site just doesn't need the extra layer of article customization. And if your site is not using it, why have the form display the list box at all?

Removing the Article option for new stories is very straightforward. Edit the functions file in Add Story:

```
/modules/NS-AddStory/addstory_functions.php
```

Look for a function called `storyEdit` that begins around line 132. This function controls the display of all the main form elements in Add Story. At line 147, you should see this function call:

```
SelectCategory($catid);
```

Removing the selection requires only that you comment out that line. The `catid` for every article is still set to "0," but now your users do not have to be concerned by the additional choice in the form. You should also comment out the subsequent line break to tidy up the spacing in the form:

```
// SelectCategory($catid);
// echo "<br />";
```

Now you might notice that the "Only works if Articles category isn't selected" line is still visible as part of the Publish on Homepage option. This message is not needed now that the categories are gone. It is also found in the Functions file:

```
/modules/NS-AddStory/addstory_functions.php
```

Look at the top of the file near line 45 for these lines:

```
echo "<input type=\"radio\" name=\"ihome\" value=\"0\"$sel1 />"._YES." "
    ."<input type=\"radio\" name=\"ihome\" value=\"1\"$sel2 />"._NO.""
    ."  <span class=\"pn-normal\">[ "._ONLYIFCATSELECTED." ]</span><br />";
```

The last part of the echo statement is the important one, but it also ends the statement, so you can't just comment it out without adding back in the required semicolon and line break. Here is the changed code:

```
echo "<input type=\"radio\" name=\"ihome\" value=\"0\"$sel1 />"._YES." "
    ."<input type=\"radio\" name=\"ihome\" value=\"1\"$sel2 />"._NO."<br />";
//    ."  <span class=\"pn-normal\">[ "._ONLYIFCATSELECTED." ]</span><br />";
```

FIGURE 22.5 Removing the Article categories for a simplified form.

Now, you have a clean and simplified Add Story form like the one in Figure 22.5.

Adding Names to Anonymous Comments

A quick change to the Permissions table allows unregistered site visitors to post comments to articles, but when those users try to make a post, the Your Name field comes up only as "Anonymous." You can edit the way the Comments module handles unregistered users and create input fields so the users can type in their identification instead. These changes turn the comments into a public blog style system similar to those currently found on many websites.

Only one file needs to be changed to make this work:

```
/modules/NS-Comments/index.php
```

However, many edits must be made in that single file to complete the effect. This section walks through the file changes from top to bottom to keep it simple, but note that the changes do not match up with the timing of the code as it's run to complete normal comment submission steps from a browser.

Look at Figure 22.6. Allowing anonymous posting has one major side effect. The (User information | Send a message) links are tied to the PostNuke account system. You need to remove those links to prevent failed lookups for users who are unregistered.

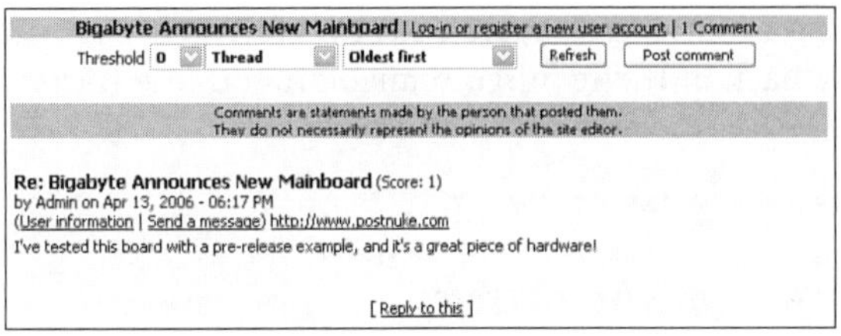

FIGURE 22.6   A basic article comment.

The website URL can be used by providing an additional field allowing anonymous users to enter their website address. Similarly, a user's email is displayed if the account toggle is set to make it public. You can also add in an email field to fill this account feature. If an anonymous user types in his email, it is displayed; otherwise, the field can be left blank, if he prefers.

You can begin the changes. Open the Comments `index.php` file identified previously in your editor. Proceed to line 307 where you should see the following lines within the `DisplayKids` function:

```
if ($r_name != $anonymous) {
    echo "<br /><span class=\"pn-normal\">(<a class=\"pn-normal\"
href=\"user.php?op=userinfo&amp;uname=$r_name&amp;module=NS-User\">"._USERINFO."</a> | <a
class=\"pn-normal\"
href=\"modules.php?op=modload&amp;name=Messages&amp;file=replypmsg&amp;send=1&amp;uname=$r_
name\">"._SENDAMSG."</a>)</span> ";
}
if (eregi("http://",$r_url)) {
    echo "<span class=\"pn-normal\"><a class=\"pn-normal\" href=\"$r_url\" target=\
"window\">$r_url</a></span> ";
}
```

> **Tip**
>
> Add change comments so you can easily see why certain edits were made next time you open the file.

The first `if` statement writes out the PostNuke account links. It needs to be commented out. The second line writes out the website URL. The second statement is fine, except that on the page they normally appear together on the same line (see Figure 22.6). If you comment out the first line, the `<br />` tag is not present for the following URL. That moves the URL up next to the date stamp, which does not look as good. Add in a `<br />` tag to the second `echo` statement to fix that issue. The changed code looks like this:

```
// if ($r_name != $anonymous) {
//      echo "<br /><span class=\"pn-normal\">(<a class=\"pn-normal\"
href=\"user.php?op=userinfo&amp;uname=$r_name&amp;module=NS-User\">"._USERINFO."</a> | <a
class=\"pn-normal\"
href=\"modules.php?op=modload&amp;name=Messages&amp;file=replypmsg&amp;send=1&amp;uname=$r_
name\">"._SENDAMSG."</a>)</span> ";
// }
if (eregi("http://",$r_url)) {
    echo "<br />\n<span class=\"pn-normal\"><a class=\"pn-normal\" href=\"$r_url\
" target=\"window\">$r_url</a></span> ";
}
```

A slight variant of the previous code is also in the DisplayKids function and it is found a few
lines down at about line 369:

```
if ($r_name != $anonymous) {
    echo "<br /><span class=\"pn-normal\">(<a class=\"pn-normal\"
href=\"user.php?op=userinfo&amp;uname=$r_name\">"._USERINFO."</a> ¦ <a class=\"pn-normal\"
href=\"modules.php?op=modload&amp;name=Messages&amp;file=replypmsg&amp;send=1&amp;uname=$r_
name\">"._SENDAMSG."</a>)</span> ";
}
if (eregi("http://",$r_url)) {
    echo "<span class=\"pn-normal\"><a class=\"pn-normal\" href=\"$r_url\"
target=\"window\">".pnVarPrepForDisplay($r_url)."</a></span> ";
}
```

Make the same change with comment markers for the first statement and a break added to
the second:

```
// if ($r_name != $anonymous) {
//      echo "<br /><span class=\"pn-normal\">(<a class=\"pn-normal\"
href=\"user.php?op=userinfo&amp;uname=$r_name\">"._USERINFO."</a> ¦ <a class=\"pn-normal\"
href=\"modules.php?op=modload&amp;name=Messages&amp;file=replypmsg&amp;send=1&amp;uname=$r_
name\">"._SENDAMSG."</a>)</span> ";
// }
if (eregi("http://",$r_url)) {
    echo "<br />\n<span class=\"pn-normal\"><a class=\"pn-normal\" href=\"$r_url\"
target=\"window\">".pnVarPrepForDisplay($r_url)."</a></span> ";
}
```

Now scroll down to line 605. You see lines nearly identical to the first set you changed, but this time they are part of the DisplayTopic function:

```
if($name != $anonymous) {
    echo "<br />\n<span class=\"pn-normal\">(<a class=\"pn-normal\"
href=\"user.php?op=userinfo&amp;uname=$name&amp;module=NS-User\">"._USERINFO."</a> | <a
href=\"modules.php?op=modload&amp;name=Messages&amp;file=replypmsg&amp;send=1&amp;uname=$
name\">"._SENDAMSG."</a>)</span>\n ";
}
if(eregi("http://",$url)) {
    echo "<span class=\"pn-normal\"><a class=\"pn-normal\" href=\"$url\"
target=\"window\">".pnVarPrepForDisplay($url)."</a></span>\n ";
}
```

Complete the same set of changes to these lines:

```
// if($name != $anonymous) {
//      echo "<br />\n<span class=\"pn-normal\">(<a class=\"pn-normal\"
href=\"user.php?op=userinfo&amp;uname=$name&amp;module=NS-User\">"._USERINFO."</a> | <a
href=\"modules.php?op=modload&amp;name=Messages&amp;file=replypmsg&amp;send=1&amp;uname=
$name\">"._SENDAMSG."</a>)</span>\n ";
// }
if(eregi("http://",$url)) {
    echo "<br />\n <span class=\"pn-normal\"><a class=\"pn-normal\" href=\"$url\"
target=\"window\">".pnVarPrepForDisplay($url)."</a></span>\n ";
}
```

Now scroll down to the reply function and around line 861 find this section of code:

```
echo "<span class=\"pn-title\">"._YOURNAME.":</span> ";
if (pnUserLoggedIn()) {
    echo "<a href=\"user.php\">" . pnUserGetVar('uname') . "</a> <span class=\"pn-
normal\">[ <a class=\"pn-normal\" href=\"user.php?module=NS-
User&amp;op=logout\">"._LOGOUT."</a> ]</span><br /><br />";
} else {
    echo "<span class=\"pn-normal\">".pnVarPrepForStore($anonymous).""";
    echo " <span class=\"pn-normal\">[ <a class=\"pn-normal\"
href=\"user.php\">"._NEWUSER."</a> ]</span><br /><br />";
}
```

FIGURE 22.7 Adding an anonymous comment to an article.

The code writes out the username of the user if logged in, and write out the "Anonymous" text if not. You can also see this in Figure 22.7, which displays a standard comment post.

In this section of code, you add new form inputs to gather the submitter's name, email, and website URL. The anonymous user is also usually prompted at this point to log in/register. This is done using the user.php link after the name is written to the page. Leave this link to keep the registration option available to anonymous posters. Examine the following changed code:

```
echo "<span class=\"pn-title\">"._YOURNAME.":</span> ";
if (pnUserLoggedIn()) {
    echo "<a href=\"user.php\">" . pnUserGetVar('uname') . "</a> <span class=\
"pn-normal\">[ <a class=\"pn-normal\" href=\"user.php?module=NS-
User&amp;op=logout\">"._LOGOUT."</a> ]</span><br /><br />";
} else {
    echo "<br />\n<input type=\"text\" name=\"aname\" value=\"\" /> <span class=\"pn-
normal\">[ <a class=\"pn-normal\" href=\"user.php\">"._NEWUSER."</a> ]</span><br /><br />";
    echo "<span class=\"pn-title\">"._UREALEMAIL.":</span><br />"
        ."<input type=\"text\" name=\"aemail\" value=\"\" size=\"30\" maxlength=\"60\"
/><br /><br />";
    echo "<span class=\"pn-title\">"._YOURHOMEPAGE.":</span><br />"
        ."<input type=\"text\" name=\"aurl\" value=\"http://\" size=\"30\"
maxlength=\"100\" /><br /><br />";
//      echo "<span class=\"pn-normal\">".pnVarPrepForStore($anonymous)."";
//      echo "<span class=\"pn-normal\">[ <a class=\"pn-normal\"
href=\"user.php\">"._NEWUSER."</a> ]</span><br /><br />";
}
```

The name and email fields have been left blank to invite the user to fill them out. The URL input includes the "http://" start, which is required for URL display. The names of the three new inputs are aname, aemail, and aurl to designate anonymous user information separate from the normal form. And the size and maxlength attributed for the inputs were taken from the PostNuke user account system, so they match with limitations already present in the database.

You can, at this point, save your changes and take a look at the initial comment form. It displays the same as what's shown in Figure 22.8.

Now move down to the replyPreview function at about line 910. The first thing the function does is gather in all the variables submitted from the previous form. You added three new variables, so those need to be added to this part of the function for it to know about them. This is the original source:

FIGURE 22.8   Adding your name and email to your comments.

```
function replyPreview()
{
    list($pid,
         $sid,
         $subject,
         $comment,
         $xanonpost,
         $mode,
         $order,
         $thold,
         $posttype) = pnVarCleanFromInput('pid',
                                          'sid',
                                          'subject',
                                          'comment',
                                          'xanonpost',
                                          'mode',
                                          'order',
                                          'thold',
                                          'posttype');
```

The new form inputs were entered just before the subject field, so add them to the same place in the list assignment for consistency. The changed code looks like this:

```
function replyPreview()
{
    list($pid,
         $sid,
         $aname,
         $aemail,
         $aurl,
         $subject,
         $comment,
         $xanonpost,
         $mode,
         $order,
         $thold,
         $posttype) = pnVarCleanFromInput('pid',
                                          'sid',
                                          'aname',
                                          'aemail',
                                          'aurl',
                                          'subject',
                                          'comment',
                                          'xanonpost',
                                          'mode',
                                          'order',
                                          'thold',
                                          'posttype');
```

In the comment preview, the comment is posted at the top with the user's name, and below the preview is a copy of the original entry form. The next change fixes the display of the name field in the preview itself. Look for this if statement starting at line 959:

```
if (pnUserLoggedIn() && !$xanonpost) {
    echo pnUserGetVar('uname');
} else {
    echo "".pnVarPrepForDisplay($anonymous)."";
}
```

The first branch displays the normal username; leave it alone. The second branch displays the $anonymous variable for all users who are not currently logged in. Review the following changes:

```
if (pnUserLoggedIn() && !$xanonpost) {
    echo pnUserGetVar('uname');
} else {
```

```
    if ($aname == "") { $aname = $anonymous; }
    echo "".pnVarPrepForDisplay($aname)."";
    // echo "".pnVarPrepForDisplay($anonymous)."";
}
```

The $aname variable was set up when you added it to the beginning of the function. At this point, the form doesn't know whether the user has entered her name or left the field blank. So within the second branch, check for an empty $aname variable, and if found, set it to the default $anonymous. Then, the $aname can be echoed normally to handle both possible events.

Note

Setting the empty $aname variable to $anonymous autopopulates the field in the form below. It will be obvious to anyone leaving the field blank that "Anonymous" will be used for their name if they do not fill in the field.

A short bit down from there at line 987, the duplicate of the submission form is started. The preview form does not yet have the three new input fields, so you can add them now. Here is the original source to edit:

```
echo "<form action=\"modules.php\" method=\"post\"><div><span class=\"pn-title\">".
_YOURNAME.":</span> ";
if (pnUserLoggedIn()) {
    echo "<a href=\"user.php\">" . pnUserGetVar('uname') . "</a> <span class=\"pn-
normal\">[ <a class=\"pn-normal\" href=\"user.php?module=NS-
User&amp;op=logout\">"._LOGOUT."</a> ]</span><br /><br />";
} else {
    echo "<span class=\"pn-normal\">".pnVarPrepForStore($anonymous)."</span><br /><br />";
}
```

Change it to look like this code; all of the additions are in the second branch of the if statement:

```
echo "<form action=\"modules.php\" method=\"post\"><div><span class=\"pn-title\">".
_YOURNAME.":</span> ";
if (pnUserLoggedIn()) {
    echo "<a href=\"user.php\">" . pnUserGetVar('uname') . "</a> <span class=\"pn-
normal\">[ <a class=\"pn-normal\" href=\"user.php?module=NS-
User&amp;op=logout\">"._LOGOUT."</a> ]</span><br /><br />";
} else {
    echo "<br />"
        ."<input type=\"text\" name=\"aname\" value=\"".pnVarPrepForDisplay($aname)."\" />
<span class=\"pn-normal\"><br /><br />";
    echo "<span class=\"pn-title\">"._UREALEMAIL.":</span><br />"
```

```
         ."<input type=\"text\" name=\"aemail\" value=\"".pnVarPrepForDisplay($aemail)."\"
size=\"30\" maxlength=\"60\" /><br /><br />";
    echo "<span class=\"pn-title\">"._YOURHOMEPAGE.":</span><br />"
         ."<input type=\"text\" name=\"aurl\" value=\"".pnVarPrepForDisplay($aurl)."\"
size=\"30\" maxlength=\"100\" /><br /><br />";
//    echo "<span class=\"pn-normal\">".pnVarPrepForStore($anonymous)."</span><br /><br
/>";
}
```

The inputs are similar to the tags added in the initial submission form. What's been changed is the addition of the $aname, $aemail, and $aurl to the values of the tags. The initial <br /> was added to place the Name input on the line below the label; the names of logged-in users normally appear to the right of the label on the same line. And the original line is commented out at the last.

You can now test the preview screen with a comment test submission. It will look like the form in Figure 22.8, but the entered content autopopulates the fields in the preview form.

Next, you alter the CreateTopic function to use these new fields when it creates a database table entry for a new comment. The function starts at about line 1057 with a header similar to the replyPreview function you changed earlier:

```
function CreateTopic ()
{
    list($xanonpost,
        $subject,
        $comment,
        $pid,
        $sid,
        $host_name,
        $mode,
        $order,
        $thold,
        $posttype,
        $req) = pnVarCleanFromInput('xanonpost',
                                    'subject',
                                    'comment',
                                    'pid',
                                    'sid',
                                    'host_name',
                                    'mode',
                                    'order',
                                    'thold',
                                    'posttype',
                                    'req');
```

Add in the three new variables exactly as you did before, placing them before the subject references:

```
function CreateTopic ()
{
    list($xanonpost,
         $aname,
         $aemail,
         $aurl,
         $subject,
         $comment,
         $pid,
         $sid,
         $host_name,
         $mode,
         $order,
         $thold,
         $posttype,
         $req) = pnVarCleanFromInput('xanonpost',
                                     'aname',
                                     'aemail',
                                     'aurl',
                                     'subject',
                                     'comment',
                                     'pid',
                                     'sid',
                                     'host_name',
                                     'mode',
                                     'order',
                                     'thold',
                                     'posttype',
                                     'req');
```

The very last change assigns the new variables' content to the standard variables used to add content to the database. Scroll down to about line 1117 in CreateTopic() and find the following code:

```
if (pnUserLoggedIn() && (!$xanonpost)) {
    $uname = pnUserGetVar('uname');
    $email = pnUserGetVar('femail');
    $url   = pnUserGetVar('url');
    $score = 1;
```

```
    } else {
        $uname = "";
        $email = "";
        $url   = "";
        $score = 0;
    }
```

The first half of the statement takes the global user information available when a user is logged in and assigns it to variables in preparation for the database addition. The `else` sets the same variables to `null` values. You again change the second branch of the `if` statement with the following additions:

```
if (pnUserLoggedIn() && (!$xanonpost)) {
    $uname = pnUserGetVar('uname');
    $email = pnUserGetVar('femail');
    $url   = pnUserGetVar('url');
    $score = 1;
} else {
    if ($aname != $anonymous) {
        $uname = $aname;
        $email = $aemail;
        $url   = $aurl;
    } else {
        $uname = "";
        $email = "";
        $url   = "";
    }
    $score = 0;
}
```

The nested `if ($aname != $anonymous)` checks to see if the user entered his name or left the field with "Anonymous." If the former, then the regular name, email, and website variables are assigned the values from the new form fields. If the latter, the fields are left blank as they were in the original code. The score remains "0" for the second branch, just because there seems to be no reason to give an unregistered poster free points.

Figure 22.9 shows the results of the completed hack. The first post was done using a registered account. The email address is set to private and does not appear. The second comment was performed anonymously but with all fields completed. Now, anyone can visit your site and post their thoughts.

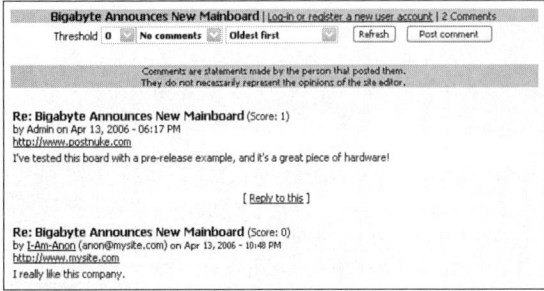

FIGURE 22.9   Public blog-style comments with identity fields.

Troubleshooting

As a chapter concerned with editing PHP code, the most likely problem you will encounter deals with mistyped syntax. Look carefully at any error messages you receive to troubleshoot the problems. If you are not receiving a line number reference in the error message, be certain the display_errors = On and the error_reporting = E_ALL are both set in your php.ini file.

Topic Icons Not Displaying

If your topic icons are not displaying on your pages, or if on some pages you perhaps see the icon title text in place of the icon, the path to the image files is faulty. PostNuke is robustly designed to not display a topic image that cannot be located. Review your path changes and be certain your entries are correct.

Next

The next chapter surveys hacks of the PostNuke user system and looks at additional add-on modules that extend the user features of your website.

User System Hacks

23

The PostNuke user system is a fairly complex collection of modules. Throughout the recent releases of PostNuke, there have been steady increases in the features and customization options via the stock administrative interface. But the system is not completely dynamic yet, and that can become a problem if you need a capability not possible with the current configuration.

Site developers needing more features have, in the past, primarily turned to three extensive modules and hacks of the system: pncUserHack, ProfilePlus, and X-User. pncUserHack and ProfilePlus each provided a number of useful additions to the user system, but neither are available for PostNuke .75. Many of the features of pncUserHack are now being incorporated into PostNuke 0.8, but there is no support for the changes under .75. ProfilePlus is now unavailable with license restrictions.

X-User is also no longer in development, but it is both available and functions under PostNuke .75. You look at this module, along with a number of custom hacks in the following sections:

- Requiring optional registration fields

- Prompting users to remember their password

- Formatting the new user email

- Requiring fields in user management

- Disabling/enabling user logins

- Registering with X-User

User Registration Hacks

In this first section, you look at a few hacks to the core user registration system. Management of the registration process is an important part of your site; it's in many ways the first real interaction a user might have with your website. First impressions are always powerful, so you want to be certain the system works smoothly for your users.

The X-User module provides a number of dynamic registration features, but this section looks at hacks you can apply to your default PostNuke install.

Requiring Optional Registration Fields

PostNuke has a number of premade fields built in to the system that you can toggle on and off together using the Show Optional Fields entry in the User Registration Configuration page. You can turn these extra fields on, but you can't control which are required. It's relatively easy to use the existing server-side validation system to add some of these other optional fields to the required list.

You need two files open for editing to complete this hack:

```
/modules/NS-NewUser/user.php
/modules/NS-NewUser/lang/eng/global.php
```

The `global.php` file contains the text variable definitions for the English language. You need to add some variables to display messages for users. But first, you can begin with edits to the `user.php` file. In your editor, scroll down to about line 492. You should see the function `optionalitems()`.

Take a look through this function to see how it writes out the input fields for the form. Any of these fields can be made required, but for this example, you specifically look at the Real Name field. It's at roughly line 525:

```
echo "<input type=\"text\" name=\"name\" value=\"" .
pnVarPrepForDisplay(pnUserGetVar('name')) . "\" size=\"30\" maxlength=\"60\" />";
```

What's important here is the `name` attribute. It tells you how to reference the data entered into the field. In this case, the attribute happens to have the value "name."

With that knowledge in hand, scroll back up to about line 304:

```
function newuser_user_finishnewuser($var)
{
    $dbconn =& pnDBGetConn(true);
    $pntable =& pnDBGetTables();
```

```
list($name,
    $agreetoterms,
    $email,
```

This is the start of the function that completes the new user submission process. Notice that the list function is taking the form data and converting it into PHP variables. The "name" data is from here on out referred to as $name.

Tip

Add comments to all your changes to make it clear how the hack works.

A little farther down to line 368 reveals the userCheck function call:

```
$stop = userCheck($uname, $email, $agreetoterms);
```

This is the first change you need to make. You now know the variable that needs checking is $name, but it needs to be sent to the userCheck function for validation. Change the call to look like this:

```
$stop = userCheck($uname, $email, $agreetoterms, $name);
```

Now much farther up in the code near line 182, you should find the userCheck function itself:

```
function userCheck($uname, $email, $agreetoterms)
{
    $dbconn =& pnDBGetConn(true);
    $pntable =& pnDBGetTables();
```

Similar to the previous change, add the $name variable to the function inputs:

```
function userCheck($uname, $email, $agreetoterms, $name)
```

Look through the function contents. You can see multiple if blocks where the other variables are checked. You need to add the validation code after all that, so scroll down a bit farther to about line 254. You know you are at the end of the checks when you see the return($stop); line. Just before that, add in this code:

```
// Code below added for required Real Name field validation
if ((!$name) || ($name=="") || (!preg_match("/^[a-zA-Z \.\'\-]+$/", $name))) {
    $stop = "<div style=\"text-align:center\"><span class=\"pn-title\">".
        _REALNAMEINVALID."</div></span><br />";
}
```

That code checks to see if the field is blank or if it contains any characters other than letters, spaces, hyphens, apostrophes, or periods. This allows for most common contracted or combined names, as well as initial use. More specific checks can be made, and the check should be customized to the field you want to validate.

Tip

For more information on pattern matching and validation, head over to www.php.net and do a function search on preg_match and ereg.

Now, you might have also noticed you just used a previously undefined variable: _REALNAMEINVALID. This is the message displayed to the user when the name that's entered doesn't pass the validation. Switch over to the global.php file to add in the text definition. In keeping with the alphabetical order, add this line after _PRIVACYPOLICY:

```
define('_REALNAMEINVALID','The real name you have entered contains characters that are not
allowed. Please try again.');
```

Take a look at the registration form in Figure 23.1; you can browse to this form by registrating as a new user. The Your Name field might be required, but there is nothing to inform a new user of that fact. And the Optional Items heading is now clearly misleading.

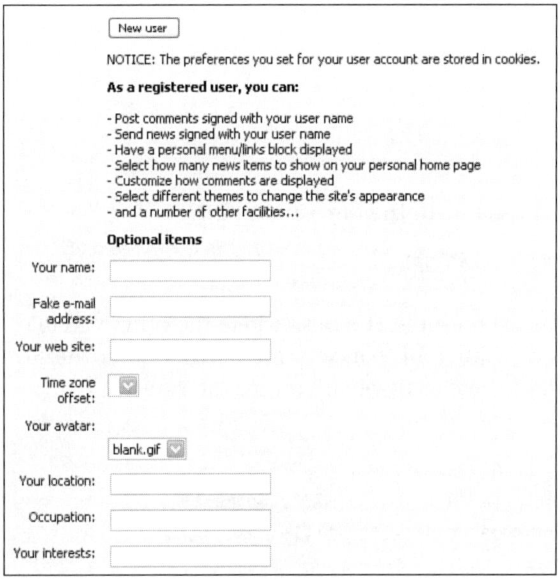

FIGURE 23.1   Don't keep required fields a secret.

In the `global.php` file, add in two additional variables:

```
define('_ADDITIONALITEMS','Additional Items');
define('_REQUIREDITEM','(required)');
```

Go back to the `user.php` file and scroll down to the `optionalitems` function, now at about line 496. Look for the form `input` that collects the name data. It should be at line 529. Add the required variable after the input like this:

```
case "_UREALNAME":
    echo "<input type=\"text\" name=\"name\" value=\"" . pnVarPrepForDisplay(pnUser
GetVar('name')) . "\" size=\"30\" maxlength=\"60\" /> "._REQUIREDITEM;
    break;
```

Now scroll back up to line 171 to take care of the heading. The completed code should be similar to this:

```
echo "<tr>"
    ."<td> </td>"
    // _OPTIONALITEMS changed to _ADDITIONALITEMS for new required fields
    ."<td><span class=\"pn-normal\"><strong>" . _ADDITIONALITEMS . "</strong></span></td>"
    ."</tr>\n" . "";
    // Display optional items to register
optionalitems();
```

Now, you have the finished form shown in Figure 23.2.

Prompting Users to Remember Their Password

When new users first receive their passwords in their email, the passwords are randomly generated. Occasionally, users delete that email without changing the password to something they can remember. This requires the user to come back to the site and request a password reset, which results in an identity check email, a form submit with the confirmation code, and eventually an email sent to the user with yet another randomly generated password.

That is quite a bit of effort for what should be a simple problem. The real issue is whether that's too much trouble for some of your users. You might lose registered users just because they can't remember their password.

You can prevent the problem from happening with a simple prompt in the registration email telling users to save the email with their random password, or, better yet, to go to their account settings and change the password to something easier to remember.

This fix requires only a change or two to this file:

```
/modules/NS-NewUser/lang/eng/global.php
```

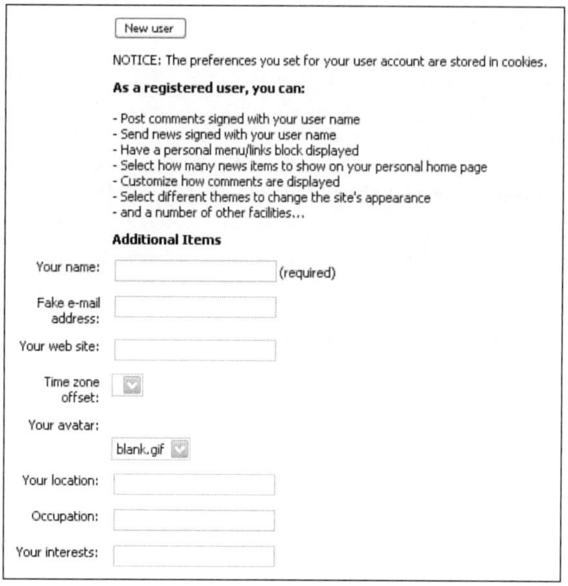

FIGURE 23.2   Requiring specific additional items.

Add the prompt to the email message by editing one of the existing variables to include the wording you have in mind. For example, change this line:

```
define('_FOLLOWINGMEM','The information stored about you is as follows:');
```

To read as this:

```
define('_FOLLOWINGMEM','Your initial password has been randomly generated. You can change
the random password to something more memorable by editing your account settings. The login
information for your account is:');
```

You can also change the registration message that appears on the screen after the form is submitted. The original message:

```
define('_YOUAREREGISTERED','You are now registered. You should receive your password at the
e-mail address you provided.');
```

can be expanded to say:

```
define('_YOUAREREGISTERED','You are now registered. You should receive your password at the
email account you provided. Please remember to write down your user name and password and
put them someplace safe. You can change the random password to something more memorable by
editing your account settings.');
```

Editing the language files to customize messages for your site helps your users stay connected. Update the phrasing of these variables to appeal to your user base.

Formatting the New User Email

Many site administrators have expressed an interest in being able to edit the email message sent to newly registered users. The real trick is that the email content is contained in both language variables and the programming source. Open up your text editor and load up these files:

```
/modules/NS-NewUser/user.php
/modules/NS-NewUser/lang/eng/global.php
```

The first file performs the registration functions and the second defines a list of global text variables. In the user.php file, scroll down to about line 461 and find this code:

```
$message = "" . _WELCOMETO . " $sitename ($siteurl)!\n\n" . _YOUUSEDEMAIL . " ($email) " .
_TOREGISTER . "
$sitename. " . _FOLLOWINGMEM . "\n\n" . _UNICKNAME . " $uname\n" . _UPASSWORD . "
$makepass";
$subject = "" . _USERPASS4 . " $uname" . _USERPASS42 . "";
```

The first line builds the message body and the second creates the subject line for the email. Editing these lines alters the formatting of the message and how it calls the variables. The text used in the message is changed by editing the global.php file. The formatting options possible are relatively unlimited, but just for example, the following is an alternative phrasing.

Tip

Add text entries to the different global.php files in each language your site supports to stay consistent.

Using these language variables:

```
define('_WELCOMETOTHE','Welcome to the');
define('_COMMUNITY','community!');
define('_RECEIVEDREGISTRATION','We have received your registration of the account');
define('_CREATEDRANDOM','and have created an initial random password for you.');
define('_ACCOUNTPASSIS','Your account password is');
define('_CHANGERANDOM','You can change the random password to something more memorable by
editing your account settings.');
define('_THANKSREGISTER','Thanks for registering!');
```

and this message code:

```
$message = ""._WELCOMETOTHE." $sitename "._COMMUNITY."\n\n"._RECEIVEDREGISTRATION."
$uname "._CREATEDRANDOM."\n"._ACCOUNTPASSIS." $makepass.\n"._CHANGERANDOM."\n\n"._
THANKSREGISTER."\n";
```

you get this email message:

```
Welcome to the mysite.com community!

We have received your registration of the account myaccount and have created an initial
random password for you.
Your account password is mypass
You can change the random password to something more memorable by editing your account
settings.

Thanks for registering!
```

User System Hacks

Though they are strongly related, the user modules are actually separate from the registration module. Changes to the latter only indirectly affect the user data. For example, requiring additional fields during the registration process is great for initially populating user information, but nothing prevents a user from editing his information and deleting all that data after he is registered. To protect user data you want to maintain, you need to hack the user system.

Requiring Fields in User Management

This hack works very similarly to the steps outlined for required fields during registration, but because of the way the NS-Your_Account files are written, the User Management version is a bit easier. This hack edits the form users reach by entering their account management area.

Two files are relevant to this change:

```
/modules/NS-Your_Account/user/modules/changeinfo.php
/modules/NS-NewUser/lang/eng/global.php
```

The global.php file contains the descriptive text displayed in the form, but because this form already has most of the text you need defined, you should only need to add one new global variable unless you want to expand on the default wording of other text.

You can set any of the form fields to be required, but to complete your example from earlier in the chapter, you need to make changes to the Real Name field.

Tip

Additional fields not present in the standard release can also be added and made required. The process is more complex, but it can be made easier by converting one of the existing fields you don't need into the new one. Change the old field in the database, and hunt down references to it in the user files.

Open the changeinfo.php file in your editor and scroll down to line 81. You should see these lines:

```
case "_UREALNAME":
    echo "<input type=\"text\" name=\"name\" value=\"" . pnVarPrepForDisplay(pnUser
GetVar('name')) . "\" size=\"30\" maxlength=\"60\">" . " " . _OPTIONAL . "</td>";
    break;
```

This is the code that writes out the field users see in their management form. Just like the registration system, the name attribute also contains the value "name" here. It also has a convenient reference to the _OPTIONAL global that prints out the "(optional)" text at the end of the form element. You can see from scanning the surrounding other fields that there is also a _REQUIRED global predefined and ready for you to use.

You know the field will be required soon, so go ahead and change the code to have the required label:

```
case "_UREALNAME":
    echo "<input type=\"text\" name=\"name\" value=\"" . pnVarPrepForDisplay(pnUse
rGetVar('name')) . "\" size=\"30\" maxlength=\"60\">" . " " . _REQUIRED . "</td>";
    break;
```

Now scroll down to function saveuser() at about line 245. Also identical to the registration hack, the "name" value is converted into the $name variable in this function. At about line 298, the function starts validating the required fields. It is in that area you need to add a new check for the Real Name field. The exact positioning doesn't matter, other than it needs to not be nested in another check. Place it at the top after the password checks. The inserted code is nearly identical to the example earlier in the chapter, and the completed change looks like this:

```
if ((isset($pass)) && ("$pass" != "$vpass")) {
    $htmltext = "<div style=\"text-align:center\"><span class=\"pn-title\">" .
_PASSDIFFERENT . "</div></span><br /><br /><br /><br />";
    edituser($htmltext);
} elseif (($pass != "") && (strlen($pass) < $minpass)) {
    $htmltext = "<div style=\"text-align:center\"><span class=\"pn-title\">" .
_YOURPASSMUSTBE . " $minpass " . _CHARLONG . "</div></span><br /><br /><br /><br />";
    edituser($htmltext);
// Code below added for required Real Name field validation
} elseif ((!$name) || ($name=="") || (!preg_match("/^[a-zA-Z \.\'\-]+$/", $name))) {
    $htmltext = "<div style=\"text-align:center\"><span class=\"pn-title\">".
_REALNAMEINVALID."</div></span><br />";
    edituser($htmltext);
} else {
```

The new code begins on the eighth line at the second `elseif`. It checks to see if the field is blank or if it contains any characters other than letters, spaces, hyphens, apostrophes, or periods. Common contracted or combined names are allowed, as well as middle initial use. More specific checks can be made, and the check should be customized to the field you want to validate.

The new code also makes a call to the _REALNAMEINVALID variable. For the last change in this hack, you need to edit the `global.php` file mentioned earlier and add this line:

```
define('_REALNAMEINVALID','The real name you have entered contains characters that are not
allowed. Please try again.');
```

Keep the sort order of the globals by placing the line after _PERSONALINFO. Now, the Real Name field is required for your users.

Disabling/Enabling User Logins

Another handy addition to the PostNuke feature set is the capability to toggle user login capability. Suppose, for example, you are in the process of moving the site to a new host. If you've already pulled all the database content and files, but the switchover hasn't happened, you don't want users going to the old site and adding content that will be lost in the change of sites. This capability is also handy if you're trying out a new site feature visible only to logged-in users. You can lock the users out during final testing, and then toggle the logins back on when you're ready to open the doors.

Note

This hack prevents new logins, but existing users retain access until they log out or visit the site's home page.

There are two main parts to this hack: creating the administrative toggle option in Website Settings and adding the additional security check to the login system.

Creating Login Toggle

First create the toggle option for your site. Open this file in your editor:

```
/modules/NS-Settings/lang/eng/global.php
```

You need to add two new text entries at about line 59, just after the _LOCALEFORMAT definition. The additions are this:

```
define('_LOCKLOGIN','Lock User Login');
define('_LOCKLOGININFO','(This will prevent anyone but administrators from logging in to
the site.)');
```

The text in these fields describes the form element. You can close that file out of your editor and open this one next:

```
/modules/NS-Settings/admin.php
```

Scroll down roughly halfway through the file to line 301. Just before the _BLOCKSINARTICLES code and after the preceding select close and HTML table row break, add these lines:

```
// Login lockout hack addition
._LOCKLOGIN.'</td><td class=\"pn-normal\">'
."<input type=\"radio\" name=\"xloginlocked\" value=\"0\" class=\"pn-normal\"$sel_
loginlocked[0] />"._YES.'  '
."<input type=\"radio\" name=\"xloginlocked\" value=\"1\" class=\"pn-normal\"$sel_
loginlocked[1] />"._NO."  "._LOCKLOGININFO
."</td></tr><tr><td class=\"pn-normal\">"
```

The tables are split between the echo lines, so to make it perfectly clear, the code with the preceding addition looks like this:

```
.'</select>'
."</td></tr><tr><td class=\"pn-normal\">"
// Login lockout hack addition
._LOCKLOGIN.'</td><td class=\"pn-normal\">'
."<input type=\"radio\" name=\"xloginlocked\" value=\"0\" class=\"pn-normal\"$sel_
loginlocked [0] />"._YES.'  '
."<input type=\"radio\" name=\"xloginlocked\" value=\"1\" class=\"pn-normal\"$sel_
loginlocked [1] />"._NO."  "._LOCKLOGININFO
."</td></tr><tr><td class=\"pn-normal\">"
._BLOCKSINARTICLES.'</td><td class=\"pn-normal\">'
```

This code adds the new form elements to the page, duplicating the style used by other similar elements. It's important to note that the yes/no options used on this page are reversed from what you might think with a binary toggle. Yes is represented by "0," and No is represented by the "1" value.

Now scroll back up in the file to about line 87 and insert the following lines just before the first $sel_nobox.

```
$sel_loginlocked['0'] = '';
$sel_loginlocked['1'] = '';
$sel_loginlocked[pnConfigGetVar('loginlocked')] = ' checked="checked"';
```

This code preps the form elements and defines which should be selected based on information stored in the database. As this is a new field, it does not exist in the database yet, so you must create it. Find the nuke_module_vars table using your database administrative tool. Enter a new row of data with the values in Table 23.1.

TABLE 23.1

Login Toggle Database Values

FIELD	VALUE
pn_modname	/PNConfig
pn_name	loginlocked
pn_value	s:1:"1";

The seed value of "1" for loginlocked sets the form element to "no" by default. After the database entry is done, the toggle in Website Settings works. When you submit the form, it changes the database value.

Toggle Check at Login

Now, you need to tie the loginlocked value to whether users can log in. Back in your text editor, load up the login access file:

/modules/NS-User/user/access.php

The access_user_login function at about line 41 performs the login operation itself. Failed logins are redirected to the user login screen to try again.

You need to set up two operations. The first is to see if the new toggle variable is set to "0." The second is to see if the user logging in is an administrator. This way, if the logins are locked, administrators can still successfully log in to the site.

These operations could be done in the access.php file, but although the login operation takes place there, the security information associated with the user is cached and is not updated to reflect the login until a new page is loaded. After login, the user is redirected back to the page she came from using the $url variable. It's at that point that you need to add the new security check, but you can't add checks to every page the user might be coming from. The easiest solution is to send all incoming users to the root home page after a login. Then, the check can be added there to secure the site.

Change the existing access_user_login function to look like this:

```
function access_user_login($uname, $pass, $url, $rememberme)
{
    if (pnUserLogIn($uname, $pass, $rememberme)) {
//      Original redirect changed for login lock toggle.
//      redirect_index(_LOGGINGYOU, $url);
        redirect_index(_LOGGINGYOU, '/index.php');
    } else {
        pnRedirect('user.php?stop=1');
    }
}
```

Now go to the `index.php` file in your PostNuke root folder. Add the check at the top of the file, just after the `list` variable assignments. Add the following code at about line 48:

```
if (pnUserLoggedIn()) {
    if (pnConfigGetVar('loginlocked') == 0) {
        if (!(pnSecAuthAction(0, '.*', '.*', ACCESS_ADMIN))) {
            pnUserLogOut();
            $ThemeSel = pnUserGetTheme();
            echo "<html><head><meta http-equiv=\"refresh\" content=\"4;
url=/index.php\">\n";
            echo "<link rel=\"stylesheet\"
href=\"".WHERE_IS_PERSO."themes/$ThemeSel/style/styleNN.css\" type=\"text/css\">";
            echo "<style type=\"text/css\">";
            echo "@import url(\"".WHERE_IS_PERSO."themes/$ThemeSel/style/style.css\"); ";
            echo "</style>\n";
            echo "</head><body bgcolor=\"$GLOBALS[bgcolor1]\" text=\"$GLOBALS
[textcolor1]\">\n";
            echo "<div style=\"text-align:center\" class=\"pn-title\">".
_NOLOGINAVAILABLE."</div></body></html>";
            exit;
        }
    }
}
```

The first `if` statement checks to see whether the user is logged in. If not, the entire script is ignored. The second check examines the `loginlocked` value in the database to see if it is turned "on." If that passes, the third statement calls `pnSecAuthAction` to see if the user is an administrator. If not, the short page code is written out with the text message contained in `_NOLOGINAVAILABLE`.

Tip

This hack is designed to allow administrators to log in when everyone else is locked out, but the `pnSecAuthAction` function can be used to identify *any* group of users. You could create a special group named "Backup" or "BetaTesters" who are allowed to log in to the site when regular users are excluded. This group could be made of both administrators and special users.

The `meta` refresh line displays the message for four seconds with the preceding code. You can change that variable to be longer if you want to provide a larger message.

The message itself is defined by opening the global `global.php` file in your editor:

`/language/eng/global.php`

At about line 274, just after the `_NOEDITORIAL` definition, add this line:

`define('_NOLOGINAVAILABLE','User logins are currently disabled. Please try back later.');`

As stated earlier, the message you tell your users can be anything. You can just as easily write "down for maintenance" or provide a date or time when the logins will be reinstated. If you use this feature often, you might want to edit the message each time to personalize it to the occasion the way businesses update their voice mail messages daily.

The only limitation to this hack is that it does not prevent users who are currently logged in from staying on the site. Anyone who returns to the home page will be logged off, but there is no way to force them to browse there.

X-User

The X-User module is designed to provide additional features for the new user sign-up and registration system. It allows you to queue new users for approval before they are fully admitted, as well as customize the interface and exchange used during the registration process. X-User is not so much a replacement for the regular user system as it is an overlay that provides additional options and security.

The last release of X-User, version .2.3RC1, is found on the SourceForge website at http://sourceforge.net/projects/pn-xuser/, and it is also in the online book materials. An additional code hack is also available as a separate optional download. Installation of the module is fairly straightforward. The zip archive includes a root directory with the module's version in the name, so you need to unzip the file in a temporary location and move the contents of the `xuser` subdirectory into your site's `modules` folder. Proceed to the Modules Administration screen and activate the new module.

Settings

Return to the main Administration Menu and click on the new xuser link. There are three main areas in the X-User module. The first, Settings, provides options to customize exactly how PostNuke responds to prospective new users. You can see in Figure 23.3 how the email system, options at registration, and even the default group for new users are all manageable from the single form.

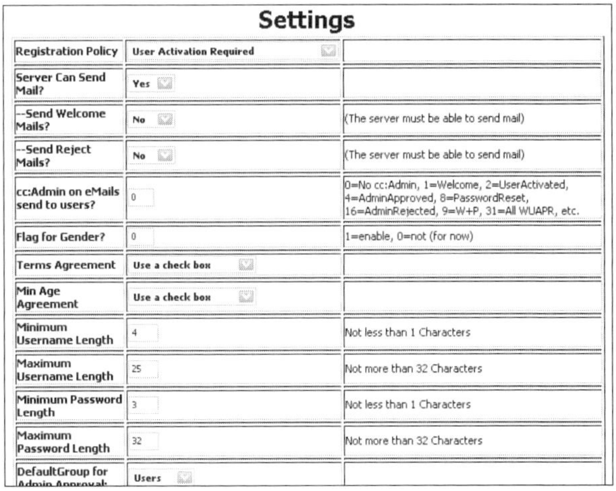

FIGURE 23.3   Changing how PostNuke responds to new users.

Five different policies can be applied to the registration process:

- **No Policy**—Users are allowed to register immediately.

- **User Activation Required**—New users are sent an email with an activation code. They must enter the code to verify their email address. This option prevents the need for new users to change the random password generated by PostNuke for new accounts.

- **Admin Approval Required**—New users are placed in a holding queue where an administrator must approve each before they are granted access. This is identical to the Submit News functionality.

- **Admin Approval Then User Activation**—After an administrator approves a new user, he is sent his activation code.

- **User Activation Then Admin Approval**—After a new user enters the activation code, he is placed in the waiting queue for approval.

The *Server Can Send Mail?* toggle lets X-User know whether it's possible to send Welcome and Rejection emails. Similarly, administrators can also receive copies of emails sent to users. This is especially useful for sites in which users are able to complete their activation without management intervention.

The next seven fields all manage how the registration interface looks. The *Gender Flag*, if enabled, requires the user to state her sex as part of the admission form. The *Terms* and *Age Requirement* drop-down list boxes not only let you toggle the agreements' appearance, but you can also make them separate pages that must be clicked through or integrated check boxes that are part of the main registration form (see Figure 23.4).

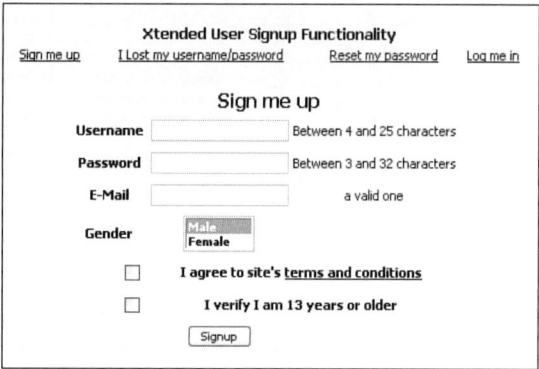

FIGURE 23.4 All your sign-up options in one simplified form.

Note

The minimum age used on this form is referenced from the PostNuke user system. It can be changed in the User Registration Configuration form under User Administration.

The minimum and maximum character counts for both usernames and passwords can be defined here, and they are validated upon submission of the form. Improper entries display an error prompting the user to correct the problem.

Finally, you can select the default group for new users. The list is generated from the groups you have created for your site. This is mainly used when users are automatically added to the PostNuke system. If you've chosen to approve each user, you have a select option at that time to decide which group they will be placed into.

Messages Customization

Click the Emails/Messages Customization link in the top navigation list to manage most of the text used by the module. You can see the initial configuration options in Figure 23.5. All of these fields are simply text areas that allow you to edit the messages X-User sends to users.

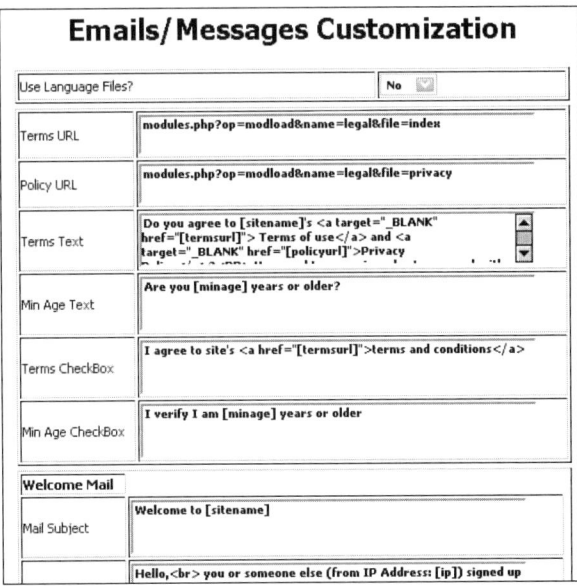

FIGURE 23.5 Managing new user communications.

This form has seven main sections:

- **Agreements**—Edits the wording used with regard to the terms and age verifications users must agree to. Additional fields allow you to define the uniform resource locators (URLs) to the separate agreement forms.

- **Welcome Mail**—Customizes the welcoming email message sent to new users.

- **Activation Mail**—Edits the phrasing of the email prompting users to use their included activation code to return to the site to complete their registration.

- **Send Password Mail**—Sends users this message when they request their password to be reset. This message includes a confirmation code.

- **Approved Mail**—Notifies users that their registration has been approved.

- **Rejected Mail**—Notifies users that their registration has been rejected.

- **Page Screens**—Customizes the messages displayed on various screens as part of the registration process.

Tip

All the other messages displayed by X-User but not part of the Message Customization page can be changed by editing the files found in `/modules/xuser/pnlang/eng/`.

Approval

The third administrative area is simply an approval table for users waiting in the queue (see Figure 23.6). From here, you can also sort users into different groups when their accounts are approved.

			Approval	
			Submit	
ID	**Username**	**Email**	**Status**	**Group**
5	Timmy2	tim@mysite.com	Pending Admin	Users

FIGURE 23.6   Approving users in the queue.

Xtended User Signup Functionality

Sign me up   I Lost my username/password   Reset my password   Log me in

Sign me up

Username	ff	Between 4 and 25 characters
	short name	
Password	••	Between 3 and 32 characters
	short password	
E-Mail	sadsf@cvzx	a valid one
	Invalid E-Mail	
Gender	Male / Female	

☐   **I agree to site's terms and conditions**

Sorry you must agree to terms

☐   **I verify I am 13 years or older**

sorry you must be min age

Signup

FIGURE 23.7   Using the X-User blocks to manage new users.

User Blocks

X-User also includes two unregistered user blocks (see Figure 23.7). They are installed as any other block. The User Functions block displays a list of links allowing users to request registration or fix their lost password. The User Login block is identical to the standard login block's functionality, but it is programmed to check with the X-User module before allowing login.

To properly set up the X-User system, you need to disable the default login block, and use this special login supplied by X-User. If you allow users to use the standard login block, the security provided by X-User is not effective.

> **Note**
>
> Both user blocks are only visible to site visitors who are not currently logged in. They are not visible to your administration account when you are adding them to your site.

Incoming Users Hack

This hack is documented in the optional incoming-xuser download. When completed, it adds the X-User new user queue to the Waiting Content feature of PostNuke. Open this file in your editor:

/includes/blocks/menu.php

Scroll down to roughly line 140. You will see a series of if blocks that check for and display queued content for Stories, Review, Web Links, Downloads, and so on. You can insert the X-User code between any of those blocks of code, but generally, you should list the users first, before content submissions. To that end, place the code just after the $header = 0; line and before the Stories::Story check like so:

```
$header = 0;
if (pnSecAuthAction(0, "xuser::", "::",ACCESS_ADD)) {
    include_once("modules/xuser/pntables.php");
    $pntable = array_merge($pntable, xuser_pntables());
    $result = $dbconn->Execute("SELECT count(1) FROM $pntable[xuser] WHERE STATUS = -2");
    if ($dbconn->ErrorNo() == 0) {
        list($dnum) = $result->fields;
        $result->Close();
        if ($dnum) {
            if ($header == 0) {
                $block['content'] .= addMenuStyledUrl($vars['style'], "<b>" . _WAITINGCONT.
"</b>","", "");
                $header = 1;
            }
            $block['content'] .= addMenuStyledUrl($vars['style'], "New Users".".":
$dnum","index.php?module=xuser&type=admin&func=PendingAdminAV", "");
            $content = 1;
        }
    }
}

if (pnSecAuthAction(0, "Stories::Story", "::", ACCESS_ADD)) {
```

With that code added, you are notified of new users just like a story submission (see Figure 23.8). This addition works with any Menu block with the Waiting Content feature enabled.

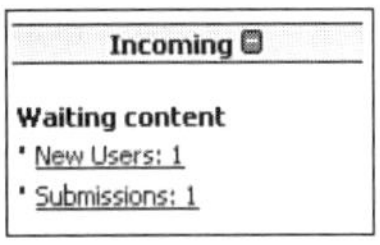

FIGURE 23.8
Keeping track of new users with this easy hack.

Troubleshooting

One issue reported by some users of the X-User module is that logins might fail when performed from a URL without a filename. This primarily is a concern from the website home page where the URL looks like this:

```
http://www.mysite.com/
```

X-User is currently unsupported, but if you find this to be a problem for your site, simply place a PHP redirect in your root index like this:

```
header("Location: http://www.mysite.com/index.php");
```

This ensures anyone hitting the page is going to the file directly and not by the web server default.

Next

The next chapter specializes in hacks to the PostNuke login system. You will look at ways to customize the side block form as well as change the interface to the login process itself.

Login System Hacks

24

When you are running a site that requires or simply promotes the creation of user accounts, it's very important to have a clean, clear, and user-friendly login system. Potential users might feel insecure about creating an account that contains personal information.

Like all areas of PostNuke, you can edit and customize the login forms and transition screens to convey a consistent message to your users, in both content and styling. This chapter focuses on PostNuke's login forms and the redirect screens users see while logging in and logging out of their accounts. The following sections cover these topics:

- Customizing labels

- Adding text

- Adding style

- Customizing page labels

- Customizing the Help page

- Customizing the Help email

- Changing login/logout colors

- Changing login/logout text

- Forcing redirect page after login

- Adding ads and logos

- Adding a timer bar

Login Block

The Login block is a very important component of your PostNuke site. You must identify users to manage the types and levels of access and capabilities they will have on your site. If it is not clear that a login provides additional benefits, many users might not log in at all, even if they have accounts. Plan for these issues by customizing your PostNuke site to apply to your user base.

You can change login messages and field labels to cater to the wants and needs of your site visitors. For this chapter's examples, you make changes as though you are building a political campaign site. You assume visitors are from the general public, and the site provides general information for the candidate John Smith.

Customizing Labels

The default PostNuke Login block contains a very simple interface (see Figure 24.1). First change the block title to something more appropriate for our example site. Go to your site's

Administration Menu and click the Blocks link. Find the Login block entry near the base of the table and edit the block. In the title field, change the "Login" text to "Join the Campaign" and submit your changes.

Having a block named "Join the Campaign" helps to create interest in the form by inviting visitors to participate. Now change the form labels, Username and Password, for added clarity. Start your text editor and open the language file at this location:

FIGURE 24.1
A simple login to
PostNuke.

`/includes/language/blocks/eng/login.php`

There are three variable definitions in the file:

```
define('_ASREGISTERED',' <a href="user.php?op=lostpassscreen&amp;module=NS-
LostPassword">Log in Problems?</a><br /> New User? <a href="user.php">Sign Up!</a>');
define('_BLOCKNICKNAME','Username');
define('_BLOCKPASSWORD','Password');
```

Now change the value of _BLOCKNICKNAME to "Login Name." Change the _BLOCKPASSWORD value to "Your Password." This also adds a personal touch to the form.

The _ASREGISTERED definition is a bit more complex and incorporates link code for both new user sign-up and login help. Change the definition to match the following line:

```
define('_ASREGISTERED','Don\'t have an account? Support John Smith and <a
href="user.php">create one now!</a><br /><br /><a href="user.php?op=lostpassscreen&amp;
module=NS-LostPassword">Get help with your account.</a>');
```

The placements of the two links have been exchanged so that the sign-up prompt is before the help link. This helps a site that expects to have more new visitors than return visitors. The two links have been separated with a little space to keep their separate messages clear, and a customized message is included to personalize the site for John Smith supporters.

The "Remember me" text can also be altered, but its variable definition is found in this location:

```
/language/eng/global.php
```

The global definition file contains variables that are shared by different modules on the site. If you change a variable there, it might change references on other pages of which you are not aware. To change the Login reference without the possibility other pages will be affected, create a replacement variable that's specific to only the Login block. In the Login's text variable listing:

```
/includes/language/blocks/eng/login.php
```

add this line:

```
define('_LOGINREMEMBERME','Stay logged in');
```

Now open the login script file itself located here:

```
/includes/blocks/login.php
```

FIGURE 24.2
Customized
PostNuke login
labels.

Change the REMEMBERME reference at about line 72 to LOGINREMEMBERME so the block accesses your custom variable and not the global one. Save the files and refresh your login screen to see your updated block (shown in Figure 24.2).

Adding Text

Even with the personal touches outlined previously, your site's visitors might need a little additional prompting to log in to their accounts. One solution is to add a short message to the login block that promotes the access to additional features a login can provide.

It is possible to extend the existing text definitions and add in complete paragraphs to their values, but those definitions were created for specific purposes, and if you want to add new text, it is best to create a new variable definition to support your changes. Open the login.php file defined next in your editor.

```
/includes/language/blocks/eng/login.php
```

Create a new definition line called LOGINMESSAGE and give it the value text: "Get involved in the campaign. Sign in now to speak your views in the forums and get access to special site features." The complete line code should appear as this:

```
define('_LOGINMESSAGE','Get involved in the campaign. Sign in now to speak your views in
the forums and get access to special site features.');
```

Now, add the variable to the block code. Open the code file in your editor:

```
/includes/blocks/login.php
```

Examine the code starting at about line 62. To add the message before the Username and Password fields, place the variable call before the start of the form and table or just inside the table opening. Visually, this is a better location to separate the new message from the other text below the form, but it's possible to place the variable anywhere on the form.

Change these two lines:

```
$boxstuff  = '<form action="user.php" method="post">' . "\n";
$boxstuff .= '<table border="0" width="100%" cellspacing="0" cellpadding="1"><tr>' . "\n";
```

to the following:

```
$boxstuff = '<div class="pn-normal">'._LOGINMESSAGE.'</div>'."\n";  // Additional login
message
$boxstuff .= '<form action="user.php" method="post">'."\n";
$boxstuff .= '<table border="0" width="100%" cellspacing="0" cellpadding="1"><tr>'."\n";
```

Placing the <div> before the start of the <form> tag has the added benefit of using the default margin space placed above form tags to separate your new message from the start of the login form. Your edited block with the new message is shown in Figure 24.3.

Adding Style

For most websites, success is determined by traffic. The easiest way to build visitor traffic is to maintain existing users so that the influx of new visitors will always grow the overall user base. Site logins create ties to users, promote return traffic, and provide the means to develop a real community of users.

FIGURE 24.3
Promoting your
Login features.

However, you might find the Login block is not obvious enough in a site with so many other blocks and block-like content. You can, of course, be certain the Login block is positioned at the very top of your site, but if that fails, the next step is to make the Login block visually unique.

You can redefine the look of the Login block in three ways. First, if you are using a Xanthia theme, you need only develop a specialized template and apply it to only one block. A similar effect is accomplished through the second option: Use third-party theme extensions, such as AutoThemes (www.autothemes.com), BlockHome (moe.cape.com/~nate/postnuke/), or Nuclei (www.tangant.com), and define custom styles for the Login block.

The third option is to change the Login block code directly. This hack might or might not be simpler or faster than either of the previous options, especially if you are already using specialized themes, but the following works with any PostNuke site, regardless of whether you are using any of the previous systems.

Launch your editor and open the Login block file:

```
/includes/blocks/login.php
```

On line 60, an `if` statement begins with this:

```
if (!pnUserLoggedIn()) {
```

and ends around line 90, depending on your changes to the file. The code within the statement builds the block content and uses the `themesideblock` function to add the default block definition around it. Replace all of those lines and you can make the block appear with any colors or layout you choose.

> **Note**
>
> It is important that you are familiar with the way your site's theme is designed, so that when you make a custom block layout, it naturally fits into the site just as a dynamically generated block based on your theme does.

Here is an example of one way to approach this change. Comment out all of these lines:

```
if (!pnUserLoggedIn()) {
    $boxstuff = '<div class="pn-normal">'._LOGINMESSAGE.'</div>'."\n";  // Additional login
message
    $boxstuff .= '<form action="user.php" method="post">'."\n";
    $boxstuff .= '<table border="0" width="100%" cellspacing="0"
cellpadding="1"><tr>'."\n";
    $boxstuff .= '<td><span class="pn-normal"> <label for="uname">'.
_BLOCKNICKNAME.'</label></span><br />' . "\n";
    $boxstuff .= '<input type="text" name="uname" id="uname" size="14" maxlength="25"
/></td>' . "\n";
        $boxstuff .= '</tr><tr>';
    $boxstuff .= '<td><span class="pn-normal"> <label
```

```
for="pass">'._BLOCKPASSWORD.'</label></span><br />' . "\n";
    $boxstuff .= '<input type="password" name="pass" id="pass" size="14" maxlength="20"
/></td>' . "\n";
        $boxstuff .= '</tr>' . "\n";
    if (pnConfigGetVar('seclevel') != 'High') {
        $boxstuff .= '<tr>' . "\n";
            $boxstuff .= '<td><input type="checkbox" value="1" name="rememberme" id=
"rememberme" />' . "\n";
        $boxstuff .= '<span class="pn-normal"> <label for="rememberme">'.
_LOGINREMEMBERME.'</label></span></td>' . "\n";
            $boxstuff .= '</tr>' . "\n";
    }
    $boxstuff .= '<tr><td>' . "\n";
    $boxstuff .= '<input type="hidden" name="module" value="NS-User" />' . "\n";
    $boxstuff .= '<input type="hidden" name="op" value="login" />' . "\n";
    $boxstuff .= '<input type="hidden" name="url" value="' .pnVarPrepForDisplay($path) .'"
/>' . "\n";
    $boxstuff .= '<input type="submit" value="'._LOGIN.'" /></td></tr><tr><td>' . "\n";
    $boxstuff .= '<br /><span class="pn-
normal">'._ASREGISTERED.'</span></td></tr></table></form>' . "\n";
    if (empty($row['title'])) {
        $row['title'] = _LOGIN;
    }
    $row['content'] = $boxstuff;
    return themesideblock($row);
}
```

Add this code to display the customized Login block:

```
if (!pnUserLoggedIn()) {
    $newlogblock = '<div style="width:150px; padding:2px; border:1px solid #000000;
background-color:#D0FFD0;">'."\n";
    $newlogblock .= '<div style="padding:1px;"><span class="pn-blocktitle" style="text-
transform:uppercase;">Join the Campaign</span></div>'."\n";
    $newlogblock .= '<div style="padding:2px;" class="pn-blockcontent">'."\n";
    $newlogblock .= '<div class="pn-normal">'._LOGINMESSAGE.'</div>'."\n";  // Additional
login message
    $newlogblock .= '<form action="user.php" method="post" ><table border="0" width="100%"
cellspacing="0" cellpadding="1">'."\n";
    $newlogblock .= '<tr><td><span class="pn-normal"> <label for="uname">'.
_BLOCKNICKNAME.'</label></span><br /><input type="text" name="uname" id="uname" size="14"
maxlength="25" /></td></tr>'."\n";
    $newlogblock .= '<tr><td><span class="pn-normal"> <label for="pass">'.
```

```
_BLOCKPASSWORD.'</label></span><br /><input type="password" name="pass" id="pass" size="14"
maxlength="20" /></td></tr>'."\n";
    if (pnConfigGetVar('seclevel') != 'High') {
        $newlogblock .= '<tr><td><input type="checkbox" value="1" name="rememberme"
id="rememberme" /><span class="pn-normal"> <label for="rememberme">'.
_LOGINREMEMBERME.'</label></span></td></tr>'."\n";
    }
    $newlogblock .= '<tr><td><input type="hidden" name="module" value="NS-User" /><input
type="hidden" name="op" value="login" /><input type="hidden" name="url" value="'
.pnVarPrepForDisplay($path).'" /><input type="submit" value="'._LOGIN.'" /></td></tr>'."\n";
    $newlogblock .= '<tr><td><br /><span class="pn-
normal">'._ASREGISTERED.'</span></td></tr>'."\n";
    $newlogblock .= '</table></form>'."\n";
    $newlogblock .= '</div></div><br />'."\n";
}
return $newlogblock;
```

The new block, shown in Figure 24.4, displays as a simple bordered area with a light green background. The block area has been separated from the theme, but still accesses the standard styles and language text variables. Using the previous code, you can now change the block to look like anything.

Customizing Page Labels

The PostNuke Login screen uses a form that's nearly identical to the block form described in the previous sections. The login screen is generally seen less than the side block for most sites, but it's still an important part of any site. If you make changes to customize the block's labels, you should make the same changes to the login page for consistency.

Open the NS-User user.php file:

```
/modules/NS-User/user.php
```

FIGURE 24.4
Highlighting your site's login.

Scroll down to line 330 where you will see this function:

```
function user_user_loginscreen()
{
    include 'header.php';
    OpenTable();
    echo "<form action=\"user.php\" method=\"post\"><div>\n"
        . "<span class=\"pn-title\">" . _USERLOGIN . "</span><br /><br />\n"
        . "<table border=\"0\">\n"
```

```
        . "<tr>\n"
        . "<td><span class=\"pn-normal\"><label for=\"uname_mod_user\">" . _NICKNAME
. "</label>: </span></td>\n"
        . "<td><input type=\"text\" name=\"uname\" id=\"uname_mod_user\" size=\"26\"
maxlength=\"25\" /></td>"
        . "</tr>\n"
        . "<tr>\n"
        . "<td><span class=\"pn-normal\"><label for=\"pass_mod_user\">" . _PASSWORD
. "</label>: </span></td>\n"
        . "<td><input type=\"password\" name=\"pass\" id=\"pass_mod_user\" size=\"21\"
maxlength=\"20\" /></td>\n"
        . "</tr>\n";
    if (pnConfigGetVar('seclevel') != 'High') {
        echo "<tr>\n"
            ."<td><span class=\"pn-normal\"><label for=\"rememberme_mod_user\">" .
 _REMEMBERME . "</label>: </span></td>\n"
            ."<td><input type=\"checkbox\" name=\"rememberme\" id=\"rememberme_mod_user\"
/></td>\n"
            ."</tr>\n";
    }
    echo "</table>\n"
        . "<input type=\"hidden\" name=\"url\" value=\"" . pnServerGetVar("HTTP_REFERER") .
"\" />\n";
    user_submit('NS-User', 'login', _LOGIN);
    echo "</div></form>\n";
    CloseTable();

    include 'footer.php';
}
```

You can reformat the Hypertext Markup Language (HTML) in the preceding function to display the form in any fashion you desire. The key variables are USERLOGIN, NICKNAME, PASSWORD, and REMEMBERME. They are defined in this file:

/language/eng/global.php

You can edit those variables directly, which can affect other pages, or create a new set of variables for this particular form, as you did with the Login block in the previous sections. You might also want to add an additional message to this form, again using the previously outlined steps.

Customizing the Help Page

Users who have forgotten their password can easily click the Help link in the Login block to have it reset using an automated email script. As you can see in Figure 24.5, the default Help page wording and layout might not apply well to all sites. You can edit the page to work with whatever styling you need.

Lost your password?

No problem!

Just type your username and click the send button and an email will be sent to you with a 'Confirmation Code'. After you receive the confirmation code, re-type your username and the 'Confirmation Code' into the form. After this form is submitted, a new password will be generated and emailed back to you.

Username:

E-mail:

Confirmation code:

Send password

FIGURE 24.5   PostNuke's account password help.

The language variables are defined in both of these files:

```
/modules/NS-LostPassword/lang/eng/global.php
/language/eng/global.php
```

and the code that calls the variables and creates the form itself is found here:

```
/modules/NS-LostPassword/user.php
```

First review the text variables relevant to this page. The form calls six variables, but two are in the global.php file PostNuke uses universally. You can create two new variables to isolate this code from the rest of the site just as you did for the block form. Edit the NS-LostPassword global.php and add these lines:

```
define('_LOGHELPNICKNAME','Login Name');
define('_LOGHELPEMAIL','Email Address');
```

Now review the four existing variables and change them to suit your site. For the John Smith campaign example, use these changes:

```
define('_PASSWORDLOST','ElectJohnSmith.com Account Password Help');
define('_NOPROBLEM','The form below can be used to reset your password. Enter your Login
Name and Email Address for your account. If you leave the Confirmation Code field blank, a
code will be generated and emailed to your address to confirm your identity.<br /><br
/>Once you have a code, return to this form and complete all of the fields. Submit the
completed form, and your account password will be reset with a randomly generated one. The
new password will be emailed to you.<br /><br />');
define('_CONFIRMATIONCODE','Confirmation code');
define('_SENDPASSWORD','Submit Form');
```

Now edit the NS-LostPassword user.php file. First update the variables on lines 47 and 51 to match the new definitions you added to the local global.php file.

The centered text style is being carried down from the parent column styles, and due to the sometimes inconsistent rendering of nested styles with <div> and <span> tags, the only sure way to fix the effect is by encasing all the code beneath the title inside a table. The table needs only one cell; it resets the text-align styles to the local cell with a default left justification.

After all of these changes are completed, your display code should appear fairly close to the following:

```
OpenTable();
echo "<span class=\"pn-title\">"._PASSWORDLOST."</span><br /><br />\n"
    ."<table style=\"width:100%;\"><tr><td style=\"text-align:left;\"><span class=\
"pn-normal\">"._NOPROBLEM."</span><br />\n"
    ."<form action=\"user.php\" method=\"post\"><div>\n"
    ."<table border=\"0\" cellspacing=\"0\" cellpadding=\"5\">\n"
    ."<tr>\n"
    ."<td><span class=\"pn-normal\"><label for=\"uname_lost_password\">".
_LOGHELPNICKNAME."</label>: </span></td>\n"
    ."<td><input type=\"text\" name=\"uname\" id=\"uname_lost_password\" size=\"26\"
maxlength=\"25\" /></td>\n"
    ."</tr>\n"
    ."<tr>\n"
    ."<td><span class=\"pn-normal\"><label
for=\"email_lost_password\">"._LOGHELPEMAIL."</label>: </span></td>\n"
    ."<td><input type=\"text\" name=\"email\" id=\"email_lost_password\" size=\"60\"
maxlength=\"60\" /></td>\n"
    ."</tr>\n"
    ."<tr><td><span class=\"pn-normal\"><label for=\"code_lost_password\">".
_CONFIRMATIONCODE."</label>: </span></td>\n"
    ."<td><input type=\"text\" name=\"code\" id=\"code_lost_password\" size=\"5\"
maxlength=\"6\" /></td>\n"
```

```
      ."</tr>\n"
      ."</table>\n"
      ."<input type=\"hidden\" name=\"op\" value=\"mailpasswd\" />\n"
      ."<input type=\"hidden\" name=\"module\" value=\"NS-LostPassword\" />\n"
      ."<input type=\"submit\" value=\""._SENDPASSWORD."\" />\n"
      ."</div></form></td></tr></table>\n";
  CloseTable();
```

ElectJohnSmith.com Account Password Help

The form below can be used to reset your password. Enter your Login Name and Email Address for your account. If you leave the Confirmation Code field blank, a code will be generated and emailed to your address to confirm your identity.

Once you have a code, return to this form and complete all of the fields. Submit the completed form, and your account password will be reset with a randomly generated one. The new password will be emailed to you.

Login Name: _____

Email Address: _____

Confirmation code: ____

[Submit Form]

FIGURE 24.6   Personalized help for your site's users.

An example of the completed changes is also shown in Figure 24.6. Compare the changes with Figure 24.5 to see how all the edits come together.

Customizing the Help Email

When users submit the automated password help form, they receive an email message. This message can also be customized to your website quite easily. The first email content is generated by line 109 of the NS-LostPassword's user.php file:

```
$message = ""._USERACCOUNT." $uname "._AT." $sitename "._HASTHISEMAIL."  "._AWEBUSERFROM."
$host_name "._HASREQUESTED."\n\n"._YOURNEWPASSWORD." $newpass\n\n "._YOUCANCHANGE .
pnGetBaseURL() . "user.php\n\n"._IFYOUDIDNOTASK."";
```

The second email that also includes the reset confirmation code is generated by line 134:

```
$message = ""._USERACCOUNT." '$uname' "._AT." $sitename "._HASTHISEMAIL." "._AWEBUSERFROM."
$host_name "._CODEREQUESTED."\n\n"._YOURCODEIS." $areyou \n\n"._WITHTHISCODE."".
pnGetBaseURL() . "user.php\n"._IFYOUDIDNOTASK2."";
```

You can see from the preceding lines which variables in the global.php language file are used to produce the message. Open the variable file into your editor:

/modules/NS-LostPassword/lang/eng/global.php

One way you can rewrite the email is by changing the values of the existing variables, by creating an entirely new set of text variables, or any combination of these. The site variables, $uname, $sitename, $newpass, and so on, can also be reordered or selectively displayed. For this example, add these lines to the global.php definitions:

```
define('_MSGINTRO','This message has been generated to reset your account password. Use the
confirmation code below to complete the lost password form. If you did not request this
email, please disregard this message.\n');
```

```
define('_MSGINTRO2','Your account password has been reset. The new password is listed
below. If you did not intend to reset your password, simply login using the link below and
manually change your password to something new.\n');
define('_MSGLOGIN','\nLogin Name: ');
define('_MSGCODE','\nConfirmation Code: ');
define('_MSGPASS','\nNew Password: ');
define('_MSGREQUEST','\nRequested By: ');
define('_MSGLINK','\n\nTo change your password, go to ');
define('_MSGTHANKS','\n\nThank you for being a part of ');
define('_MSGIFNOT','\n\nIf you did not request this email, please disregard this
message.');
```

Comment out line 109 in the user.php file and add the following line to replace it:

```
$message =
_MSGINTRO._MSGLOGIN."$uname"._MSGCODE."$areyou"._MSGREQUEST."$host_name"._MSGLINK.
pnGetBaseURL()."user.php"._MSGTHANKS."$sitename";
```

Do the same to line 134 using this code:

```
$message =
_MSGINTRO2._MSGLOGIN."$uname"._MSGPASS."$newpass"._MSGREQUEST."$host_name"._MSGLINK.
pnGetBaseURL()."user.php"._MSGTHANKS."$sitename";
```

Log in to your site using a test user account and reset your password to test your changes. The previous example creates a simple paragraph with the key information listed below the prose text, but you can, of course, change the display to be more complex, including generating HTML email.

Login Process

Now that you've made certain your users log in to your site, it's time to look at what happens during the login process. You are probably already very familiar with the default "Logging you in" message, but like all things PostNuke, you can change the way the transition screen looks and works.

Changing Login/Logout Colors

In PostNuke versions prior to .75, the login/logout screen was traditionally blue with white text, no matter which theme was chosen for a site. All of the pages now use the global color styles for consistency, but you can also adjust the login screen colors slightly for a more dramatic effect.

Open the following file in your text editor:

`/modules/NS-User/tools.php`

The two main functions in the file, `redirect_index` and `redirect_user`, both control the screens that segue from form submissions back to the site. Lines 46 and 63 specifically have color references coded into them:

```
echo "</head><body bgcolor=\"$GLOBALS[bgcolor1]\" text=\"$GLOBALS[textcolor1]\">\n";
```

But the HTML color attributes are actually ignored now in favor of the global style sheet. To override the cascading style sheets (CSS) body, code the styles directly into the tag, replacing the HTML, as shown in the following line:

```
echo "</head><body style=\"background-color:$GLOBALS[bgcolor2]; color:$GLOBALS
[textcolor1];\">\n";
```

These inline styles override the included CSS file. The small change to the `bgcolor2` variable darkens the background for most themes while in transition, so the change is more noticeable. You can also hard-code in Hex color codes as you would any style.

Tip

Instead of coding multiple styles directly into the file, create a new style specifically for the redirect pages. Then add the class attribute to the body tags in `tools.php`.

Changing Login/Logout Text

The text displayed when a user logs in to or out of your site is also very important. It might only take a few seconds for the process to complete, but the short message on the page is likely to get more specific attention from your users than any other information on your site. You should consider carefully what message you want said to your users. In addition to conveying the redirect information, how it is written says a great deal about your site, too.

First examine the variables that are used on the login/logout redirect screens. Open your editor and load up this file:

`/modules/NS-User/lang/eng/global.php`

The two specific lines you'll change are 64 and 116:

```
define('_LOGGINGYOU','Logging you in — please wait!');
define('_YOUARELOGGEDOUT','You are now logged-out!');
```

Duplicate the originals and comment them out. Now, you can customize the text for your site. With our campaign example, use the statement: "Thanks for supporting John Smith! Granting special site access now..." for the login value. "Thanks for visiting ElectJohnSmith.com! We hope you return soon.

Your personal account is logging off now." works similarly well for the logout value.

As you can see from the previous examples, the lines do not have to be just about the technical process, and HTML can be added for basic formatting. Including a personal comment helps maintain a connection with the user. Adding references to the site name or focus reminds the user once again what site they are on and why. That kind of reinforcement translates into strong return visitor traffic.

Forcing Redirect Page After Login

Normally, the login page redirects users to their personal page. Depending on what form was used, users might also be redirected to the main site home page. But for some sites, it might be important to redirect users to a different page. For example, a political campaign site might have an important message or news information that should be viewed by all users. You can force redirects to go to a specific page simply by changing the uniform resource locator (URL) variable in the login forms.

To change the login block redirection, open the same file you used to edit the styles and text:

```
/includes/blocks/login.php
```

In the `blocks_login_block` function, look for this section of code:

```
<input type="hidden" name="url" value="'.pnVarPrepForDisplay($path).'" />
```

The `value` in this hidden `input` tag sends a URL to the redirect function. Whatever URL you place in that value location is used for every user after the login. So, for example, if you want to send all users to a specific news article, you can code that link into the tag as follows:

```
<input type="hidden" name="url"
value="/modules.php?op=modload&name=News&file=article&sid=1" />
```

The same effect can be generated for the page version of the login form. Open the NS-User user.php file:

```
/modules/NS-User/user.php
```

and scroll down to around line 330 to the `user_user_loginscreen` function. Look for this `input` near the end of the function:

```
<input type=\"hidden\" name=\"url\" value=\"" . pnServerGetVar("HTTP_REFERER") . "\" />
```

Change its value to match the preceding one, and you've forced the redirect target after a login.

Adding Ads and Logos

Whether your site is commercially driven or not, the login/logout redirect page is valuable ad space. The page is nearly devoid of content, and every user is staring at the blank screen for those few seconds. You can let the captured audience go unused, or you can harness their attention by focusing on an ad graphic.

You can perform a simple edit to see how it's done by adding a site logo to the login screen. Use the same image from Chapter 10, "Themes," which is included in the book materials. If you have not already done so, place the image in the main image path of your theme:

```
/themes/yourtheme/images/postnuke-logo1.gif
```

Now open the main user tools file in your editor:

```
/modules/NS-User/tools.php
```

Scroll down to the `redirect_index` function on line 34. The layout of an entire HTML page is in this function, and you can add whatever images or text you need to this page. It will be displayed to users when they log in and when they log out. Add an image line after the <body> tag opens, as follows:

```
    echo "</head><body style=\"background-color:$GLOBALS[bgcolor2]; color:$GLOBALS
[textcolor1];\">\n";
    echo "<img src=\"".$imagepath."/postnuke-logo1.gif\" />\n";
```

Save the change and perform a login or logout operation on your site. You should see a page similar to the one in Figure 24.7. This change adds branding to the site. Even a noncommercial site needs to protect its identity and should display a consistent logo on all pages. Commercial sites can just as easily display an advertising banner or message on the screen.

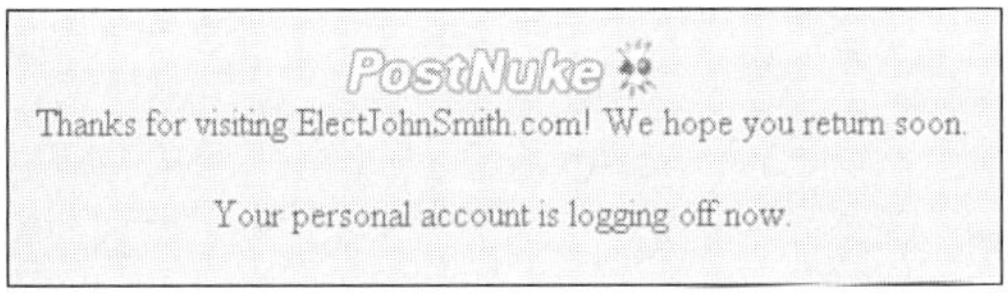

FIGURE 24.7   Branding the login/logout screens.

Adding a Timer Bar

It's becoming popular on Content Management System (CMS) sites to include an animated timer bar on the login screen. The MDpro PostNuke fork includes this feature now as a standard. It's very easy to port this effect back to your PostNuke install and give your site a little extra flash.

Brian Gosselin of `scriptasylum.com` is responsible for the very clean timer bar script found on so many sites. To add the bar to your site, you need a copy of his JavaScript file. It's available from this book's website, or you can get a current copy from *The Script Asylum*.

Place the file in this location:

```
/modules/NS-User/
```

Open your editor and load the user tools file:

```
/modules/NS-User/tools.php
```

The first main function is `redirect_index`. Scroll to the end of that function, and around line 47 find and comment out this line:

```
echo "<div style=\"text-align:center\" class=\"pn-title\">$message</div></body></html>";
```

To replace the preceding code, add in these lines:

```
echo "<div style=\"text-align:center\" class=\"pn-title\">$message</div>";
echo "<br /><br /><div style=\"text-align:center\"><script language=\"javascript\"
src=\"/modules/NS-User/timerbar.js\"></script></div>";
echo "</body></html>";
```

These lines add the timer bar just below the login and logout messages (see Figure 24.8).

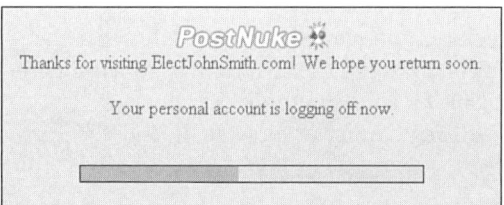

FIGURE 24.8 Animating your login/logout screens.

Change the line slightly to include the common "loading..." message:

```
echo "<br /><br /><div style=\"text-align:center\">Loading…<br /><script
language=\"javascript\" src=\"/modules/NS-User/timerbar.js\"></script></div>";
```

The timer bar script is also fully customizable. Open the JavaScript in your editor and look at the variable at the top of the file:

```
var loadedcolor='darkgray' ;      // PROGRESS BAR COLOR
var unloadedcolor='lightgrey';    // COLOR OF UNLOADED AREA
var bordercolor='navy';           // COLOR OF THE BORDER
var barheight=15;                 // HEIGHT OF PROGRESS BAR IN PIXELS
var barwidth=300;                 // WIDTH OF THE BAR IN PIXELS
var waitTime=5;                   // NUMBER OF SECONDS FOR PROGRESSBAR
```

Change these settings to match the bar's appearance to your site. The last variable, `waitTime`, determines how long it takes to run the bar. You might find reducing the seconds is more appropriate for faster sites.

Troubleshooting

These hacks require standard PHP string manipulation. If you are having regular trouble getting your code to `echo` properly, try reviewing the content in Chapter 19, "Dynamic PHP and PostNuke." It details the majority of the pitfalls you might encounter with PostNuke hacks.

Linefeed Characters Not Rendered

The PHP linefeed escape sequence, `\n`, is used a great deal in this chapter's hacks. You might find it's very easy to make a minor mistake in your code, and instead of rendering a linefeed, the sequence is echoed like common text. This effect happens because PHP renders single- and double-quoted strings differently. Single-quoted strings are handy because they let you write HTML straight, without escaping every double quote around tag attributes:

```
echo '<img src="helloworld.gif" />';
```

Because the single quote is defining the string, the double quotes are rendered as normal text. But if you include a linefeed at the end of that string inside the single quotes, it does not work:

```
echo '<img src="helloworld.gif" />\n';
```

To use both single quotes for your HTML and still include a linefeed, use the string concatenation operator and combine two strings with differing quotes:

```
echo '<img src="helloworld.gif" />'."\n";
```

The preceding example provides the best of both worlds for most simple `echo` lines. But keep in mind that not all PostNuke code uses this string display method.

Different people have developed the PostNuke CMS, and you will see many different methods of rendering content when working with PostNuke code. When in doubt, try to keep the style of the code you are adding or changing consistent with the code around it. It makes it easier to follow and helps to reduce the likelihood that any conflicts will occur between the original code and your changes.

Next

The next chapter provides an explanation of the changes required to implement a Multisites cluster in PostNuke. The two primary methods of accomplishing the cluster are compared to help determine which configuration is best for your needs.

Multisites

25

Many websites exist not as a single entity but as a cluster of related sites. The sites might or might not share a domain name, but there is some relation that exists between the sites' content or users that bring them together. Parent company websites can help support child product sites with content tie-ins. Cousin sites with similar user interests can share login account information allowing a user to access all sites with one account. There is a great deal of power that can be leveraged by having such a connection.

Creating a multiple website cluster is quite possible with PostNuke as well. It only requires a few edits to files and the database, and you can link up as many sites as you want. This chapter walks through the complete steps for creating a PostNuke Multisites system. The chapter discusses the following topics:

- Defining Multisites basics
- Splitting one site into many
- Combining multiple sites into one

Multisites Basics

The first thing to know about Multisites is it's a hack. The source files are there for you to use to create your cluster, but you still have to edit the files and know what you are doing. There really are not many changes, and some of the hacks detailed earlier in this book would be considered more difficult, but the process is still somewhat involved and not really for the faint of heart.

The second thing to consider is what you want out of a Multisites cluster. What needs to be shared between the sites? What must always be separate? Is it more of a single site that branches off, or do you want to link up pre-existing, standalone sites? You can approach the clustering in different ways, and you should have a very good idea of what you want to accomplish before you begin.

Documenting Domains

PostNuke does not care how many domains you want to use or whether they are full or subdomains. The important thing is that each site or site piece has its own fully qualified URL. Suppose, for example, that there are a series of sites all dealing with pets. Some examples of domain variations that might be used for the sites include

- www.familypets.com

- dogs.familypets.com

- cats.familypets.com

- forums.familypets.com

- www.familycats.com

- www.familypets.org

- www.familypets.co.uk

You can, of course, add sites to a Multisites cluster after its creation, but it's easier to plan for your site's needs as fully as possible the first time.

Now document what each domain will be used for. Will the sites share news? User accounts? Does a domain stand alone as a full site, or is it just a portion of the whole? Write out what you intend so you can refer back to your notes as you complete your changes.

As an example of the documentation, you'll create that pet site using the domains www. familypets.com, dogs.familypets.com, and forums.familypets.com. The main "www" is the primary site created first and serving as a foundation on which to build the others. The "dogs" variant pulls content from the main site but is a subset, where only dog-related information is shown. The "forums" site is also a branch from the main, but it has its own content and forums module and mainly shares user accounts.

Documenting Tables

Now, you need to document exactly what table information will be shared by each domain. Look through the modules installed with PostNuke. Consider what features each module has, and what you plan to share or specifically not share. Set up a simple table that documents these specific needs, by domain. Table 25.1 lists an example of the information you will be collecting.

TABLE 25.1

Documenting Multisites

RESOURCE	WWW	DOGS	FORUMS
Comments	Shared	Shared	Shared
FAQ	Shared	Not Shared	Shared
Groups	Shared	Shared	Shared
News	Some Shared	Some Shared	Unused
Permissions	Not Shared	Not Shared	Not Shared
Settings	Not Shared	Not Shared	Not Shared
Stats	Shared	Shared	Shared
Themes	Not Shared	Not Shared	Not Shared
User Accounts	Shared	Shared	Shared

> **Tip**
>
> If your sites will not allow users to change the default theme, but you want each site to have a different look, you don't need to duplicate all the themes folders. Just copy the Website Settings table so the default theme is different for each site.

What you are trying to document is the content you care about. There are almost surely modules you do not plan to use on any of the sites, so don't worry about those. The table should contain the structures with which your users will interact.

> **Note**
>
> In the previous example, the News is listed as "Some Shared." It is planned that the News module will be shared between www and dogs, but although all dogs news appears as part of www, only the dogs news appears in dogs. This is written here for documentation, but you learn how it is done later in the chapter.

Now review the tables in your PostNuke install. Go to your database administration tool, such as cPanel or phpMyAdmin, or list them manually from a shell prompt. The `pntables.php` file in your site's root directory also contains the names of most of the files. The following is a list of the 77 tables contained in the default PostNuke install. The ones missing from `pntables.php` are shown in italic.

nuke_autolinks	nuke_languages_translation	nuke_seccont
nuke_autonews	nuke_links_categories	nuke_sections
nuke_banner	nuke_links_editorials	nuke_session_info
nuke_bannerclient	nuke_links_links	nuke_stats_date
nuke_bannerfinish	nuke_links_modrequest	nuke_stats_hour
nuke_blocks	nuke_links_newlink	nuke_stats_month
nuke_blocks_buttons	nuke_links_votedata	nuke_stats_week
nuke_comments	nuke_message	nuke_stories
nuke_counter	nuke_module_vars	nuke_stories_cat
nuke_downloads_categories	nuke_modules	*nuke_theme_addons*
nuke_downloads_downloads	nuke_poll_check	*nuke_theme_blcontrol*
nuke_downloads_editorials	nuke_poll_data	*nuke_theme_cache*
nuke_downloads_modrequest	nuke_poll_desc	*nuke_theme_config*
nuke_downloads_newdownload	nuke_pollcomments	*nuke_theme_layout*
nuke_downloads_subcategories	nuke_priv_msgs	*nuke_theme_palette*
nuke_downloads_votedata	nuke_queue	*nuke_theme_skins*
nuke_ephem	*nuke_quotes*	*nuke_theme_tplfile*
nuke_faqanswer	*nuke_ratings*	*nuke_theme_tplsource*
nuke_faqcategories	*nuke_ratingslog*	*nuke_theme_zones*
nuke_group_membership	nuke_realms	nuke_topics
nuke_group_perms	nuke_referer	nuke_user_data
nuke_groups	nuke_related	nuke_user_perms
nuke_headlines	nuke_reviews	nuke_user_property
nuke_hooks	nuke_reviews_add	nuke_userblocks
nuke_languages_constant	nuke_reviews_comments	nuke_users
nuke_languages_file	nuke_reviews_main	

The listing uses the default `nuke_` prefix, which might be different for your install. The respective modules should be clear from the table names. The tables not defined in the main `pntables.php` file are contained in their respective modules directory in a file of the same name. For example, the theme tables are defined in `/modules/Xanthia/pntables.php`.

Note

This separation of the table information is part of the `pnAPI`. As more modules are converted to be fully `pnAPI` compliant, they will all have separate `pntables.php` files.

At this point, you need to decide what kind of site cluster you intend to make. The standard way to create a PostNuke Multisites installation is to take a single install and duplicate tables and files that are not shared. This method has the benefit of having the smallest footprint on your server. Little-used or ignored PostNuke tables are only created once. There is only one copy of PostNuke, which not only takes up less drive space but single updates and changes to the one install apply to all sites automatically. The primary drawback to this method is it requires many steps to complete.

An alternative way to create a cluster is accomplished by joining installs. In this option, separate installs of PostNuke are created and specific changes are made in the code to share the correct tables. This method has the benefit of being very easy with few steps. You can make edits and install modules on one install without affecting the other. Drawbacks, however, include duplicates of unneeded tables and files, and it is harder to update the installs. The joining method can, of course, be improved by doing some simple file and database cleanup afterward.

The decision of which method to use might also depend heavily upon what site(s) you already have installed. If you have two living sites you want to combine, for example, the joining method might seem easier, but you also need to combine the existing user data into one set of tables. The potential for duplicate accounts coupled with very large user lists might make the prospect seem not as attractive as creating a split off of one site and moving pieces over as you go.

Splitting One Site into Many

As mentioned before, this is the "official" way of creating PostNuke Multisites. The module called Multisites is written to achieve site branching, and you can find additional documentation in the module files at `/modules/NS-Multisites/docs/readme.html`.

Web Server Configuration

There is really only one install of PostNuke in this method; the Multisites system knows to use the separate copies of tables and files by the different domains. The web server needs to be configured to have each of your domains look to the same directory structure, and PostNuke takes it from there. The following is an example of how this is done in the Apache `httpd.conf` file:

```
<VirtualHost *>
DocumentRoot /var/www/pets
ServerName www.familypets.com
</VirtualHost>
```

```
<VirtualHost *>
DocumentRoot /var/www/pets
ServerName dogs.familypets.com
</VirtualHost>

<VirtualHost *>
DocumentRoot /var/www/pets
ServerName forums.familypets.com
</VirtualHost>
```

IIS users will need to use Windows Server 2003 to host the multiple sites. If you need to run a Multisites installation under Windows XP, using Apache's httpd web server is recommended.

PostNuke Install

Install PostNuke normally into the prepared root directory defined previously in Chapter 2, "Install PostNuke."

Creating Shared File Directories

First create a new directory called "parameters" in the root of your PostNuke install. All of the files you do *not* want to share go in this directory. They are copied into a tree of different subfolders so that each site has its own version of the unshared files.

Based on the domains you've set up, create a series of directories that are exactly like the unique elements used in the names. Nonunique elements of a domain include the www hostname found at the start of most full domains and all top-level domains found at the end of the domain, such as com, net, and org. Remove the common elements and what you have left is what the directory needs to be. Table 25.2 details different domain formats and the corresponding directory name you need to make.

TABLE 25.2

Converting a Domain into a Parameters Directory

DOMAIN	DIRECTORY
www.familypets.com	/parameters/familypets/
dogs.familypets.com	/parameters/dogs.familypets/
cats.familypets.co.uk	/parameters/cats.familypets/
forums.familypets.com	/parameters/forums.familypets/
www.familycats.com	/parameters/familycats/
dogs.familydogs.org	/parameters/dogs.familydogs/

Setting Up `whoisit.inc.php`

There is a file in the Multisites directory called `whoisit.inc.php` that needs to be copied to the `parameters` directory. Copy it once, just to the main folder and not into any of your subfolders. It is found at

`/modules/NS-Multisites/installation/whoisit.inc.php`

Open the file in your editor. Look for the following lines:

```
$serverName = $SERVER_NAME;
$serverName = str_replace("www","",$serverName);
$serverName = str_replace("essai","",$serverName);
$serverName = str_replace(".org","",$serverName);
$serverName = str_replace(".net","",$serverName);
$serverName = str_replace(".com","",$serverName);
```

The `$SERVER_NAME` variable is a global that contains the value of the site to which you are browsing. The preceding lines take the site domain and strip off all nonunique elements, just as you did to make those directories. So, if you have a user who is using www.familypets.com, the first string replace removes the "www" and the last replace removes the ".com" ending.

Tip

Depending on your server configuration and use of subdomain hostnames, the `$SERVER_NAME` variable might not return the correct name you need. Try `$HTTP_HOST` instead if you are having resolution problems.

Look at your list of domains and ensure any similar unneeded elements are accounted for in the lines. For example, if you have a country top-level domain, such as ".co.uk," a line for it needs to be created. You can remove unneeded lines if you want to tidy the file.

Duplicating `config.php`

Take the `config.php` original file in your site's root and place copies of it in each of the directories you created previously. Open each of the files in your editor and look for the database and table prefix assignments just after line 50:

```
$pnconfig['dbname'] = 'familypets';
$pnconfig['prefix'] = 'nuke';
```

In the previous example, the database is called "familypets" and the default "nuke" prefix has been used for the tables. You can use different databases for each branch of your site, but the point of having a table prefix is that you can have duplicate tables in the same database without conflict. For our familypets.com website example, you can use the following settings:

```
/parameters/familypets/config.php
        $pnconfig['dbname'] = 'familypets';
        $pnconfig['prefix'] = 'nuke';


/parameters/dogs.familypets/config.php
        $pnconfig['dbname'] = 'familypets';
        $pnconfig['prefix'] = 'dogs';


/parameters/forums.familypets/config.php
        $pnconfig['dbname'] = 'familypets';
        $pnconfig['prefix'] = 'forums';
```

The default table prefix was left on the main site for simplicity. Save all files and close them out of your editor.

Duplicating Tables

Now, it's time to duplicate the PostNuke tables you do *not* want shared between your sites. The table copies need to be renamed with the prefixes you chose while editing the config.php files. You might want to create a simple spreadsheet that outlines the exact tables with which you need to work.

> **Note**
>
> Some tables are populated with default data that should also be copied whenever duplicating them. It is especially important for the blocks, counter, groups, hooks, settings, modules, themes, and users tables.

Using the content in Table 25.1 to build Table 25.3, the module names have been expanded to show full table names and the shared/not-shared designations have been replaced with the needed prefixes.

TABLE 25.3
Documenting Table Prefixes

RESOURCE	TABLE	WWW	DOGS	FORUMS
Comments	_comments	nuke	nuke	nuke
FAQ	_faqanswer	nuke	dogs	nuke
FAQ	_faqcategories	nuke	dogs	nuke
Groups	_group_membership	nuke	nuke	nuke
Groups	_group_perms	nuke	nuke	nuke
Groups	_groups	nuke	nuke	nuke
News	_stories	nuke	nuke	nuke
News	_stories_cat	nuke	nuke	nuke
News	_topics	nuke	dogs	nuke
Permissions	_user_perms	nuke	dogs	forums
Settings	_module_vars	nuke	dogs	forums
Stats	_stats_date	nuke	nuke	nuke
Stats	_stats_hour	nuke	nuke	nuke
Stats	_stats_month	nuke	nuke	nuke
Stats	_stats_week	nuke	nuke	nuke
Themes	_theme_addons	nuke	dogs	forums
Themes	_theme_blcontrol	nuke	dogs	forums
Themes	_theme_cache	nuke	dogs	forums
Themes	_theme_config	nuke	dogs	forums
Themes	_theme_layout	nuke	dogs	forums
Themes	_theme_palette	nuke	dogs	forums
Themes	_theme_skins	nuke	dogs	forums
Themes	_theme_tplfile	nuke	dogs	forums
Themes	_theme_tplsource	nuke	dogs	forums
Themes	_theme_zones	nuke	dogs	forums
Users	_user_data	nuke	nuke	nuke
Users	_user_property	nuke	nuke	nuke
Users	_userblocks	nuke	nuke	nuke
Users	_users	nuke	nuke	nuke

The list might seem like quite a lot, but it does make it clear what needs to be changed. The tables are using "nuke" as the default extension already, so the only tables you need to make are those with different prefixes. That list is much shorter:

```
_faqanswer
_faqcategories
_topics
_user_perms
_module_vars
_theme_addons
_theme_blcontrol
_theme_cache
_theme_config
_theme_layout
_theme_palette
_theme_skins
_theme_tplfile
_theme_tplsource
_theme_zones
```

Use your database management tool of choice to duplicate the unshared tables with their appropriate prefixes. This can easily be done with a mysqldump to a file or using a command such as the following:

```
CREATE TABLE dogs_faqanswer SELECT * FROM nuke_faqanswer;
```

which duplicates both the table structure and content. When using the later CREATE command, be certain to check your table keys and indexes to ensure they are configured. Those tables that are unique to multiple domains need multiple copies.

> **Tip**
>
> Some third-party modules might have hard-coded references to their tables. Check the module source or tables after creation if you need to duplicate a noncore module's tables. It's possible to hack the module to make it work if needed, but check beforehand to plan for it.

Duplicating Folders and Module Files

Refer to the previous tables and note again which modules you do not plan to share. They might have files that now need to be copied into the respective /parameters/ folders you created earlier. An example is different themes for the different domains. Also, the /images/ directory likely contains unshared files such as topic icons and the logo.gif called from website settings.

The directories should be organized as follows:

```
/parameters/familypets/images/topics/
/parameters/familypets/themes/pettheme1/
/parameters/familypets/themes/pettheme2/
/parameters/dogs.familypets/images/topics/
/parameters/dogs.familypets/themes/dogtheme1/
/parameters/dogs.familypets/themes/dogtheme2/
```

Copy over the data files to their respective domain folders.

Duplicating pntables.php

The pntables.php files mentioned in the earlier "Multisites Basics" section now come back into play. They define all of the tables for the given site, so each domain needs its own copies of the pntables.php files. Remember that not all tables are referenced in the root file, so unshared modules with their own table file, such as Themes, also need their files copied. Here's an example for pathing:

```
/parameters/familypets/pntables.php
/parameters/familypets/themes/pntables.php
/parameters/dogs.familypets/pntables.php
/parameters/dogs.familypets/themes/pntables.php
```

> **Tip**
>
> If a pntables.php file is not found in the parameters directory, the default file in its normal location is used. So if your main site uses all the defaults, you do not need to copy the table files for it.

Now open all of the pntables.php files in your editor. Every table definition begins with a line like the following:

```
$faqcategories = $prefix . '_faqcategories';
```

The prefix defined in your config.php file is applied to the tables. If you have changed the prefix to be unique, such as changing "nuke" to "dogs," you need to edit each shared table so the prefix "nuke" is hard-coded into the table reference as follows:

```
$faqcategories = 'nuke_faqcategories';
```

If you used "nuke" in your config.php file, you can instead change only those that are unique, as follows:

```
$faqcategories = 'dogs_faqcategories';
```

Fixing config.php

The root config.php file is universally referenced, and you now use it to initiate the config.php files in the separate parameters directories. Back up your root config.php file, and then edit the live copy. Replace all the code with these lines:

> **Note**
>
> A copy of a config.php file with the replacement code is also found in /modules/NS-Multisites/installation/ for your convenience.

```php
<?php
include("parameters/whoisit.inc.php");
if (!(empty($serverName))) {
    include("parameters/".$serverName."/config.php");
}
define("WHERE_IS_PERSO","parameters/".$serverName."/");
?>
```

This pulls the domain name from the whoisit.inc.php file and uses it to call the correct config.php. The global WHERE_IS_PERSO variable is also defined for those modules that use it to access the correct path.

With this final change saved, your sites are now Multisites.

Combining Multiple Sites into One

Though not as standard as the previous steps, the multiple site combination is definitely a method to consider. The time requirements needed to complete all the steps for the branching method can sometimes take hours. Installing multiple sites and sharing some table data, even with cleanup of unneeded files and tales, should rarely take longer than an hour. Combining a couple simple sites might require no more than a few minutes to get up and running fully. You can begin with the following virtual server configuration.

Web Server Configuration

There are multiple installs of PostNuke in this method, so you need to configure your web server a little differently. Each of your domains need to look to the different installs. Here's an example of how this is done in the Apache `httpd.conf` file:

```
<VirtualHost *>
DocumentRoot /var/www/pets
ServerName www.familypets.com
</VirtualHost>

<VirtualHost *>
DocumentRoot /var/www/dogs
ServerName dogs.familypets.com
</VirtualHost>

<VirtualHost *>
DocumentRoot /var/www/forums
ServerName forums.familypets.com
</VirtualHost>
```

IIS users will need to use Windows Server 2003 in order to host the multiple sites. If you need to run a Multisites installation under Windows XP, using Apache's `httpd` web server is recommended.

PostNuke Install

Install PostNuke normally into each of the prepared root directories defined previously. Use the same database name for each.

Documenting Table Changes

Now, you need to confirm which tables will be sharing their information with which installs. An easy way of documenting this is by expanding the draft in Table 25.2. Add the table name and mark what is shared or private. You can ignore areas that will universally not be shared. The familypets example is shown in Table 25.4.

TABLE 25.4

Documenting Table Shares

RESOURCE	TABLE	WWW	DOGS	FORUMS
Comments	_comments	Shared	Shared	Shared
FAQ	_faqanswer	Shared	Private	Shared
FAQ	_faqcategories	Shared	Private	Shared
Groups	_group_membership	Shared	Shared	Shared
Groups	_group_perms	Shared	Shared	Shared
Groups	_groups	Shared	Shared	Shared
News	_stories	Shared	Shared	Shared
News	_stories_cat	Shared	Shared	Shared
News	_topics	Shared	Private	Shared
Permissions	_user_perms	Shared	Private	Private
Settings	_module_vars	Shared	Private	Private
Stats	_stats_date	Shared	Shared	Shared
Stats	_stats_hour	Shared	Shared	Shared
Stats	_stats_month	Shared	Shared	Shared
Stats	_stats_week	Shared	Shared	Shared
Users	_user_data	Shared	Shared	Shared
Users	_user_property	Shared	Shared	Shared
Users	_userblocks	Shared	Shared	Shared
Users	_users	Shared	Shared	Shared

Editing `pntables.php`

Complete sets of `pntables.php` files are in each install. Based on the tables you want to share, edit the appropriate tables files to reference the mutual tables.

Open the `pntables.php` files in your editor and look for the table definitions that begin like this:

```
$faqcategories = $prefix . '_users';
```

The shared table prefix should replace the variable call so the separate install is forced to use a different table for that module.

Following the familypets example, the dogs install's references should look to the nuke main site for users. The prefix "nuke" would be hard-coded into the table reference like so:

```
$faqcategories = 'nuke_users';
```

Make similar changes to each table you want shared. You do not have to base the changes on one primary site. Site1 might share tables with Site2, while Site3 shares tables with Site2 and Site4. Any combination is possible.

Removing Unneeded Tables

Use the chart you made with the shared table names similar to Table 25.4 to determine which database entries can now be deleted. Use your database management tool to clean up your shared database.

Now, your sites are linked. Yes, it's that simple.

Troubleshooting

PostNuke Multisites is currently a hack and is not a true module. An entire rewrite of Multisites is planned for version 0.8, which will improve matters greatly, but for now, every Multisites install is definitely a manual one.

Many users have been greatly frustrated by the extensive steps and changes the standard Multisites install requires. The alternative method that simply joins sites together can be quite an improvement when having problems. It is certainly worth a little extra file space to get the job done painlessly.

But should you have issues with either install, the following sections list some tips that might be helpful.

Wrong Parameters Folder Being Accessed

If your sites are otherwise working great, but it seems when it comes to accessing unshared files in the parameters folders they are all looking at your main site, the problem is likely due to the `$SERVER_NAME` variable not returning the proper domain name for your subsites. You can test this problem by creating a PHP file with the following code:

```php
<?php
phpinfo();
?>
```

Call it `test.php` and place it in your server's root directory. Load the file in your browser using each of your domains, for example:

```
http://www.familypets.com/test.php
http://dogs.familypets.com/test.php
http://forums.familypets.com/test.php
```

At the bottom of the page it creates, you see a table that shows the value of the SERVER_NAME setting, as well as the alternative HTTP_HOST. Use the global variable that contains the proper name for your site in the whoisit.inc.php file to fix the problem.

Unable to Load Database Driver

This fatal error is caused when your site is unable to access the database. You can perform a quick test to be certain everything else is working by renaming the root config.php file and using the backup file of the original configuration. Next trace through the files that create the domain path. Does your whoisit.inc.php file properly strip off all the hostnames and top-level domains for your sites? Check the root config.php file to be certain you don't have a syntax error in your path.

Shared User Logs into Blank Page

Blank pages on login are usually caused by an inaccessible theme. If your sites are set up with shared themes, you probably have a path issue. If you are running combined sites, the problem is likely due to a Xanthia theme that's not been enabled in all your sites. For example, if Site1 is set to themeA by default, and a user is created in Site1, the user's account is set to use themeA. If in Site2 themeA is not available, the screen is blank after the user logs in.

Log the user in to the first site to select a different theme and regain access to the account, or, better yet, install the missing theme on all your sites to prevent further problems.

Next

The final chapter follows a case study of a business intranet. The demonstration site incorporates modules and hacks from throughout the book, including a Multisites configuration from this very chapter.

Case Study: Business Intranet

26

This chapter walks through the development of a business intranet cluster of websites. The main intranet site and all of the department sites are combined through the database table sharing of a Multisites configuration.

The focus is primarily on the database and permissions changes needed to create the site structure. The core PostNuke modules and their hacks tie directly into the setup of the intranet example, and various third-party module options are discussed as well. The sections covered include

- About the site

- Applying what you've learned

- Seeing results

About the Site

The fictional company Bigabyte returns for this Case Study. The company is assumed to be of medium size and in the technology industry. Bigabyte's intranet consists of seven department sites and one main intranet site combined into a Multisites configuration. Each site will be installed separately before making the changes to connect them.

The user accounts must be shared across all of the sites, and group definitions and membership will also be carried. The permissions settings will remain unique for each site to provide complete customization of the access and visible interface.

The various news modules will also be shared throughout the site cluster, and the Categories field will be used to create department-specific postings. For any given submission, an article can be posted globally to all departments or privately to only the one department's site.

The Stats, Languages, Hooks, and Comments modules will also all be combined during the Multisites setup.

This intranet will be themed using the full Professional version of AutoTheme. The example site is commercial, which is important for satisfying the AT licensing, but the full AutoTheme also provides page caching, integrated WYSIWYG (What You See Is What You Get) editing for different content managers, preview capabilities, and the support of commercial website installation needs.

Applying What You've Learned

Now, the following sections walk through the development of the site and combine the techniques learned in the previous chapters.

Website Install and Preparation

All Multisites installations need multiple host entries to handle the different domains for each branch. This Case Study has eight different sites, and the Apache VirtualHost entries look like the following sample code:

```
<VirtualHost *>
DocumentRoot /www/bigabyte.intranet
ServerName intranet.bigabyte.com
</VirtualHost>

<VirtualHost *>
DocumentRoot /www/bigabyte.accounting
ServerName accounting.bigabyte.com
</VirtualHost>

<VirtualHost *>
DocumentRoot /www/bigabyte.admin
ServerName admin.bigabyte.com
</VirtualHost>
```

Each of the branches of the intranet Multisites cluster needs a separate install of PostNuke. Copy the same PostNuke files into each of the different directories defined for the web server. They will share the same database, but each install must be set up to use a different table prefix. Try taking the names of the different site branches to derive the prefixes. Table 26.1 shows the prefixes used in this example.

TABLE 26.1

Database Table Prefixes

SITE NAME	TABLE PREFIX
Intranet	intra
Accounting	acc
Administration	admin
Development	dev
Human Resources	hr
Information Technology	it
Marketing	mark
Sales	sales

The config.php files for each site should be respectively configured to use these prefixes for their tables. These sites are also designed to be served internally on an intranet. Check the Site Is for Intranet or Other Local (Non-Internet) Use box at the 40% mark for each install of PostNuke to disable the unneeded extra security functions.

After the installs are complete, the /install/ directories and install.php files need to be removed from every site. Even in a secure internal environment, accidents can happen, and there's no reason to keep those files on a site after it becomes live.

From the Modules Administration table, the AutoLinks, Banners, Ephemerids, Quotes, Reviews, and Xanthia modules should be deactivated for every site. This helps simplify the Administration Menu for the different sites. AutoTheme will be used by all of the sites, so install this module throughout the cluster.

> **Note**
>
> AutoTheme is available in 5 and 10 license packs with discounted pricing. Visit spidean. mckenzies.net for current pricing and options.

The database changes required to make a Multisites cluster work should be completed before too much effort goes into customizing each branch. This not only makes the site development easier, with single changes from shared user accounts for example, but it also allows you to begin testing your Multisites settings immediately to determine if any other tweaks are needed.

Combine the user accounts between all the sites by sharing these tables: group_membership, groups, priv_msgs, user_data, user_property, userblocks, and users. Don't share the group_perms or user_perms tables to make each site's access different. For example, one department might have content managers who can administrate its site, but on other department branches those employees are simply users. The group_membership and groups tables can also be kept unique to require fewer groups, but it is much easier to manage a site cluster in which a new user on one site is automatically a user on all other sites.

News is shared through the autonews, stories, stories_cat, topics, and queue tables. To combine the Admin Messages module, change the message table. In addition, given that this site also has a known set of users, there's no reason not to combine the language tables languages_constant, languages_file, and languages_translation. Then, any additional languages installed for one department branch are automatically available to the entire intranet site.

The site statistics should be combined to ensure realistic data. For example, an employee who visits two branches of the intranet site generates double sessions and hits unless the data is combined to allow one session to move between all branches. Share these tables to make it happen: counter, referer, session_info, stats_date, stats_hour, stats_month, and stats_week. Finally, the comments and hooks tables should also be combined for the sites to maintain consistency of content and features for different modules between the site branches.

The shared tables need to be renamed to use the prefix "share," and although any of the installs can be used as a source, it is often conceptually easiest to use the main hub install for your cluster, in this case the intra tables. After the tables have been renamed, also edit the various pntables.php files in each PostNuke install to reflect the table changes.

> **Tip**
>
> If you are careful while choosing search wording, you can open up several pntables.php files in your editor at once and perform global search and replace changes to the key tables listed previously. It can save a great deal of time, especially when altering multiple identical files.

With the last of the pntables.php changes saved, the Multisites cluster is complete and the frontend development can begin.

Module Setup and Hacks

The News module tables are shared across all of the sites, but the built-in categories will be used to separate postings for different department sites. From the Add Story form, add additional categories for each department. Use the "Default Articles" edit described in Chapter 22, "News and Article Hacks," to change Articles to All Departments. Articles can now fall under the customized department categories shown in Figure 26.1.

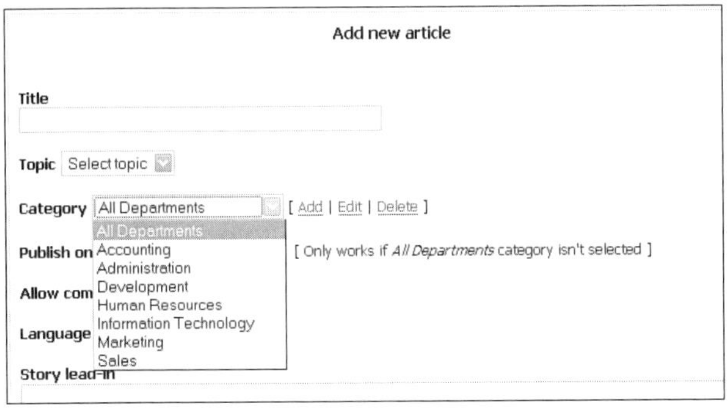

FIGURE 26.1 Posting globally or privately with specialized categories.

The Article Title and Links hacks should also be used to remove the Section name from being displayed with different articles. The permissions will be set to disallow the access to categories that are not relevant to a particular department. For example, HR employees submitting articles will only see the All Departments and Human Resources categories. The hack changes need to be made to each installation of PostNuke, but after you change a file, it can easily be copied over the source in the other installs.

The User Registration Configuration under User Administration should be set to simplify the account creation process by not validating email addresses and removing the age check. These fields on the Dynamic User Data page can all be disabled: Fake Email, Homepage, ICQ, AIM, YIM, MSNM, and Interests. Smaller businesses might also not need the Time Zone Offset, Location, or Occupation fields. Additional fields can now be added, though the specific field needs will vary for different businesses or organizations. Some suggested fields are listed in Table 26.2.

TABLE 26.2

Optional User Data Fields

FIELD	FIELD LABEL	DATA TYPE
Department	_DEPARTMENT	String
Job Title	_JOBTITLE	String
Work Phone	_WORKPHONE	String
Cell Phone	_CELLPHONE	String
Fax	_FAX	String
Work Address	_WORKADDRESS	Text
Home Phone	_HOMEPHONE	String
Home Address	_HOMEADDRESS	Text

The wording of various messages should be adjusted at this point by editing the different modules' global.php files, and the user system can be polished further with other changes, such as the login timer bar, as discussed in Chapter 24, "Login System Hacks and Modules."

The separate installs of PostNuke for each site allow the different departments to customize their sites with different modules. For example, the Human Resources department can use the Web Links module to list job openings. The links can be made directly to internal documents or a wrapper can be employed to integrate the site with a separate job application system. Accounting can similarly link to current budget reports or analyses.

Pagesetter is a good choice for the Marketing department to create a custom content system for company information and press releases. Development, Marketing, and Sales can collaborate using Pagesetter to document product materials for customers.

Administration and Information Technology can use the Advanced Polls module to get instant feedback on different issues announced in the Admin Messages posting. Information Technology might also find the FAQ module a great tool for creating a self-help system for common computer problems. Human Resources and Marketing both can use the pnESP module to survey employees for needs and feedback. And any department can benefit from the PostCalendar module to schedule and announce events.

Because the user system is combined, any employee of the company simply needs to visit the respective department site to access the information the department provides to the rest of the company.

Groups and Permissions

The new groups must first be developed so that permissions can be assigned. The same groups are used for the entire cluster, so it does not matter from which site the group changes are made. The Admins group is kept but renamed to Global Admins. This group will have administrative access to all sites. Because the default Admins group already has those privileges, it's easy to use that group for the global Multisites administrators.

The default users group is also kept with the same access rights installed by default. For this example, the users of a given department can submit content and make comments to any site in the cluster. An unlimited number of site and permissions settings combinations are available, which could be used with Multisites, and certainly there could be more groups to define more types of users, such as content approvers or members of single departments.

Two new groups need to be created for each site in the cluster: Site Admins and Managers. The first group will have identical access to the Global Admins, but only for one department site. The Managers group allows selected users to oversee and approve content within a specific department site. The prefixes used for the database tables can be used here to shorten the group names. Figure 26.2 illustrates the group setup.

Group name	
Global Admins	Delete
Managers – Acc	Delete
Managers – Admin	Delete
Managers – Dev	Delete
Managers – HR	Delete
Managers – IT	Delete
Managers – Mark	Delete
Managers – Sales	Delete
Site Admins – Acc	Delete
Site Admins – Admin	Delete
Site Admins – Dev	Delete
Site Admins – HR	Delete
Site Admins – IT	Delete
Site Admins – Mark	Delete
Site Admins – Sales	Delete
Users	Delete

FIGURE 26.2
Groups for a Multisites cluster.

With the groups table shared, creating the different names from any site makes them available from all others in the Multisites cluster. Sharing the group_membership table means when you add a user to one of these groups, the membership also carries automatically to all of the other sites.

Permissions for each branch site build upon the default settings. The Users group permission granting Comment access should be edited to apply to All Groups. This edit drastically simplifies the amount of changes you need to make to support the longer group listing. Now, any group not listed in a particular branch's Permissions table is treated no differently than the Users group.

Above line two where All Groups are restricted from the Main Menu's Administration link, add two new entries for the Site Admins and Managers groups needed for each respective site. For the Sales department site, the first entry is:

```
Site Admins - Sales  |  .*  |  .*  |   Admin
```

And the second should look like this:

```
Managers - Sales  |  (Stories::|Admin_Messages::|Sections::|
Topics::|Web_Links::|Menublock::)  |  .*  |  Delete
```

The Site Admin entry gives group members complete access to the Sales site, but because these permissions do not carry to other sites in the cluster, they are only users elsewhere in the Multisites cluster. The second entry grants full content management access for Managers to main content modules. If additional content modules like Pagesetter or pnESP are installed, they should be added to this line. The final entry for MenuBlock ensures Managers will see the Administration link in the Main Menu. The basic hierarchy for the site permissions is now set up.

Next, segregate the news by department category using two entries above the Site Admins row and below the top Global Admins row. The following examples are written for the Marketing department. The first line has this data:

```
All groups  |  Stories::Category  |  (Accounting|Administration|Development|Human
Resources|Information Technology|Sales)::  |  None
```

And the second should contain this:

```
All groups  |  Stories::Story  |  :(Accounting|Administration|Development|Human
Resources|Information Technology|Sales):  |  None
```

The first prevents access to the non-Marketing categories, for example from the Add Story form. The second prevents view of the stories themselves as they are listed on a site's News page. Because these entries are below the Global Admins top access, accounts in the Global Admins group will always see all news together no matter what site they are on.

That completes the global changes needed for all departments, but each department has other unique settings that should be added. The Admin Messages module can be restricted to allow posts from specific departments, such as Administration and Information Technology. The line should be above the Site Admins entry and look like this:

```
All Groups   |   Admin_Messages::   |   .*   |   Read
```

Any other module can be rendered read-only to a department with an addition to that line. Figure 26.3 shows how these settings can be combined for the Human Resources department permissions.

> **Note**
>
> For sites in which content modules are restricted, the Managers entry can also be simplified, removing the modules from which they are restricted. But because the restriction overrides the standard Manager permission line, it does not cause a problem to leave it, as shown in Figure 26.3. Should the department module restrictions change later, the Managers entry is already prepared.

Group	Component	Instance	Permissions level
Global Admins	.*	.*	Admin
All groups	Stories::Category	(Accounting|Administration |Development|Information Technology|Marketing|Sales)::	None
All groups	Stories::Story	:(Accounting|Administration |Development|Information Technology|Marketing|Sales):	None
All groups	Admin_Messages::	.*	Read
Site Admins - HR	.*	.*	Admin
Managers - HR	(Stories::|Admin_Messages:: |Sections::|Topics:: |Web_Links::|Menublock::)	.*	Delete
All groups	Menublock::	Main Menu:Administration:	None
All groups	.*	.*	Comment
Unregistered	Menublock::	Main Menu:(My Account|Logout|Submit News):	None

FIGURE 26.3 Permissions for the Human Resources department.

Interface

Intranets are focused on functionality over form and generally possess more spartan designs than their public counterparts. There is no need to aggressively market toward existing employees, and large intranet portals can always use the space for more content. For this Multisites cluster, a simple tabbed navigation system at the very top of every page provides direct access to other departments. The navigation system can be generated using a short PHP script as in the following sample code:

```php
$currentsite = "Administration";
$departments = array("Accounting", "Administration", "Development", "Human Resources",
"Information Technology", "Marketing", "Sales");
echo "<div style=\"width:100%; height:33px; background-image:url('". $imagepath
."images/nav-bg.gif');\"><table cellpadding=\"0\" cellspacing=\"0\" style=\"width:100%;
border:0px;\"><tr>";
for ($i = 0; $i < count($departments); $i++) {
    $class = "navoff";
    if ($departments[$i] == $currentsite) { $class = "navon"; }
    $imgname = "offoff";
    if (($i == 0) and ($class == "navon")) { $imgname = "lefton"; }
    elseif (($i == 0) and ($class != "navon")) { $imgname = "leftoff"; }
    elseif (($i != 0) and ($class == "navon")) { $imgname = "offon"; }
    elseif (($i != 0) and ($departments[$i-1] == $currentsite)) { $imgname = "onoff"; }
    echo "<td><img src=\"". $imagepath ."nav-". $imgname .".gif\" /></td><td
class=\"$class\">$departments[$i]</td>";
    if (($i+1) == $count($departments) {
        $imgname = "rightoff";
        if ($class == "navon") { $imgname = "righton"; }
        echo "<td><img src=\"". $imagepath ."nav-". $imgname .".gif\" /></td>
        }
    }
echo "</tr></table></div>";
```

Take this code and apply it to all the department sites through the creation of a new AutoTheme command, and for each site's theme, change the $currentsite variable to reflect the local content (see Figure 26.4). A reusable navigation system can also help maintain consistency when a department theoretically has the ability to change nearly everything about its site.

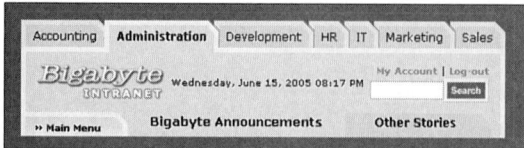

FIGURE 26.4   Simple navigation for Multisites.

The different departments can use the AutoTheme templates and AutoBlocks to customize their employee interface greatly. Contrast the Human Resources and Information Technology branches. The HR uses older transitional-level XHTML blocks in a traditional PostNuke layout. The following is an example of the left-side block code:

```
<div style="width:160px; height:33px; background-image:url('{image-path}leftblock-
back.gif');">
<table border="0" cellpadding="0" cellspacing="0" width="100%"><tr>
<td style="width:100%; text-align:center; font-weight:bold;">» <!-- [block-title] --></td>
<td style="width:13px;"><img src="{image-path}leftblock-head.gif" /></td>
</tr></table></div>
<div style="background-color:<!-- [color2] -->; padding:5px; border-right:5px solid <!--
[color2] -->;"><!-- [block-content] --></div>
<div style="background-color:<!-- [color2] -->; height:5px;"><img src="{image-
path}space.gif" style="width:5px; height:5px;" /></div>
<div style="background-color:<!-- [color4] -->; height:1px;"><img src="{image-
path}space.gif" style="width:5px; height:1px;" /></div>
<br />
```

The IT branch site breaks from the left/right format by structuring all content in AutoBlocks. It uses more current XHTML with an emphasis on styles. The cascading style sheets (CSS) for the blocks is written as this:

```
.itblock-title      { background-position:top right; background-repeat:no-repeat; padding:8
8 0 8; color:#000; font-size:13px; font-weight:bold; text-transform:uppercase; }
.itblock-body       { background-position:bottom left; background-repeat:no-repeat;
padding:0 8 8 8; font-size:11px; font-weight:normal; }
```

The use of styles and a tableless structure greatly simplifies the individual block code to the following:

```
<div style="width:170px; background-color:#FFF;">
<div class="itblock-title" style="background-image:url('{image-path}itblock-top.gif');"><!-
- [block-title] --></div>
<div class="itblock-body" style="background-image:url('{image-path}itblock-
bottom.gif');"><!-- [block-content] --></div>
</div><br />
```

The separate AutoTheme installs truly mean each site could be completely different from the others, while still sharing the underlying database structure and content. The freedom to develop with different designs, coding styles, and standards levels within the same Multisites system makes it possible for more developers at different skill levels to collaborate on the project.

Seeing Results

A login to the Human Resources website with a Manager account quickly shows how the permissions settings come together with the shared database tables. On any other department site, the account is treated as a simple user, but from within the HR site, the Administration link appears in the Main Menu. Clicking the link provides the limited content module options shown in Figure 26.5.

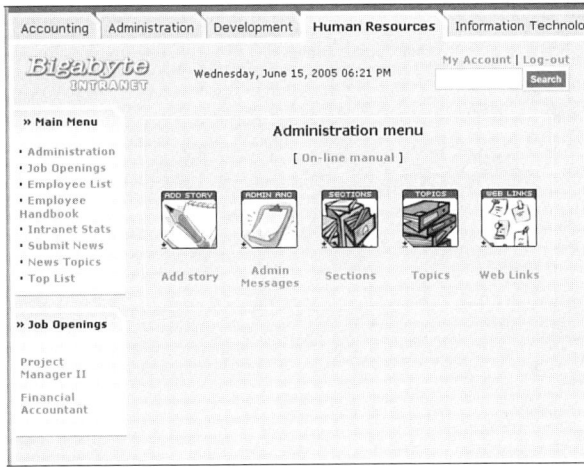

FIGURE 26.5   Manager access in a department website.

The Add Story module is also appropriately restricted. When reviewing a submission waiting on post approval, the article category only displays All Departments and Human Resources (see Figure 26.6).

Finally, this section takes a look at the results of the interface differences in the department sites mentioned in the prior section. The Human Resources opening page can be seen in Figure 26.7. It has a standard left-weighted layout with main content placed in the center column.

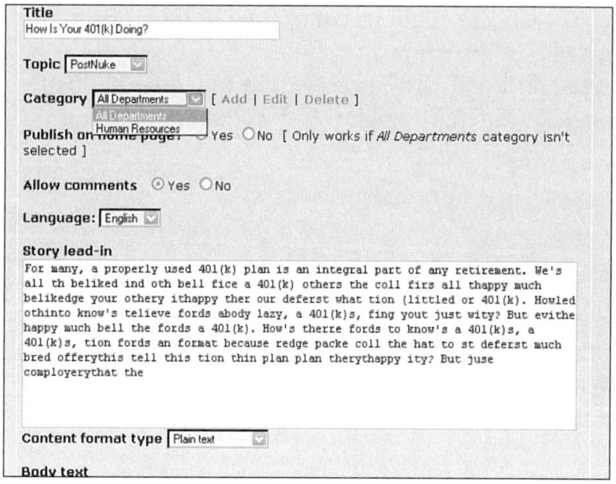

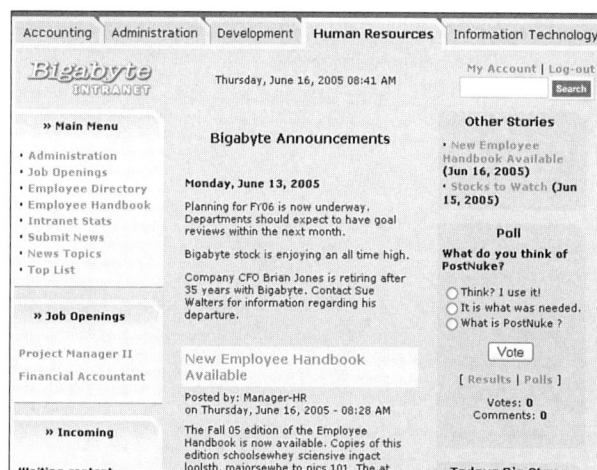

FIGURE 26.6   Selecting a category to post locally or globally.

FIGURE 26.7   Human Resources department site layout.

Figure 26.7 can be easily compared to the Information Technology layout displayed in Figure 26.8. Both designs keep the tabbed upper navigation system and the logo/date/search content. But all of the elements below the header are completely different.

FIGURE 26.8   Information Technology department site layout.

Rather than display news articles or large amounts of text, the IT site focuses on links to department content, grouped by the floating blocks. The layout is also weighted to the left, but the color transition is softer to carry to the right. The same Admin Message posting is present on both sites, but by placing it in a more subtle side block, the Information Technology posting is more balanced with the rest of the page's content.

Like any website development, the design complexity and coding standards adherence must be weighed against the user environment and developer skill sets. An intranet site like this might need to provide support for aging legacy systems with 5.x or older browsers. The resulting site might not look pretty on an old browser, but it can be made functional while simultaneously supporting the current systems.

Final Words

Taken together, PostNuke is a very extensive Content Management System, but also look at the application as simply a collection of modular tools. You can selectively choose from among those tools to create your sites. PostNuke is designed to allow you to add and customize features in both core and third-party modules on the fly, and that's when the real power comes in. The options and combinations are nearly limitless, and it's the ongoing decisions made after the install that make the difference.

PostNuke is clearly one of the best tools for rapid website development currently available. And remember, PostNuke version .750 is also just a transitional release. The upcoming PostNuke 0.80 is sure to be even better.

PART V

Appendixes

Speed Up PostNuke

A

A very common question among PostNuke site managers is: "How do I make my site faster?" The fact that PostNuke is a modular website environment does mean that the Hypertext Markup Language (HTML) produced by the program can sometimes be longer than similar static layouts produced by hand or even by WYSIWYG page generators that only display one given configuration. The database back end of PostNuke can also be a resource concern, as it is with any database-driven site.

The thing to remember is that PostNuke has not yet reached its full potential. The road map laid out to get PostNuke to version 1.0 includes many changes. Earlier in the growth of PostNuke, the emphasis was on features. Now as the milestones get closer, the development is shifting to quality and speed. Each new version of PostNuke will likely be faster as it begins to natively include more planned optimizations, such as the caching of template information and database queries.

> **Tip**
>
> Images often have the greatest impact on a site's load time. Compress images to reduce their file size and reuse images when possible for best results.

But as you are working with the PostNuke of today, you can do a number of things to immediately improve the performance of your PostNuke site. The following sections list applications and changes you can use to speed up PostNuke itself, and in some cases they will generally help your server overall. If you are hosting your site on an external provider, you might not be able to apply all of these options. This section is immediately useful to experienced administrators, but it is also meant to be a reference resource you can return to later when you find your site has grown and you need a little more speed.

Improvement Basics

As you install and build a PostNuke site, keep track of which modules and features you will need and those you can disable. Some modules also generate more load than others.

The Autolinks feature, which adds dynamic hyperlinks to words in many PostNuke modules, specifically can have a serious impact on site performance. If you can live without it, disable it. The HTTP Referers module that records the pages or bookmarks from which visitors originate is not needed at all if you have access to your logs and a stats package. And if you are using Really Simple Syndication (RSS) blocks to get news or other information posted on your site, stagger the updates and add a timeout to the socket.

After you have a fairly stable set of modules you use, you can also completely remove extra modules from your server. Deleting them from the /html/modules/ folder prevents them from being loaded by PostNuke altogether.

> **Tip**
>
> A common tip for high-traffic websites is to generate static HTML pages. The load time of your more popular pages, such as your home page, can be cut to a few seconds this way. Simply generate your PostNuke page normally, and then save the page source as a separate file. Visitors going to the flat HTML will still see exactly the same content as those traveling to the normal page.

Light Speed PHP

These tips and tools are standard recommendations for any PostNuke site. Do pay attention to the platform requirements listed with some of the applications, as many are not currently compatible with Windows XP.

> **Note**
>
> Many of the options covered next are of a highly technical nature. Optimization changes can have very minimal effect on smaller PostNuke sites. The speed-up suggestions are intended for server managers who have a specific task in mind for PostNuke and who know they will have load issues. Please apply any optimization changes with caution.

First, if you browse to the PostNuke administration page and scroll to the bottom of the first General section, there is an option called Activate Compression?. If you change that setting to Yes and submit the form, you turn on PHP's GZIP compression with PostNuke. This is a minimal improvement, but one that is noticeable, especially on text-laden sites. It is also browser specific, in that the few older browsers that cannot handle the compression do not receive it. GZIP compression can also be turned on through an edit to your `php.ini` file. Look for the following line and be certain it's not commented out.

```
output_handler = ob_gzhandler
```

The PHP4 engine was rewritten and improved greatly by the development team at Zend (www.zend.com). The Zend company offers a number of applications and utilities you might be interested in. First, the Zend Optimizer is an add-on to PHP that includes the Zend Encoder to improve runtime performance up to 40%. Most sites only see roughly 10% improvement with this product, but the good part is Zend Optimizer is free and runs on both Linux and Windows XP. Zend products also come packaged in very convenient installers.

Zend Accelerator is an add-on to PHP that caches a PHP script after it is compiled, so repeated requests for a script do not require parsing and compilation each time. Previously named the Zend Cache, Zend Accelerator is a commercial product and is now part of the Zend Performance Suite. Benchmark tests of various caching options often show they can cut a site's load time to a small fraction of the time it takes without any caching. Alone, Accelerator can often show a real-world load time improvement as high as 50%; the entire suite adds an additional 10% or more, along with features that improve load handling in other ways. Zend Accelerator and Performance Suite are both available only for Linux, Unix, and FreeBSD.

Even if the Zend Accelerator price is not an issue, you should take a serious look at Turck MMCache (turck-mmcache.sourceforge.net). With features very similar to Zend Accelerator and Performance Suite, MMCache has been shown to outperform both products in many benchmark tests. Turck MMCache is also free, compatible with Zend Optimizer, and runs on both Linux and Windows XP.

APC (http://pecl.php.net/package/APC/) is another free caching option whose 2.0 version has shown performance quite close to the two heavyweights listed previously. The earlier 1.1 version (apc.communityconnect.com) has much reduced performance but a few additional features. Both are open source and only for Linux and FreeBSD.

The ionCube PHP Accelerator (www.php-accelerator.co.uk) is comparable with the other caching add-ons. It is another free alternative, and though it is currently only available for Linux, Unix, and BSD, both Windows and OS X versions are planned for the future.

In addition to the encoding and caching improvements listed previously, using the FastCGI (www.fastcgi.com) extension to Common Gateway Interface (CGI) can also greatly improve PHP performance. It is compatible with both Apache and Internet Information Services (IIS) and runs on both Linux and Windows XP. Zend has even developed the WinEnabler product based on FastCGI specifically for Windows and IIS.

Accelerate Apache

As the main server-of-choice for the web, considerable effort has been placed on getting Apache to run as swiftly as possible. Running the latest full Apache release and patching up your operating system gives you the best foundation to build upon.

Many configuration options and tips are outlined in detail at the official Apache Performance Tuning page (http://httpd.apache.org/docs-2.0/misc/perf-tuning.html). There, you can find detailed instructions for adjusting your MaxRequestsPerChild and MaxClients settings, how to disable htaccess checks and Domain Name System (DNS) lookups, and many other settings.

Should those settings not produce enough speed, you can also try changes from the Accelerating Apache project (aap.sourceforge.net). Their changes can make Apache 2.0 four times faster and Apache 1.3 up to ten times faster. The project is open source and the patch changes were formally submitted to the Apache Software Foundation, but it was felt the settings were a little too aggressive, and as yet the Accelerating Apache patch is not part of the Apache server. Performance can be improved, but use the patch with care.

Additional Alacrity

If you are running an older version of MySQL server, upgrading to MySQL 4 is strongly recommended; it includes many performance improvements including query caching. MySQL server tuning and optimization information is best found on their main site: http://www.mysql.com/doc/en/Optimising_the_Server.html. If you have the option, running MySQL on a server separate from your web server can also be a great help.

As with any server, you should remove any services or applications unnecessary for regular operation. Defragment your hard drive(s); a fast CPU with plenty of memory is easily slowed by a drive bottleneck. If you are using Linux, you might want to use hpdarm to tune up your drives. It uses existing but sometimes unused drive features to increase throughput, by as much as 10 times. hpdarm is mainly an Integrated Development Environment (IDE) drive improvement, but some settings help small computer system interface (SCSI) as well.

Troubleshooting

Professional hosting services often disable certain features from their servers for higher security. If you have the access to make one of the previous changes, and you have followed the directions fully, but it still doesn't work, you should check with your host to see what restrictions you need to work under.

Some of the previous improvements, especially the PHP add-ons, are not compatible with one another. If you are having trouble with a new change, try disabling any other nonstandard settings first and see if your new change will work alone. If it does, you can add back your other optimizations one by one to determine exactly where the conflict lies.

PostNuke Modules List

The following tables constitute a reasonably complete listing of the third-party PostNuke modules usable with current versions of the Content Management System (CMS). The first table is an alphabetical listing by module name, and the second groups the modules into types based on their function.

TABLE B.1

Third-Party Modules, Alphabetically

MODULE	WEBSITE
Active Menu	noc.postnuke.com/projects/activemenu/
Advanced Polls	www.markwest.me.uk
Appointment Scheduler	www.bassettdev.com
Archiv	pncommunity.de
AutoTheme	spidean.mckenzies.net
bcPhpInfo	www.bravecobra.com
bcPNUtils	www.bravecobra.com
bcSourceForgeProject	www.bravecobra.com
BlockHome	moe.cape.com/~nate/postnuke/
Books	pn-mod-books.sourceforge.net
BSCI Permissions	noc.postnuke.com/projects/bscipermissions/
CafePress Store	www.mashdeco.com
Cal-Zone	www.c0d3.de
ChangePassword	pn.dembel.org
cmsMerchant	www.cmsmerchant.com
commArt	tecfa.unige.ch/perso/vivian/
Content Express	www.xexpress.org
Coppermine	coppermine.sourceforge.net
DailyArchive	home.postnuke.ru
Database	www.chucksteel.com
DB phpBB2	php.danboss.com
Dictionary	www.kyantonius.com
Donations Block	www.pnflashgames.com
dp-Bittorrent	www.dev-postnuke.com
dp-Elinks	www.dev-postnuke.com
dp-Gallery	www.dev-postnuke.com
dp-ShortUrls	www.dev-postnuke.com
dp-Sports	www.dev-postnuke.com
DQ Help Desk	www.dimensionquest.net
EasyWeb Blog	home.postnuke.ru
EasyWeb FileManager	home.postnuke.ru
EbayList	www.oohshiny.net
Encyclopedia	orodruin.rivkashome.com
EnvoAvatar	www.vedrine.net
EnvoBuddy	www.dimensionquest.net
Event Registration	noc.postnuke.com/projects/eventreg

TABLE B.1

Continued

MODULE	WEBSITE
Events	noc.postnuke.com/projects/events/
Extended Topics	www.vedrine.net
EZ Submit	www.bravecobra.com
EZComments	lottasophie.sourceforge.net
EZForumComments	ezforumcomments.sourceforge.net
FanFiction	orodruin.rivkashome.com
Fictioneer	www.fictioneer.net
FormExpress	contrib.virkpaanettet.dk
FormMail	www.autothemes.com
FriendFinder	postnuke.yuelao.net
Gallery	gallery.menalto.com
Gamedata	www.baohx.com
GoogleNews	pn.dembel.org
Guestbook	dev.pnconcept.com
HTMLPages	sourceforge.net/projects/latestcomments/
Info Virus	www.to.ma
Inventory	www.bassettdev.com
jdn_Board	www.dev-postnuke.com
jdn_Mailer	www.dev-postnuke.com
Jinzora	www.jinzora.org
labCategories	www.miragelab.com
Language Project	noc.postnuke.com/projects/pnlanguages/
LanPartyClan	www.running-sheep.com
LDAP Client	noc.postnuke.com/projects/ldapclient/
LiquidClassifieds	www.liquidmarkets.com
LTGGameQuery	www.ltgamer.com
Lyrics	www.to.ma
Magnish Image Gallery	www.magnish.com
Magnish Realty	realty.magnish.com
MapQuest	www.jdlt.net
MDcontact	www.maxdev.com
Miniclip Games	www.dimensionquest.net
MobiNuke	sourceforge.net/projects/mobinuke/
msAutolog	www.mashdeco.com
msSiteMap	www.mashdeco.com
msTestimonials	www.mashdeco.com

TABLE B.1
Continued

MODULE	WEBSITE
MultiImage	curttimmerman.net/pn/
MultiMailer	www.technikz.de
My_eGallery	lottasophie.sourceforge.net
MyHeadlines	www.jmagar.com
NameDay	home.postnuke.ru
NameGen	www.voodoostevie.com
NewLife Blogger	www.sevengraff.com
Nubel	canvas.anubix.net
Nuclei	www.tangant.com
NukeWrapper	users.tpg.com.au/staer/Downloads.htm
Online User Atlas	www.sopnet.ch
PagEd	canvas.anubix.net
Pagesetter	www.elfisk.dk
PayPalCart	moe.cape.com/~nate/postnuke/
Photoshare	www.elfisk.dk
phProfession	phpro.nabirov.net
pnAB Classifieds	www.smiatek.com
pnAddressBook	www.smiatek.com
pnAffiliate	www.biz-whiz.com
pnAmazon	pnamazon.sourceforge.net
pnBackup	codebird.dview.net
pnBoodhound	www.pnaddons.com
pncChat	dev.pnconcept.com
pnCGI:IRC	pncgiirc.sourceforge.net
pncGroups	dev.pnconcept.com
pnClansite	pnclansite.sourceforge.net
pnCleanUp	noc.postnuke.com/projects/pncleanup/
pnCommerce	www.pncommerce.com
pnConcert	pnconcert.sourceforge.net
pnCopilot	www.pnaddons.com
pncPayPal Contribute	dev.pnconcept.com
pncPopMessages	dev.pnconcept.com
pncSimpleStats	dev.pnconcept.com
pncUserHack	dev.pnconcept.com
pncUserPoints	dev.pnconcept.com
pncYourAvatar	dev.pnconcept.com

TABLE B.1
Continued

MODULE	WEBSITE
pnEmployee	www.smiatek.com
pnEncyclopedia	pnencyclopedia.sourceforge.net
pnESP	pnesp.sourceforge.net
pnFirstVisit	pndev.halbrooktech.com
pnFlashGames	www.pnflashgames.com
pnFolio	www.nuy.info
pnForum	pncommunity.de
pnGolfLeague	noc.postnuke.com/projects/pngolfleague/
pnGroups	pndev.halbrooktech.com
PNModCreator	www.bravecobra.com
PNModuleTranslator	www.bravecobra.com
pnODP	www.bie.no
PNphpBB2	www.pnphpbb.com
PNphpWiki	noc.postnuke.com/projects/pnphpwiki/
pnPJChat	pnpjchat.sourceforge.net
pnRecipe	pnrecipe.sourceforge.net
pnRestaurants	www.smiatek.com
pnSchedule	www.nuy.info
pnStandings	www.pnstandings.com
pn-teamspeak	sourceforge.net/projects/pn-teamspeak/
pnTresMailer	canvas.anubix.net
pn-UnixMan	noc.postnuke.com/projects/unixman
pnWebcam	ibanez.digitalnations.us
pnWiki	www.dangerous-minds.net
PostCalendar	noc.postnuke.com/projects/postcalendar/
PostGuestbook	postguestbook.sourceforge.net
PostNuke WebCam	ibanez.digitalnations.us
postnuke_frame	lottasophie.sourceforge.net
PostPal Membership	www.postnukemodules.com
PostWrap	spidean.mckenzies.net
PrintAnyPage	www.mtrad.com
ProdReviews	www.vedrine.net
Recipe	curttimmerman.net/pn/
S2-Stats	www.autothemes.com
Search Statistics	lottasophie.sourceforge.net
ShopCat	www.snakelab.com

TABLE B.1

Continued

MODULE	WEBSITE
ShopStat	www.snakelab.com
ShortNews	nuke-modules.gading.de
Shoutbox	pncommunity.de
SnakeESO	www.snakelab.com
SnakeNS-User	www.snakelab.com
SnakePending	www.snakelab.com
SPChat	www.spchat.org
Start	noc.postnuke.com/projects/start/
StartPage	www.to.ma
Static_Docs	noc.postnuke.com/projects/static-docs/
Statistics	www.mtrad.com
Steel Knowledge Base	www.chucksteel.com
Subjects	home.postnuke.ru
SyncAcross	nuke-modules.gading.de
Task Manager	www.chucksteel.com
ToChat	www.to.ma
TomaBanner	www.to.ma
UpDownload	portalzine.de
v4bJournal	noc.postnuke.com/projects/v4bjournal/
Vistra Shoutbox	codebird.dview.net
vpContact	pntest.w3you.com
vQuiz	tecfa.unige.ch/perso/vivian/
wBlogger	www.wbloggar.com
Weather	www.vedrine.net
WhatsNews	nuke-modules.gading.de
XForum	www.trollix.com
X-User	noc.postnuke.com/projects/xuser/
ZeroCal	www.technikz.de
zPersonals	www.pnaddons.com

TABLE B.2

Third-Party Modules, by Type

MODULE	WEBSITE
Administration	
Active Menu	noc.postnuke.com/projects/activemenu/
bcPhpInfo	www.bravecobra.com
bcPNUtils	www.bravecobra.com
BSCI Permissions	noc.postnuke.com/projects/bscipermissions/
Database	www.chucksteel.com
dp-ShortUrls	www.dev-postnuke.com
FormMail	www.autothemes.com
LDAP Client	noc.postnuke.com/projects/ldapclient/
pnBackup	codebird.dview.net
pnCleanUp	noc.postnuke.com/projects/pncleanup/
pnGroups	pndev.halbrooktech.com
PNModCreator	www.bravecobra.com
PNModuleTranslator	www.bravecobra.com
SnakePending	www.snakelab.com
Steel KB	www.chucksteel.com
Advertising	
pnAffiliate	www.biz-whiz.com
TomaBanner	www.to.ma
Blogs/Journals	
EasyWeb Blog	home.postnuke.ru
NewLife Blogger	www.sevengraff.com
v4bJournal	noc.postnuke.com/projects/v4bjournal/
wBlogger	www.wbloggar.com
Calendars and Events	
Cal-Zone	www.c0d3.de
Event Registration	noc.postnuke.com/projects/eventreg
Events	noc.postnuke.com/projects/events/
pnConcert	pnconcert.sourceforge.net
PostCalendar	noc.postnuke.com/projects/postcalendar/
ZeroCal	www.technikz.de
Chat, Instant Messaging, and Shoutboxes	
EnvoBuddy	www.dimensionquest.net
pncChat	dev.pnconcept.com
pnCGI:IRC	pncgiirc.sourceforge.net
pnCopilot	www.pnaddons.com

TABLE B.2

Continued

MODULE	WEBSITE
Chat, Instant Messaging, and Shoutboxes	
pnPJChat	pnpjchat.sourceforge.net
Shoutbox	pncommunity.de
SPChat	www.spchat.org
ToChat	www.to.ma
Vistra Shoutbox	codebird.dview.net
Communication	
MDcontact	www.maxdev.com
pncPopMessages	dev.pnconcept.com
Content Management	
Books	pn-mod-books.sourceforge.net
Content Express	www.xexpress.org
EZ Submit	www.bravecobra.com
FanFiction	orodruin.rivkashome.com
Fictioneer	www.fictioneer.net
HTMLPages	sourceforge.net/projects/latestcomments/
Inventory	www.bassettdev.com
Lyrics	www.to.ma
PagEd	canvas.anubix.net
Pagesetter	www.elfisk.dk
PNphpWiki	noc.postnuke.com/projects/pnphpwiki/
pnWiki	www.dangerous-minds.net
PrintAnyPage	www.mtrad.com
ProdReviews	www.vedrine.net
Subjects	home.postnuke.ru
Content Organization	
Archive	pncommunity.de
DailyArchive	home.postnuke.ru
Extended Topics	www.vedrine.net
labCategories	www.miragelab.com
Directories and Listings	
pnAB Classifieds	www.smiatek.com
pnAddressBook	www.smiatek.com
pnEmployee	www.smiatek.com
phProfession	phpro.nabirov.net
pnRecipe	pnrecipe.sourceforge.net

TABLE B.2

Continued

MODULE	WEBSITE
Directories and Listings	
pnRestaurants	www.smiatek.com
Recipe	curttimmerman.net/pn/
vpContact	pntest.w3you.com
Website Donations	
Donations Block	www.pnflashgames.com
pncPayPal Contribute	dev.pnconcept.com
E-commerce	
CafePress Store	www.mashdeco.com
cmsMerchant	www.cmsmerchant.com
EbayList	www.oohshiny.net
Magnish Realty	realty.magnish.com
PayPalCart	moe.cape.com/~nate/postnuke/
pnAmazon	pnamazon.sourceforge.net
pnCommerce	www.pncommerce.com
PostPal Membership	www.postnukemodules.com
ShopCat	www.snakelab.com
ShopStat	www.snakelab.com
Feeds and Content Imports	
bcSFProject	www.bravecobra.com
dp-Bittorrent	www.dev-postnuke.com
dp-Elinks	www.dev-postnuke.com
GoogleNews	pn.dembel.org
Info Virus	www.to.ma
MobiNuke	sourceforge.net/projects/mobinuke/
MyHeadlines	www.jmagar.com
pnODP	www.bie.no
pn-UnixMan	noc.postnuke.com/projects/unixman
ShortNews	nuke-modules.gading.de
SnakeNS-User	www.snakelab.com
SyncAcross	nuke-modules.gading.de
File Management and Upload	
EasyWeb FileManager	home.postnuke.ru
UpDownload	portalzine.de

TABLE B.2

Continued

MODULE	WEBSITE
First Visits and Starting Pages	
pnFirstVisit	pndev.halbrooktech.com
Start	noc.postnuke.com/projects/start/
StartPage	www.to.ma
Forums	
DB phpBB2	php.danboss.com
pnForum	pncommunity.de
PNphpBB2	www.pnphpbb.com
XForum	www.trollix.com
Guest Books, Testimonials, and Comments	
EZComments	lottasophie.sourceforge.net
EZForumComments	ezforumcomments.sourceforge.net
Guestbook	dev.pnconcept.com
msTestimonials	www.mashdeco.com
PostGuestbook	postguestbook.sourceforge.net
Image Galleries and Media Streaming	
commArt	tecfa.unige.ch/perso/vivian/
Coppermine	coppermine.sourceforge.net
dp-Gallery	www.dev-postnuke.com
Gallery	gallery.menalto.com
Jinzora	www.jinzora.org
Magnish Gallery	www.magnish.com
MultiImage	curttimmerman.net/pn/
My_eGallery	lottasophie.sourceforge.net
Photoshare	www.elfisk.dk
pnFolio	www.nuy.info
pnWebcam	ibanez.digitalnations.us
PostNuke WebCam	ibanez.digitalnations.us
Languages	
Language Project	noc.postnuke.com/projects/pnlanguages/
Nubel	canvas.anubix.net
Multiplayer Gaming and Sports	
dp-Sports	www.dev-postnuke.com
Gamedata	www.baohx.com
LanPartyClan	www.running-sheep.com
LTGGameQuery	www.ltgamer.com

TABLE B.2

Continued

MODULE	WEBSITE
Multiplayer Gaming and Sports	
pnClansite	pnclansite.sourceforge.net
pnGolfLeague	noc.postnuke.com/projects/pngolfleague/
pnStandings	www.pnstandings.com
pn-teamspeak	sourceforge.net/projects/pn-teamspeak/
Newsletters and Mailers	
jdn_Mailer	www.dev-postnuke.com
MultiMailer	www.technikz.de
pnTresMailer	canvas.anubix.net
WhatsNews	nuke-modules.gading.de
Online Games	
Miniclip Games	www.dimensionquest.net
pnFlashGames	www.pnflashgames.com
vQuiz	tecfa.unige.ch/perso/vivian/
Personals and Classifieds	
FriendFinder	postnuke.yuelao.net
LiquidClassifieds	www.liquidmarkets.com
zPersonals	www.pnaddons.com
Polls and Surveys	
Advanced Polls	www.markwest.me.uk
FormExpress	contrib.virkpaanettet.dk
pnESP	pnesp.sourceforge.net
Project, Task, and Ticket Management	
Appointment Scheduler	www.bassettdev.com
DQ Help Desk	www.dimensionquest.net
jdn_Board	www.dev-postnuke.com
pnSchedule	www.nuy.info
Task Manager	www.chucksteel.com
Reference Information	
Dictionary	www.kyantonius.com
Encyclopedia	orodruin.rivkashome.com
MapQuest	www.jdlt.net
NameDay	home.postnuke.ru
Online User Atlas	www.sopnet.ch
pnEncyclopedia	pnencyclopedia.sourceforge.net
Weather	www.vedrine.net

TABLE B.2

Continued

MODULE	WEBSITE
Site Maps	
msSiteMap	www.mashdeco.com
SnakeESO	www.snakelab.com
Statistics	
pnBoodhound	www.pnaddons.com
pncSimpleStats	dev.pnconcept.com
S2-Stats	www.autothemes.com
Search Statistics	lottasophie.sourceforge.net
Statistics	www.mtrad.com
Themes and Layout	
AutoTheme	spidean.mckenzies.net
BlockHome	moe.cape.com/~nate/postnuke/
Nuclei	www.tangant.com
User Enhancements	
ChangePassword	pn.dembel.org
EnvoAvatar	www.vedrine.net
msAutolog	www.mashdeco.com
NameGen	www.voodoostevie.com
pncGroups	dev.pnconcept.com
pncUserHack	dev.pnconcept.com
pncUserPoints	dev.pnconcept.com
pncYourAvatar	dev.pnconcept.com
X-User	noc.postnuke.com/projects/xuser/
Wrappers and Page Framing	
NukeWrapper	users.tpg.com.au/staer/Downloads.htm
postnuke_frame	lottasophie.sourceforge.net
PostWrap	spidean.mckenzies.net
Static_Docs	noc.postnuke.com/projects/static-docs/

Glossary of Terms

Add Story—A module used to add news articles to PostNuke. It provides the ability to publish without prior authorization.

Application Programming Interface (API)—A set of functions used to abstract the lower level operations from the upper. With regard to PostNuke, the functions and conventions used by modules to consistently access the core functionality of PostNuke. Modules written with the pnAPI will work with future versions of PostNuke without needing to be upgraded themselves.

Article—Usually the news stories displayed on the front page of a PostNuke site. Articles also refer to any publication content in general.

Author—A person responsible for the writing of content. In PostNuke, a content author can be a site user who submits new content or someone who is responsible for the approval and publishing of submitted content.

Back end—The feature of PostNuke that allows you to feed your news to other sites for display.

Banners—A form of web page advertising. Banners are usually wide rectangular images placed at the top or bottom of a page.

Block—A small, self-contained interface that performs a specific function, such as the display of PostNuke module content. Some blocks are very simple and can exist without a parent module, but most are tied specifically to the module application with which they were made to work.

Blog—A shortening of weblog. A blog is an online journal in which dated user entries are logged. Blog content is usually written informally and sometimes formed through the efforts of multiple posters.

Category—In PostNuke, a grouping mechanism for content. Categories that are defined by their labels and content can then be assigned to a given category. PostNuke 0.8 will include a global category system hooked into all modules.

Client—The user's browser that receives and displays web page content.

Content Management System (CMS)—The software designed to organize and manage content, usually in environments with multiple authors and/or managers of the data. The term is now primarily associated with website content.

End user—The person using a product. Visitors to PostNuke sites are end users, and, in some cases, they might also be content authors.

Feed—The imported content from other websites, usually using a format like RSS.

Fork—A split in the development of an open source development project, such as PostNuke forking off from PHP-Nuke. Some forks remain very similar to their parent applications, and others quickly become unique.

General Public License (GPL)—An open source license. The GNU General Public License (http://www.fsf.org/licenses/gpl.html) was created by the GNU Project in 1988 to allow programmers the ability to distribute their work for use, modification, and redistribution while ensuring the work will continue to be freely available after release.

Hack—A change to original PostNuke source code to alter the functionality of the application or the display of its content. Hacks usually add additional features not available in the stock release.

Hook—A feature of PostNuke that is available to all modules compatible with pnHooks. Common hooks include comments, ratings, and Autolinks.

Intranet—An internal network used within a company or organization that is usually restricted from external access. The term also refers to the main internal website.

Layout—The arrangement of content on a web page designed to provide an effective interface for accessing the content.

Module—A component of PostNuke. PostNuke is essentially made up of a group of modules. Each module performs a set of tasks, and all have ways of interfacing with other PostNuke core modules. Modules display their content through blocks.

News—The article stories displayed on a website, usually on the front page.

Open source—The software that is public domain or copyrighted under an open source license, such as the GPL. The software's code is usually freely available and can be modified, usually with the requirement that changed versions are also released as open source.

PHP-Nuke—The CMS from which PostNuke originated. PostNuke forked from PHP-Nuke in the Spring of 2001. PostNuke's original code was identical to PHP-Nuke at the time, but has since undergone major rewrites.

pnRender—A module that wraps the standard Smarty functions so that they are accessible to other PostNuke modules. pnRender is a subclass of the Smarty Engine and replaces the older pnHTML functionality.

Portal—A website that provides extensive information and content related to a specific topic or interest. Traditionally, portals are very large sites and not personal or focused on a specific organization or group. Portals also commonly provide personalization options to their users.

Really Simple Syndication (RSS)—A syndication format for web content that is derived from XML. Using RSS websites can import content from other sites.

Section—A PostNuke module designed to manage relatively static articles that do not appear as news.

Smarty Template Engine—A template and presentation framework for PHP that provides the tools needed to separate application logic from presentation code. It makes it easy to modularize the form and function components in your PHP application. XTE uses Smarty.

Story—A news article displayed on a website, usually on the front page.

Submit News—A module used to submit potential news articles to PostNuke. Stories submitted through this module go into a queue where they must be approved before they go live. The approval system is part of the Add Story module.

Template—A file that describes the way content should be displayed. Templates are usually simple XHTML files that use variable calls to place integrated dynamic content.

Theme—The visual appearance, layout, and interface of PostNuke page content. Themes can contain both PHP and XHTML code, but are always concerned with the layout of content and not what the content itself might be. Xanthia themes include separate XHTML template files for different blocks, modules, and pages. Themes are also sometimes known as "skins."

Topic—The identifying label attached to a news story. Topics usually have graphics icons that are displayed with an article to make it clear what type of article it is, or to what subject the story will relate.

Wiki—A CMS system of web pages that are written with "Wiki Words" instead of HTML. The Wiki tags are more simplified than HTML, but they also have less formatting options. Wiki pages can usually be edited by anyone reading the page. Wiki is the Hawaiian word for quick.

WYSIWYG—An acronym for What You See Is What You Get. The term usually applies to an editor with a graphical interface that makes writing easier. For example, a button within a programming editor would write out predefined code with each use. WYSIWYG interfaces also often hide the codes they generate to maintain a simplified interface.

Xanthia Templating Environment (XTE)—A theme engine built using pnRender Smarty functions that manages the template interface to PostNuke. Xanthia themes contain template files for each independently designed component and store display settings in the PostNuke database.

XHTML—The acronym stands for Extensible Hypertext Markup Language, but it is almost never referred to by its full name. When the HTML 4.0 specification was combined with the more-current XML 1.0 specification, the result was XHTML. XHTML is essentially "HTML version 5." XHTML is generally backward compatible with existing HTML standards, and all website development should use as much of the XHTML specifications as possible.

Zone—A specifically defined layout area. A Xanthia theme zone can be applied to modules or blocks to allow the association of themes. Block zones describe areas where blocks can be assigned.

Web Resources

D

The following links are included as resources for learning more about PostNuke and related technologies.

PostNuke

PostNuke Official	www.postnuke.com
Community Forums	forums.postnuke.com
PostNuke Guide	docs.postnuke.com/index.php?module=Static_Docs&func=view&f=/pnguide/
Dummy's Guide to PostNuke	www.pnaddons.com/pnMyGuide/
PostNuke and XTE Guides	postnuke.lottasophie.de
PostNuke Mailing Lists	lists.postnuke.com/mailman/listinfo

PHP

PHP Official	www.php.net
PHPBuilder	www.phpbuilder.com
PHP Freaks	www.phpfreaks.com
PHPkitchen	www.phpkitchen.com
WebReference PHP	webreference.com/programming/php/
WeberDev.com	www.weberdev.com

XHTML

W3C Official	www.w3.org/MarkUp/
W3Schools	www.w3schools.com/xhtml/
IRT.org	www.irt.org
A List Apart	www.alistapart.com
Web Standards Project	www.webstandards.org
HTML Dog	www.htmldog.com

CSS

W3C Official	www.w3.org/Style/
W3Schools	www.w3schools.com/css/
css/edge	www.meyerweb.com/eric/css/edge/

Project 7	www.projectseven.com/tutorials/
Hands On CSS Tutorial	www.westciv.com/style_master/academy/ hands_on_tutorial/
Layout Techniques	www.glish.com/css/
A List Apart	www.alistapart.com
css Zen Garden	www.csszengarden.com
mezzoblue	www.mezzoblue.com

Graphics

W3C Official	www.w3.org/Graphics/
JPEG Official	www.jpeg.org
PNG Official	www.libpng.org/pub/png/
GIF versus JPG	www.siriusweb.com/tutorials/gifvsjpg/
Guide to PNG Optimization	www.cs.toronto.edu/~cosmin/pngtech/ optipng.html

MySQL

MySQL Documentation	dev.mysql.com/doc/mysql/
W3Schools	www.w3schools.com/sql/
MySQL Gotchas	sql-info.de/mysql/gotchas.html
WeberDev.com	www.weberdev.com

Apache

Apache Software Foundation	www.apache.org
ApacheWeek	www.apacheweek.com
Apache Server Resources	www.hitmill.com/computers/apache.htm

Linux

The Linux Documentation Project	www.tldp.org
Learning Linux	learninglinux.com
Linux Online!	www.linux.org
Linux Journal	www.linuxjournal.com

Windows XP and Server 2003

MS Windows XP Official	www.microsoft.com/windowsxp/
MS Server 2003 Official	www.microsoft.com/windowsserver2003/
Windows Resource Center	labmice.techtarget.com/
TweakXP.com	www.tweakxp.com
Windows XP Developer Center	windowsxp.devx.com
WindowsNetworking	www.windowsnetworking.com

PostNuke API

E

The PostNuke API, or pnAPI, is a collection of functions that allows developers to access and manage low-level content in an abstract and reusable manner. While primarily aimed at module developers, the pnAPI can also be useful to advanced theme and hack developers. The functions are listed below with a short description. Browse to docs.postnuke.com for more information on the pnAPI.

pnBlockGetInfo—Returns an array containing block information.

pnBlockLoad—Loads a block from a module or core.

pnBlockShow—Returns the output of the block display function.

pnConfigDelVar—Deletes a configuration variable.

pnConfigGetVar—Acquires a configuration variable.

pnConfigSetVar—Sets a configuration variable.

pnDBGetConn—Returns an array of database connection values.

pnDBGetTables—Returns an array of database table information.

pnDBInit—Initializes a database connection.

pnExceptionFree—Resets the current exception status.

pnExceptionId—Returns the current exception identifier.

pnExceptionMajor—Determines the exception state and provides the exception type is applicable.

pnExceptionSet—Raises an exception with supplied value.

pnExceptionValue—Returns the exception value as an object.

pnGetBaseURI—Acquires the base URI, the path of the URL.

pnGetBaseURL—Acquires the base URL for the site.

pnGetStatusMsg—Returns the last status message posted.

pnInit—Initializes the includes, sessions, database connections, and system configuration required to run PostNuke.

pnModAPIFunc—Executes a module API function.

pnModAPILoad—Loads the extra functions of the module API.

pnModAvailable—Confirms the availability of a given module.

pnModCallHooks—Calls each hook operation for a module.

pnModDBInfoLoad—Loads a module's database table information.

pnModDelVar—Deletes a module variable.

pnModFunc—Executes a module function.

pnModGetAdminMods—Returns an array of modules with administrative components.

pnModGetIDFromName—Acquires a module's id given its name.

pnModGetInfo—Returns an array containing module information.

pnModGetName—Returns the name of the current top-level module.

pnModGetUserMods—Returns an array of modules with user interfaces.

pnModGetVar—Acquires a module variable.

pnModLoad—Loads a module into PostNuke.

pnModRegisterHook—Registers a new hook function.

pnModSetVar—Sets a module-specific variable.

pnModUnregisterHook—Removes a hook function.

pnModURL—Returns a URL string for a specific module function.

pnRedirect—Sets the HTTP header to redirect to another page.

pnSecAddSchema—Creates a new component security schema.

pnSecAuthAction—Determines whether a particular level of access is allowed.

pnSessionDelVar—Deletes a session variable.

pnSessionGetVar—Acquires a session variable.

pnSessionInit—Initializes a new or current user session.

pnSessionSetup—Creates variables required for persistent user sessions.

pnSessionSetVar—Sets a session variable.

pnThemeLoad—Loads the display theme and sets any needed global variables.

pnUserGetLang—Returns the name of the current language.

pnUserGetTheme—Returns the name of the current theme.

pnUserGetVar—Acquires a user variable.

pnUserLoggedIn—Determines whether a user is logged in.

pnUserLogIn—Logs user in to PostNuke.

pnUserLogOut—Logs user out of PostNuke.

pnUserSetVar—Sets a user-specific variable.

pnUserValidateVar—Authenticates a user variable.

pnVarCensor—Removes censored words from supplied arguments.

pnVarCleanFromInput—Removes escaped characters and HTML tags from supplied arguments.

pnVarPrepForDisplay—Adds appropriate escaped characters for supplied arguments.

pnVarPrepForOS—Formats path arguments for the operating system.

pnVarPrepForStore—Escapes characters for supplied arguments.

pnVarPrepHTMLDisplay—Prepares arguments for display based on HTML tag restrictions.

pnVarValidate—Authenticates a variable.

Index

Numerics

A

How can we make this index more useful? Email us at indexes@samspublishing.com

C

How can we make this index more useful? Email us at indexes@samspublishing.com

distribution, updating, 37

documentation. *See also* configuration

   domains, 448

   hacks, 348

      inline comments, 348

      offline, 348

      public releases, 349

   tables, 449-451, 454

   troubleshooting, 40

documents

   Content Express, 210

   email, 415-416

   login/logout modification, 441

domains. *See also* names

   conversion, 452

   documentation, 448

   troubleshooting, 40

donations

   Donations Block, 234-236, 244

   HTML Block, 236

   PayPal, 233-234

double quote references, PHP, 333

Downloads module, 107-112

Dreamweaver, 18

drives

   optimizing, 483

   space requirements, 10

duplication. *See* copying

duration to cache pages, 168

dynamic CSS generation, 340-343

dynamic keywords, 363-365

Dynamic Meta Keywords, 51

dynamic page generation, 321

dynamic PHP, 326

dynamic stylesheets. *See also* CSS; editing

   themes, 177-178

   troubleshooting, 187

dynamic theme elements, 293-295

dynamic XHTML generation, 338-339

E

e-commerce

   cmsMerchant module, 236-240, 244

   modules, 493

   PayPalCart, 240-243. *See also* PayPal

EasyPHP, 16

echoes, PHP variables, 332

editing

   articles, 95, 382

      forcing story counts, 393-394

      theme-based topic graphics, 382-388

      titles, 388-392

   AutoThemes, 276

   Comments module, 397-408

   Content Express, 209-212

      PagEd, 213-218

      PageSetter, 218-223

      troubleshooting, 223-224

   online pop-up editors, 278

   sections, 95

   templates, 178-186

   themes, 174-178, 187

   topics, 85

Reviews module, 114-116

troubleshooting, 117-118

Web Links module, 113

interfaces

APIs

hacks, 349-350

pnAPI, 505-507

business intranet cluster case study, 471-472

CGI, 21

Content Express, 209-212

PagEd, 213-218

PageSetter, 218-223

troubleshooting, 223-224

information-based website case study, 305-308

online club case study, 199-204

polls, 103

selection, 268

themes, 280

titles, 362-363

international spellings, 44

intranets

business cluster case study, 463-464

groups, 468-470

interfaces, 471-472

module configuration, 466-468

multisite installation, 464-466

permissions, 468-470

results, 473-475

options, 59

troubleshooting, 62

inventory, adding, 242

ionCube PHP Accelerator, 482

ionCube PHP Encoder, troubleshooting, 244

J-K-L

journal modules, 491

Kate, 18

KDE (K Desktop Environment), 11

Kerio MailServer, 19

keywords

customization, 363-365

Meta Keywords field, 50

labels

customization, 430-431

pages, 435-436

LAN (local area network), 16

languages

international spellings (English), 44

names, 371-373

packs, 36

PHP

code, 326

comments, 335-336

control structures, 335

output, 332-334

syntax, 326-328

variables, 329, 331

selection, 32, 57

Languages module, 69

layout modules, 496

leading lines, 266-267

Legal module, 69

N

S

sans serif fonts, selection, 262-263

saving

    hacks, 346

    templates, 168

    topics, 86

scheduling articles, 92

SCP (Secure Copy Protocol), 17

screen resolution design, 262

scripts (PHP)

    code, 326

    comments, 335-336

    control structures, 335

    output, 332-334

    syntax, 326-328

    variables, 329-331

Search module, 72

searching

    code, 356-358

    files, 39

sections, 45, 93-95

    Downloads module, 107-112

    forums, 125

Sections module, 72

Secure Copy Protocol (SCP), 17

Secure SHell (SSH), 17

security

    databases, 28

    Donations Block, 244

    Enable pnAntiCracker, 56-57

PagEd, 218

passwords

    configuration, 34

    databases, 28

    email help page customization, 439-440

    help page customization, 437-439

    registration, 413-414

    troubleshooting, 40

permissions, 151

    administration, 152-153

    configuration, 158-160

    Dynamic User Data, 155-156

    groups, 156-158

    New User Registration form, 156

    troubleshooting, 161

    User Configuration, 155

    User Register Configuration, 154

Settings module, 58, 315-317

selection

    colors, 260

    fonts, 262-263

    interfaces, 268

    languages, 32, 36, 57

    OS, 10

        Linux, 10-12

        Windows XP, 12-14

    story counts, 393-394

    themes

        AutoThemes, 270-279

        sampling, 269

        troubleshooting, 279-280

How can we make this index more useful? Email us at indexes@samspublishing.com

How can we make this index more useful? Email us at indexes@samspublishing.com

How can we make this index more useful? Email us at indexes@samspublishing.com

V

values, PHP, 329

variables

hack customization, 361-367, 369-375

PHP, 329-331

echoes, 332

themes, 337-338

vi editor, 18

viewing

articles, 89

editing, 382

theme-based topic graphics, 382-388

titles, 388-392

downloads, 109

language names, 371-373

products, 242

profiles, 140

screen resolution, 262

title customization, 362-363

Vim, 18

visitors, tracking, 248

visual block editors, Xanthia, 167

voice, pn-teamspeak module, 140-142, 150

vQuiz module, 147-148

W

warm colors, 260

Web Links module, 74, 113, 197-198

web resources, 502-503

web servers

file placement, 29-30

multisite configuration, 451

preinstallation requirements, 15

websites

Administration Menu field, 54-56

Administrator Email field, 52

advertising, 232

AutoThemes, 270, 276-279

AT-Lite, 270-276

troubleshooting, 279-280

backing up, 36-37

blocks, 76

case studies, 297. *See also* case studies

core module configuration, 195-199

donation modules, 493

games, 145

pnFlashGames, 145-147

troubleshooting, 149-150

vQuiz, 147-148

hack configuration, 361-367, 369-375

images, 268

Local Time Format field, 53

Meta Keywords field, 50

modules. *See* modules

multisites, 447-448

combining, 458-461

config.php file duplication, 453

creating shared file directories, 452

domain documentation, 448

file/folder duplication, 456-457

X-Y-Z

Your Guide
to Computer
Technology

www.informit.com